Pursuing Excellence
in Higher Education

Pursuing Excellence in Higher Education

Eight Fundamental Challenges

Brent D. Ruben

JOSSEY-BASS
A Wiley Imprint
www.josseybass.com

Published by Jossey-Bass
A Wiley Imprint
989 Market Street, San Francisco, CA 94103-1741   www.josseybass.com

Jossey-Bass books and products are available through most bookstores. To contact Jossey-Bass directly
call our Customer Care Department within the U.S. at 800-956-7739, outside the U.S. at 317-572-3986
or fax 317-572-4002.

Jossey-Bass also publishes its books in a variety of electronic formats. Some content that appears in
print may not be available in electronic books.

Library of Congress Cataloging-in-Publication Data

Ruben, Brent D.
  Pursuing excellence in higher education : eight fundamental challenges
/ Brent D. Ruben.— 1st ed.
      p. cm. — (The Jossey-Bass higher and adult education series)
Includes bibliographical references and index.
  ISBN 0-7879-6204-X (alk. paper)
  1. Education, Higher—Aims and objectives—United States. I. Title.
II. Series.
  LA227.4.R83 2004
  378.73—dc21

                              2003011190

Printed in the United States of America

FIRST EDITION
HB Printing 10 9 8 7 6 5 4 3 2 1

10/25/04

Contents

For Jann—
With gratitude for continuing support and
encouragement in this and all things

Foreword

This book is about change and responses to change in higher education. Change itself has created tensions about the mission and the values of higher education. Some of these tensions are healthy and creative; others are threatening and destructive. Succinctly expressed, these tensions are rooted in the interplay of an historic public mission and new market-based strategies. A set of public values and a long commitment to public investment in higher education have yielded a public good, but increasingly resource allocations designed to serve that public good are based on market conditions. On each side of this equation, we have different but not necessarily irreconcilable values. But if reconciliation is possible or desirable, we need to be clear about the changes that drive these current tensions.

The changes in higher education over the past decade are probably greater in magnitude and scope than during any period since the 1960s. For example, it is unlikely that the dramatic reductions in direct state support for higher education will return to the high levels of the post–World War II era. For long, public universities were able to restrict their budget planning to anticipated increments to their base budgets. The growing dependence on tuition, often to offset reductions in state support; the expansion of both private and corporate donations; the strategic management of endowments; and the growth of targeted federal research support have profoundly altered the revenue mix of institutional budgets. These shifts decisively redefined the role of the president or chancellor and other administrative officers, who became engaged in a more active and strategic management of our institutions.

We often identify this change in the budget process as the means by which market forces have an impact on our mission. But we should also recognize that many institutions were unclear and vague about their mission, and the process of rethinking our direction was necessary and beneficial. Although market forces ignited the rethinking process, other critical educational objectives, including efforts to improve the undergraduate learning experience, also influenced discussions of the mission of higher education. Budget reallocations are without question a source of tension, but it is an unavoidable tension that is derived from changes in support for higher education. Until recently, the higher education community viewed changes in public support as an oscillation encouraging us to wait out bad times until better times returned. During the 1990s, the ball fell off this oscillating pendulum, and we are now facing unprecedented and irreversible change.

Concurrent with these changes in revenue sources and strategic management have been shifts in student financial aid and concerns about access to higher education. In response to the increase in tuition, there has been a corresponding expansion of financial aid. However, the growth of loan obligations and the continuing underrepresentation of students from families in the lowest quartile of the nation's income distribution is a persistent source of complaint and concern. This access challenge is a matter not only of affordability but also of academic preparation and campus hospitability. Recent rapid increases in tuition have also raised questions about the growing financial challenge for the vast middle ranks of American society. Ultimately this issue is a public policy debate about uniformly moderate tuition as a social entitlement or differential tuition reduced by financial aid proportionate to student needs. The reconfiguration of revenues has amplified and created a sense of immediacy in this debate. Although the reduction of college costs could reduce the upward pressure on tuition, reductions in state support of higher education have accounted for most of that upward pressure. There will be a continuing debate about whether the growth of student support through grants and loans is adequate to address limitations on access. In short, is rising tuition offset by grants for those least able to afford the increase a fairer solution than an exhaustive political campaign to keep tuition low for every student irrespective of wealth and income?

Perhaps the most potent impact of market forces on higher education is to be found in the growth and success of several for-profit providers. Most currently serve adult students, and their programs are geared to professional or vocational requirements. The impact of direct competition is at the present time restricted to specific segments of higher education. More critical, however, is the precocious development of new pedagogies based on information technology and the integration of distance learning into the course schedules, which may well create an alternate delivery process—with enormous competitive implications. Traditional residential learning has certainly adapted some of the potentialities of information technology, but they are often fragmentary and eclectic; the impact of new technologies has been more transformative in administrative services and communication processes. Eventually, traditional institutions may expand their own alternative delivery systems to participate in this new marketplace where adult students in particular are prepared to pay for either a second chance or a second kind of qualification.

This emerging market of alternative providers will amplify another market-driven issue in higher education. Capacity as well as access is now a key issue for higher education. In those parts of the country in which immigration has swelled population growth, there will be a surge in demand by first-generation college applicants and the likelihood of a capacity crisis in several regions. Part of the solution will necessarily be the need for students to start at one kind of institution and complete their requirements at one or more other institutions. This process is often cumbersome, and although many students are already completing their degree programs at more than one institution there will be pressure to clarify and ease the process of credit transfer. The dilemma of how to maintain consistent quality control and facilitate credit transfer will become extremely critical under conditions of a capacity crisis. Capacity stress will also create pressure to improve the articulation of distance education and residential education, and perhaps of the for-profit and traditional segments of higher education. The challenge of transferability among institutions ought not to compromise quality control, but it remains one of the great frustrations of those who necessarily have their education at multiple locations.

Cumulatively, these changes have already created a more differentiated set of higher education options. We have long celebrated the range of choices in American higher education. Choices among public and private, based on size, program, and location, will be further refined; although some large institutions will remain comprehensive, the vast majority will define a specific niche. A generation ago, under conditions of rapid enrollment growth, many institutions aspired to become large comprehensive research institutions. Now, market pressures and resource constraints are driving most institutions to define their mission in relation to their niche in the demand for higher education. This more highly differentiated range of higher education opportunities may be related to a more competitive market environment for resources and students, but concerns about access and quality remain part of a set of enduring values. Indeed, over the past century, the high value placed on institutional autonomy often stimulated intense academic competition, and especially a preoccupation with the ordinal ranking of institutional quality. In contrast, a greater emphasis on mission niches may well promote greater interinstitutional collaboration by means of alliances, partnerships, and even virtual systems of both similar and differing institutions.

This undocumented and incomplete transformation of higher education is also global in scale and context. One of the great paradoxes in disciplinary studies of globalization is how little attention is given to higher education as a defining part of that process. Higher education is an instrument of globalization; the sciences and the English language have, in many ways, become measures of globalization. The international currency of higher education by means of student exchange or off-shore programs will complicate changes at the national level. These changes are occurring at different rates and in different forms worldwide. But largely because of the unique public-private partnership and enormous scale that defines U.S. higher education, our experience is a source of special interest and expectations. Here the interplay of markets and mission may have proceeded further than elsewhere in the world; it is expressed primarily through resource reallocations made necessary by the changing demands and needs of society. These strategic reallocations do reflect some of the impacts of market pressures on higher education, but many new priorities are also part of independent efforts to enhance or refine our mission to meet the changing needs of students and new ways to advance knowledge.

The most curious aspect of our role in the advancement of knowledge is our lack of curiosity about higher education as an institution and its place in society. Colleges and universities are not only places of learning but also organizations and cultures with their own deliberative and reactive relationships to society at large. Higher education is often judged to be slow to change, but it should also be an arena where debate about public and private values, about access and quality, about tradition and change, and about market-driven and value-driven decision making are fully and openly explored.

David Ward
President, American Council on Education and Chancellor Emeritus, University of Wisconsin–Madison

Introduction

It's difficult not to be incredibly grateful to the colleges and universities that have helped to shape our lives. There is essentially no facet of our existence that would be precisely as it is were it not for the contributions of the academy to our personal, social, occupational, cultural, and intellectual development.

I must confess, however, that I have not always held this view. As an undergraduate student at a large research university, it was difficult not to have very mixed feelings about the academy. I had been told many times about the benefits of a college education, and in a theoretical sense I never doubted its value. The experiences of living on my own, making new acquaintances, and interacting with other students on a variety of topics were positive ones. It never fully occurred to me at the time, however, that these were "college" experiences, in the sense of being among the opportunities the academy had created. If pressed, I probably would have described them as "personal" experiences, in the sense that I saw myself, rather than the institution, as making them what they were.

Even as I had been frequently reminded by my parents, and other older and wiser relatives and friends, that college was providing me "the best years of my life," it seemed I was encountering a great many experiences that didn't fit all that well with the prophecy. Heading out at 7:00 A.M. on the long walk to Earth Science 101 lab, where I would rub rocks together to determine their relative hardness, just wasn't my idea of a good time. I also found no particular joy in studying late into the night to prepare simultaneously for three final exams all scheduled for the same day, or driving endlessly around parking lot after parking lot in search of a space. Sitting in large lectures trying to write as rapidly as the professor (for whom English was a second language) read from his notes wasn't all that wonderful either. I still remember another professor who wouldn't allow me to take a makeup quiz when I missed class and didn't have sufficient verification that I had been ill, and more generally having great difficulty finding instructors "in" during the offices hours posted on their doors. I also have fading recollections of waiting in long lines for various things, and of having to quite literally beg my way into an oversubscribed course that I needed so I could graduate in my major. I could go on.

I may have suffered from a less informed appreciation of the academy in those days, but I am pleased to report that I've since come to a more mature understanding of my undergraduate experience and now recognize the many character-building experiences higher education fashioned for me. Still, it has been strangely cathartic to talk to many others over the years who have faded recollections of experiences similar to mine, and to hear their reports that even dozens of years after graduation they have had dreams, as I do, of forgetting to drop a course before the final cut-off date, losing the only copy of a paper the day it was due to be turned in, or arriving at graduation day two credits short.

As therapeutic as these conversations and insights are to me personally, from my perspective as an educator and advocate for higher education, they have not been nearly so reassuring. Some forty years after my undergraduate years, for example, I found myself on various occasions talking with my children and their friends about their college experiences and discovered something curious. Although there have been many changes in higher education, their stories—and their complaints—are remarkably similar to those I had some four decades earlier. Amid their positive recollections about interactions with peers and cocurricular activities were many stories of frustration resulting from interactions with the institution's administrative services and some members of the faculty and staff. When I am in a situation such as this, I always do my best to provide professorial explanations of the time-honored traditions of the academy, pointing to the great benefits that come from overcoming personal and organizational challenges and adversity. Of course, I always dutifully remind them that these *are* the best years of their lives.

Fortunately, as someone who works in higher education, I have had the opportunity to develop a much broader perspective of the many benefits of the college experience. I have also read broadly about higher education and gained a good deal of first-hand experience as a faculty member and administrator. No doubt my greatest learning has come about during the past ten years in my capacity as executive director of the Center for Organizational Development and Leadership (ODL) at Rutgers University. This position has given me the opportunity to work with leaders from throughout the university, including administrators at the senior level, in business services, student life, and auxiliary services, as well as in academic affairs, greatly expanding my personal knowledge of the work across the organization. I have also been able to interact and learn from senior administrative and faculty leaders from many other institutions around the country, and through active participation in the National Consortium for Continuous Improvement in Higher Education. Finally, my position has given me many more opportunities than I had had previously to represent the academy in dealings with people from business, health care, and government, and to hear how they think about our colleges and universities, and higher education in general.

As a result of my experiences these last ten years, I've come to recognize that many of the concerns that I tended previously to think were personal, situational, or campus-specific are not. I have also arrived at the inescapable conclusion that, for all the many changes in the world around us, much that is higher education has remained quite the same for many years—the good, the bad, and the ugly. I have also come to recognize, as I listen to the voices of external constituencies, that much of what is best about the academy and the experiences it offers is abstract, intangible, and easily overlooked in the moment, while much of what is not so good smacks you in the face and is difficult, if not impossible, to ignore or forget.

When it comes to self-reflection and learning, higher education should afford society an unequalled standard of excellence. With regard to institutional self-reflection, learning, and improvement, however, it is difficult to argue that we have been fully successful in achieving this ideal, though it is most certainly a noble and worthy pursuit. Clarifying this vision, recognizing challenges and obstacles to its realization, and identifying concepts and cases that help to meet these challenges and close these gaps are the guiding purposes of this book.

Is this a book about the core academic mission of the academy? The answer is yes and no. The focus is not on the academic components of our mission per se, in the sense that it is not about the content of courses, programs, instruction, research, or public service. Instead, this book is very much about the nature and dynamics of teaching and learning; about the importance of scholarship and research being communicated to and valued by the many constituencies of higher education; and about the centrality of public service, outreach, and engagement that extend beyond the boundaries of the campus experience. *Pursuing Excellence in Higher Education,* then, does indeed have broad implications for thinking about our academic mission, and other important aspects of our work, as they play themselves out in everyday interactions with our students, visitors, alumni, employers, policy makers, the general public, and others.

The use of the term *we* in the previous paragraphs raises the referential question. Who are the *we* who have not "been fully successful?" Who is the intended audience for this message, and for this book: faculty? administrators? staff? The answer is yes to all of the above. This book is for all those who care deeply about the purposes and directions of higher education—most especially, college and university faculty, staff, and administrators. Indeed, one of the central themes of this volume is that all who work in higher education, regardless of their role, *are* the academy. Although it is perhaps inevitable to differentiate between roles as we go about our daily tasks, all of us who work at a college or university share responsibility for the experiences in higher education. We are all learners, all teachers, all accountable for the impressions higher education creates and the mission it serves. So this is a book for faculty, administrators, and staff—and for all others who are concerned with the future and high purposes of the academy—for all who have a role to play in helping to ensure excellence in practice within higher education.

Specifically, the book focuses on the challenges and problems facing the academy today. The first chapter sets the context and outlines the dimensions of eight of our most basic challenges. Each subsequent chapter explores one of these issues in greater depth and is followed by several brief narratives written by some of the many individuals who are working to address them. The final chapter addresses what is perhaps the most fundamental challenge posed in the book: developing a broadened vision for higher education, one that emphasizes excellence in practice and asks more of our institutions and of each of us working in them.

There are, of course, any number of challenges facing the academy. The factors that guided the selection of the eight challenges addressed in *Pursuing Excellence in Higher Education* are these: the issues are of major significance, are broad in consequence, are relevant throughout most if not all of the higher education community, are of long-standing concern, and are challenges to the academy's fundamental values. Perhaps most important, in each case the means of addressing the problem are within our control; we have the power, expertise, resources, and ingenuity to bring about change.

As I have mentioned, Chapter One lays the foundation for the book and summarizes each of eight challenges to be examined in greater depth. Beginning with Chapter Two, one chapter is devoted to exploring each challenge in some detail. Each chapter is followed by several brief narratives describing promising efforts to address these challenges, told by those who are leading the efforts. I am most grateful for the willingness of these individuals to contribute their insights and energies to this book. The narratives are intended to present both information and inspiration. Given the purposes at hand and limitations on space, authors were asked to emphasize *what* is being done, and *why,* rather than *how.* A short introduction prefaces each set of narratives. As will become apparent, the placement of the narratives is arbitrary in some instances, since a number of initiatives described are relevant to themes that are explored in more than one chapter. Where such linkages exist, they are noted in the introductory sections for each set of narratives. A disclaimer is also warranted: the narratives that are included are a sampling of the many developments under way nationally and internationally. The collection is neither comprehensive nor necessarily representative, but I hope it will be as useful for readers of the book as it has been for me. Chapter Ten furnishes a summary and offers further observations and reflections.

Our colleges and universities are the best in world. Wonderful things are happening, but still there are many ways to improve and enhance what we're doing. This book is intended to contribute to the conversation about ways to improve the work of the academy in its efforts to better serve our students, our communities, our global society, and one another.

Acknowledgments

The impetus for this book was my selection as the 2000 recipient of the Daniel Gorenstein Memorial Award for outstanding scholarship and distinguished service to Rutgers University, an honor for which I was, and am, deeply appreciative. With this esteemed award comes the privilege of delivering a university lecture on a topic germane to one's scholarly interests; I chose "The Ivory Tower 2000: Images, Ironies, and Opportunities."

Preparing that lecture gave me an occasion to integrate a number of disparate thoughts regarding the issues facing higher education, and in the process I found myself engaging in a good deal of reflection as to how my thinking on the subject had evolved over the years, and on the many individuals and influences that have helped to shape my current viewpoint. The response of family members, friends, and colleagues to the lecture was very gratifying. A number of individuals encouraged me to use the Gorenstein Lecture as the foundation for a more extensive exploration of the challenges facing colleges and universities. *Pursuing Excellence in Higher Education* is the result of those urgings.

Many of the influences and individuals that have been important to the development of my perspective are identified in the references and notes accompanying the text of this book, and the Introduction alludes to a few less scholarly influences. Others, of a more personal nature, I want to mention here.

It is difficult to know where to begin to acknowledge the many individuals who have contributed to the ideas discussed in this book. I should start by acknowledging my family, and college friends and faculty at the University of Iowa, with whom I engaged in my first discussions about higher education. My parents, Nate and Ruth Ruben; my wife, Jann; son Marc and daughter Robbi; son-in-law Matt; and other relatives and friends have continued to be an important influence in my thinking.

My years as a faculty member and administrator at Rutgers have provided me with a magnificent source of learning. I have benefited particularly from discussions with colleagues in the Department of Communication, an academic unit that has always placed a high premium on educational innovation and quality instruction. Scores of other past and present colleagues in the School of Communication, Information, and Library Studies and other units at Rutgers should be acknowledged in this regard, but unfortunately there is space to mention just a few: Dan Fishman, Gus Friedrich, Kathy Blackstone, Barbara Bender, Dorothy DeMaio, Irving Horowitz, Karen Stubaus, Jay Kohl, Daryl Lund, Ian Maw, Clay Alderfer, Kevin MacConnell, Michael Quinlan, Ed Kozack, Paul Brightman, Kim Manning Lewis, Cal Maradonna, Joe Potenza, Pam Blake, Barry Qualls, Marilynn Rison, Sandy Russell, Tricia Torok, Gene Vincente, David Burns, Bill Walker, Emmet Dennis, David Christensen, and Matt Weismantel. I've spent many hours discussing higher education issues with each of them over the years, and I want to express my thanks for their generosity and indulgence.

Serving as executive director of the Center for Organizational Development and Leadership for the past ten years has been a special privilege, and the most significant learning experience of my career. Thanks to Fran Lawrence, Christine Haska Cermak, Richard Norman, Joe Seneca, Nancy Winterbauer, and members of the previous cabinet for creating this learning opportunity; and to Dick McCormick, Karen Kavanagh, and others in the new administration of the university for their continuing support and encouragement of this work.

I also feel fortunate to have had the opportunity to interact and learn from academic and administrative leaders at a number of other institutions, and I particularly want to thank Phyllis Hoffman, John Cummins, Ron Coley, Bob Berdahl, Christina Maslach, Don McQuade, and others at Cal-Berkeley with whom I've worked; Maury Cotter, Kathleen Paris, and David Ward at the University of Wisconsin-Madison; Louise Sandmeyer, Ann Dodd, and Carol Everett at Penn State; Richard Norman and his associates at Miami University; and other colleagues from whom I've learned a great deal at MIT, Kent State, SUNY-Buffalo, Cornell, Raritan Valley, Belmont, and the University of Cincinnati.

I have also come to understand much more about the nature and complexity of higher education from my involvement with a number of associations during my years with ODL, especially the National Consortium for Continuous Improvement in Higher Education (NCCI), of which I was proud to serve as a founder and first chair of the executive committee; the National Association of College and University Business Officers (NACUBO); the Kellogg Commission on the Future of State Universities and Land Grant Colleges (NASULGC) Implementation Committee; the Kellogg Foundation Leadership for Institutional Change Initiative (LINC); and the International Association of College and University Housing Officers (ACUHO-I). I especially want to acknowledge the support of Jay Morley, Susan Jurow, Donna Klinger, and Connie Adamson at NACUBO; Gail Emig at the Kellogg Foundation; and John Byrne, executive director of the Kellogg Commission.

For a broadened knowledge of organizational assessment, planning, and improvement, I am most indebted to a number of individuals at Johnson & Johnson, AT&T, and the Cedar Group. In this regard, I want to particularly acknowledge the collegiality and support of Donnie Young, Bill Quinn, Mike Burtha, Jerry Cianfrocca, Bob Bury, Denis Hamilton, and Jeff Nugent at J&J; Phil Scanlan and Marilyn Resnik at AT&T and the AT&T Foundation, respectively; and John Harrison, Katharin Brink, and Susan Blanchard at Cedar.

My coworkers at ODL—Sherrie Tromp, Joe Lopez, Ann Volpe, Barbara Corso—are a continuing source of energy and inspiration, and I feel most grateful for such exceptional colleagues and friends. Thanks also to the many graduate students who have worked with us, among them Lisa Mahajan, Lily Arasaratnam, Jocelyn DiAngeles, Jennifer Lehr, and John Fortunato.

Special thanks to those who have helped with the review of this manuscript, among them Dan Fishman, Bob Berdahl, Jay Morley, David Ward, Gus Friedrich, Ron Rice, John Byrne, Jim Hyatt, Nancy Winterbauer, Daryl Lund, Chet Warzynski, Maury Cotter, Phyllis Hoffman, Richard Norman, and Dick McCormick, who read and provided helpful comments on drafts of chapters. A special place in heaven should be reserved for Barbara Bender, Christine Haska Cermak, Sherrie Tromp, and Amy Vames, who read and commented on drafts of many of the chapters, some more than once.

Throughout the editorial review and publication process, I have very much appreciated the encouragement and helpful guidance of David Brightman and Melissa Kirk at Jossey Bass, and of Cathy Mallon and Tom Finnegan, who edited the manuscript for Jossey-Bass and offered extremely helpful suggestions.

Finally, I want to thank the many colleagues who have helped me learn about the challenges faced by higher education, and particularly those who have so generously contributed narratives to this book to illustrate some of the ways in which these challenges are being addressed.

To all of you, and the many helpful friends and colleagues I have inadvertently failed to acknowledge, I express my gratitude, but promise that you will not be held accountable for any of my indiscretions herein.

About the Authors

Brent D. Ruben is professor of communication and organizational psychology, and executive director of the Center for Organizational Development and Leadership, at Rutgers University. He has held various administrative positions, including graduate program director and department chair. His scholarly and professional work focuses on communication in relationships, health, organizational, intercultural and educational settings, and he is the author of numerous books and articles in these areas. Ruben was founding chair of the National Consortium for Continuous Improvement in Higher Education (NCCI). He has served as a member of the Implementation Committee of the Kellogg Commission on the Future of State Universities and Land-Grant Colleges, the Malcolm Baldrige Quality Award Program's Education and Healthcare Pilot Advisory and Evaluation Team, and the National Association of College and University Business Officers (NACUBO) professional development faculty. He is a recipient of awards for his scholarship, teaching, and service and was the 2000 recipient of the university's Daniel Gorenstein Memorial Award. He received his B.A., M.A., and Ph.D. from the University of Iowa.

Ruth C. Ash presently serves as dean of the Orlean Bullard Beeson School of Education and Professional Studies at Samford University in Birmingham, Alabama. Previously she served in public school systems in Alabama as a teacher, assistant principal, director of curriculum and staff development, assistant superintendent, and superintendent. She is currently a Malcolm Baldrige National Quality Award judge and is past president of the Alabama Association of Colleges for Teacher Education. She is an arbitrator with the Better Business Bureau and a member of Leadership Birmingham and Leadership Alabama. She has been honored by Auburn University as a distinguished alumnus and, in 1997, was named one of Birmingham's Top Ten Women in Business. She was awarded the 2002 Truman Pierce Award for outstanding "contributions which significantly influence the direction of education in Alabama." Ash is a member of the board of directors for A+: the Coalition for Better Education and serves as chairman of the Governor's Committee on Teacher Enhancement for the State of Alabama. She received her B.S. degree from Auburn University, her M.S. degree from the University of South Alabama, her A.A. Certificate from the University of Alabama in Birmingham, and her Ed.D. from Auburn University.

Barbara E. Bender is associate dean of the Graduate School–New Brunswick and director of the Teaching Assistant Project at Rutgers, the State University of New Jersey. She earned her bachelor's degree at SUNY Cortland; her master's degree at SUNY Albany; and her doctorate at Teacher's College, Columbia University. She has worked in both public and independent institutions for more than twenty-five years in such roles as associate provost and dean of students. At Rutgers University, Bender founded the Teaching Assistant Project in 1987. She served as editor of the *NASPA Journal,* the journal of student affairs administration, research, and practice, and received the National Association of Student Personnel Administrators National Award for Outstanding Contribution to Literature or Research. Most recently, the National Association of Student Personnel Administrators' Foundation named her as a leading contributor to the profession.

Robert M. Berdahl has served as chancellor of the University of California, Berkeley, since 1997. Previously, he was president of the University of Texas at Austin. He also served as vice chancellor for academic affairs at the University of Illinois at Urbana–Champaign, dean of the College of Arts and Sciences at Oregon, and a member of the history faculty at Oregon. Berdahl received his B.A. degree from Augustana College, his M.A. degree from the University of Illinois, and his Ph.D. from the University of Minnesota. He is the recipient of a Fulbright Research Fellowship, and a National Endowment for the Humanities Independent Study and Research Fellowship; he also served as a research associate at the Institute of Advanced Study in Princeton and at the Max-Planck Institute for History in Göttingen, Germany. He is currently the chair of the Association of American Universities, and a member of the American Academy of Arts and Sciences.

Jean Ann Box is associate dean of the Orlean Bullard Beeson School of Education and Professional Studies at Samford University and chair of the Teacher Education Department. She has presented at state and national conferences addressing issues such as teacher education renewal, early childhood literacy development, curricular changes, improving teachers and increasing K–12 achievement, preparing teachers for the twenty-first century, literacy development for the at-risk child, helping children develop as writers, overcoming writing problems, and restructuring higher education. She received the George Macon Teaching Award from Samford University in 1992 and the Outstanding Alumni Early Childhood Education Award from the University of Alabama at Birmingham in 1997. Box received her B.S. degree from Auburn University, where she majored in early childhood education, and her M.S., Ed.S., and Ph.D. degrees from the University of Alabama at Birmingham, also in early childhood education. Previously she taught kindergarten and first grade in the Birmingham City School System and in France.

John V. Byrne is president emeritus of Oregon State University, having served as OSU's twelfth president from 1984 through 1995. He previously served as administrator of the National Oceanic and Atmospheric Administration under President Reagan (1981–1984) and as a U.S. Commissioner to the Whaling Commission (1982–1985). Byrne has been active in the private and public sectors, participating in several national committees and boards, including serving as executive director of the Kellogg Commission on the Future of State and Land-Grant Universities (1995–2000). He continues to be active as a consultant in higher education.

Christine Haska Cermak is associate provost at the Naval Postgraduate School with responsibility for a number of areas, including information technology and institutional research. For ten years previously, she served as vice president for planning at Rutgers, overseeing information technology, university communications, institutional research, and strategic planning. Cermak oversaw the Rutgers universitywide strategic plan and the development of IT plans to support the larger university plan. She was principal investigator for a series of Technology Innovation Challenge Grants totaling more than $8 million, oversaw the planning and implementation of a $100 million university networking project, and worked with state officials to arrange for the development of a university high-speed network linking campuses using the state's electronic toll infrastructure. Now at the Naval Postgraduate School, she is currently working on a Monterey Peninsula consortium, linking K–12 schools, government organizations, higher education institutions, and research centers with the statewide high-performance research network.

Brian F. Chabot is a professor in the Department of Ecology and Evolutionary Biology. He earned a B.S. in 1965 from the College of William and Mary and a Ph.D. in 1971 from Duke University. He served as department chair and then for eighteen years was a senior administrator in the College of Agriculture and Life Sciences. For nine years, he was senior associate dean with responsibilities for personnel and planning. In this role, he participated in or helped develop many of the programs in the area of leadership development.

Mary Sue Coleman, now president of the University of Michigan, was president of the University of Iowa from 1995 until 2002. She received her Ph.D. in biochemistry from the University of North Carolina at Chapel Hill. After a nineteen-year career as a biochemistry faculty member and Cancer Center administrator at the University of Kentucky in Lexington, where her laboratories were continuously funded by the National Institutes of Health, she served as associate provost and dean of research, and as vice chancellor for graduate studies and research at the University of North Carolina at Chapel Hill, and then as provost and vice president for academic affairs at the University of New Mexico.

Ron Coley is associate vice chancellor of business and administrative services at UC Berkeley. He joined Berkeley in 1998 after serving more than six years as a senior county administrator on the team of professionals who helped Orange County, California, recover from the largest municipal bankruptcy in history. Previously, he completed twenty years of active service (1972–1992) as a Marine Corps pilot.

During his military career, he helped adapt the Marine Corps to the extreme economic environments of the extraordinary defense build-ups in the 1980s and the subsequent drawdowns in the 1990s. In his present position at Berkeley, he oversees eight units with a combined workforce of more than eleven hundred staff and an operating budget of $120 million. He holds a bachelor of science degree in business administration and industrial relations from Drexel University, and an MBA degree from the Wharton School of Business.

Stacey L. Connaughton is an assistant professor in the Department of Communication at Rutgers University. She received her Ph.D. from the University of Texas at Austin. Her research interests include identity, identification, and leadership, particularly as they relate to virtual organizations and political parties. At Rutgers, she teaches graduate and undergraduate courses in organizational communication theory, leadership, interviewing, and stakeholder groups; she is the director of the Leadership Certificate Program in the Department of Communication. She has led workshops for corporate, governmental, educational administrative, and student groups on leadership, team building, organizational assessment, and work relationships.

Maury Cotter is director of strategic planning and quality improvement at UW-Madison. As a member of the provost's and chancellor's staffs, she coordinates campus planning and improvement efforts, leading a staff of internal consultants who help administrative and academic departments across campus with their planning and improvement initiatives. She consults with other universities, including a semester-long engagement at UC Berkeley, and she is helping David Ward with planning efforts at the American Council on Education. She coordinated the national Total Quality Forum, a collaboration between higher education and major U.S. corporations. She is on the executive council of the National Consortium for Continuous Improvement, the implementation committee for the Kellogg Commission on the Future of State and Land-Grant Universities, and the operating committee of the Juran Center for Leadership in Quality. She speaks nationally and has authored books and articles on planning and improvement in education.

John Dew is director for continuous quality improvement at the University of Alabama. Reporting to the provost, he facilitates strategic planning activities for the university and assists academic and administrative units in improving work processes, understanding stakeholder needs, and improving teamwork and collaboration. He received his doctorate in education from the University of Tennessee. Prior to joining the university, he worked for twenty-three years with the Lockheed Martin Energy Group as a quality and training professional. Dew's work supported the government's nuclear fuel program, research activities at the Oak Ridge National Laboratory, and production activities in the nation's nuclear weapons complex. In addition to his work with Lockheed Martin, he has provided consulting support to NASA, the Brookhaven National Laboratory, and numerous hospitals in their efforts to diagnose and prevent medical errors.

Paul K. Dimond is principal administrative analyst in the office of the associate vice chancellor of business and administrative services at UC Berkeley. He has been coordinator of the Balanced Scorecard Pilot since its inception in 1999. A twenty-one-year staff member at Berkeley, he began his career as an electrician in the campus's Physical Plant Department. He holds a bachelor of science degree from Boston College and an MBA from San Francisco State University.

Carol Lindborg Everett is the associate director of the Office of Planning and Institutional Assessment at Penn State University. She consults with the heads of academic and administrative units to define their customers or constituents, identify the academic and administrative department's critical work processes, and assist in the formation of quality improvement teams around those processes. Everett participates in the development and implementation of the office's marketing plan, which promotes and recognizes diversity planning, improvement, and assessment activities. She cochairs the Quality Expo Planning Team. She served as an examiner for the Pennsylvania Quality Leadership Award in 1996. She has a B.A. in French from the University of Montana; an M.A. in Education from the University of North Carolina, Chapel Hill; and an MBA from Penn State.

Conrado M. (Bobby) Gempesaw II is vice provost for academic and international programs at the University of Delaware. He previously served as vice provost for academic programs and planning and as chairperson of the Department of Food and Resource Economics. He completed his B.A. in economics at Ateneo de Davao University in the Philippines, his M.S. in agricultural economics at West Virginia University, and his Ph.D. in agricultural economics from Penn State.

Adolph Haislar is currently the senior associate vice president for auxiliary services and excellence in higher education initiatives at Miami University. He has been affiliated with the university's housing, food service, conference, and student center operations for more than twenty-five years. Prior to his employment at Miami, he worked for Marriott Hospitality Services, Sheraton ITT, Intercontinental Corporation, and various hospitality management companies. All of his professional experiences have involved dining and hospitality management. He has a B.A. and M.A. in psychology and an M.S. in food service management. He is a frequent presenter for many regional and national associations and business organizations.

W. James Haley is currently the associate vice president for facilities at Miami University, having served in that role since 1999. He joined the staff in 1995 as executive assistant to the vice president for finance and business services following his retirement from the U.S. Navy. His extensive Navy experience includes serving as a flight instructor in F-4 Phantom and F-14 Tomcat aircraft; as an operations officer and maintenance officer in Fighter Squadron 2 from the *USS Enterprise;* executive officer and commanding officer of Fighter Squadron 213, flying Tomcats from the *USS America;* navigator and executive officer of the *USS Kitty Hawk;* commanding officer of the *USS San Jose;* sales liaison; deputy director, Force Level Plans Division on the Chief of Naval Operations staff; and professor of Naval Science. He holds a B.S. in major construction management and an M.S. in systems procurement management. He is active in several professional organizations and supports the community through his involvement with various civic organizations.

Phyllis Hoffman is the director of the Center for Organizational Effectiveness (COrE) at UC Berkeley. Prior to her appointment to this position in 1999, she was the chief administrative officer for University Health Services (UHS) on the Berkeley campus. In that capacity, she directed daily operations for all administrative functions and led the organization's strategic planning and continuous improvement efforts. Prior to her positions at Berkeley, she was a departmental manager at a medical center and the assistant administrator of two psychiatric hospitals. She has a bachelor's degree in educational psychology from the University of Pennsylvania and a master's degree in public administration from California State University, Hayward.

Francis L. Lawrence served as president of Rutgers from 1990 to 2002. He was previously provost of Tulane University, where he also served as president of the Association of Graduate Schools. During his tenure as president at Rutgers, he was a member of the executive committee of the Association of American Universities and represented the AAU on the board of directors of the American Council on Education. As a member of the Kellogg Commission on the Future of State and Land-Grant Universities (1996–2000), he drafted the commission's report on the learning society. He is currently on an NCAA task force developing a plan for academic reform in intercollegiate athletics. Lawrence was an early proponent of Baldrige-based quality improvement in higher education. As president emeritus and university professor, he is now active in the advancement of student leadership development programs and serves as director of the Leadership Forum of the Rutgers Center for Organizational Development and Leadership. His Ph.D. is in French classical literature. In recognition of his contributions to scholarship and cultural exchange, he has been awarded the title Chevalier dans l'Ordre des Palmes Academiques by the French government.

Diane Moen is vice chancellor of administrative and student life services at the University of Wisconsin-Stout. She began her career with UW–Stout in 1978; she has held several positions, including budget analyst, controller, and assistant chancellor. She is active in professional organizations, including the Central Association of College and University Business Officers, and she also serves as an executive council member for the National Consortium for Continuous Improvement in Higher Education. She received a bachelor of science degree in business administration and a master's of business administration from the University of Wisconsin–Eau Claire.

James E. Morley, Jr., is president of the National Association of College and University Business Officers (NACUBO). His twenty-three-year career on four campuses includes ten years at Cornell University, serving first as vice president and treasurer and then as senior vice president. His years at Cornell were preceded by tenures as vice president, finance and administration, at Rensselaer Polytechnic Institute; vice president, business and finance, and treasurer at Rider College; and comptroller at Syracuse University. Morley was instrumental in establishing School, College, and University Underwriters Limited (SCUUL) and the United Educators Reciprocal Risk Retention (UERRR) Group Insurance Co., both of which provide insurance for schools, colleges, and universities. He also served on the American Council of Education's board of directors from 1997 to 1999. He received his undergraduate degree from Rensselaer and an M.S. from Syracuse University.

Richard M. Norman became vice president for finance and business services and treasurer at Miami University in 1999. Prior to joining the staff at Miami, he served for eleven years as the vice president for administration and the associate treasurer at Rutgers University. He has more than twenty-five years of experience in higher education, having served twelve years at the Ohio Board of Regents and three years at Central State University in Wilberforce, Ohio. His responsibilities over the past twenty-five years have included capital planning, investment management, human resources, and labor relations, as well as oversight of physical facilities, information technology, faculty relations, and police services. He has a B.A. in political science and English and a master's degree in business administration.

Leonard E. Pollack is manager of the Human Resources Development Center and is affiliated with the College of Education at Penn State. In addition to leading overall development and implementation of the programs in Excellence in Leadership and Management, he also teaches components in several of the seminars.

Mo Qayoumi is currently the vice president for administration and finance and chief financial officer at California State University, Northridge. He is also a tenured professor in the Department of Manufacturing Engineering and Engineering Management. He is a licensed professional engineer and a certified management accountant. He has more than twenty-five years of industrial and higher education experience; has published more than sixty-five articles, seven books, and several chapters in various books, and has made presentations in many conferences across the United States and internationally on topics in the areas of quality, energy, and systems theory. He also served as a Malcolm Baldrige National Quality Award examiner from 1998 to 2001 and as a senior examiner for the Missouri Quality Award Program from 1997 to 2000.

Michael C. Quinlan is acting associate vice president for business services and formerly was director of the Environmental Health and Safety Department (REHS) for Rutgers University. He is a certified industrial hygienist and a member of the New Jersey Public Employees Occupational Safety and Health Advisory Board in the Campus Safety, Health, and Environmental Management Association.

Louise Sandmeyer is the executive director of the Office of Planning and Institutional Assessment at Penn State University. The office facilitates the university's planning, quality, and assessment initiatives by using quality principles to help administrative and academic units develop strategic plans, improve key work processes, and assess performance. She currently serves as the chair of the executive committee of the National Consortium for Continuous Improvement and is a co-convener for the Kellogg Leadership for Institutional Change Initiative at Penn State. She was appointed by the U.S. Department of Commerce, National Institute of Standard and Technology, to serve as an evaluator on the 1995 Education and Health Care Pilot Evaluation team of the Malcolm Baldrige National Quality Award. Sandmeyer has a B.A. in English from Penn State and an M.A. in higher education administration from the University of Denver.

Robert Secor is program coordinator of the Committee for Institutional Cooperation's Academic Leadership Program, and vice provost for academic affairs at Penn State. After serving as head of

Penn State's Department of English from 1990 to 1995, he took on the role of vice provost for academic affairs, where his responsibilities include overseeing Penn State's leadership development activities. He is a former Fellow of the CIC's Academic Leadership Program and served as Penn State's liaison to the program for five years, before assuming the role of overall program coordinator in 2002. He is also Penn State's liaison for the CIC's Department Executive Officer Program, which Penn State proposed to the CIC and for which he served as coordinator during its first four years.

D. Michael Shafer is professor of political science at Rutgers University and director of both the Rutgers Citizenship and Service Education (CASE) Program and www.njserves.org, the virtual home of New Jersey's nonprofits. He received his B.A. from Yale and Ph.D. from Harvard. Shafer is author of *Deadly Paradigms; The Legacy;* and *Winners and Losers;* and numerous journal articles. He has been teaching at Rutgers since 1984 and has taught overseas at Korea University, the University of Colombo, the University of Cape Town, and the University of Natal. He is a member of the Council on Foreign Relations and lectures worldwide on issues of foreign and defense policy as well as political economy. As director of CASE, he has worked with colleges and universities across the United States to develop service-learning programs, and has helped to establish service-learning programs modeled upon CASE at universities in Costa Rica, Estonia, Lebanon, Poland, and South Africa, and he is currently engaged in establishing similar programs in Latvia, Lithuania, Moldova (in the former Soviet Union), and Korea.

Charles W. Sorensen is chancellor of the University of Wisconsin–Stout. He served as a teacher, historian, academic dean, and academic vice president prior to joining the UW-Stout staff in 1988 as the sixth person to head this century-old institution. He holds a Ph.D. in history from Michigan State University and has more than twenty-two years of experience as an administrator. UW-Stout was selected by the U.S. Department of Commerce for the prestigious 2001 Malcolm Baldrige National Quality Award in the education category. Sorensen has been invited to present at several national and international conferences, as well as hosting a number of colleges and universities on the UW-Stout campus, to share the university's quality journey.

Stephen D. Spangehl is director of the Academic Quality Improvement Project (AQIP), an initiative of the Higher Learning Commission, which is a division of the North Central Association of Colleges and Schools. From 1997 to 2002, he served as a member of the board of examiners of the Malcolm Baldrige National Quality Award program and has adapted both the values and processes of quality award programs in making AQIP an alternative to traditional accreditation. Prior to joining the Higher Learning Commission in 1991, he was an administrator and professor in several U.S. universities. He earned a Ph.D. in English philology, literature, and linguistics from the University of Pennsylvania, and graduate and undergraduate degrees in English from New York University; he has written and spoken widely on quality principles, assessment, accreditation, developmental education, and other higher education issues.

Graham B. Spanier has served since 1995 as president of Penn State. He is a national leader in higher education and is chair of the board of directors of the National Association of State Universities and Land-Grant Colleges and co-chair of the Association of Academic Health Centers Council on Health Sciences and the University. Previously, he served as chair of the NCAA Division I board of directors and was a founding member of the board of directors of the University Corporation for Advanced Internet Development (Internet2, the next-generation use of the Internet for teaching and research). A distinguished researcher and scholar, he has written more than one hundred scholarly publications, including ten books. He is a family sociologist, demographer, and marriage and family therapist. He earned his Ph.D. from Northwestern University and his bachelor's and master's degrees from Iowa State University.

Marie L. Sutthoff works with the quality service within the Administrative Services and Facilities Management Departments of the University of Cincinnati. During her eleven-year career at the university, she has specialized in communication and administrative management for the Division of Administrative and Business Services, and she currently administers the university's *UC Is Listening* Web-based communication program.

James R. Tucker is vice president for administrative and business services at the University of Cincinnati. His twenty-five-year career at the university includes international recognition in the fields of continuous quality improvement, energy management techniques, utility contract negotiations, return on investment projects, and facilities management.

David Ward is president of the American Council on Education and chancellor emeritus of the University of Wisconsin–Madison. As provost and chancellor at the UW-Madison, he led the campus in advancing an ambitious agenda for improvement and innovation. He now heads the American Council on Education. He chaired the board of trustees of the University Corporation for Advanced Internet Development, a nonprofit group spearheading the development of Internet2. He also served on the board of directors of the National Association of State Universities and Land-Grant Colleges and was a member of the Kellogg Commission on the Future of State and Land-Grant Universities. He was born in Manchester, England, and received his bachelor's and master's degrees from the University of Leeds. He earned a Fulbright travel award to the United States in 1960 and received a doctorate from UW-Madison in 1963.

Chester C. Warzynski is the director of organizational development services in the Office of Human Resources and a lecturer in the department of Human Resource Studies in the School of Industrial and Labor Relations, Cornell University. He is responsible for providing management consulting services, including leadership development, strategic planning, organization design, team building, performance management, and conflict resolution, to academic and administrative units of the university. He earned a B.A. and M.A. in sociology from Southern Illinois University and the University of Western Ontario respectively and completed postgraduate studies in educational planning at the University of Toronto. He is a member of the Academy of Management and served on the board of the National Consortium for Continuous Improvement in Higher Education.

Susan G. Williams is professor of management in the Jack Massey Graduate School of Business at Belmont University in Nashville, Tennessee. She teaches management, strategy, negotiation and decision making, and organizational assessment and design. She is the author of many publications on continuous improvement, adult learning, and higher education systems. She serves on the panel of judges for the Malcolm Baldrige National Quality Award. A former national examiner, she has also been a member of the board of directors and panel of judges for the Tennessee Quality Award. Williams is an executive board member and officer of the National Consortium for Continuous Improvement in Higher Education (NCCI). A public speaker and consultant for many businesses, she presents regularly at national and international conferences on topics related to negotiation, adult learning, and continuous quality improvement. She holds a Ph.D. from the University of Georgia.

Billie S. Willits is assistant vice president for human resources at Penn State University and is affiliated with the Smeal College of Business, where she teaches a management course. She serves as a consultant in leadership professional development and oversaw the creation of the Excellence in Leadership and Management series at Penn State.

Pursuing Excellence
in Higher Education

Chapter One

Excellence in Higher Education
Eight Fundamental Challenges

Higher education is a vital and indispensable sector within society, and those of us who work in colleges and universities have some of the most important jobs anywhere. The academy contributes in fundamental, pervasive, and lasting ways to the personal and professional lives of the more than thirteen million students enrolled annually in degree-granting programs, and more generally to the cultural, intellectual, and economic vitality of our communities and our society (NASULGC, 2001; NCES, 2002a).

As eloquently described by Frank Rhodes, president emeritus of Cornell, higher education "informs public understanding, cultivates public taste, and contributes to the nation's well-being as it nurtures and trains each new generation of architects, artists, authors, business leaders, engineers, farmers, lawyers, physicians, poets, scientists, social workers, and teachers as well as a steady succession of advocates, dreamers, doers, dropouts, parents, politicians, preachers, prophets, social reformers, visionaries, and volunteers who leaven, nudge, and shape the course of public life" (Rhodes, 2001, p. xi).

Our colleges and universities have always taken their academic role very seriously, and higher education institutions go to great lengths to document and evaluate their accomplishments. This is done in various ways, including accreditation reviews; disciplinary self-studies; and periodic peer evaluations of individuals, programs, and institutions. Assessments focus on student qualifications, faculty teaching and scholarship, research-funding levels, instructional programs, library holdings, computing facilities, and many other dimensions of quality. With regard to scholarship and academics, higher education institutions are the gold standard, the model to which other organizations throughout the world compare themselves and the ideal to which they aspire.

Why Isn't Higher Education More Fully Appreciated?

With all that higher education does—and does so well—why isn't support from the beneficiaries of our work much stronger? Why has public funding for higher education been relatively flat in recent years? Why is there perpetual critique by students, parents, alumni, employers, mass media, taxpayers, public officials, and other constituencies?

Complaints abound—about perceived problems of rising tuition costs, accountability, classroom crowding, difficult-to-understand teachers, outdated facilities, getting the courses needed to graduate in four years, faculty tenure, graduates unprepared for the workplace, inadequate advising, inaccessible faculty, inappropriate courses, unconcerned staff, cumbersome bureaucratic procedures . . . the list goes on. The perceived deficiencies are recurring themes in social conversation, and favorite topics of news and feature stories in the popular press.

It would seem that the scholarly tradition[1] has served society well in a great many ways. Yet for all that higher education contributes, its institutions, administrators, faculty, and staff often do not receive the level of recognition, support, and appreciation one would expect and hope for. There is, as Donald Kennedy (1997, p. 2) has observed, "a kind of dissonance between the purposes our society foresees for the university and the way the university sees itself." Increasingly, the image of the ivory tower—the protected sanctuary, disengaged from contemporary societal concerns,[2] which has been the embodiment of the scholarly tradition—is increasingly under siege in many quarters. Also being challenged is the autonomy that has been a defining characteristic of the academy.

The Academy's Response

One response for some in the academy has been to ignore or dismiss the mounting criticism, and to point out that critique of higher education is to be expected. The academy, it is argued, has always been the subject of controversy, and it always will be. Colleges and universities are, after all, institutions whose mission it is to hold up a mirror to society and to challenge conventional ways of thinking. Such purposes are seldom achieved without arousing some discomfort and discontent. From this perspective, it follows that the task facing those of us in higher education today is to insulate ourselves from the influence of outside voices. They threaten our intellectual detachment and institutional self-determination, long regarded as essential to academic excellence. Reflecting this point of view are comments by James Carey, in *The Engaged Discipline:* "Contemporary academics are often embarrassed and defensive about the invidious contrast between the academy and the 'real world'. . . . I take that distinction as a tribute, for the relevant contrast is not between the real and the imitation but between the sacred and the profane. The gates of the university mark a passage not only from the city to the campus but from the vulgar and ordinary to the hallowed and unique" (Carey, 2000, p. 6).

Indeed, a dismissal of outside perspectives may be justified by asserting the academy's superior insight about such things, or by suggesting that detractors are uninformed, unsophisticated, or poorly educated. The critics, it is often alleged, focus on the wrong things and ask the wrong questions. They don't understand higher education's mission, and they don't have all the facts. Thus time spent listening to critics—or pondering the details of their messages—is wasteful activity that simply distracts from the important work of the academy. These arguments are persuasive for some, but many in the academy find it difficult to disregard the rising chorus of discontent. Having one's institution criticized, one's work misunderstood, and one's contributions undervalued is not only disheartening and demoralizing but also difficult to ignore.

Mounting economic pressures are also hard to overlook. There is nothing particularly new about the notion of competition between institutions for students, faculty, research support, funding, prestige, and athletic prominence. Nor is there anything novel about the need for change in higher education. Indeed, the academy has been evolving in a variety of ways since colleges and universities first opened their doors to students, and the literature reminds us that each era brings its own calls for innovation and change (Koepplin and Wilson, 1985). Increasingly, however, colleges and universities are competing for scarce resources not only with one another but also with P–12 systems, for-profit educational and research providers, and even state prisons, transportation, and other publicly funded agencies. Many observers contend that the forces of change, the level of competition, and the economic pressures fueling the competitiveness are intensifying more rapidly than ever before.[3] Newman and Couturier (2001) have offered a list of some of the developments that help to explain the present circumstance:

- New educational options for students, including more than 650 for-profit degree-granting universities and colleges
- Courses and programs targeted for older, working students
- Student aid programs used to attract and recruit students
- An increased number of researchers applying for federally funded research grants
- Growing online courses and distance education opportunities
- Developing global higher education institutions such as the British Open University, Monash University of Australia, New York University, the University of Maryland, and the University of Phoenix
- Emerging corporate universities, of which there are now more than two thousand
- New collaborative arrangements between community colleges and four-year institutions
- Intercollegiate athletics (Newman and Couturier, 2001, pp. 12–13)

Confronted with daily reminders of the external critique, complexity, and growing competition for resources, many inside and outside higher education have concluded that colleges and universities have no choice but to acknowledge and adapt to the changing environment in which the academy finds itself. As Barry Munitz, former chancellor of the California State University System, comments: "Higher education (continues) . . . to manage itself as if today's colleges and universities were still snug, little, collegial communities of 2,000 or so souls as they were in the 1920s. Colleges and universities have become huge, fragmented and very expansive enterprises" (Munitz, 1995, p. 4).

To be successful in the increasingly complex, demanding, and competitive setting, it is argued, the academy must recognize the leadership challenges it faces and devote increasing attention to expectations and concerns articulated by the external constituencies that provide the moral and financial support necessary to our functioning. The list of such groups is a long one: present and potential students, parents, alumni, members of advisory and oversight groups, employers, public officials, community groups, taxpayers, funding agencies, donors, and the general public. From this perspective, colleges and universities are viewed as providers of educational services. As with other service providers, changes in marketplace needs and expectations create intensifying demands and emerging opportunities. Organizations must adapt or risk obsolescence and atrophy.

Academic Excellence Versus Marketplace Expectations

For many in the academy—particularly some members of the faculty—discourse that positions higher education institutions in a marketplace or service context is not likely to be enthusiastically received.[4] In essence, the concern is that these images and metaphors lead inevitably to corporate models for the academy. They are seen as promoting an inappropriate emphasis on marketing, consumerism, and corporate management approaches, all of which are regarded as fundamental threats to the traditions of academic excellence. Trout (1997a), for example, writes: "In the marketplace, consumerism implies that the desires of the customer reign supreme . . . and that the customer should be easily satisfied. . . . When this . . . model is applied to higher education, however, it not only distorts the teacher/student mentoring relationship but renders meaningless such traditional notions as hard work, responsibility, and standards of excellence" (Trout, 1997a, p. 50).

Noble (2001) discusses specific issues related to the commercialization of intellectual property but does so in the context of much broader concerns. He argues passionately of the need to reaffirm "the traditional ideals of academic purpose and promise . . . and to recapture the ideological, rhetorical, and political initiative and the moral high ground in the debates about higher education in order to reinvigorate a noncommercial conception of higher education and to reconsecrate the intrinsic rather than the mere utility value of universities" (Noble, 2001, p. 32). From this perspective, the "faculty represent the last line of defense against the wholesale commercialization of academia, of which the commodification of instruction is just the latest manifestation" (Noble, 2001, p. 32).

Critical Challenges

The conflict of perspective and priority is a very real one, and the stakes are high if we are to become what the Kellogg Commission describes as the architects of change rather than its victims (Kellogg Commission, 1997). Is the academy best served today by redoubling its commitment to the traditional academic model in spite of the growing critique and the competitive realities of the marketplace? Or must colleges and universities focus their attention on identifying and responding to the needs and expectations of the contemporary marketplace? Should the academy reaffirm its commitment to academic quality, or realign priorities to more effectively meet changing marketplace demands and expectations?

Customary and appealing though it may be to pose such options as mutually exclusive alternatives, they need not be. A first step in reconciling what are often presented as irreconcilable differences is achieved by the simple act of replacing *or* with *and,* and asserting the necessity, if not the virtue, of simultaneously pursuing the goals of academic quality and the expectations of the marketplace. A further step is to reconceptualize the conflict between the academic quality model and the marketplace capacity model not so much as a *problem* to be solved or eliminated but as a potentially creative and productive *tension* to be better understood, valued, and perhaps even nurtured in order to propel the academy to a new and higher standard of excellence.

That said, how does one proceed with reconciliation, and how can we more effectively make use of the tension between the two models? For most of us in the academy, the benefits and values of the traditional perspectives on higher education purpose are clear, and always have been. What may be less apparent are the reasons some of our constituencies do not fully embrace this model as we do, and what might be done to constructively resolve differences that often seem to be irreconcilable. As Kennedy (1997, p. 14) has noted, "it seems strange and unfair to those who live and work in [colleges and universities] that the public view is so negative when the record of accomplishment seems so strong."

Listening methodically to the voices of one's critics is seldom a joyous endeavor, for many of the reasons alluded to previously. In this case, however, it is the place the analysis must begin. Indeed, it seems quite likely that the future of the academy could depend on how we as a community are able to understand our critics and respond to the challenges they pose. This does not necessarily imply that the academy should set its course on the basis of external points of view. With a more informed understanding of contrasting views come various options for addressing gaps. Institutional change is one such option. The development of more effective communication strategies to enhance stakeholder commitment to the academy's traditional values is another, and the negotiation of more appropriate and aligned expectations by all involved is a third. In each case, the gap between what is anticipated and what is actually encountered is diminished, and dissatisfaction is reduced or eliminated. It seems clear that unless we begin to devote greater attention to our critics and their criticisms, the full measure of support and appreciation the academy desires will drift increasingly out of reach.

It is not a difficult matter to construct a lengthy list of the specific concerns that are voiced by external constituents, many of which have been noted previously in this chapter. The common complaints, however, seem often to be symptoms and manifestations of what are quite often far more basic issues:

- Broadening public appreciation for the work of the academy
- Increasing our understanding of the needs of workplaces
- Becoming more effective learning organizations
- Integrating assessment, planning, and improvement
- Enhancing collaboration and community
- Recognizing that everyone in the institution is a teacher
- Devoting more attention and resources to leadership
- More broadly framing our vision of excellence

Broadening Public Appreciation for the Work of the Academy

Beyond classroom teaching, the work of higher education is not well understood or fully appreciated by many of our publics. All too often, for instance, faculty members find themselves explaining what they do, that they don't really have summers "off," and why an answer to the question "How many hours are you teaching this semester?" isn't a full description of their work responsibilities. College and university administrators and staff find themselves not only explaining their own work and justifying the activities of the faculty but also describing the reasons many colleges and universities need to have bureaucracies as extensive as those of many towns or municipalities. In this context, it is probably not surprising that 63 percent of the respondents in a *Chronicle of Higher Education* national survey (Selingo, 2003) said colleges could cut their costs without adversely affecting quality.

The work of higher education is not well understood, and constituents often have incomplete or incorrect impressions of our day-to-day responsibilities, our roles, our institutions, and the principles that guide the work of the academy. Many of the questions one often hears from those outside the academy are quite straightforward: Why don't colleges and universities focus their efforts exclusively on instruction and advising? In what ways are instruction, scholarship, and outreach complementary endeavors when they seem like distinct activities that compete against one another for resources? Why do faculty members in some institutions teach only one or two (and sometimes no) classes in a semester? How is it possible for some members of faculty to come to work only two days a week? Why aren't popular magazine rating systems necessarily a good way to judge the quality of a college? Why are there so many part-time instructors and foreign teaching assistants? Why are some departments understaffed and turning interested students away, while other departments have a large number of faculty and very little student demand?

There is ample evidence that many of our constituents do not have answers to these questions, and where they do, the answers are often not the ones we wish they had. The problem is not that we are unable to address these issues at length, but rather that we often don't have concise, uncomplicated answers to give that respond to the fundamental concerns motivating them. Often, what is required are brief and compelling answers that can be shared in the two, three, or four sentences that most nonacademics are willing to invest in listening to us talk about such matters. We need answers that can be given during an elevator ride, or while exchanging pleasantries at a social or neighborhood gathering with acquaintances or friends from business, health care, or government.

The responsibility for the communication failure, and the fix, falls squarely on the shoulders of all of us. It is tempting to look to people who are employed in university public affairs and public information offices to correct this problem; clearly, professionals in these departments have an important role to play. However, the nature and magnitude of the problem is such that it cannot be meaningfully addressed by a single department within an institution, or a series of brochures or public service advertisements on television, no matter how well-crafted and persuasive. Meaningfully addressing this challenge requires the collective and concerted effort of all who work in or value higher education.

To be effective ambassadors for the higher education community, we all need to be adept at translating our *own* understandings of our purposes and priorities into messages that speak more clearly and directly to the needs and concerns of our beneficiaries and the publics to whom we look for support. Given our values, our commitment, and our expertise in teaching-and-learning and research, there is no group better prepared than ours to excel in this kind of effort. Others expect higher educators to have these capabilities, and the expectation seems quite reasonable. This work is an important component of our teaching and public service, and we should seek out opportunities to engage in constructive dialogue with those who question, misunderstand, and criticize. In these efforts, as institutions and individuals, we must aspire to the same level of excellence that we do in other academic endeavors. The goal is a simple one: to foster mutually beneficial dialogue and enhanced understanding of the multiple perspectives of higher education, its purposes, and its priorities.

Increasing Our Understanding of the Needs of Workplaces

With the exception of community and career colleges, higher education generally does not devote a great deal of time or effort to thinking about the needs of the contemporary workplace. This is particularly true in the arts and humanities and other "nonprofessional" disciplines. This is often quite troubling to external constituencies, many of whom—92 percent, according to one recent study (Selingo, 2003)—believe it is one of the most fundamental reasons for the existence of higher education. Researchers at one university found that 80 percent of entering students felt career preparation was a very important goal for attending college, yet only 20 percent of the faculty shared this view (Kuh, 2001b; Sax, Astin, Arredondo, and Korn, 1996). Our inattention to these matters often confronts many of our stakeholders—students, parents, employers, and alumni in particular—as a particularly poignant demonstration of higher education's arrogance and self-preoccupation, and as confirmation of our lack of interest in the realities of the external world.

It does not seem unreasonable to expect that higher education would be vitally interested in the educational needs of contemporary workplaces. Since most students eventually work in one sector or another, an understanding of needed workplace capabilities would seem to be a priority among all disciplines, liberal arts as well as professional disciplines. This same logic suggests that college faculty and staff would be resolute in their efforts to determine whether graduates leave their institution with the disciplinary knowledge, skills, and competencies that are appropriate for workplace effectiveness and leadership. It would also seem that colleges and universities would want to know how well curricular and cocurricular programs prepare students in these areas, and how the relevant teaching-and-learning processes could be enhanced. For reasons that are somewhat difficult to grasp—and nearly impossible to explain to our beneficiaries—we generally do very little systematic analysis of these topics.

The goal of a higher education is clearly not limited to vocational training. Still, most would agree that there should be an important connection between the knowledge and skills that are being cultivated in universities and the ability of graduates to make meaningful contributions through the various work-related activities in which they will engage over the course of their lifetimes. Even among those who do not regard workplace preparation as a primary goal of higher education, there is the possibility—perhaps the responsibility—of explaining this point of view, since it is not necessarily well understood or appreciated by our publics.

There is a good deal being written on the topic of workplace competence in the popular and professional press. The general conclusions of these writings, and inferences that can be drawn from them, are quite interesting and point to the value of further and more systematic attention to the subject. First, it is interesting to note that there is a reasonable level of agreement on many of the capabilities that are valued in the workplace. Second, many of the topics judged to be critical to success in the workplace—ethics, critical reasoning, leadership, written and oral communication, group and collaborative skills, cultural and cross-cultural under-standing—are not domain-specific subjects but instead fall within the realm of the arts and humanities (Pfeffer and Fong, 2002; Ruben and DeAngelis, 1998). Parenthetically, many of these same competencies that are identified as important in occupational settings are generally viewed as equally important in other inter-personal, group, and social contexts. Third, writings in the area point to the value of student life and cocurricular programs as an important complement to traditional coursework.

In sum, there is a reasonably good level of agreement on many of the needed competencies, and many, if not most, of the work-place needs identified in the literature are consistent with the goals of university programs—not only in professional schools but also in the humanities. Generally speaking, however, this compatibility and correspondence are often not well recognized by the academy or by external constituencies, because of differences in language, level of analysis, and publication venue. There is no question that more systematic research is needed on these topics. Equally impor-tant is increased dialogue on this topic among faculty, staff, students, parents, alumni, and employers. Such exchanges would clarify areas of difference, broaden the awareness of shared per-spectives and goals, and encourage new collaboration in research.

Becoming More Effective Learning Organizations

Nothing is more basic to the purposes of the academy than the development of environments that value and support learning. A learning community need not be defined by the boundaries of a campus, nor limited to the years one is enrolled in classes. Rather, the values of learning that the academy endorses are lifelong pursuits, and the role colleges and universities are playing in support of these endeavors is increasingly expansive. Again, in the words of the Kellogg Commission, it should be a fundamental goal of the academy to "ensure that the remarkable growth in demand for education throughout the lifetime of virtually every citizen can be satisfied [and to] . . . demonstrate that we can meet this need at the highest level of quality imaginable, along with the greatest efficiency possible" (Kellogg Commission, 1999a, viii).

To achieve these noble purposes, colleges and universities must themselves be effective learning environments, what David Garvin (1998) describes as "organizations skilled at creating, acquiring, and transferring knowledge, and at modifying its behavior to reflect new knowledge and insight" (p. 51). Organizational learning requires clarity of goals, supportive facilities and work processes, effective evaluation, and most fundamentally openness and receptivity to a range of information and information sources.

Goal Clarification and Evaluation

The clarification of goals and evaluation of the impact of the academy's work is one of our most formidable and enduring challenges as a learning organization (Gardiner, 1994). The importance of the task has increased with the introduction of new educational programs and services and new educational technologies, serving increasingly varied constituencies.

The need to clearly articulate goals and develop corresponding measures to evaluate the extent to which they are being met is being given particular urgency by demands for greater accountability and performance measurement. In 1997, eighteen states were using performance-based assessments in funding or budgeting for higher education; in 2000, nearly three quarters had such a program (Burke and Serban, 1997; Burke and Minassians, 2001; Rockefeller Institute, 2000).

There is little argument about the importance of evaluating the work of colleges and universities. But given the complexity of the academy's mission and of the measurement issues involved, questions about what to evaluate and how to make these evaluations are matters of long-standing debate and controversy. Those within the academy understand better than others that many of the most important areas to assess in relation to research, instruction, and outreach are often the least amenable to straightforward quantitative analysis (Astin, 1993). How does one assess the value and impact of a course or program, a residential learning experience, an advising program, participation in cocurricular campus programs, or interactions with faculty or staff? How do we measure the contribution of a program or institution to occupational preparation, aesthetic appreciation, civic engagement, or lifelong learning? How does a course, department, or institution assess its impact relative to others in any of these regards?

The same complexity is apparent in evaluating research and scholarly contribution. It is considerably more difficult to discern the long-term significance and impact of one's work for academic peers or for society generally than it is to calculate the number of single and coauthored publications, dollar level of grant funding, and professional activities—as important as these indicators may be in their own right.

The tasks are no less daunting in other areas of institutional functioning. If we hope to have the traditional concerns of higher education appropriately reflected in evaluation systems that are developed and used, our attention and expertise are needed. It is instructive to note, for example, the five most commonly employed performance indicators in eight states that were leaders in instituting performance-based measures: (1) retention and graduation rates; (2) faculty teaching load; (3) licensure test scores; (4) successful transfer rates; and (5) the use of technology, telecommunications, and distance learning (Burke, 1997). As Joseph Burke, director of the Rockefeller Institute, Public Higher Education Program, observes, these performance indicators ". . . respond to external complaints about the quality and quantity of faculty teaching and student learning, the preoccupation with graduate studies and research and neglect of undergraduate education, the lack of priorities and productivity, the allowance of mission creep and program sprawl, and the swelling of administrative positions and support staff" (1997, p. 19).

If such measures do not fully represent the goals of the academy, it is incumbent upon members of the higher education community to become much more involved in the dialogue on what's worth measuring, why, and how. Critique and commentary alone do not lead to the development of more comprehensive and useful measures of excellence.

Supportive and Facilitative Processes

On campuses across the country, we find many striking examples of innovative facilities and processes that support learning. Among these are new and more flexible learning spaces, online information and library services, high-tech classrooms, widely accessible computing facilities, wired residence facilities, Web page support and enhancement of classes, and an increasing array of distance learning and lifelong learning programs and services. There are many other advances, such as the creation of increased opportunities for student involvement in faculty research activities, collegewide first-year courses, a renewed emphasis on undergraduate teaching, and new programs to promote improvements in classroom instruction and to support student learning.

Alongside our examples of best practice, we also find a significant number of anything-but-best-practices, many of which we have come to simply take for granted over the years: buildings, classrooms, and classroom furniture that look and feel very much like those used by previous generations of students, academic and academic support units operating on schedules that don't correspond well to the needs of today's learners, transportation and parking problems that limit ease of access, and so on. Additionally, there are perennial problems of multiple sections of the same course that vary widely, sequences of prerequisite courses that don't articulate well with one another, uneven courses and instructor quality, and more.

Receptivity to a Range of Information and Information Sources

A third issue of concern for the academy is openness to learning from other organizations and other sectors. When talking with faculty and staff, one hears a great deal about the uniqueness of each academic or administrative unit. Passions are even stronger when it comes to discussing similarities and differences between higher education and other sectors, as for example between higher education and health care or government, and especially between higher education and business.

Learning organizations are characterized by active efforts to look beyond their own departmental, institutional, and sector boundaries in the quest for knowledge and insight—"to act with the benefit of knowing how others have addressed similar issues and opportunities . . ." (Burtha, 2002, n.p.). Certainly every academic and administrative department is unique in many respects, but there are also many commonalities across organizations, and these similarities provide the potential for learning directly and by analogy.

The use of comparisons and peer review has always been fundamental in evaluating education and improving scholarship. "Benchmarking," as it is often termed in the parlance of contemporary organizational studies—has also been useful in identifying and sharing effective practices in academic and student life areas (Schuh and Bender, 2002; Jackson and Lund, 2000; Qayoumi, 2000).

The approach can be equally useful as it relates to organizational practices (Doerfel and Ruben, 2002). Even when there is agreement on the value of comparisons with other colleges and universities, there is often resistance to the idea that higher education can benefit from comparison with other sectors. The major barrier is the common perception that higher education is *different* from other organizations. But there are any number of areas where there are fundamental similarities, even if not obviously so. Consider, for example, a problem faced by a university admissions department: the goal is to improve the handling of applications so that your prospective students can easily check on the status of their applications. But the objective is to do this without assigning a large staff to respond to phone inquiries. Where do you look for a model? The most obvious place is other colleges and universities, of course. But what if they are not handling this any more effectively or efficiently than your institution? The guidance that comes from leading businesses when it comes to analyzing and improving processes is this: think more broadly. Think about your problem in generic terms. Look to the best (Camp, 1995).

In this case, thinking generically leads to the realization that the so-called applicant status checking problem could be more broadly conceptualized as a tracking problem. Who does tracking the best? Arguably, Federal Express or UPS. Studying their systems and how they track packages could lead a university to develop a

Web-based tracking system for prospective students that embodies the same features as a package-tracking process.[5] A university learning from a delivery service; who would have thought?

For colleges and universities, there is often a great deal to learn even from what seem like quite different organizations. Theme parks—Disneyland or Disney World, for example—could be a valuable source of organizational learning when it comes to identifying effective approaches for welcoming and managing large groups of people, handling a wait, and maintaining consistently high standards of cleanliness and courtesy. There are also a number of institutions outside of higher education from which valuable lessons can be learned when it comes to using technology to support instruction, mobilizing resources to collaborate on research projects, and designing and maintaining teaching-and-learning environments.

A preoccupation with uniqueness and the differences between our own institutions and others (or other sectors) can be a significant barrier to organizational learning. To the extent that colleges and universities—and their constituent departments—are conceived to be wholly unique, they have nothing to learn from others. This is certainly not the ideal posture for an institution where discovery, teaching, and learning are core values. Colleges and universities should be society's best examples of learning organizations, the standard of excellence when it comes to establishing clear goals, supportive work processes and facilities, and openness and receptivity to learning from any and all sources.

Integrating Assessment, Planning, and Improvement

A fourth challenge is the integration of assessment, planning, and improvement activities. The issue is not that there is an absence of assessment, planning, or improvement activity within higher education. To the contrary, most universities have institutional research departments that collect and organize data to meet various reporting needs. Assessment also occurs within academic units, where the quality of programs, courses, faculty, and students is addressed in a variety of ways, among them disciplinary self-studies and accreditation review processes. Planning and improvement activities may also be a part of the work of many other administrative, student life, and service departments within an institution.

The challenge here is that assessment, planning, and improvement are often not as well integrated as they might be, and typically episodic rather than continuous. Moreover, the focus of assessment, planning, and improvement is generally on individual faculty members, programs, or services, rather than on organizations—(departments, divisions, colleges). It is often the case, also, that information and insights gained through assessment are not fully, effectively, or efficiently translated into improvements, and they may not be coordinated or aligned throughout the university (National Center for Postsecondary Improvement, 1999). These concerns are not new to higher education; the frameworks adopted by the regional accrediting associations have evolved in recent years to address these issues more directly (Middle States Commission on Higher Education, 2002; North Central Accrediting Association, 2002; Spangehl, 2003).

Awareness of the need for integrated approaches to assessment, planning, and improvement activities is not unique to higher education, and considerable effort has been directed toward these challenges in other sectors. One particularly powerful framework is that embodied in the Malcolm Baldrige National Quality Awards program (Baldrige National Quality Program, 2002a, 2002e). The Baldrige program, initially developed in 1987 for use in the business sector, is sponsored by the National Institute of Standards and Technology (NIST) to address three basic goals:

1. To identify criteria for organizational effectiveness
2. To recognize leading organizations
3. To promote dissemination of effective practices

The Baldrige program has been an extremely influential force in organizational improvement efforts in the United States and internationally. Since 1988, almost eight hundred organizations have submitted applications for awards, nearly sixty have received recognition for their accomplishments, and the framework serves as the prototype for awards programs in forty-three states and ten regional or local programs (Baldrige National Quality Program, 2002b, 2002c, 2002d). The program also serves as a model for many international programs (Johnson, 2002).

In recent years, efforts have been made to apply the Baldrige framework to education. The intention has been to do so in a manner that avoids what has been described as the tendency of colleagues and universities to borrow innovations and jargon developed in other settings and to apply them uncritically to the work of the academy (Allen and Chaffee, 1981; Birnbaum, 2001). In 1995, a broadly oriented education version of the Baldrige framework was developed by NIST. In that same year, *Excellence in Higher Education (EHE)*—a version of the Baldrige framework tailored especially to the needs, language, and culture of higher education—was developed (Ruben, 1995b, 2000b, 2001c, 2003a, 2003c; Ruben and Lehr, 1997). The Baldrige criteria and approach have also had a significant impact on professional school and regional accreditation. Of particular note is the Academic Quality Improvement Project (AQIP), introduced by the North Central Association as an optional accreditation process (Spangehl, 2000, 2003).[6]

EHE and other Baldrige-based frameworks encourage critical self-examination and learning in seven areas: leadership, strategic planning, external (stakeholder) focus, measurement and knowledge utilization, workforce and workplace focus, effectiveness of work processes, and organizational outcomes and achievements compared with peers and leaders. The approach identifies organizational strengths and needs, helps define priorities, encourages immediate and continuous improvement, creates a common language for dialogue among faculty and staff across the institution, and focuses attention on factors associated with the quest for collective excellence. Of particular importance in this context, Baldrige-based approaches give colleges and universities a well-tested and integrated approach to assessment, planning, and improvement.

Enhancing Collaboration and Community

Another fundamental challenge facing the academy is the need to increase commitment to collaboration and community. The need exists *within* departments, but it is most pronounced *across* academic and administrative department lines. This is a complex and important topic, and one that has a number of facets. Faculty are socialized into a culture that positions them at the center of the institution, linked directly to the instructional, research, and public service mission of the university; hence the rationale for the phrase "the faculty are the university."[7] Unfortunately, this is a way of thinking and talking that can marginalize other university employees, foster resentment, contribute to a fundamental cultural divide, and undermine efforts to promote a shared sense of purpose and community.

Dramatizing the point is this letter to the editor published in the *Chronicle of Higher Education.* Paul Irgang, a member of the physical plant staff at a large university, comments on the problem from the staff perspective:

> At colleges and universities . . . physical plant employees are often unappreciated and undervalued, the campus equivalent to Ralph Ellison's "invisible man."
>
> Those who work in academe inhabit an unofficial, yet undeniable caste system. Tenured Ph.D.'s constitute the Brahmin sect, followed by untenured faculty and staff members, and research associates, librarians, secretaries, food-service personnel, and finally, the untouchables: physical-plant employees. . . .
>
> Here at U.M., my colleagues and I are most appreciated whenever a hurricane . . . approaches campus. It is usually during this "emergency-preparation phase" that our dean provides us with a free catered lunch and unlimited kudos [Irgang, 2000, p. B8].

These challenges in higher education are not limited solely to overcoming the gap *between* faculty and staff cultures. It is also not uncommon to find role- and discipline-based cultural divisions within each of these groups, as when the faculty member in the sciences questions the value of a humanities department, or a social scientist wonders out loud about the contributions of this or that professional school, and so on. Then there are the academic advisors throughout our institutions, each of whom has his or her own hierarchical view of the academic landscape. As Carey has noted, "borders . . . are . . . firmly entrenched between departments and disciplines, students and teachers, administrators, researchers and faculty and above all, between types of faculty: adjuncts, assistants, part time, tenured, and tenure track" (Carey, 2000, p. 12).

All too often, personal prejudices, role-based stereotyping, and disciplinary profiling have damaging consequences and undermine the standard of excellence to which we aspire. They interfere with

our ability to work together effectively, reveal themselves in interactions with our constituents in ways that undermine our ability to
serve, and diminish the stature of our institutions. Here, too, there
are great ironies, as we look in the mirror and find ourselves
confronted with practices that are so at odds with our core values
and with the very concept of a university. To change our institutions,
we need to change the conversation (R. Dickeson, personal correspondence, Aug. 2001). Universities *are* communities—what Tierney
(1993) calls communities of differences—not simply collections of
disparate disciplines and scholars, technical specialties, administrators and staff. We need to regularly remind ourselves what it
means to be responsible, contributing members of these communities (C. H. Cermak, personal correspondence, Nov. 2001).

There are certainly a number of examples in every institution
in which faculty and staff members work together across cultural
lines in pursuit of common purposes. Our challenge is to create
many more boundary-spanning and community-building activities
like these on our campuses—activities that reaffirm our common
purposes, increase institutional cohesion, and call into question
the patterns of thought and action that undermine it. In these collective endeavors, quality means that the *whole* must be something
more than the simple sum of the distinguished parts.

Recognizing That Everyone in the Institution Is a Teacher

A sixth challenge is recognizing that we are all teachers. Each day,
at institutions of higher education all over the country, tens of thousands of faculty members enter classrooms to help discharge a key
element in the mission of their institution: the sharing of knowledge.

At every college and university in the country, there are also
many more employees of the institution who are not faculty. So
what in the world do all those nonfaculty people do? We know, of
course, that they fulfill a variety of functions necessary to the operation of the institution and the support of its core mission, but in
truth their roles are much more fundamental: they are teachers.
We are all teachers—not only the full-time and part-time faculty and
TAs, but also each and every administrator and staff member. Some
teach in the classroom; some teach through student life programs;
and many more teach in the dorms, the dining halls, the buses, and

the administrative offices. We teach through every single interaction with students, guests, and one another as we engage in thousands of interpersonal encounters daily on our campuses. We are all the face of higher education, and the voice of its values.

Many students come to college or university at a time in their lives when they are first assuming responsibility for the management of their lives—living away from home, paying their own bills, overseeing their own health care, and in some cases living and interacting for the first time with people with whom they may have little in common. Clearly, they are gaining important knowledge inside the classroom. But they are also being taught poignant and enduring lessons outside the classroom as they watch how faculty and staff relate to them and to one another; strive to understand and adapt to institutional policies and procedures; and learn how a large, complex system functions (Light, 2001; Ruben, 1995d).

Together, faculty, administrators, and staff provide lessons for the next generation of teachers, government workers, corporate managers, and health care providers. What kinds of organizations and environments are they learning how to create? We *are* teaching—and students *are* learning—but what? What kinds of behaviors are we collectively reinforcing? How confident are we that our lessons are formulated by design, rather than by default? Are we teaching the values and practices that are needed to create the world we want to exist, or merely reproducing spare parts for a world whose frustrations we know all too well?

We should devote more effort to thinking about our collective teaching function, and to studying the kinds of learning that result. Perhaps one of our most fundamental tensions as it relates to teaching-and-learning is the fact that the instructional goals and intentions of the teachers on the one hand and the learning agenda, "goals," and learning outcomes of students on the other hand may not necessarily or automatically align particularly well. Improving our understanding of "teacher-learner" communication processes and beginning to explore the implications of the shared instructional role of administrators, faculty, and staff constitute an important challenge to be addressed in our efforts to reconcile competing perspectives on higher education, and to achieve the level of excellence that justifies our claim to leadership in this area.

Devoting More Attention and Resources to Leadership

Given the many pressing challenges facing the academy, perhaps no need is greater than for strong leadership at all levels of higher education: board members, presidents, senior administrators, deans, directors, chairs, faculty, and all members of the academic community who serve in a leadership capacity of one type or another. The tasks confronting leaders are daunting in many respects. The unique character of the academy presents unique opportunities, but also special challenges.

Well-developed leadership capacities are essential in any organization. The recognition of the importance of leadership and of the scope of the requisite knowledge and skills has led business, health care, and government to invest substantial time and resources in this area. The leadership challenges in higher education are arguably more complex and difficult than in other sectors. In most private sector organizations leaders possess considerable authority. Typically, reporting lines are clear; the goals and measures of organizational success, the so-called bottom line, is well defined; and the people in leadership roles throughout an organization have considerable resources, incentives, and sanctions available to motivate and encourage organizational innovation, advancement, and change.

In higher education, where independence is prized and shared governance is highly valued, the leadership challenge is enormous. It requires of individuals with insight and competence not simply to create and articulate vision, goals, and action plans but also to meaningfully engage one's colleagues throughout the institution—and sometimes external stakeholders—in the process of their formulation. For all the deliberations, delays, and difficulties that collaboration involves, failure to adopt this value sometimes leads to less useful ideas, and almost always to resisting implementation—even when the ideas are not particularly contentious. In higher education leadership, the maxim "pay now or pay later" truly applies.

Despite the incredible challenges associated with developing effective leaders in higher education, historically little attention has been devoted to this issue. It has generally been assumed that distinguished faculty or staff would quite naturally make equally distinguished leaders. The record demonstrates, however, that the knowledge and competencies needed for excellence in leadership are not capabilities that faculty or staff members naturally possess simply because they are outstanding teachers, scholars, or subject matter experts. The needed capabilities go well beyond the intellectual capability, subject matter expertise, and experience that come with mastery in one academic, technical, or occupational field.[8] Also critical are knowledge and competencies in collaborative decision making, planning, process analysis, interpersonal and organizational communication, consensus building, conflict resolution, and various other organizational and people skills.

There is a substantial body of academic and professional literature about leadership, and relevant concepts and competencies can be taught and learned as with other subject matters. We promote continuous and lifelong learning for others, recognizing that new learning needs come with changing life responsibilities. To address this most critical need in higher education, we must devote more attention to leadership issues within the academy; this can begin by applying the same continuing education philosophy and resources to leadership development for internal groups that we so enthusiastically advocate for others outside the academy.

More Broadly Framing Our Vision of Excellence

Perhaps the most fundamental and pervasive challenge confronting higher education has to do with the way we conceive of excellence, and the vision to which we aspire as a consequence. How we think about excellence has fundamental implications for illuminating and reconciling differences in perspective and priority within the academy.

Academic Excellence

Colleges and universities have long been regarded as the gold standard when it comes to academics, as noted earlier. As described by Frederick Balderston: "The university is . . . society's main repository of systematic knowledge and its main contributor to tomorrow's scientific and humanistic understanding. [It] . . . is designed precisely for that mission. . . . Other types of enterprises and institutions may therefore need to pay special attention to the university as the archetype of the organization where discovery and transmission of knowledge are both the reasons for existence and the occasion for enduring satisfaction" (1995, p. xvi).

Even with regard to academics, as we know, there are challenges that confront us in the pursuit of excellence. There are questions about mission balance and mission creep, the roles of tenure-track and part-time faculty, access and diversity, the appropriate extent of faculty participation in continuing education initiatives, the relationship between academic matters and student life issues, alignment between faculty incentives and institutional goals, the proper role of athletics, and any number of other issues.

However, beyond issues related to academics and academic excellence—where the consensus is that higher education generally performs with distinction—there are at least two other dimensions of excellence where we fall considerably short of that standard. For lack of better labels, these can be termed *service* excellence and *operational* excellence.

Service Excellence

The term *service excellence*[9] can be used to refer to the complex set of communication processes through which we create and maintain relationships with those with whom we interact through our instruction, research, public outreach, and also through our administrative, student life, service, and other activities. *Service* is a way of talking about *all forms of interaction* between the academy and its many constituencies—what the Kellogg Commission has called *engagement* (Kellogg Commission, 1999b).

To clarify the concept of excellence in service, consider simple examples of situations where it is notable by its absence:

> A faculty member is in her office carefully preparing material for a class lecture. When a student arrives at her door during office hours with the hope of discussing a question from class, she reacts to the interruption abruptly and with annoyance. She tells the student that this is not a good time and to come back later.

The professor here is hard at work maintaining higher education's reputation for *academic* excellence. Unfortunately, at the same time, she's making a less exemplary contribution to *service* excellence.

And another:

> Just before graduation day, a student and his family gather eagerly around the dining room table to open a letter from the university that the student attends. The student begins to read to all assembled what they hope will be a note of congratulations from the dean.
>
> The letter reads: "Dear Student: Your diploma will be withheld because of an outstanding parking violation. In order to receive your diploma, you are required to first satisfy this obligation." It is signed "The Parking Department."

The issue in this case is not whether the student should meet his financial responsibilities to the institution, of course, but rather how we communicate those obligations so that we don't undermine our broader set of goals.

Both situations illustrate the challenges of excellence in service, communication, and relationship development. Events like these help to explain why some of our beneficiaries fail to fully appreciate the work of higher education. When such situations occur—and most would agree that they occur much more often than we would like in many institutions—students and others who are touched by the event may be left with a tainted impression of their college or university experience, and too few kind thoughts about the institution, its faculty, and its staff. Unfortunately, many of the manifestations of academic excellence are deferred and intangible; deficiencies in the area of service are generally immediate and visible. In extreme cases, an accumulation of negative experiences can result in students concluding that graduating—and other positive outcomes they associate with their college experience—are things they did *in spite of* our efforts, rather than *because* of them.

Unfortunately, it doesn't take many negative experiences to create an impression, leave a lasting memory, or sour a relationship; negative events are far more likely to be remembered and retold than those that are positive.[10] What this means is that not-so-wonderful encounters have a disproportionately large impact, not only on the individuals who experience them but also on an organization's reputation and on stakeholders' images of our departments, our institutions, and higher education in general.

Collectively, these impressions can have a significant influence on applicant preferences, patterns of financial and moral support, attitudes toward higher education, and perhaps even attitudes toward learning.

It is important to point out that the fundamental issue is *not* one of treating students—or family members, visitors, or members of the public—in a particular way because they are *customers,* but rather because they are *people.* Casting the issue solely in marketplace terms is an all-too-convenient way of dismissing what are in actuality much more basic issues of human relationships, respect, and dignity—issues that should be basic to the work we do and the values we espouse.

Operational Excellence

A second dimension of relevance is *operational excellence,* matters having to do with the effectiveness and efficiency of how our institutions function. Operational issues affect external constituencies—students, parents, visitors, and others not employed by the institution—and they also affect internal users, such as faculty and staff.

Here are two examples:

> An eager transfer student and her parents find themselves traveling from one administrative office to another to pay the tuition, secure the appropriate forms to register, have previous course work evaluated, and secure library or parking privileges; ultimately they learn that there are no spaces left in any of the required courses she'll need for the major she came to the university to pursue.

> A faculty member finds that the process for peer review and action on a new course being proposed to the college could take nine months, and require the same faculty members to review the same course proposal several times as members of different committees and constituted bodies.

Beyond the impact of the delays and frustrations involved, operational impediments such as these mitigate against academic and service excellence. Dysfunctional work processes create waste and rework, undermine faculty and staff morale, and in many cases interfere with our ability to efficiently achieve our academic goals and serve our external constituencies effectively. Like issues of service, their impact is often quite immediate and tangible.

Beyond "The Ivory Tower": Virtue and Necessity

The term *ivory tower* was apparently first used in 1837, in a poem by Charles Augustine Sainte-Beuve (1869). In its original usage, the ivory tower referred to a kind of sanctuary, a retreat from the realities of the day. According to the dictionary, today the phrase refers to "a condition of seclusion or separation from the world; protection or shelter from the harsh realities of life."

The ivory tower presents an image of the academy as a place that is different and disconnected, a sort of academic fantasyland where students prepare for their transition into the so-called real world. When they depart, they leave behind the faculty who are the perpetual guardians of the light in this scholarly enclave on the hill. It's an interesting image.

Indeed, colleges and universities do strive to maintain a protected environment, one where we pursue the noblest of goals—research and discovery, teaching and learning. And yet at a time when we are confronted with diverse perspectives and priorities, the academy can and should embody much more, and in so doing respond genuinely to the expressed concerns of external constituencies.

This book is devoted to an exploration of important issues around which there is often substantial polarization and disagreement. These differences in point of view—and in the underlying understanding of the purposes of the academy they imply—may appear irreconcilable, much as Thomas Kuhn (1970) had in mind when he discussed the problem of incommensurable paradigms. Tensions are unmistakable between those who are alarmed about the erosion of commitment to traditional academic values and those who are focused on the realities and opportunities of the rapidly changing external environment. In this instance, however, these differences need not be irreconcilable; indeed, there is considerable danger in allowing ourselves the luxury of creating rhetoric or reality that suggests that they can or should be.

Colleges and universities must embody the values of both continuity and change (J. J. Seneca, personal communication, 2002).

This is not a simple call for improved public relations, but a call for a fresh look at what excellence in higher education ought to mean as we begin a new millennium. This is a period when information technologies are creating many new opportunities for enhancing scholarship in all fields. Yet it is also a time when, because of these same technologies, the academy is no longer the sole proprietor of knowledge, and no longer the sole arbiter in its quality or dissemination. It is a time when a remarkable array of new teaching-and-learning opportunities are presenting themselves, when higher education is no longer confined to our campuses, to a particular time of day, or to particular demographic groups. But it is also a time when there is increasing competition from other institutions and other sectors, a period of increasing pressures for productivity, accountability, and responsiveness to constituent needs. It is, finally, a period in which effective human interaction and satisfying relationships continue to be of vital importance and increasingly difficult to achieve and maintain.

The academy needs a new, more encompassing vision of excellence—a vision that takes account of opposing views of higher education's purpose and underscores the importance, interdependence, and useful tensions among the goals of academic excellence *and* those of service and operational excellence. It should identify the academy as a place that not only *advances* knowledge but also one that *applies, tests,* and *uses* that knowledge—one that practices what we teach, and that genuinely aspires to excellence in all that we do.

Notes

1. This phrase was introduced by Harold Innis in the title of a paper delivered during World War II at the University of New Brunswick. His "plea for the university tradition" cautioned against influence from constituencies and forces external to the university. See discussion by Carey (2000), Noble (2001), Scott (2002), and Slaughter (2001).
2. See Wolff, (1992, p. xxx), who indicates that "at its best . . . [the university must be] a protected sanctuary . . . preserved for undergraduate liberal education"; and Carey (2000), who argues for disengagement and "the independence of the university . . . keeping its internal needs and nature at the forefront" (p. 6), so that the university can execute its responsibility of standing in opposition to the dominant forces and fashion of public opinion at any particular point in time.

3. For example, see Collis (2001); Marchese (1998); Meister (1994); Newman and Couturier (2001); Frank (2001); Shulman and Bowen (2001); Ramsden (1998); Rhodes (2001); Selingo (1999); Winston (2001).

4. Apprehension about the influence of business on the academy is anything but new. In 1918, T. Veblen (1957, p. 65) wrote: "the intrusion of business principles in the universities goes to weaken and retard the pursuit of learning, and therefore to defeat the ends for which a university is maintained. This result follows, primarily, from the substitution of impersonal, mechanical relations, standards and tests, in the place of personal conference, guidance and association between teachers and students; and also from the imposition of a mechanically standardized routine upon the members of the staff, whereby any disinterested preoccupation with scholarly or scientific inquiry is thrown into the background and falls in abeyance." Current writings that voice concerns about the influence of business on higher education include McMillan and Cheney (1996), Noble (2001), Schwartzman (1995), Scott (2002), Slaughter (2001), and Trout (1997a).

5. This approach was used by the Office of Undergraduate Admissions, Rutgers University.

6. See discussion by Biemiller (2000). The North Central Association accredits colleges and universities in Arizona, Arkansas, Colorado, Illinois, Indiana, Iowa, Kansas, Michigan, Minnesota, Missouri, Nebraska, New Mexico, North Dakota, Ohio, Oklahoma, South Dakota, West Virginia, Wisconsin, and Wyoming.

7. George O'Brien (1998, p. 15) presents this account of the origin of the phrase: when General Dwight Eisenhower, who served as president of Columbia University from 1948 to 1953, first addressed the faculty, he opened his remarks by commenting how pleased he was to be meeting with "employees" of the university. Professor I. I. Rabi, a distinguished senior faculty member and later Nobel Prize winner, responded, "Sir, the faculty are not the employees of Columbia University, the faculty is Columbia University."

8. Authors who have dealt with these issues include Cherniss and Goleman (2001); Daly and Wiemann (1994); Goleman (1997, 1998a, 1998b); O'Hair, Friedrich, Wiemann, and Wiemann (1997); Kealey and Ruben (1983); Ruben and Kealey (1979).

9. There is no fully satisfactory term or phrase to convey this idea. Whether one selects "engagement," "interaction," "relationship," or "service" there is a potential for misinterpretation. The reference to "service" and "service excellence" used by the author in Ruben (2001c) and earlier (in "The Ivory Tower—2000: Images, Ironies and Opportunities," Rutgers University Daniel Gorenstein Memorial

Lecture, Apr. 17, 2000) is being continued here for purposes of consistency. The intended meaning of *service* in this context is generic, referring to the full range of interactions that occur between colleges and universities and their constituencies, and not the more limited usage of the term, as implied by "public service" or "support services." The concept is discussed in detail in Chapter Nine.

10. According to studies conducted by the Technical Assistance Research Program (TARP) for the White House Office of Consumer Affairs, the average consumer who has a problem with an organization tells nine to ten people. The research also indicates that organizations don't hear from 96 percent of those who are dissatisfied. See discussion in Albrecht and Zemke (1985).

Chapter Two

Broadening Public Appreciation for the Work of the Academy
Committing Ourselves to Dialogue

It would be ideal if the academy's many contributions to society were self-evident and universally appreciated. Unfortunately, this is not the case. Evidence of the lack of full understanding and support of the traditional values of higher education abounds, and the consequences are numerous and significant. This lack of understanding and support is seen in the flat or modest increases in funding from legislatures, student complaints about their experiences as "consumers," calls for increasing accountability from governing boards and advisory groups, growing attraction of for-profit and other competitors, and a public perception often quite at odds with those of the higher education community (Selingo, 2003; Hebel, 2003).

Clearly, one of the most essential tasks facing higher education is to broaden understanding and support for our work among our many constituencies and publics. As Donald Kennedy (1997) notes: "conversation among thoughtful, well-intentioned graduates of the very institutions they are discussing exposes the degree to which the participants fail to understand how colleges and universities actually *work*—how they are structured, organized, and financed, what their faculties do, and who is responsible for securing their future. Academic institutions remain mysterious to the many millions of Americans who have attended colleges and universities. . . . When they were students, there was neither

31

opportunity nor incentive to study their institutions. The resulting misunderstandings are damaging" (p. 15).

A clearer public understanding of higher education and its purposes does not automatically guarantee that our institutions and our work will be as fully appreciated and supported as we would like. It is, however, the place our efforts must begin.

There may be nearly as many ideas about how higher education should be changed as there are individuals thinking about this subject, but neither avoidance nor denial—strategies we sometimes seem to adopt—serves a constructive purpose. Dialogue can help us better understand the perspectives of those who have questions and concerns, more clearly and effectively respond, clarify areas of misunderstanding, and identify areas where change may be appropriate.

Higher Education's Multiple Missions and Many Stakeholders

Being misunderstood is not altogether surprising when one considers the many activities of colleges and universities, and the number and variety of groups and organizations for which programs and services are provided.

Multiple Missions, Multitudinous Programs and Services, Many Employee Groups

Considered in terms of organizational complexity, diversity of function, and variety of employee roles, institutions of higher education have considerably less in common with *a school* than they do with a city or a large corporation. The core mission of most colleges and universities includes instruction, scholarship, and outreach, though, as we know, the extent of emphasis and operational definitions of each vary considerably from institution to institution. Boyer (1997) described these mission-critical functions as discovery and integration of knowledge, teaching, and service; more recently, the Kellogg Commission introduced the terms discovery, learning, and engagement to describe these activities (Kellogg Commission, 2001b). Of these, teaching-and-learning is clearly the activity most widely associated with the work of colleges and universities in the perceptions of external stakeholders. Teaching-and-learning takes place through programs and courses in lectures, laboratories, and libraries, and at other locations through service learning, the Internet, or technological support systems. Though perhaps less obvious to those outside the academy, teaching-and-learning also occurs through many other activities sponsored by colleges and universities, among them advising, student life programs, and cocurricular activities that occur under the auspices of the institution.

Research and scholarship also have numerous dimensions, as we know, including conference attendance, professional activity, publication, grant development, and applied scholarship of various types. The numerous outreach and public service initiatives to the community and public groups define the third category of mission-critical component, with a variety of associated activities.

The work of higher education doesn't end here. Beyond these core mission-related activities are any number of support, service, and administrative functions performed by colleges and universities: the tasks of financial aid offices, physical plant maintenance operations, postal services, recreational facilities, transportation systems, police and fire departments, offices of computing services, human resources, budgeting, institutional research, printing, development, public relations, research and sponsored programs, and on and on.

Each of these mission-critical and support areas has its own array of employee roles, ranging from those highly trained faculty, staff, and administrative specialists to relatively unskilled generalists. Many, but not all, are full-time. The part-time group may include undergraduate support staff, graduate student research and teaching assistants, adjunct faculty, and various staff positions. Thus, in addition to the multiplicity of programs, services, and activities that define a college or university—some widely understood and appreciated, others perhaps less so—there are a great many individuals with wide-ranging levels of expertise, education, and institutional commitment serving in an array of roles. All of these employees function as "official" representatives of the institution in interactions with students, alumni, visitors, and the general public.

An Endless List of Stakeholders

Just as there is a seemingly endless list of programs and services—
and diverse employees—associated with the mission of the academy, so are there myriad groups that colleges and universities
serve, or with which we collaborate (Figure 2.1). The academy's
activities touch the lives of many stakeholder groups—variously
termed constituencies, publics, audiences, or beneficiaries. By
whatever name, the defining characteristic of such groups is that
they have a stake in higher education's work. They are influenced
and affected by, and in turn have the potential to influence and
affect, our institutions.

Current students are certainly the most obvious stakeholders
relative to teaching-and-learning activities. Prospective students,
parents, alumni, employers, and graduate and professional schools
to whom graduates apply for further degree work are also significant (and often vocal) constituencies relative to this dimension of
our mission.

A quite different group of stakeholders relates most directly to
our scholarly and research activities: disciplinary and professional
peer groups, funding agencies and organizations, journal editors
and review boards, national scholarly academies and organizations,
and the faculty and graduate students from other colleges and universities.

Yet a third set of constituencies is associated primarily with the
academy's outreach and public service functions. This cluster of
stakeholders is composed of community and state agencies and
organizations, professional groups, policy planning and legislative
groups, donors, alumni, and the general (in the case of publicly
assisted institutions, the taxpaying) public.

In addition to these groups—which most directly affect and are
affected by the academy's activities—there are members of groups
that relate to our institutions in still other ways. For residents of
the adjacent community, the focus may be upon the institution as
a neighbor. For the vendor community, the institution is a business.
For fans of campus sports or cultural events, the institution may be
seen primarily as a source of entertainment or personal enrichment. Another important stakeholder is the federal government,
which is a source of resources—and also of regulations and
requirements. Indeed, identifying the many stakeholder groups

Figure 2.1. Higher Education's Multiple Missions and Stakeholders.

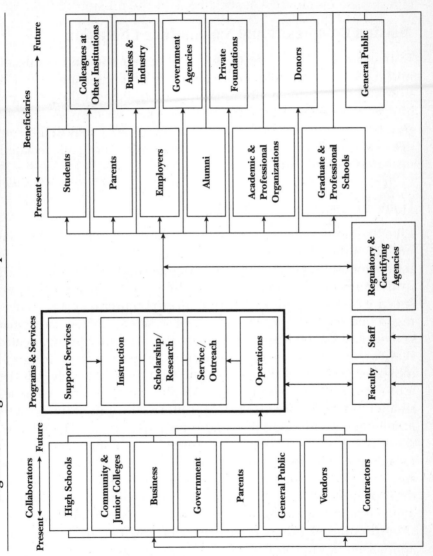

for a single academic or administrative department—let alone an entire institution—is a formidable task and, no doubt, the list could be extended considerably.

Mission Complexity and Stakeholder Confusion

Even cursory reflection on the scope of higher education's mission and the list of stakeholders reveals a fundamental irony: the richness and complexity of our work, the multiplicity of the programs and services we offer, the variety of workers we employ, and the number and diversity of the beneficiaries we serve may well be our greatest *obstacle* when it comes to being understood, appreciated, and appropriately supported.

Limited Perspective on the Whole

Like the blind man who feels one part of the elephant and thinks he knows the whole creature, our stakeholders are quite likely to have a focused understanding of some of what we do, and a fuzzy understanding of other parts and the whole. Consider the perspective of undergraduates: their concerns center on classes, advising, scheduling, financial aid, housing, residence life, cocurricular activities, social activities, parking, transportation, dining, health services, and whether the institution is preparing them for good jobs after graduation. From this viewpoint quite naturally flow the all-too-familiar questions and complaints: Why aren't classes smaller, offered more often, and at more convenient times? Why aren't papers and exams read and returned more quickly? Why are there professors who teach only one class per semester? Why is money spent on improving research facilities when it could be spent on classrooms that are in disrepair, or on building more student parking? Why are courses and labs sometimes taught by adjunct faculty rather than professors? Given their vantage point, it should come as no great surprise that most students may not appreciate the appropriateness of faculty "release time" from teaching to work on research, travel money for faculty to report on their work to colleagues at national conferences, or increases in tuition that go in part to fund staff salary increases.

Likewise, should we be startled to learn that students or others who "pay the bills" are more concerned with campus safety, access to courses, the size of classes, and intelligibility of the instructor than with faculty members' research experience or publication records? It also should help to explain why these beneficiaries may value the accessibility, courtesy, and helpfulness of faculty and staff more than they do the percentage of Ph.D.s on the faculty, the hours the library is open, the number of research journals to which the library subscribes, or the appearance and safety of the campus rather than the adequacy of support for faculty professional development.

Stakeholders whose connection with higher education is focused on scholarship and research—or service and outreach functions—are likely to have quite different perspectives and concerns. Some undergraduate students, parents, and others who look to the academy primarily for instruction *may* be interested in the institution's scholarship and research. For other funding constituencies—agencies, disciplinary and professional peer groups, national academies and organizations, and the faculty and graduate students from other colleges and universities, for example—these activities are *the* critical basis for institutional linkages. As mentioned previously, public service and outreach activities are the foundation for relationships with community and state agencies and organizations, professional groups, policy planning and legislative groups, donors, alumni, and the general public.

An Intricate Web of Collaborative Relationships

The web of stakeholder relationships for any college or university is exceedingly intricate, and each linkage is vitally important to the support, vitality, and advancement of our institutions. Today's students are tomorrow's alumni—and potential donors, employers, and parents of potential students. Employers are potential students, parents of potential students, and potential research sponsors or donors. The general public benefits from the work of colleges and universities, and in turn is an important source of financial and moral support.

Perhaps to a greater extent than in organizations in other sectors, the relationship between the academy and its stakeholders can truly be described as a set of elaborate and interconnected *partnerships*. This is the case at the institutional (macro) level as suggested in the examples just given, and also at the micro level, when looking for the best way to characterize learning relationships between a teacher and a student, a researcher and sponsor, or a faculty member engaged in public service with the community. This insight has often been overlooked in organizational models that characterize students as customers in that such approaches fail to capture the fundamental sense in which successful teaching—and learning—requires a *partnership*. As in the case of the doctor-patient relationship—to which the teacher-student relationship is quite analogous—each party brings specific perspectives, capabilities, and resources. The most desirable outcomes are possible only when collaboration and mutual investment are present. To the extent that either institutional or individual partners fail to recognize or appropriately assume their role, the effectiveness of the endeavor and the satisfaction of the parties involved are jeopardized.

At both interpersonal and institutional levels, the academy's mission is fundamentally dependent upon its many partnerships. The viability of each of these partnerships in turn depends upon shared understandings of the nature of the relationships, shared expectations of associated roles and responsibilities, and shared appreciation of the contribution of the other parties involved.

Increasing Economic Dependence on External Stakeholders

The institutional web of relationships is particularly important from an economic point of view. Higher education depends on a mix of private and public support from many individuals, groups, and organizations; in this sense, colleges and universities have always been dependent on the marketplace for their sustenance and growth. The academy has generally enjoyed a comfortable and empowered position within this web of relationships—a position that has allowed a high degree of independence and self-determination. This state of affairs has led to organizational excellence and advancement on one hand, and also to the stereotypic image of the ivory tower as remote, removed, disconnected, unresponsive, and unrealistic on the other.

With changes in marketplace conditions, the consequences of stakeholder misunderstanding and narrow vision of our purposes and aspirations become increasingly problematic. The challenge comes from a marketplace that seeks new terms of relationship, new accountability, and evolving concepts of partnership. Unquestioning acceptance and unconditional positive regard are gone from the relationships between the academy and a number of its stakeholders; in its place are what sometimes seem to be irreconcilable differences that require a new commitment, new humility, and new infusion of attention and energy directed toward reconciliation. This issue was once purely academic, but it now has considerably more pragmatic consequences.

Communication and Perspective

Misunderstanding, failure to appreciate our work, and questions about purpose and value are symptoms. They signal a need to reexamine the web of relationships and to take a much more proactive role in reframing our partnerships with stakeholders.

At its core, the challenge facing the academy is one of improving communication, and in this process devoting more attention to the perspectives and concerns of our stakeholders. The challenge is substantial: multiple missions, multiple jobs, multiple constituencies, multiple perspectives . . . multiple sources of misunderstanding. Are we doing the right things, and doing things right? Are the things we do, and the reasons we do them, understood and appreciated? We need to do a far better job of telling higher education's story, explaining the nature and significance of our work, soliciting support where it's warranted, and identifying priorities for change where they are needed. The goal is the creation of shared perspectives—or at least of shared understanding of perspectives—on matters of purpose and priority in higher education.

Perspective Taking

The events of the day are powerful sources of communication. Consider these instances:

- A faculty member informs students in her course that five class sessions will be canceled during the semester because she will be attending conferences.
- An adult part-time student takes time off from work to meet with his professor at a mutually agreed time and drives an hour to campus, only to learn that the professor left for home earlier in the day.

- A visitor to campus stops in several buildings in search of an administrator with whom he has an appointment and is treated rudely by a staff member when he enters the wrong building and asks for directions.
- A graduate student waits for months for comments on a preliminary draft of her dissertation from members of her committee.

Most would agree that although these may not be everyday occurrences, neither are they all that uncommon. Faculty members understand why it isn't always possible to offer immediate turnaround on papers and exams, or why attending a conference is important to one's research and classroom instruction. We all can relate to the stress that staff members experience during certain peak periods, and the reactions that may lead to "if just one more person asks me just one more question . . . " But can we expect others to naturally understand our faculty and staff perspectives and priorities as we do? In the preoccupation we have with our own work—and the value we and our disciplinary colleagues associate with those endeavors—it is perhaps understandable that we may fail to fully appreciate the perspectives of others who lack our frame of reference. Consciously or unconsciously, however, our actions and inactions are important elements of the stories our institutions are telling—stories that sometimes undermine the respect and support we enjoy from our many publics. Faculty and staff actions are perpetual sources of impression-creating messages about the academy, its purposes, and its standards. Indeed, the public image of higher education is created at least as much through small stories, such as those presented earlier, as it is by our institutions' large and glossy stories in publications and professionally produced videos, or by our scholarly articles and books.

A poignant example of the communication challenges facing the academy was described in an article in the *Chronicle of Higher Education* titled "It's 10 A.M. Do You Know Where Your Professors Are?" (Wilson, 2001a). The purpose of the article was ostensibly to discuss reactions of Boston University faculty members to a proposal from a university committee to require faculty to be in their offices at least four days a week. But comments by those interviewed for the article, and in letters to the editor regarding the article, offer insight into why students and the public at large might sometimes fail to understand and fully appreciate the faculty and its work. The article begins with a scenario:

> All the student at Boston University wanted to know was whether he could make up a quiz in his Greek mythology course. But after he set out to track down his professor, he realized that getting an answer wouldn't be easy.
>
> First the senior went to the classical studies department during the two hours each week the professor calls his "office hours," but the professor wasn't in. The student considered sending an e-mail message, but the professor's address isn't listed in the printed campus directory. And he would have called the professor at home, but the number is unpublished. Finally, an administrator in the classical studies department reached the professor, who then called the student to set up an appointment. Eventually, the two met [Wilson, 2001a, p. 1].

"If you want to get in touch with him," says the student, "you really have to try hard" (Wilson, 2001a, p. 1). A faculty member from another department at Boston University, who was also interviewed for the article, had this to say: "I don't get paid for hanging around my office. I get paid for preparing for classes and because I publish books and articles and reviews" (Wilson, 2001a, p. 2). Two other faculty members offered these observations in subsequent letters to the editor: "Any professor worthy of the title ought to be willing to hold a minimum of four office hours a week," and "In no case should a faculty member need to be on call for more than 10 hours per week" (*Chronicle of Higher Education Almanac*, 2002, p. 1). Commenting on the general issue, another faculty member said of a colleague: "One law professor . . . does so much outside legal work . . . that he has insisted on scheduling important committee meetings at 8 A.M. so he can make a timely escape to a downtown law firm" (Wilson, 2001a, p. 4).

This situation is certainly not the typical one, but the general themes it touches upon are all too familiar. The vignette reminds us that the issue of perceived availability and ease of access to faculty is a salient concern, a frequent topic of dissatisfaction, and a theme of the folklore of higher education. Negative personal experiences are powerful impression-shaping events. When situations such as this occur, they are far more likely to be remembered and retold than positive events, and also likely to contribute to exaggerated stereotypes about life in the academy.

The core issue here is perspective taking. The communication challenge—which is quite simple to verbalize, but very difficult to enact—is to avoid being so engrossed in one's own frame of reference that it becomes difficult to comprehend and connect with others'. In some instances, perspective taking is as simple as pausing to ask oneself "What would I want—or need—to know if I were a student, parent, or visitor in this or that situation?" or "How would I like my son, daughter, or family member to be treated in this circumstance?" Simply stated, we need to listen more to our many stakeholder groups to gain a better sense of what they know and don't know about higher education, and about the issues that concern them.

The goal of perspective taking is not simply to collect information, complaints, and suggestions, nor to fix every concern that is voiced; rather, it is to be informed by them, and use the insights gained to negotiate increasingly shared perspectives. Perhaps ideally from the academy's point of view, dialogue would result in stakeholders understanding higher education and its challenges precisely as we do, and with a new appreciation of our work and renewed commitment to help provide the support, recognition, and resources we need to advance the academy. Unfortunately, many of the groups with whom improved communication is most critical may seem— and, in fact, may be—generally less well-informed, less educated, narrower in perspective, more short-term in their outlook, and less systematic in their thinking about higher education than are we. But the impact of their points of view and opinions is not diminished by these shortcomings; sometimes, to the contrary, it leads to forcefully articulated and influential—if frustrating—perspectives on the role colleges and universities should play within society.

For such publics, the challenge begins with finding compelling ways to explain the complex missions of our institutions, and how the various components of that mission are interrelated and mutually reinforcing. For research institutions, then, it is essential to be able to tell a simple story about how the commitment to scholarship leads to efforts to recruit the best and brightest minds and to support efforts to advance the frontiers of knowledge. The institution and students benefit from working with the most informed and knowledgeable faculty in their disciplines. These individuals are current with advances in their field; understand how knowledge is created; are leaders in their disciplines; and are able to bring cutting-edge knowledge, methods, and applications to the classroom, their students, and society. All of this is obvious to those within the academy, but often far less so to those outside.

If the issue is an instructor whom students can't understand, the conversation may need to be quite basic in its explanation of why some college teachers are not native English speakers, the importance of the role U.S. higher education plays for the world, the vast wealth of experience that individuals with international experience bring to the classroom, the important source of learning that international instructors can be in a time when the world is becoming a progressively global community, and so on. Similar discussions can be held around many other typical sources of concern:

- How do colleges and universities contribute to the economic and social development of their communities, states, regions, and nation?
- How do new faculty research facilities benefit students?
- How can a faculty member be fully contributing to an institution while teaching only one or two courses?
- In what ways are athletic and cultural events potentially important parts of education and community development?
- Why is faculty travel and support for faculty development vital to improved teaching?
- Can we use virtual learning technologies to eliminate the need for campus-based teaching and residential learning experiences? What will be the differences in the quality of education and student development if such approaches are used?
- Why is it important to create an environment where graduate students work with faculty to learn teaching competencies?
- Why is adequate funding for staff salaries and administrative services critical to the core institutional mission?

Viewed from an external perspective, these are all reasonable concerns, and for each there are informative answers that we can offer. In the process of engaging in dialogue relative to these issues, the academy's partnerships with its stakeholders can be strengthened, and the areas of shared understanding increased. But these answers are of little value if only those within the academy know them, or if they are not addressed persuasively and meaningfully with messages tailored to the perspectives of the multiple stakeholder groups, which have varying levels of sophistication and knowledge about higher education and their own individualized interests.

Whether the concern is broad or narrow, the communication process and intended outcomes are essentially the same: learning from stakeholders, acknowledging the legitimacy of their point of view and concerns, working to broaden their perspective and the areas of shared understanding, and identifying areas where changes are appropriate to improve the institution and strengthen relationships with stakeholders.

Communication with Stakeholders: Who Is Responsible?

Whose responsibility is it to improve relations with stakeholders and the public? At the national level, organizations such as the American Council on Education (ACE), the American Association for Higher Education (AAHE), and the National Association of College and University Business Officers (NACUBO) as well as initiatives such as the Kellogg Commission on the Future of State Universities and Land-Grant Colleges have important contributions to make in this regard.

Within each college and university, the department charged with external or public relations has a most obvious responsibility in this regard. As noted previously, important contributions to the effort can be made through publications, video, and Web-based information packages. Opportunities for improving communication don't stop there, however. They also include publication of documents such as the undergraduate and graduate prospectus, recruitment brochures, posters, Websites, alumni publications, events, reunions, media relations, publicity for research, annual reports, and numerous other media and activities (Albrighton and Thomas, 2001).

The advancement or development office also has an important role to play. Those involved in external relations and fundraising are essential in developing positive relations with alumni, corporations, and friends of the institutions. The offices of undergraduate and graduate admissions, alumni relations, athletics, and others also have a vital role to play. A most essential role is played by the college or university president or chancellor, the senior administration, and other leaders from throughout the institution with access to many key opinion leaders—in the community, state, and region, and in various academic and professional fields (Figure 2.2).

Figure 2.2. Impressions of the Academy and Their Consequences.

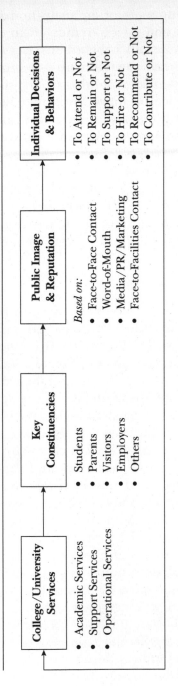

In every institution, there are many individuals in a number of departments who have jobs dedicated to communication and engagement with various stakeholders. But the magnitude of the challenge is such that it requires a much broader effort to be successful. Each and every administrator, faculty, or staff member employed by a college or university is quite literally the face of that institution. In many respects, students and alumni also contribute in much the same way. Intentionally or not, each of us creates impressions and conveys information about the institution—by what we say, by how we say it, and by the way we present ourselves. Each interaction is an opportunity to strengthen the relationships between the academy and its stakeholders, to broaden and deepen understanding of the institution and its work, and to respond constructively to questioning and critique whenever it's encountered.

Concluding Comments

For all that higher education does, and much of it so well, it is disappointing that our contributions are not more universally recognized and respected. This is apparent from the continuing criticism of higher education by many of our stakeholders. Suggestions about what colleges and universities can and should do to improve come from all quarters, and the academy is often viewed as isolated, resistant, and sometimes arrogant in the face of a need for change.

Clearly, there *are* gaps between those within the academy whose views of the purposes of higher education are deeply rooted in the classical traditions of the academy, and those constituents who contend that colleges and universities should be more attentive to the needs and expectations of a highly competitive and rapidly changing marketplace. Some of these gaps signal differences in the sense of purpose and priority that can only be resolved by new or redirected resource allocations, revised priorities and goals, or other fundamental institutional changes. At least as many of these gaps, however, result from a misunderstanding of higher education's purposes and priorities, the work of faculty and staff, and the multiplicity of important goals served by the academy.

Regardless of whether the gap points to a need for institutional change, improved understanding, or altered expectations, the process of reconciliation must begin with a more passionate commitment to communication on the part of administrators, faculty, and staff from throughout the academy. Every discussion, every encounter with a student, parent, alum, or member of the general public is what Noel Tichy (1997) calls a teachable moment—an opportunity to reframe and refine how the academy and its work are understood and valued, and to inform the decisions stakeholders make that have a significant and lasting impact on higher education. Even if engaged dialogue does nothing more than clarify the significant gaps in expectations relative to perceived priorities, the process of genuine engagement can only serve to increase mutual respect, understanding, and support for the challenges and complexities we face.

Narratives

Broadening Public Appreciation for the Work of the Academy: Committing Ourselves to Dialogue

Enhanced understanding results from dialogue and engagement. It comes about when there are genuine efforts to better grasp the perspectives of those who benefit from the programs and services we provide. Also important is the sharing of carefully crafted messages that articulate plans and aspirations in terms that make sense and seem responsive to the purposes of the academy on the one hand, and to the needs of stakeholders and a complex, competitive, and rapidly changing environment on the other.

What better way to enhance perspective taking than for a president of a land-grant university to serve as the personal tour guide for a journey around the state for new faculty? For faculty whose primary institutional loyalty is to their own discipline or prior employer, the tour is a dramatic introduction to their new institution and the state, while fostering opportunities for interaction with the senior administrator and colleagues from other disciplines. This novel approach is used by Graham Spanier at Penn State and Richard McCormick at Rutgers (and previously at the University of Washington). In the first narrative in this section, Spanier, president of Penn State University, describes his Road's Scholar Program, and the goals it is designed to achieve.

In the second narrative, former University of Wisconsin Chancellor David Ward and Maury Cotter, director, services for planning and improvement, describe the process through which stakeholder needs and expectations—those of faculty and staff, as well as students and taxpayers—were blended with innovative plans for the future of the institution.

Additional narratives in the book speak to issues of dialogue and engagement, perspective taking and perspective sharing in the context of other activities. Following Chapter Three, Ruth Ash and Jean Ann Box describe a teacher preparation program that involves close collaboration with the educational community, and John Dew describes how the University of Alabama formalized its involvement with corporate leaders in the state. The narratives by Mary Sue Coleman and Susan Williams following Chapter Four describe how the perspectives of students, alumni, and other stakeholders were included in the University of Iowa and Belmont University's system for assessing outcomes. In their Chapter Six narrative, Francis Lawrence and Christine Haska Cermak describe a strategic planning effort at Rutgers that had as one goal broadening public knowledge and support of the institutions and its academic strengths. Finally, the narratives following Chapter Seven, by James Tucker and Marie Sutthoff at the University of Cincinnati and by Michael Shafer and Barbara Bender of Rutgers University, offer further examples of other approaches to dialogue and engagement. The University of Cincinnati vignette describes an innovative system for soliciting student and visitor questions and concerns, and the Rutgers teaching assistant program narrative is an overview of an initiative to enhance graduate student instructional knowledge and skills. The service learning program at Rutgers is a most interesting model of civic and community service that promotes engagement of the institution with its constituencies, while advancing the education needs of students.

Professional organizations and foundations such as the AAHE, the ACE, the NACUBO, the Pew Charitable Trust, and the Kellogg Foundation also play an important role in telling higher education's story and in fostering increased dialogue and engagement. In the narrative following Chapter Eight, President James Morley describes the role the NACUBO plays in this area. In the narratives following Chapter Nine, Kellogg Commission Executive Director John Byrne presents an excellent description of the commission's role in addressing these communication needs.

The Road Scholars Program

Graham B. Spanier
President, Pennsylvania State University

Penn State makes a difference in the lives of people throughout the Commonwealth of Pennsylvania and beyond. However, some of our teachers and researchers, especially those newly hired, have not had an opportunity to witness firsthand the depth and breadth of our university's impact. Knowing how your work benefits the community is particularly important at a land-grant institution, with its emphasis on service to society.

Background

When I was provost at Oregon State University, and later chancellor of the University of Nebraska (both land-grant schools), we developed programs in which new faculty took statewide bus tours to see how their institutions affected the everyday lives of the citizenry. When I became president of Penn State in 1995, I knew a similar program would be worthwhile because Penn State is truly a geographically dispersed university. In addition to the administrative and research hub at the University Park campus, we have twenty-three other locations, ranging from small campuses that offer the first two years of baccalaureate-degree studies along with a limited number of four-year degrees, to highly specialized locations such as Penn State's Milton S. Hershey Medical Center, the Pennsylvania College of Technology, the Great Valley Graduate Center near Philadelphia, and the Dickinson School of Law.

So with the help of many units throughout the university, we devised the first Road Scholars tour, scheduling it for mid-May 1996, just after the close of the spring semester. I invited all newly hired faculty from all of our campuses to join me on a three-day bus tour of southeastern Pennsylvania, with the university covering all the costs of the trip. The itinerary included a bit of history, some current economics and government, exposure to Pennsylvania geography, traditional Pennsylvania culture, and visits to some of our campuses. I wanted to focus on areas related to Penn State's outreach initiatives, especially the Cooperative Extension Service, and to its research and technology transfer strengths.

I recall quite clearly our first early morning departure, in two bus loads, from University Park: seventy-some academics, most of them unsure that this was the best way they could spend the next three days, some surely having second thoughts about the prospect of spending a couple of nights in campus dorms, and a few undoubtedly present mainly because their deans thought it would be a good way to keep the new president happy. A diverse lot, I realized, but at the same time I hoped that our adventure would change forever their perceptions about Penn State and put into broader perspective their own work as teachers and researchers.

Our Itinerary

Our first stop was at the state capitol building in Harrisburg, where we witnessed the legislature in action and met with the university's governmental affairs representative. We heard how well respected the university was in the legislature but also were warned that "not all legislators love Penn State." One of the reasons for our tour was to change perceptions and to help faculty understand the challenges confronting a comprehensive public research university. Then it was on to the Penn State's medical center in Hershey for a look at the latest advances in health care and the products of Penn State medical research.

Over the course of the next two days, we toured an Amish farm in Lancaster County, which presented us with an excellent opportunity to discuss Penn State's contributions to agriculture, along with our environmental initiatives, which were helping Amish farmers avoid polluting local water supplies. Then we visited the Berks campus, to see firsthand how a Penn State campus served one of the many diverse areas of the state. We saw manufacturing in action at Carpenter Technology in Reading, a company that employs scores of Penn State alumni and has active ties to our engineering research. We were then hosted by that city's Police Athletic League, a venue for Penn State educational outreach programming among teen-aged youth. Our final stop before returning to University Park was at the Pennsylvania College of Technology, a Penn State affiliate in Williamsport, which has a stellar reputation for hands-on education and meeting employers' needs for graduates with a high degree of technical skills. As one faculty member on the tour observed, "We gobbled up miles of territory and scads of information and ideas faster than the Pentium chip of a desktop computer moves bits and bytes!"

The Road Scholars has become an annual event. Beginning with the spring 2000 tour, all faculty—not just new hires—have been eligible to participate, and we've invited some staff as well. I serve as a host for one of the buses and ask senior administrators or faculty to host the other bus. I move back and forth from one bus to the other, and between stops I give talks about the origins and concept of land-grant universities, discuss issues in higher education, explain Penn State's unusual multicampus university and its governance system, and talk about our budget and state politics. In the course of each annual tour, I answer dozens of questions about these and other matters in a free-flowing Q&A format on the buses.

Other places the Road Scholars have visited include historic sites such the Eckley Coal Miners' Village, where faculty can gain a deeper appreciation for the people and accomplishments of Pennsylvania's past; manufacturing plants such as the Harley-Davidson motorcycle factory in York, which has cooperative education programs with the Penn State York campus, and Hershey Foods' chocolate factory (Penn State has the nation's largest cocoa research program); and high-tech facilities such as Lockheed Martin Management and Data Systems in King of Prussia, a world leader in systems engineering and software development and a wonderful tie-in with our newly established School of Information Sciences and Technology. We have also visited many places that are just plain fun, such as Philadelphia's famed multiethnic Reading

Terminal market, mushroom farms, the Gettysburg battlefield, state parks, museums, Longwood Gardens, and the H. J. Heinz food plant in Pittsburgh.

A Program with Many Benefits

Invariably I receive positive and thoughtful feedback from the faculty who participate in these Road Scholars events. "It's difficult to venture to any part of the state or in any discipline that has not been touched by Penn State," one observed. Another remarked, "Being new to Penn State and new to Pennsylvania, I was struck by the admiration the university has in the eyes of the business and community leaders, citizens, and congressmen that we met." Still another noted, "I get so involved in the day-to-day routine, it's really nice to be able to step back and see the big picture." One participant summed up his experience this way: "One of the things I took away from the tour was an appreciation for the diversity of the state. Penn State can provide outreach across a vast range from rural to urban, industrial to agricultural, but it can also draw on the vast and diverse resources of Pennsylvania." Such comments convince me that these faculty will be more effective and more knowledgeable teachers and researchers when they return to their classrooms and labs.

The flip side of the Road Scholars program is that it gives Pennsylvanians a chance to learn more about our university, to see the myriad ways in which Penn State, the Commonwealth's flagship public university, influences their daily lives. It is vital to the university that our constituents know who we are and what we are all about, if we are to retain their confidence and support. The Road Scholars tour is an effective tool in that context.

To promote the visibility of the scholars, we work with our Department of Public Information to invite local news reporters (electronic and print) and photographers to meet us at many of our stops. We also encourage the student newspaper, the *Daily Collegian,* to send a representative. On the 2002 tour, we had the good fortune to be accompanied for the full three-day itinerary by a reporter and photographer from the Associated Press. The stories that result usually further the grass roots' understanding of the university's mission and the specific academic achievements and

interests of many of our Road Scholars. For example, when we visited Gettysburg we made sure to include faculty experts from our
newly established Civil War Era Center, both to serve as guides and
to make them available for press contacts. The resulting newspaper coverage raised public awareness of this significant addition to
our liberal arts curricula. Even when coverage by the news media
is not immediate, contact between the faculty expert and the news
reporter can pay off in the form of later stories related to that faculty member's area of expertise.

Another positive offshoot of the Road Scholars program is that
it gives our new faculty a splendid opportunity to bond with one
another. Participants no sooner board the buses on the first day
than they're eagerly getting to know their colleagues' academic
and personal interests. Two faculty members who were on a recent
tour have announced their engagement. That news caused me to
reflect a bit: over the first seven years, we've had three marriages
and a baby come out of the tours. As I tell our participants at the
Road Scholars orientation, "Feel free to get acquainted to whatever degree you wish to get acquainted."

Admittedly, three days is not nearly enough time to get
acquainted with all the ways Penn State affects Pennsylvania. Nevertheless, the sampling that our Road Scholars do receive broadens
their perspective on the university's mission and accomplishments,
and I am confident it makes them better teachers and researchers.
It also reminds the Commonwealth's citizens that Penn State, some
150 years after its founding, is still committed to making their lives
better.

Responding to Wants: Innovating to Address Needs

David Ward
President, American Council on Education;
Chancellor Emeritus, University of Wisconsin–
Madison

Maury Cotter
Director, Strategic Planning and Quality
Improvement, University of Wisconsin–Madison

Since 1990, under the leadership of three chancellors, the University of Wisconsin–Madison has pursued a few key objectives that have given consistency and momentum to an evolving strategic plan.

By way of background, the University of Wisconsin–Madison is the flagship university of the State of Wisconsin's twenty-six-campus public university system. UW-Madison enrolls more than forty thousand students in a range of academic studies, including 138 undergraduate majors, 158 master's degree programs, and 115 doctoral programs. Recognized as one of the nation's leading research universities, UW-Madison annually ranks among the leaders in research spending, the number of doctorate degrees conferred, and the volume of gift and grant money received.

This campus strategic plan is rooted in the self-study prepared as part of the accreditation process in 1989. The plan has been updated periodically on the basis of progress checks and feedback from constituents, with a major update as part of the accreditation self-study in 1999.

A Campus Plan Driven by Constituents' Concerns

One of the underlying principles of UW-Madison's strategic plan was to develop a clear link between the strategic priorities and internal and external concerns and anxieties about higher education. Diminished state resources had discouraged efforts to reform and innovate, but the 1989 self-study created a sense of urgency about the need both to address the quality of undergraduate education and to improve public recognition of the value of research. Public criticism of higher education stressed the neglect of undergraduate education, while the business community expressed reservations about the contributions of higher education to the competitive challenges of economic development in an increasingly global and high-tech world. Clearly, the university needed to find a way to become more connected to our external constituencies. We had to understand their concerns and needs, and they had to know that our decisions and actions were aligned with those needs.

The university initiated a number of venues for better listening and connecting. Campus and community constituents were invited to open forums for a variety of specific issues, from agriculture to binge drinking to parking ramps. As part of the 1989 and 1999 self-studies, open forums invited discussion on any topics of concern to constituents. We added staff for external liaison functions, increasing our involvement with local, state and federal constituencies. The Wisconsin Alumni Association established a formal network of alumni who became voices for the campus. External advisory councils in schools and colleges were expanded and used more effectively. A speaker's bureau was established, greatly expanding the number of faculty and staff who were better connected with the people of the state.

The long-held "Wisconsin idea" tradition of service to the state meant that we already had extensive connections with Wisconsin citizens. We came to see that it would be important to connect with them in a new way. It was easy to simply "dispense" knowledge to citizens of the state. It was a shift to convert those contacts into a time for listening, engaging, and partnering. As we did, however, we began to learn more about how we needed to revise our priorities.

A message we took from these constituent interactions was that the state did not want to invest new resources in activities that were an expected part of our mission. For instance, we were already *expected* to deliver quality undergraduate education, and there was little interest in providing additional funding for this activity.

It also became clear that the faculty and staff were skeptical of any planned efforts to respond to external criticism. If we were going to make progress on addressing the needs and concerns of external constituencies, such initiatives would have to resonate with faculty and staff as well. The faculty-led accreditation self-study identified external concerns and thus lent a kind of legitimacy to efforts addressing them. The key was to root strategic changes in that self-study and to identify as pilot ventures programs designed either to improve undergraduate education or to amplify economic impacts of research. Ultimately, initiating these programs on the basis of the self-study results and our mission helped better connect the university with the external constituencies we serve. Other more innovative reforms that would require new funds or reallocations of existing funds were expressed as a part of our vision, which was described as areas where we wanted to *do things differently and to do different things.*

Success in implementing our mission—improving what we were already doing—would constitute a ramp to more visionary efforts. Keeping our mission in the forefront and linking our strategic goals to that mission greatly facilitated communication with outside constituencies. Our first priority was to tap existing efforts to improve undergraduate education. On the basis of surveys, town meetings, and focus groups, we decided to address the first-year student experience. Most responses stressed the need to offer greater rewards for teaching, but our surveys indicated that the much-publicized indifference of faculty to undergraduate teaching was exaggerated. Student surveys revealed a high opinion of teaching and the curricula but a low opinion of advising and frustration with class access. Our response was to accelerate and to expand existing proposals to improve communication with high schools, to create an orientation for newly admitted students, and to reserve or create a class schedule that would guarantee the availability of appropriate first-year classes. To recognize faculty and staff contributions to teaching and learning and to encourage them to discuss their achievements, we created a Teaching Academy. The discussion and subsequent approval of the Teaching Academy by the Faculty Senate reflected skepticism about deliberative reform and apprehension about extradepartmental entities, but also the commitment of a respected segment of the faculty to innovation in undergraduate education.

Moving Beyond Wants and Demands to Addressing Needs Innovatively

Once we had addressed some of the most pressing constituent concerns, our efforts matured into a series of increasingly innovative programs. These programs moved beyond responding to problems by creating programs that enhanced and expanded our offerings and, in some cases, attracted new resources.

One such example was the development of several thematic residential learning communities. The inclusion of the residence halls in the academic planning of the university was a reversal of almost three decades of indifference to out-of-classroom student life. Community members, faculty, and staff were engaged in various aspects of these residential learning community efforts, including advisory committees, visiting speakers, and participating in programs.

Another related program funded by alumni support was a center and information system designed to match student interests and skills with the service needs of the community and nation and to review service-learning opportunities in the curriculum. Again, constituents were engaged in the design and development of these efforts and are partners in or recipients of dozens of service-learning projects that are resulting from the program.

A program to support faculty-supervised undergraduate research projects during the summer between the third and fourth year was supported with endowment funds and proved to be so successful that the state appropriated additional funding. This program also broke down the stereotypical association of research exclusively with graduate education and gained external recognition of the value of research at the undergraduate level.

Our mission had grown into a vision of an integrated learning community. Our goals were formally expressed in our planning documents. The energy and creativity came from the participants, while much of the funding came from special appropriations or alumni gifts. The implementation of the plan clearly restored communication with our external constituencies, and they responded by investing in new programs.

Our second commitment was to improve knowledge transfer. The "Wisconsin idea" had for almost a century captured the role of the university in serving the social and economic needs of the state. In part because of the separation of Extension from UW-Madison at the time of the creation of the UW system, the contributions of the campus to the state were less obvious. The symbol of the renewed partnership was the University Research Park. After a slow start, the park became the local focus of several high-tech and biotech companies based on innovations developed at UW-Madison. Collaboration among the parties devoted to seeding research, communicating research, patenting research, and facilitating corporate organization was rewarded by a state investment in a Biotechnology Center. Similar collaborations occurred in engineering, business, and education, and eventually new curricula and new delivery mechanisms were developed to respond to local needs. The establishment of the Research Park and its ensuing success involved extensive partnerships with an expanded constituency. The results are visible and tangible to the economic well-being of the state and thus have created a growing, committed constituency among the business community, as well as government.

International programs, previously segmented by area and topic, were constituted as an International Institute, which facilitated the integrated study of the local and the global, and also gave greater emphasis and visibility to the area. The Institute's Center for World Affairs and the Global Economy brought faculty expertise to business and government leaders seeking to participate in global economic markets. The Asian Partnership Initiative reconnected the campus with UW alumni overseas and opened doors to Asian markets and educational institutions.

Perhaps the most innovative development was the cluster-hiring program. This project created faculty positions in clusters drawn from several programs that were connected by common research or curricular interests. This idea was based on the belief that new knowledge lies in the space between our traditional departmentally organized disciplines. Many social problems and opportunities for economic development can best be addressed by collaborative efforts across disciplines. For example, new approaches for minimally invasive medical procedures are being developed through collaborative efforts among faculty from engineering, biological sciences, and medicine. Our initial program involved twenty positions in five clusters of four. Almost one hundred proposals were received. Instead of tiresome negotiations about fractional positions, each department received a position in return for a collaborative proposal with related programs. Proposals included genetics, international studies, religious studies, nanotechnology, and many others. The highly specialized intellectual division of labor that has dominated twentieth-century academic life was decisively enriched by efforts to cross-wire disciplines and to integrate knowledge. Many of the cluster appointments created interesting stories that were actively communicated to the public. Reallocated funds were used to support the initial round of cluster hire appointments, but these initial ventures were used as leverage for a successful proposal for state funding that resulted in the creation of approximately one hundred additional positions. As with so many specific objectives of the planning process, small and innovative pilot efforts embedded in the vision attracted both private and public support.

Communicating Our Strategic Plan

With the multiplicity of stakeholders, each with their own needs and expectations, it was critical to find a way to explain our vision and to connect it with their varied perspectives. In addition to a concise and unpretentious strategic planning document, we developed a one-page diagram that concisely captured the main elements of our plan. Each presentation of the plan was tailored to highlight elements, initiatives, examples, and data that were of most interest to that particular audience. But the fundamentals were consistent across all constituents (see Figure 2.3).

Figure 2.3. Communicating the Strategic Plan.

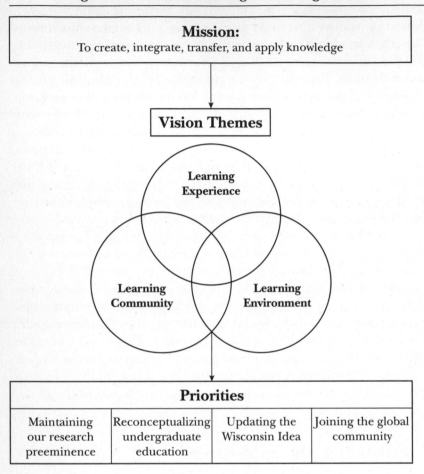

Mission:
To create, integrate, transfer, and apply knowledge

Vision Themes

Learning
Experience

Learning
Community

Learning
Environment

Priorities

Maintaining our research preeminence	Reconceptualizing undergraduate education	Updating the Wisconsin Idea	Joining the global community

Priority Systems

Maximizing our human resources: employees	Maximizing our human resources: students	Rethinking our organization and encouraging collaboration	Using technology wisely	Renewing our physical environment

The plan as well as outcomes and results were communicated extensively through the media, advisory bodies, speaking engagements, campus reports and publications, and events on campus. The many new partnerships and activities to engage constituents provided natural venues for communicating our strategic priorities and results. We took every opportunity to communicate and to tell stories about efforts and advancements in the issues we knew the public cared about. The strategic priorities were the framework for speeches, campus events such as the sesquicentennial celebration, annual reports and other campus publications, news releases, and so on. Indeed, if these were our priorities, then they should be the subject of our communications. Our communication and education efforts were not separate activities but rather infused into our everyday opportunities to connect.

Outcomes and Benefits

As a result of addressing the expressed concerns of our constituents, increasing trust began to develop among the stakeholders. This trust was first displayed by the growing involvement in and support of a series of small-but-bold pilot projects. That trust expanded into broad public support of innovative programs with state appropriations for new faculty positions, salary increases, and student program initiatives. Private giving also rose dramatically in response to plans and innovations. External research awards increased, raising the campus to number two in the nation for research expenditures/volume. Over $800 million has been allocated to a rebuilding of the campus infrastructure. Virtually every aspect of our budget improved. Specific outcomes related to our mission included:

- Over 150 new faculty lines were awarded to jump-start more than fifty new areas of knowledge through the cluster hiring program.
- As of 2001, 218 firms were identified as start-ups or spin-offs with close ties to UW-Madison, accounting for $1 billion in gross annual revenues and employing sixty-seven hundred people, mostly in high-wage professional jobs.

- Students are actively engaged in living communities, service learning in the community, undergraduate research projects, and enhanced first-year programs, all of which enhance their learning through an extension beyond traditional classroom teaching.
- Students participate in international learning opportunities, and many new international partnerships have been established to enhance learning and research.
- The number of student applicants has risen steadily, as has their level of qualifications.

Many of these outcomes can be traced at least in part to the level of stakeholder and constituent trust and engagement that was built over time by means of a widely publicized, clear set of priorities and a commitment to implement them.

Grounding the plan in constituent needs and engaging them in our efforts has helped the campus stay focused on strategic priorities and initiatives in spite of changes in leadership. The strategic priorities have become a part of the institution and have been successfully transitioned through three chancellors without losing momentum. They are part of the institution.

Lessons Learned

These outcomes would not have been possible with an "ivory tower" approach. Public trust had to be built over time, with listening and action. Being explicit about our priorities, communicating them broadly through multiple venues, and then acting on them built trust and credibility. The public began to believe we would do what we said we would do, and funding followed. Building internal legitimacy had to come first, which was accomplished by using the self-study as the framework for action. The approach was aligned with academic culture and constituted a "pull" rather than a "push" to action.

We had to first ensure our mission was being carried out effectively by making improvements in undergraduate education. After that, we were able to move to innovative programs, including technology transfer and cluster hiring. In essence, we had to address the wants first, and then move to opportunities for innovations that went beyond what anyone expected.

The current declining economy is presenting the ultimate test of this approach. As our constituents face difficult economic choices, it is critical they understand the long-term benefits the university can bring to the economic well-being of the state. They also need to trust that we will deliver. Engaging our constituents, communicating with them, and building trust have become essential to carrying out our mission.

Chapter Three

Better Understanding and Addressing the Needs of Workplaces

Bridging the Gap Between the World of the Academy and the World of Work

One of the most vivid examples of misunderstanding of the sort discussed in the previous chapter is the disconnect that exists between the world of the academy and the world of work. With the exception of community and career colleges, some of which are now accredited baccalaureate degree-granting institutions, and professional schools, a common criticism is that colleges and universities are not sufficiently concerned with the needs of the workplace, and that we don't pay attention to the preparation of graduates for work roles. The concern is a significant one for many students, potential employers, and others (Hebel, 2003; Selingo, 2003). In some sense, misunderstanding is part of a more general gap that sometimes exists between the perspective of the academy and that of the marketplace, each seeing itself as concerned with more essential matters, and the other as more focused on peripheral concerns.

Ironically, there is a good deal of evidence that the disconnect may be considerably less extensive than has been claimed. Indeed, a review of research on the subject suggests that higher education is, in fact, addressing much of what is perceived to be important for workplace success, but our critics are not fully aware that this is the case—and neither are we in the academy.

What Does It Take to Succeed in the Workplace?

Approximately 1.2 million students graduated from U.S. colleges and universities with a bachelor's degree in 2000 (NCES, 2002b). Each year, the great majority of these graduates enter the marketplace in search of jobs that are the first step in what they hope will be meaningful and successful careers in business, health care, education, government, or other areas. Although the positions these graduates assume vary substantially from sector to sector and organization to organization, in each case individual performance is critical to success. What knowledge and competencies are needed by graduates to be successful in these workplaces? What is the appropriate role for colleges and universities in preparing students for the work? Both questions are of great significance to private and public sector organizations as they look to higher education for graduates with the potential for contributing to excellence in their organizations (Meister, 1994). They are also of vital importance to students as they select their majors and courses of study and plan their careers (Table 3.1).

Much has been written relative to success in the workplace; there are narratives and case studies as well as rigorous quantitative analyses. On the basis of a review and analysis of forty-five of these publications appearing in the last decade, it is clear that it is not a simple matter to define the set of competencies needed for success in the workplace (Ruben and DeAngelis, 1998). However, it is equally clear that there is a good deal of shared perspective on this topic, and it is possible to begin to identify clusters of workplace capabilities that are generally regarded as important across a variety of positions, organizations, and sectors. In a review of this literature (Ruben and DeAngelis, 1998), six categories of competencies were identified, each defined by a cluster of experiences, knowledge, or skill sets mentioned as important in the literature:

1. *Personal competencies:* analytic and cognitive capability, academic achievement, positive attitude, self-motivation, flexibility, adaptability to change, integrity, loyalty, active learning, problem-solving capability, decision-making ability, and commitment to continuous improvement

Table 3.1. Graduates by Major 1999–2000.

Field	Percentage of Total Graduates
Business	20.8
Social Sciences and History	10.3
Education	8.7
Health Professions	6.3
Psychology	6.0
Biological and Life Sciences	5.1
Visual and Performing Arts	4.7
Engineering	4.7
Communication	4.5
English and Literature	4.1
Computer and Information Sciences	2.9
Liberal Arts and Sciences, Humanities, and General Studies	2.9
Multidisciplinary/Interdisciplinary Studies	2.2
Protective Services	2.0
Agricultural and Natural Resources	2.0
Public Administration and Services	1.6
Recreation, Leisure, and Fitness Studies	1.5
Physical Sciences and Technologies	1.5
Home Economics	1.4
Foreign Language and Literatures	1.2
Engineering-Related Technologies	1.1
Mathematics	1.0
Architecture	.7
Philosophy	.7
Theological Studies/Religious Vocations	.6
Area, Ethnic and Cultural Studies	.5
Transportation and Material Movement	.3
Law and Legal Studies	.2
Communications Technologies	.1
Precision Production Trades	.1
Library Science	.1
R.O.T.C. and Military Technologies	.1
Not Classified by Field	.2

Source: National Center for Education Statistics (2002b).

2. *Communication competencies:* writing, listening, public speaking, interpersonal and group communication, networking, and teamwork
3. *Organizational competencies:* work experience, extracurricular activities experience, task and project skills, leadership and management skills, meeting skills, systems perspective, business understanding, computing and information technology skills, knowledge of economics and statistics
4. *International/intercultural competencies:* cross-cultural experience, knowledge of other cultures, international knowledge, second-language capability, and international organizational or business experience
5. *Sector- or domain-specific competencies:* knowledge or skill sets specific to a particular type of work, occupation, or sector, such as completion of a program or courses in a particular disciplinary area, or work experience in a particular kind of job
6. *Other competencies:* strategic skills and having responsibility for working to contribute funding for one's education

Some of the skills and competencies noted in the workplace-needs literature are specific to a particular occupational domain or sector, but surprisingly, they were mentioned as critical to workplace success in far fewer instances than the more general competencies, as shown in Figure 3.1. The competencies most frequently mentioned in the literature were generic and listed across occupations and sectors.

Higher Education's Role in Workplace Preparation

Although it is a preliminary and limited analysis, the study's results have a number of interesting implications that are helpful in thinking about the present and potential role of colleges and universities in preparing graduates for the workplace.

We know that many of the instructional activities within our institutions are organized around particular professional fields, with the purpose of providing domain-specific knowledge. Clearly, domain- or sector-specific information is important to one's preparation for entry into and effectiveness in the workplace. However, we are also reminded by this and other studies (Ruben and DeAngelis, 1998; Pfeffer and Fong, 2002) of the critical role that is played by the

Figure 3.1. Frequency of Mention of Workplace Competencies.

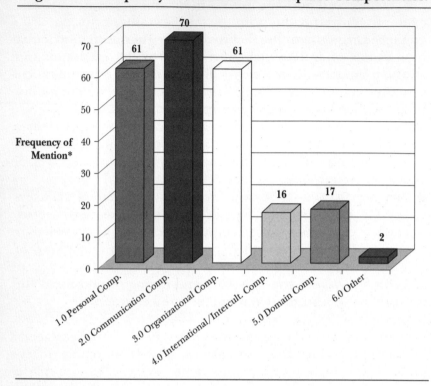

Note: Frequencies were computed by adding the total number of competencies mentioned in each article and categorizing them by competency type.

Source: Ruben and DeAngelis (1998).

humanities, communication, the social sciences, and other disciplines that emphasize what might be termed more generic workplace competencies. It is within these curricular areas that one would logically expect to find a primary emphasis on topics, knowledge, and skills associated with personal, communication, organizational, and international/intercultural competencies.

Although some allege that critical workplace competencies are not taught in colleges and universities, even a preliminary analysis indicates that many, if not most, skills mentioned as important in the literature *are* taught. Why then the criticism? In some instances, this instruction is probably taking place in programs, courses, and curricular and cocurricular activities that are not obvious to external publics, and perhaps not even to some students. A simple example illustrates the point. A business student or potential employer may lament the fact that courses in international business are not offered or taken but may overlook the preparation afforded by relevant coursework in history, foreign language, cultural studies, international politics, or intercultural communication. Or a student or potential employer may be disturbed by the absence of college or university programs or coursework in leadership or teamwork but may fail to consider the many opportunities to develop these competencies through participation in cocurricular activities, or project leadership and group work required in courses offered in a variety of disciplines. The fact that a particular topic may not be explicit in the title of a course or program does not mean that it is not taught, nor that it cannot be learned as a part of one's college or university experience. Thus in some instances the lack of understanding or appreciation of the work of the academy comes as a result of differing expectations relative to how teaching and learning experiences are structured and labeled, or in the manner or locale within the institution in which they are offered.

Another potential explanation for a perceived gap in the preparation of students may be found in contrasting perceptions of appropriateness of particular teaching and learning methodologies. Traditionally within the academy, instruction in many areas emphasized knowledge and information transfer by way of lectures, discussions, and other didactic methods. These methods may not be nearly as well suited to some learning needs and goals as are more experiential instructional methodologies (Ruben, 1999). Thus, even though students have been exposed to information regarding particular competencies, they may not have internalized this information or be able translate it into behavioral or performance skills that are important in the workplace (Pfeffer and Fong, 2002).

What Can Be Done?

Further discussion, research, and development on workplace competencies would certainly contribute to a broadening of shared perspectives between the academy and other stakeholders as to the purposes and important contributions of higher education. Specifically, the goals of this work might include:

- Broadening the base of studies and organizations used as sources in identifying needed competencies. In addition to expanding the analysis of existing studies, more extensive analysis of workplace needs and expectations could be undertaken by national associations and individual institutions, focusing broadly on workplace needs across organizations and sectors.
- Refining category and associated skill-set definitions. Further studies could include a review and refinement of the categories and the specific competencies associated with each one.
- Identifying methods to assess workplace competencies behaviorally. Most efforts to assess workplace competencies within higher education focus on cognitive and verbal measures, evaluated through written examinations or papers. Such methods are helpful for determining the extent to which students are knowledgeable about relevant concepts and competencies, but they are generally inappropriate for assessing the extent to which the corresponding skills and competencies have been integrated behaviorally. If educational goals include cognitive as well as behavioral dimensions, additional approaches to evaluation are needed. Methods of this sort used in personnel screening and placement, and in some research settings, might profitably be applied to classroom assessment (Kealey and Ruben, 1983; Ruben and Kealey, 1979; Ruben, 1976).
- Encouraging discussion on these issues within colleges and universities. Expanded discussion of these issues would be appropriate not only in business, engineering, and other professional schools but perhaps especially in the liberal arts, communication, and social sciences, where it appears some of the most sought-after competencies are being taught. The discussion should consider the full range of educational opportunities and outcomes—cocurricular as well as curricular—and broadly involve appropriate faculty *and* staff. It seems quite likely that such an analysis would help to clarify and reaffirm some of the important educational values of the institution, and help clarify the particular contributions of curricular,

cocurricular, and residential components of the campus learning environment.

Concluding Comments

There are, no doubt, any number of explanations for the perceived gap in perspectives between the academy and the workplace. One is that there probably are a number of areas of simple mismatch among the needs, expectations, and aspirations of the two groups. But there are also many more areas of convergence in perspective and priority than may be apparent to either group. Without a more dedicated effort to engage in dialogue, compare expectations, analyze language use and differences, and discuss alternative instructional venues and methods and their impact, it's difficult to know whether and where genuine disagreements reside.

In any case, there is a need for increased dialogue with students, employers, and other relevant external stakeholders to better understand their concerns, and to clarify our philosophy and approach to developing workplace competencies. For those competencies that are already being effectively taught and learned, better communication is essential to make this clear. For knowledge and skill sets that are determined to be appropriate to the teaching and learning mission of a particular institution but that are not being effectively addressed, new initiatives and approaches should be explored; there may be opportunities to do this in collaboration with workplace leaders. For those competencies judged to fall outside the parameters of an institution's mission, this decision—and the rationale for it—should be articulated. For such competencies, students could be encouraged to seek alternative learning experiences, such as cocurricular activities, internships, community service activities, volunteerism, or part-time employment.

In all these respects, more extensive dialogue among faculty, staff, students, and workplace leaders from government, health care, and business could only be beneficial. Such discussions, particularly if they are systematic and ongoing, can do a great deal to identify educational gaps of shared concern, create opportunities for collaborative research and development, clarify the needs and expectations of all parties, and at the very least enhance understanding and mutual respect.

Narratives

Better Understanding and Addressing the Needs of Workplaces: Bridging the Gap Between the World of the Academy and the World of Work

A criticism often voiced by students, employers, and various other external groups is the lack of attention they believe the academy devotes to understanding the needs, expectations, and perspectives of the workplace. It is also argued that many colleges and universities have too little concern for equipping graduates with the knowledge and skill sets necessary for effectiveness and success in the workplace. These concerns seem to manifest more general tensions that often exist between the two worlds relative to perceptions of what kinds of learning are most important.

For both noble and pragmatic reasons, it is important that colleges and universities undertake initiatives to foster increased communication and mutual understanding on these issues. When dialogue is initiated, the result is often discovery of surprisingly common perspectives and any number of mutual benefits.

In the first narrative, Ruth Ash and Jean Ann Box explain how the Samford University School of Education and Professional Studies has partnered with P–12 school systems—the external professional community/workplace—to design a teacher preparation program that ensures preparation of high-performing teachers.

The second narrative is a description of how a professor of communication and a campus director of environmental health and safety collaborated on a unique project to demonstrate how the classroom and the workplace can be brought together without leaving the campus. Their collaboration led to a unique partnership through which students studied, learned, and applied an array of communication and organizational competencies to address actual challenges facing the institution.

The final narrative is a brief overview of how the University of Alabama has engaged leaders from prominent corporations to provide counsel on organizational assessment, process improvement, and strategic leadership for the university, and in the process enhanced collaboration and mutual understanding.

Indirectly, Chapters Four and Five and their accompanying narratives also speak to the value of closer collaboration between higher education and other sectors. Chapter Four explores contemporary concepts of organizational learning, institutional effectiveness, and the evaluation of excellence, each of which benefits from ideas and approaches advanced in business and health care. Similarly, the organizational assessment, planning, and improvement models discussed in Chapter Five also draw upon developments and workplace applications in other sectors.

Preparing High-Performing Teachers

Rush C. Ash
Dean, Orlean Bullard Beeson School of Education and
Professional Studies, Samford University

Jean Ann Box
Associate Dean, Orlean Bullard Beeson School of
Education and Professional Studies, and Chair,
Teacher Education Department, Samford University

In 1994, the faculty and staff in the Teacher Education Department in Samford University's Orlean Bullard Beeson School of Education and Professional Studies collectively decided that, upon graduation, all students must be high-performing teachers. It was this clear, simple, challenging, yet vital decision that initiated a complete restructuring of the Teacher Preparation program.

After numerous meetings and a great deal of discussion, faculty and staff agreed that a quality educational process depends on the practice of continuous improvement, creation of opportunities for free and open exchange, encouragement of innovative practices by promoting risk taking and reducing the fear of failure, use of data to make decisions, and teams working together. Using these principles, and on the basis of multiyear data gathered from multiple sources, we have redesigned the teacher education program to meet the learning needs of P–12 students. *Partners* magazine, a publication of the Economic Development Partnership of Alabama, in an article titled "Rewriting the Book on Teacher Education," praised Samford's teacher education program for its "approach to planning, assessment, continuous improvement, and meeting the needs of their customers."

The development of continuous connections with the P–12 community underpins all the improvements we have made and ensures effective preparation of teacher education graduates. Collaboration with P–12 schools occurs in each phase of the teacher preparation; program goals and daily operations reflect this collaboration. Data gathered from the schools, employers, graduates, and current students furnish the information and knowledge needed for the department to monitor the achievement of our goals. These data also drive improvement in all program components within teacher education.

Process: The Evolution of Our Program

Since 1994, current students, graduates, and employers have been surveyed annually to determine program strengths and areas for improvement. Each semester, all graduating seniors complete the American College Testing Student Opinion Survey, which evaluates the effectiveness of their programs and gives suggestions for improvement.

Each year since 1994, first-year graduates with seven months of teaching experience have been asked, "What did you need to know and be able to do in your first year of teaching that we did not provide for you?" Also, employers of recent graduates have been asked, "What could the teacher education department at Samford have done to better prepare your new teachers?"

Annually, faculty and advisory groups comprising school leaders explore the questions "What do teachers need to know and be able to do?" and "What are the qualities of your most effective teachers?" Through these focus groups, we identify, in greater detail, needs and problems discovered through the surveys, create and sustain an ongoing dialogue with our students and customers, and determine the probable effectiveness of solutions.

An analysis of all of this information is completed each year and is used to evaluate and revise programs and identify opportunities for graduates. Graduates are contacted each year to determine the percentage who are employed in their chosen fields, and to identify additional help they may need. These data are used as a check for program viability and for employer satisfaction with graduates' knowledge and skills.

Student achievement results—such as course grades, GPAs, and nationally standardized tests—are used to evaluate and revise courses and programs. Every student completes the Teacher Education Capstone Experience. It includes a student portfolio, a videotaped lesson taught during the internship, and a formal presentation; it is assessed by professors and outside evaluators.

When people in organizations are involved in gathering and using data to make decisions, improvement often flows from the growth in their understanding. Therefore, in 1994, after we established clear processes for collecting data, a faculty team identified intake, process, and output key performance indicators and began collecting baseline data. According to Peggy Connell, superintendent of the Talladega County School System, "In my twelve years as a central office administrator and superintendent, I have seen no other college or university seek and use data, as well as information from practitioners, to make improvements in their programs as vigorously and accurately as Samford's School of Education." Midcourse and end-of-course evaluations by students are completed in every course each semester; they give faculty, department chairs, and the dean individual assessments of professor and course effectiveness. The faculty uses these evaluations to make adjustments during the year to improve the effectiveness of instruction.

In 1998, after four years of data and information analysis, it became obvious that graduates of teacher preparation programs must be more proficient than they currently were in three areas:

1. Graduates needed to be able to work with a diverse population of students, particularly children with special needs.
2. They must be able to solve problems and work in teams with colleagues as soon as they graduate.
3. Finally, graduates should be more than just aware of different kinds of technologies; they should be technologically able in several areas.

These were the challenges. How could we make certain that our graduates would be able to ensure learning for special-needs children as well as for typical learners, work in teams to solve authentic problems of practice immediately upon graduation, and use technology to increase student achievement and inspire learning? Faculty and staff first took the extraordinary action of discarding the entire curriculum. They then started over, building a curriculum and instructional program based on what teachers need to know and be able to do when they graduate from a teacher preparation program.

Results: What Does the Teacher Education Program Look Like Now?

To address the first area of need, every student who began Samford in the fall of 1998 and who plans to teach at the P–6 grade levels now receives certification in four areas: early childhood education, early childhood special education, elementary education, and elementary collaborative special education. This furnishes graduates with the knowledge and skills to adapt lessons to meet a variety of individual learning needs, and to ensure learning for children with diverse needs.

In response to the second area of need, problem-based learning gives prospective teachers opportunities to experience the complexity of real-life classrooms throughout their college years, rather than just during student teaching. All courses include problems that teachers are faced with daily, thus authentically connecting class work with P–12 school experiences. Teachers, administrators, and other practitioners assist in the development of courses and in the problem-solving process.

To further meet this second area of need, clinical experiences have been significantly extended in the teacher education program. The Early Childhood, Elementary, Special Needs Curriculum includes thirty weeks of clinical experiences; the secondary program includes twenty-four weeks. Clinical experiences are developmentally designed, and students are evaluated on their performance throughout the program. Clinical rotations include extensive work in inclusion classrooms with special education children and take place in urban, rural, and suburban schools.

The third area of need is met through technological requirements that have been included in every teacher education course. Before teacher education students graduate from Samford's program, they must demonstrate competence in many technologies, among them computer-based presentations, spreadsheets, two-way audio and video interactions, and television news broadcasting and editing. More importantly, they know how to build technology into instruction to improve student achievement.

Samford teacher education graduates are prepared throughout their program to improve the learning of P–12 students. A study of eleven area elementary schools confirms that all Samford graduates were effective in helping all of their students improve their learning in reading and mathematics, as demonstrated by achievement test scores.

In addition to improving P–12 student achievement, all performance measures have shown significant increases since 1994. Here are examples:

- Graduates employed within three months of graduation: up from 85 percent to 100 percent
- Major Field Assessment Test mean score: from 159.1 to 163.6 (national mean 157.3)
- Enrollment: from 492 to 750 students, a 52 percent increase
- Faculty involvement in scholarship: from 30 percent to 100 percent
- Faculty involvement in service: from 31 percent to 100 percent
- Students involved in research projects: from 20 percent to 60 percent

In the 1999 article "Transforming Teacher Education: The Samford University Example," John Norton begins his description of Samford's teacher education program with this introduction: "The results Samford is achieving are not only a testament to the hard work of its education faculty and staff but positive proof that a well-designed university program can prepare graduates who can 'hit the ground running'—ready to teach and manage today's students effectively."

Pat Hodge, principal of Mountain Brook Elementary School, said, "In my system, it has long been a tradition to hire only experienced teachers. However, I have hired a number of first-year teachers from Samford University because they are so thoroughly prepared to help my students achieve to their highest levels. And Samford University is the *only* university from which I regularly hire first-year teachers." Samford's program has also been highlighted throughout the southeast as exemplary. According to a white paper on education reform in South Carolina, "Samford University has yielded some impressive results."

Samford University recently was awarded the U.S. Department of Education's first National Award for Effective Teacher Preparation; Teacher Education was described as a "cutting edge program that provides powerful examples for others seeking to ensure that their graduates make a measurable difference in the achievement of P–12 students."

Learning Leadership Competencies as Campus Consultants

Stacey L. Connaughton
Assistant Professor of Communication, Rutgers,
State University of New Jersey

Michael C. Quinlan
Director, Environmental Health and Safety
Department, Rutgers University

In September 2001, professors Brent Ruben and Stacey Connaughton, faculty members in the Department of Communication at Rutgers University, launched an innovative classroom structure designed to give undergraduate students firsthand experience with leadership and organizational processes. Students enrolled in Leadership in Groups and Organizations, jointly taught by Ruben and Connaughton, and formed Millennium Leadership, Inc. (MLI), a classroom-based leadership and communication consulting organization. MLI's first client was the Rutgers Environmental Health and Safety Department (REHS). This department agreed to build a collaborative relationship with MLI to gain assistance in developing and executing a communication plan that would encourage universitywide compliance with federal Environmental Protection Agency (EPA) regulations. The MLI classroom model and the subsequent collaboration between MLI and REHS represent a novel approach to teaching and learning about leadership competencies, particularly as they relate to building relationships across unit and divisional boundaries. This chapter relates the history, processes, and results of this intrauniversity collaboration. It outlines the challenge that REHS faced, explicates the MLI model, discusses the leadership competencies that students developed, and highlights the outcomes of this joint endeavor.

The Challenge

In an effort to better evaluate and enforce universities' regulatory compliance with a range of environmental programs, the EPA began an aggressive enforcement program in August 2000. A December 1999 letter from the EPA Region 2 administrator notified all institutions of the pending enforcement inspections. With a rather ominous tone, the letter stated: "The U.S. Environmental Protection Agency (EPA) Region 2 is planning to conduct inspections of colleges and universities within our region . . . during the upcoming year, to determine their compliance with hazardous waste and other regulations. It has come to our attention that some colleges and universities do not fully comply with environmental regulations. If inspections determine noncompliance, formal enforcement action with monetary penalties against significant violators is possible."

Colleges and universities have reason to listen attentively. Failure to meet compliance regulations has prompted the EPA to levy extensive fines against noncomplying institutions, such as those shown in Table 3.2.

These enforcement actions have fueled negative publicity for higher education institutions. For instance, a *Wall Street Journal* headline on January 17, 2000, noted "Poison Ivy League Is a Real Dump." The poor compliance record of some schools prompted the EPA to issue an Enforcement Alert in July 2000 declaring "Universities, Colleges Not Receiving Top Marks for Environmental Compliance."

To meet these challenges, the EPA promoted its policy for "self-audits." This program gives a regulated unit the opportunity to self-report violations to the EPA in exchange for avoiding some penalties. To have penalties waived, the unit must (1) correct all violations, (2) adopt a commitment to preventing a recurrence of the violations, and (3) "cooperate" with the EPA.

In November 2001, REHS decided to pursue the self-audit policy. The unit believed that doing so would (1) demonstrate the university's commitment to environmental protection; (2) exhibit

Table 3.2. Examples of Fines Levied Against Universities by the Environmental Protection Agency.

INSTITUTION	YEAR	PENALTY	COMPLIANCE ISSUES
Stanford University	1994	$995,000	Hazardous waste
Yale University	1994	$348,500	Hazardous waste
University of New Hampshire	1997	$229,000	Hazardous waste
Boston University UST, SPCC	1997	$771,000	Hazardous waste
University of Colorado	1997	$343,000	Hazardous waste
University of Missouri	1998	$582,296	Hazardous waste

Note: UST = underground storage tanks; SPCC = spill prevention, countermeasure, and control.

Source: Website for the College and University EHS Roundtable (http://roundtable.healthsafe.uab.edu).

leadership among academic institutions; (3) encourage cultural change within the university; (4) foster a positive image of Rutgers; and (5) avoid penalties, enabling scarce resources to be allocated for environmental improvements. The self-audit approach was also consistent with the department's core beliefs of protecting people and the environment and promoting compliance with regulatory requirements.

But embarking on the self-audit policy was challenging to REHS. There were limited resources to conduct the audits, a large and diverse population was involved in potentially noncompliant activities, and the university had an extremely decentralized management structure. Considering that Rutgers has more than one thousand laboratories distributed among numerous academic disciplines and on multiple campuses, how would REHS promote and sustain environmentally friendly values and behaviors among the Rutgers research staff?

REHS quickly realized that the self-audit program's success would be contingent on effective communication with all stakeholder groups. REHS sought advice on how to communicate its message to academic research staff members across the university—hence, the unit's collaboration with MLI began.

The Model: Millennium Leadership

The MLI model was designed to be simultaneously a classroom activity and an organizational experience. At the classroom level, MLI is a simulated organization that seeks to engage students in organizational and leadership processes, and to foster critical inquiry and self-reflection about these processes. MLI is also a consulting organization that provides service to clients on communication matters.

Students built MLI from the ground up. They formed five divisions: research and development, planning, creative I (behaviors), creative II (values), and media. Each division had a student who served as "group manager," a positional leader who recruited and hired divisional members. Together, the students wrote MLI's mission, vision, and goals statements, developed communication norms for the divisions and the organization, designed and executed tasks, managed internal conflicts, coordinated with each other, engaged in problem solving and troubleshooting, and interfaced with and made presentations to their client, REHS. The students worked on a communication campaign for REHS; by the end of the semester, they had created a strategic plan with an implementation timeline that their client could follow.

Learning Leadership Competencies

The MLI model is an excellent means of demonstrating that leadership is a multifaceted and communicative process. MLI students gleaned many leadership lessons through their collaboration with REHS, lessons that are captured in the dimensions of Komives, Lucas, and McMahon's relational leadership model (1998). Komives and colleagues contend that leadership is about building and maintaining relationships. Their model focuses on five leadership competencies:

1. Being *purposeful* and committed to common goals
2. Being *inclusive* of people and diversity
3. Being *process-oriented*
4. *Empowering* others
5. Being *ethical* in thoughts and actions

Leaders encourage a sense of *purpose* from organizational members. That is, by collaborating and finding common ground with others, leaders help to establish shared vision and trajectories. The MLI model helped students learn about purposefulness in several ways. For example, as members of MLI, the students created the organization's mission and vision. Involvement in these creative processes encouraged them to buy into MLI's purpose, since they had helped create it. The students learned how mission and vision statements could be used as motivational and sense-making tools, as they periodically consulted these statements in designing the communication plan for REHS. Each MLI division also created its own vision and goals, and the divisional members then had to articulate how their unit's mission contributed to that of the organization, as well as how their unit would contribute to the REHS project.

Leadership is also about *inclusivity*—understanding, valuing, and engaging diversity in others' ideas, styles, approaches, and backgrounds. At MLI, students regularly practiced inclusivity. They confronted and learned to accept the diversity of their colleagues. They learned how to leverage diversity, using it to construct a cohesive and innovative final product for REHS. Students also engaged in inclusivity by seeking to understand the needs of their client, REHS. The REHS unit spoke a different "language" than what communication students were accustomed to, one that used scientific and technical jargon. Students had to "decipher" and then "translate" between these two languages to design a communication strategy that would meet their client's goals.

Being thoughtful and attentive to how organizational members act and interact is another key leadership competency, what Komives and colleagues call *being process-oriented*. Communicative activities such as collaboration, conflict management, and meaning making are examples of these processes. The students engaged in several of these behaviors during their MLI experience and collaboration with REHS.

Oftentimes, how educators teach and evaluate students centers on *individual* achievement. Yet when students enter organizations, they are expected to work in teams. At MLI, collaboration with fellow division members, with other MLI divisions, and with REHS was a central activity. Working in a collaborative format taught students several valuable lessons related to teamwork that will stay with them in their professional lives. One student articulated it this way: "Group cohesion is VERY important in order to be successful; [teams] can have conflict but must be able to resolve and/or compromise. . . . [It is] very important to listen to the client, do proper research, and pay attention to details."

Additionally, students learned how to (and how *not* to) deal with conflict. One organizationwide event in particular presented valuable lessons in conflict management. The planning division (in charge of overseeing the development of the communication plan and coordination of four other divisions) had sent an electronic memo to the other divisions that recipients construed as invasive and disrespectful of their ability to perform their own tasks. The e-mail caused such intraorganizational disharmony that the president met with the five divisional leaders and facilitated a discussion about motivations, intentions, perspective taking, and moving forward. The meeting was heated at times, as meetings like this can be in a professional context, but it concluded on a positive note, with divisional leaders expressing understanding about how they felt and why they acted the way they did. At the next class meeting, the CEO and president informed other MLI members of the meeting's process and outcomes. Meetings such as this one helped students make sense of why the conflict developed and how, as leaders, they could deal with similar conflicts in the future.

Students both saw and practiced meaning making throughout the MLI process. For instance, the CEO, president, and positional leaders made sense of events when updating MLI members. All students had the opportunity to manage meaning in designing their final presentation of their communication plan to REHS. Here they were faced with the challenge of selling their ideas to a group of professionals, a task that required them to remind their client of the unit's needs; outline recommendations; and convince their client that these steps would meet, and exceed, their needs.

Along with being process-oriented, leadership involves *empowering* others. That is, members feel a sense of ownership over a project or process, and the organization is set up in such a way that expression and diverse thinking are encouraged. At MLI, students were the organization; they developed the organizational climate. They also came to realize that the success of the organization rested on their shoulders. At times, students felt burned out; at other times, they felt inspired. After presenting their communication plan to REHS, most students were quite proud. As one MLI member articulated: "After putting in the work, I felt a great commitment to the end product presented to REHS. I identified with MLI and the class as though I represented the organization and its accomplishments, as well as the organization and its image represented me." MLI requires that students exert a great deal of effort, but the model also teaches them about empowerment and commitment, important components of leadership.

Further, leadership is about endorsing and practicing *ethical* behavior. Leaders are expected to do the right thing and serve others, behaving with character and integrity, even if their final goal is not attained. By working closely with each other on a real project for a real client, students watched and learned from one another. They witnessed various leadership styles. Positional leaders led by example, and MLI members modeled exemplary behavior. After completing the course, students reported being inspired to work for those positional leaders whose attitudes and behaviors they admired. Students also learned that they were accountable not only to each other but also to their client. Excuses for not having work completed were no longer matters strictly between student and professor. At MLI, students quickly learned that failure to complete assignments had consequences for the entire group, and positional leaders learned tactics for encouraging follow-through from their team members.

Outcomes

This collaborative endeavor was beneficial to students, REHS, the professors, and the university at large. In addition to the leadership competencies, students gained other valuable lessons from the MLI model and their work with REHS: developing a communication strategy, a tangible product they can highlight on their resumes and in upcoming job interviews; networking with each other and with members of the Rutgers community with whom they might not otherwise have had contact; and learning how the knowledge imparted in their university classes enables them to be productive and competent organizational citizens. REHS gained promising strategies and time lines to reach its goals. The professors were able to witness a functioning organization during class meetings and through electronic mail and listserv interactions. Such exposure prompted us to think of research questions for future projects. The university community benefited, both through the exposure that the collaborative endeavor created as well as through the synergies that enabled it to happen. After hearing of this innovative classroom experience, the university admissions office decided to feature it in a publication. In April 2002, REHS was given an award from the EPA in recognition of its self-audit program. The honor brought national visibility to Rutgers University.

The MLI model and collaboration with REHS enabled students to gain firsthand experience in developing leadership competencies. By having purpose, engaging in perspective taking, focusing on process, empowering themselves and others, and acting ethically, students learned about the challenges that leaders face, as well as the satisfaction and pride they enjoy. Many members of the university community were able to reap the rewards of this innovative classroom approach.

Formalizing Corporate Engagement

John Dew
Director, Continuous Quality Improvement,
University of Alabama

In 1997, the University of Alabama launched a continuous quality improvement effort modeled on successful programs at Pennsylvania State University and the University of Wisconsin–Madison. To maximize the involvement of academic units, the new initiative was placed under the provost and reported directly to that office.

As part of the planning process, the university recruited a panel of advisers from companies that had won the Malcolm Baldrige National Quality Award.[1] We knew that the Baldrige criteria were a clear framework for defining organizational quality, and we were confident that advice from companies committed to that framework would be extremely useful to the university. We were aware also that as a part of their involvement with the Baldrige Program, award-winning companies agreed to share their experiences with other organizations, and working with the university would fit this requirement.

Although no Baldrige-winning companies had corporate headquarters in Alabama, a number of winners had a presence within the state, including Boeing, Federal Express, Milliken, and Ritz-Carlton. Each company generously agreed to collaborate with us, and representatives were selected to serve on a newly formed Quality Corporate Advisory Board.

Assessment and Improvement Activities

The board meets twice a year with the president of the university and all of the senior executive staff. These meetings are a forum for the exchange of perspectives and an opportunity for corporate leaders to share their companies' experiences in their quality improvement efforts. University leaders may originally have thought of organizational quality simply in terms of improving work processes, which is certainly an important element of the approach. Over time, however, administrators have discovered the applicability of corporate quality principles to broader issues of organizational management, including issues of continuous improvement of processes, strategic planning, institutional leadership, measurement of processes, the system of governance, and ongoing development of faculty and staff.

One useful contribution of members of the advisory board is the sharing of their candid perceptions as institutional "outsiders," who are quite knowledgeable about effective organizational practices. After the first two advisory board meetings, the corporate representatives made three observations:

1. More attention should be directed toward recognizing and celebrating faculty and staff accomplishments and collective successes within the institution. The university, the board members noted, was quite like their own companies: highly sensitive to problems that needed to be addressed, and often failing to fully recognize the progress already being made.

2. Process improvement was a continuing need. Although the university had made significant progress in analyzing and improving several processes, a great deal remained to be done. Like most institutions, the University of Alabama focused first on the processes that were receiving the most criticism from parents, students, and faculty, and significant progress was being made in those areas. Board members pointed out that although this was an excellent starting place, it was important to be certain that process improvement efforts were continued in other areas of the institution.

3. Members of the executive staff and each vice president were encouraged to personally commit to improving processes, stimulating performance, and improving stakeholder satisfaction in their own administrative units. Board members considered this to be an important step in demonstrating to others in the institution that high-level administrators were personally and genuinely committed to improvement. They also pointed out

the important role senior administrators must play in bringing improvement to processes that involve the collaboration of multiple offices.

With the encouragement of the board, the university conducted a self-assessment using the Alabama Quality Award criteria, a state award program based on the Baldrige. A team of individuals from across the campus coordinated the effort with the support and guidance of the corporate advisors. The self-study process raised numerous questions about how the university manages important processes and compares its performance with that of other institutions. Subsequently, the university submitted an application to the Alabama Quality Award program, becoming the first research university to apply for a state quality award. After a review of the application and a site visit by the staff of the state program, the university was named a finalist for the 2001 Alabama Quality Award.

Consequences of the Corporate Collaboration

With the guidance of the Quality Corporate Advisory Board, in combination with the recommendations of a Baldrige state site review team, a number of institutional improvement priorities were identified, among them enhanced use of comparative data, an increase in the number and scope of cross-functional and cross-departmental process improvement teams, expanded recognition for staff, broader use of surveys and focus groups to gather feedback, and a continued aggressive approach to redesigning work processes.

One new initiative involved collecting and analyzing outcome-oriented, comparative data on student learning. In 2002, the university participated in the National Survey of Student Engagement, and the results provided comparative feedback regarding students' experiences related to the level of academic challenge, active and collaborative learning, student interactions with faculty, enriching educational experiences, and student satisfaction with the campus environment. The process was a helpful one in many respects; results indicated that Alabama students gave the university significantly higher marks than were given to the comparative group of institutions in the level of academic challenge, involvement in active and collaborative learning, student and faculty interactions, and supportive campus environment. Feedback from seniors regarding opportunities outside the classroom that augment academic programs matched the national average for research universities. As a next stage in data gathering, plans are in place to use the ACT's Alumni Outcome Survey to obtain comparative data from alumni.

To address additional improvements in processes that involved more than a single department, additional cross-functional teams were formed. To ensure that faculty governance was not short-circuited, the teams were structured to include representation from the faculty senate, and to more broadly encourage input from faculty and students. An initiative to project campus health needs in the year 2010 is one example of a universitywide effort that involves faculty, staff, and students. Faculty members with expertise in public health, psychology, nursing, and social work are playing an active role in this initiative; participants are benchmarking policies and practices at fifteen other top fifty public universities. The comparison data and results from campus surveys and focus groups have been used to prioritize issues, leading to an initial focus on policies and programs to reduce binge drinking among students.

Faculty and students have also worked together to establish a new Environmental Management Council, facilitated by the Office of Continuous Quality Improvement, to address campus environmental issues, including recycling, planting additional trees, and complying with regulations related to chemical storage and use. The council was established after we conducted benchmarking of similar programs at other leading universities; it is a formal mechanism for students, faculty, and staff to work out the details to support recycling efforts, and to explore how environmental issues are being addressed at other institutions.

Increasing recognition for outstanding work is another area where the influence of the Quality Corporate Advisory Board has been noteworthy. Data indicated that there was adequate recognition for faculty excellence in teaching and research, but feedback from staff indicated that many employees felt their contributions went unrecognized. To address this gap, the university initiated two major awards programs targeted for staff. The first, the Sam S. May award, named for a custodian in the chemistry department in the 1940s who became a tutor to students, is given to teams that have contributed to process improvement and increased stakeholder satisfaction. The award is presented by the president at the annual fall campus gathering and has been presented to work groups (such as the warehouse team) and cross-functional groups (such as the distance education team). The second, the Crimson Spirit Award, was created to recognize staff members for their commitment to institutional spirit and pride. To be selected, staff members must be nominated by a peer or a representative of one of the groups or organizations served by the university. Award winners are announced twice a month, with their photos and a description of their accomplishments appearing in the campus newspaper.

Another continuing influence of the advisory board can be seen in ever-increasing attention to gathering feedback from stakeholders through the use of surveys and focus groups. Although recognition that data are important in decision making is certainly not new, efforts to gather pertinent information systematically have become far more frequent. It is common now, when an issue is being discussed, for administrators to initiate a survey or focus groups to solicit input from the various affected groups. Recently, for example, to assess the quality of the student experience at the university, administrators requested a survey of student expectations and experiences in the classroom. Similarly, as a part of planning for improved student recruitment and retention, focus groups were conducted with honors students, transfer students, and minority students. On the basis of responses from student surveys, Academic Affairs and the Office of Continuous Quality Improvement have organized a faculty team focused on improving classroom teaching. The team is developing an emphasis on the scholarship of teaching and is addressing issues related to teaching large science classes; benchmarking best practices at other universities; and organizing workshops, faculty interest groups, and campuswide presentations on best practices.

The recommended emphasis on process redesign has likewise been sustained, in part because of encouragement from the Quality Corporate Advisory Board. Admissions and student financial aid processes were flowcharted and redesigned over the past two years. The university library conducted a detailed process analysis of the acquisitions and cataloging process for new books during the fall of 2002. Maintenance and engineering staff have developed detailed flow charts and redesigned processes to improve support for new campus construction and building refurbishments.

Continuing Support

The concept of the Quality Corporate Advisory Board has fit very well into the overall philosophy of the quality effort at Alabama, and the board has made important contributions to the university. For those within the institution who have tended to view the university and its circumstances as wholly unique, corporate leaders have helped the institution understand that our challenges and opportunities are similar in many ways to those in any large and complex organization. In their advisory capacity, they have brought extremely valuable insights and suggestions from their own organizational experience and have encouraged, supported, and helped to motivate our improvement efforts. Particularly, the emphasis on leadership and management principles, organizational self-assessment, employee recognition, systematic stakeholder data gathering, cross-functional process improvement, and benchmarking have been quite helpful.

Board members have continued to be most supportive of Alabama's quality improvement efforts, and of its accomplishments in many target areas, notably increased research; enrollment; freshman ACT scores; retention rates; alumni giving; faculty and student diversity; and satisfaction with the academic program among students, parents, and alumni. The board members are probably as pleased as everyone on campus as the University of Alabama has continued its climb in the *U.S. News and World Report* rankings of national research universities (passing one hundred universities in the rankings in the past five years) and emerged into the top fifty public universities ranking for the first time in 2001.

Boeing, Federal Express, Milliken, and Ritz-Carlton are very different businesses. All, however, share a common passion for quality, and all have launched major efforts to improve their management systems. The University of Alabama, though different from these organizations in many respects, is equally passionate about quality, and administrators, faculty, and staff throughout the institution have found that we have a great deal to learn from the wealth of expertise and experience of corporate leaders in our own efforts to advance institutional excellence.

Note

1. The Malcolm Baldrige National Quality Award Program is administered by the National Institute of Standards and Technology, Department of Commerce. For further information, see www.quality.nist.gov/qnew.htm; and the 2001 Criteria for Education Performance Excellence (Washington, D.C.: Baldrige National Quality Program, National Institute for Standards and Technology, 2001), also available at the same Website.

Chapter Four

Becoming More Effective Learning Organizations

Clarifying Goals and Evaluating Outcomes

One of the pervasive themes of contemporary organizational learning theory and practice is the emphasis on *information* and *measurement* for evaluating and enhancing excellence. There is little argument about the value of assessment, measurement, and the use of the information that results, but the question of what should be measured and how that information should be used has been more problematic.[1] In business, where financial measures have traditionally been the primary focus, a broadened range of performance indicators is being introduced to more fully represent key success factors for an organization. Examples include measures of consumer perceptions, employee satisfaction, and innovation. As issues of defining, measuring, and documenting excellence become increasingly consequential in higher education, an understanding of the concerns motivating these changes within the private sector and the new measurement frameworks that are emerging can be extremely useful.

Accounting-Based Measures of Organizational Excellence

Traditionally, business and industry have measured organizational performance using a financial accounting model that emphasizes profitability, return on investment, sales growth, cash flow, or economic value added:

The accounting systems that we have today—the historical cost-based numbers that we all love to hate—have developed over hundreds of years. They can be traced back to the first "joint stock" or publicly owned companies of the 14th century and even earlier.

Financial measures provided a basis for accountability and comparability. Take the case of the East India Trading Company, which was an early joint stock company. Let's say they had a manager 4,000 miles away running a trading post, and they shipped that person a boatload of goods. The purpose of accounting was to ensure that the manager used those goods to serve the company's interests and not just his own [Zimmerman, 1993, p. 6].

The need for external accountability and standardized measures for financial comparison across corporations continues today. In recent years, however, questions have increasingly been raised regarding the exclusive reliance on these measures. There is a growing sense that these financial performance indicators, used alone, fail to capture many of the critical success factors required for external accountability and are of limited value for addressing internal management needs (Brancato, 1995; Hexter, 1997).

The Harvard Business School Council on Competitiveness noted the constraints of conventional financial performance in an analysis of differences in investment patterns in U.S. corporations compared to organizations in Japan and Germany. Among the conclusions of the study (Porter, 1992, p. 73) were that the U.S. approach to excellence measurement:

- Is less supportive of long-term corporate investment because of the emphasis on improving short-term returns to influence current share prices
- Favors those forms of investment for which returns are most readily measurable; this leads to an overinvestment in assets whose value can be easily calculated
- Leads to underinvestment in intangible assets—in internal development projects, product and process innovation, employee skills, and customer satisfaction—whose short-term returns are more difficult to measure

More generally, it is noted that accounting-based measures (Brancato, 1995):

- Are too historical
- Lack predictive power
- Reward the wrong behavior
- Are focused on inputs and not outputs
- Do not capture key business changes until it is too late
- Reflect functions, not cross-functional process within a company
- Give inadequate consideration to difficult-to-quantify resources such as intellectual capital

One might also add to the list that a preoccupation with a small set of financial indicators encourages efforts to "spin," or in some cases even "cook," the numbers to create a positive image to colleagues, managers, and the investor community. The general conclusion is that financial indicators alone are limited in their ability to adequately represent the range of factors associated with organizational excellence. Accounting-based measures, for instance, may not capture key elements of an organization's mission, customer satisfaction and loyalty, employee satisfaction and turnover, employee capability, organizational adaptability or innovation, environmental competitiveness, research and development productivity, market growth and success, and other important company-specific factors (Brancato, 1995; Kaplan and Norton, 1996a, 1996b).

The Quality Approach and Expanded Measures of Excellence

Many major corporations now couple financial indicators with other measures selected to reflect key elements of their mission, vision, and strategic direction. Collectively, these "cockpit" or "dashboard" indicators, as they are sometimes called, are used to monitor and navigate the organization in much the same way a pilot and flight crew use the array of indicators in the cockpit to monitor and navigate an airplane. The usefulness of these indicators extends beyond performance measurement per se and contributes also to self-assessment, strategic planning, and the creation of focus and consensus on goals and directions within the organization.

One approach that addresses this need systematically is the "balanced scorecard" developed by a study group composed of representatives from major corporations, including American Standard, Bell South, Cray Research, Du Pont, General Electric, and Hewlett-Packard (Kaplan and Norton, 1992, 1993, 1996a, 1996b, 2001). As described by Kaplan and Norton (1996a, p. 2), "The Balanced Scorecard translates an organization's mission and strategy into a comprehensive set of performance measures that provides a framework for a strategic measurement and management system." Specifically, Kaplan and Norton (1996a, p. 10) explain: "The Balanced Scorecard should translate a business unit's mission and strategy into tangible objectives and measures. The measures represent a *balance* between external measures for shareholders and customers, and internal measures of critical business processes, innovation, and learning and growth. The measures are *balanced* between outcome measures—the results of past efforts—and the measures that drive future performance. And the scorecard is balanced between objective, easily quantified outcome measures and subjective, somewhat judgmental, performance."

Organizations that adopt this approach report that they are able to use the approach to:

- Clarify and gain consensus about vision and strategic direction
- Communicate and link strategic objectives and measures throughout the organization
- Align departmental and personal goals to the organization's vision and strategy
- Plan, set targets, and align strategic initiatives
- Conduct periodic and systematic strategic reviews
- Obtain feedback to learn about and improve strategy (Kaplan and Norton, pp. 10, 19)

One company executive describes the approach and critical questions it addresses this way (Brancato, 1995, p. 42): "A balanced business scorecard is an information-based management tool that translates our strategic objectives into a coherent set of performance measures. We start with the vision. What are the critical success factors to attain our vision? What are the key performance measures to measure our progress against those success factors? What are the targets, initiatives, and what is the review process to ensure that this balanced business scorecard is the key management tool to run the businesses? And, finally, how do we tie in the incentives?"

Excellence Indicators in Higher Education

Organizations of all types are reconceptualizing the excellence indicators they use, and the uses to which these indicators are being put. For those in higher education, what is of particular significance is not so much the particulars of the dashboard, balanced scorecard, or other measurement-based approach, but rather the widespread movement to reexamine the measurement process and its role in evaluating, monitoring, and advancing organizational excellence.

In higher education, as in business, there are time-honored traditions regarding measurement of excellence. Rather than emphasizing primarily financial measures, higher education has historically emphasized academic measures. Motivated, as with business, by issues of external accountability and comparability, measurement in higher education has generally emphasized those academically related variables that are most easily quantifiable. Familiar examples are student and faculty demographics, enrollment, grade point average, scores on standardized tests, class rank, acceptance rates, retention rate, faculty-student ratios, graduation rates, faculty teaching load, counts of faculty publications and grants, and statistics on physical and library resources.

As important as the traditional indicators are, they do not capture some of the key success factors for a college or university; nor do they necessarily reflect specific dimensions of a department or institution's mission, vision, or strategic direction. Traditional indicators are subject to other limitations as well. For example, our most popular and familiar measures relative to teaching and learning emphasize inputs—resources, student test scores, faculty credentials, attributes of the facility, and so on. These have been highly valued in various rating systems, but they do not necessarily provide useful information on what an institution itself has contributed to these outcomes.

Measures of student qualifications and institutional selectivity are examples. Student grade point averages and standardized test score measures of selectivity may be good descriptions of the capabilities students bring with them to our institutions, but they say little about the value our courses, programs, or institutions add through the teaching and learning process; nor do they help to evaluate the cumulative benefits derived from having attended a particular institution. As Pascarella (2001) and others have noted, considerably more attention has been devoted to measuring the reputation and resources of institutions than to determining what impact they actually have on the breadth and quality of students' learning.

Other efforts to assess excellence have focused on measures such as student or alumni occupational success or income levels, but these also fail to identify and isolate the contribution of the college teaching and learning experience from particular socioeconomic, networking, and other patterns that may characterize students who attend particular institutions (Pascarella, 2001). Although higher education assessment studies (for example, Astin, 1993) have advanced our understanding of the teaching and learning process, the insights gained from this research have generally not been translated into indicators that are useful for monitoring, intervening in, or comparing institutional excellence (Johnson and Seymour, 1996).

As with business, higher education indicators have tended to be primarily historical, have been limited in predictive power, are often incapable of alerting institutions to changes in time to respond, and have not given adequate consideration to important but difficult-to-quantify dimensions. Ironically, the emphasis on easy-to-quantify, limited measures has, in a manner of speaking, come home to haunt in the form of popularized college rating systems with which educators are generally frustrated and critical but that are consistently used as the measures against which they are evaluated by their constituents (Wegner, 1997).

A promising development in this area is the National Survey of Student Engagement, which collects, analyzes, and disseminates student perceptions on teaching and learning engagement at hundreds of institutions. The survey includes sixty key items that address issues of academic challenge, opportunities for active and collaborative learning, extent of student interaction with faculty members, opportunities for enriching educational experiences, and supportiveness of the campus environment. The resulting database provides comparative information across nearly three hundred institutions (Kuh, 2001a).[2]

Even though new criteria are being suggested, most evaluative frameworks use quite traditional criteria. In a study conducted for the Educational Commission of the States on measures used in performance reporting in ten states (Ewell, 1994), the most common indicators were:

- Enrollment and graduation rates by gender, ethnicity, and program
- Degree completion and time to degree
- Persistence and retention rates by grade, ethnicity, and program
- Remediation activities and indicators of their effectiveness
- Transfer rates to and from two- and four-year institutions
- Pass rates on professional exams
- Job placement data on graduates and graduates' satisfaction with their jobs
- Faculty workload and productivity in the form of student-faculty ratios and instructional contact hours

Absent from this and many other lists of higher education performance indicators are short-term or long-term measures that isolate the contributions of the institution to student learning. Also missing are indicators that capture the extent to which student, faculty, and staff needs and expectations are being met by a college or university, despite the widely shared view that attracting, retaining, and nurturing the best and brightest people is a primary goal and critical success factor. Even in evaluative systems that gather information from students about their satisfaction with particular courses and services, little effort has been devoted to systematically measuring the expectations of prospective students and their parents, and the extent to which those expectations are subsequently realized or altered over the course of the college experience. National studies examining these issues reveal significant gaps that are generally not measured or addressed at an institutional level (Selingo,

2003). Even less attention is generally directed toward measuring faculty and staff satisfaction levels within particular units or an institution as a whole, though this may be one of the better upstream predictors of the ultimate quality of instruction, research, administrative, and support services within an institution.

A Balanced Scorecard for Higher Education

The fundamental purpose of a dashboard or scorecard is to translate the often abstract mission, aspirations, plans, and goals of an organization into more tangible criteria that can be measured, monitored, communicated, and used to motivate and guide the advancement of excellence. Given that the academic mission of colleges and universities is the creation, sharing, and application of knowledge—traditionally described in terms of teaching and learning, scholarship and research, and public service and outreach—the primary challenge in developing an academic dashboard is to determine how best to measure these activities.

Many of the basic dimensions of excellence in these pursuits are common across various types of colleges and universities. Institutions of all kinds need qualified and competent faculty and staff, credible scholarship, innovative and engaging teaching and learning processes, appropriate technology and facilities, capable students, and support from various external publics.

Although less often acknowledged, excellence in communication and a service-oriented culture, appropriate visibility and prominence within the state and beyond, a welcoming physical environment, a friendly and supportive social environment, expectations of success, accessible and effective systems and services, and a sense of community are also generally important indicators of present and future success. These characteristics generally translate into successful engagement with internal and external stakeholder groups. For each such group, desired and potentially measurable outcomes can be identified:

- *Prospective students:* applying to a program or institution as a preferred choice, informed about the qualities and benefits they can realize through enrolling

- *Current students:* attending their program or institution of choice with well-defined expectations and a high level of satisfaction relative to all facets of their experience; feeling that they are valued members of the academic community with the potential and support to succeed
- *Families:* proud to have a family member attending the program or institution, supporting and recommending it to friends and acquaintances
- *Alumni:* actively supporting the institution and its initiatives
- *Employers:* seeking out program or institution graduates as employees; promoting the program or institution among their employees for continuing and professional education
- *Colleagues at peer and other institutions:* viewing the institution as a source of intellectual or professional leadership and an enviable workplace
- *Governing boards:* being supportive of the institution and enthusiastic about the opportunity to contribute personally and professionally to its advancement
- *Local community:* viewing the institution as an asset to the community; actively supporting its development
- *Friends, interested individuals, donors, legislators, and the general public:* valuing the institution as an essential resource; supporting efforts to further advance excellence
- *Faculty:* pleased to serve on the faculty of a respected, well-supported program, department, or institution
- *Staff:* regarding the department or institution as a preferred workplace where innovation, continuing improvement, and teamwork are valued; recommending the department or institution to others

How excellence is conceptualized and the weights associated with various criteria that emerge vary with the institutional type. The importance of particular criteria also varies as a consequence of one's perspective. For faculty and many administrators, academic quality as judged by peers and professionals is of paramount importance. To students, employers, alumni, the public, and other external audiences, the extent to which colleges and universities are responsive to their articulated needs and expectations is also important. As employees, faculty and staff may have other criteria that enter into judgments of the level of excellence of the department or institution. Factors associated with operational and administrative accountability may define a fourth perspective and set of criteria (Ruben, 2003a). These perspectives are not mutually exclusive and are, in fact, complementary in many respects. Collectively, they define four ways of thinking about departmental or institutional excellence, in terms of which evaluations can be made:

1. The quality of programs, services, and activities as judged by peers and professionals
2. The extent to which programs, services, and activities are perceived to meet the needs of and expectations of their beneficiaries
3. The quality of the organizational climate, and the satisfaction of faculty and staff from their perspective as employees
4. The effectiveness and efficiency of operational and financial dimensions of the organization

Building on these concepts, excellence indicators can be developed for any department or institution, given clarity on the mission, vision, and goals. The process essentially involves translating these higher-level concepts into more tangible dashboard indicators. Some of the indicators are likely to include traditional and familiar measures, and others might be quite unique and specific to purposes and aspirations of particular institutions.

For the sake of illustration, consider a college or university with a mission that emphasizes learning, discovery, and engagement equally. The dashboard ideally includes indicators that reflect each of the four perspectives on the excellence associated with teaching and learning, scholarship and research, and public service and outreach at the institution. Thus indicators are included that focus on the quality of mission-critical activities, the extent to which academic programs and services meet the needs and expectations of stakeholders, workplace climate and faculty and staff satisfaction, and operational and financial performance. For an academic institution or department, this translates into a dashboard composed of five areas: teaching and learning, scholarship and research, service and outreach, workplace satisfaction, and administration and operations (Figure 4.1).

Figure 4.1. A Hypothetical Dashboard for an Academic Department.

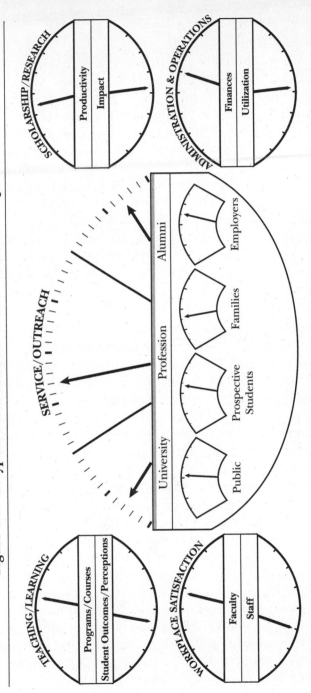

Teaching and Learning

In the proposed framework, teaching and learning are composed of quality assessments in two primary areas: (1) programs and courses and (2) student outcomes. This framework points to the value of incorporating multiple dimensions, multiple perspectives, and multiple measures in evaluating the quality of academic programs and courses, and student outcomes. Appropriate to these assessments are systematic inputs from peers or colleagues (at one's own institution and perhaps others), students (at various points in their academic career), alumni (affording retrospective analyses), and employers or graduate directors (providing data on workplace and graduate or professional school preparation).

Each group can contribute pertinent and useful insights. Collectively, these judgments yield a comprehensive and balanced cluster of measures that help to address concerns associated with reliance on any single perspective of measure (American Association of Higher Education, 2002; Trout, 1997b; Williams and Ceci, 1997).

Colleagues from one's own or another institution can offer critical assessments of instructor qualifications and the scope, comprehensiveness, rigor, and currency of programs or course content, and so on. Students and alumni can provide valuable assessments of the clarity of course or program expectations; curricular integration; perceived applicability; extent of interaction with faculty; opportunities for involvement with faculty research; and the instructor's delivery skills, enthusiasm, interest in students, accessibility, and other dimensions.

Examples of possible indicators are listed in Table 4.1. In the case of academic and academic-support programs and services, the cascade of measures[3] might well include clarity of mission of programs and courses, disciplinary standing, need, coherence, rigor, efficiency, qualifications of instructors, currency and comprehensiveness of materials, adequacy of support services, and teaching and learning climate. These can be assessed in any number of ways. Typically, evaluations of disciplinary standing are derived from external review, accreditation, or other peer review systems. The need for particular programs and courses can be assessed by considering such factors as unfulfilled demand, offerings at other institutions, and systematic input from employers or alumni. Coherence considers measures of internal curricular linkage and integration, and rigor assessment is likely to include data on assignment standards and grading practices with student and alumni input. Efficiency can include cost-student enrollment ratios, student-faculty instruction ratios, and the like. Qualifications of instructors (or in the case of academic-support programs, of staff), course content, and delivery assessments can be based on peer review and other inputs (American Association of Higher Education, 2002; Braskamp and Ory, 1994).

Student outcomes can include measures of program or course preferences, selectivity, involvement, learning outcomes (knowledge and competency acquisition), fulfillment of expectations, satisfaction, retention, preparedness, placement, motivation for lifelong learning, and other variables that may be appropriate to the mission, vision, and goals of the institution or program. Preference measures, for instance, document answers to questions such as "Was this college/program my preferred choice?" Selectivity reflects input measures of the "quality" of students enrolled in courses or programs, and learning outcomes assessment measures cognitive and behavioral competencies. Thus, in addition to content learning, assessment may also include the ability to engage in collaborative problem solving; appreciation of diversity; leadership skills; interpersonal and presentational communication skills; ethical thinking; and other capabilities appropriate to the mission, vision, and goals of the institution or program.

In addition, student satisfaction with academic support and other services—for instance, libraries, advising, facilities, computing, placement, housing, health services, recreation, or transportation—should also be included in the dashboard.

Surveys and focus groups with student and alumni groups can be the basis for evaluating and tracking satisfaction with academic programs and support services over time. For instance, alumni can be asked some years after graduation whether they would choose the same university or program if they were enrolling today.[4] Preparedness for careers or further graduate study might be assessed through input from graduates, recruiters or employers, and graduate program directors. Placement measures can be derived through systematic alumni tracking.

Table 4.1. Possible Cluster Measures for Higher Education Dashboards.

Teaching/Learning Indicators	Public Service/Outreach Indicators	Scholarship/Research Indicators
PROGRAMS, COURSES, SERVICES	**EXTERNAL STAKE-HOLDER GROUPS**	**PRODUCTIVITY**
• Mission clarity	Prospective students	• Presentations
• Disciplinary standing	University	• Performances
• Need	Profession/discipline	• Submissions
• Coherence	Research agencies	• Publications
• Rigor	Alumni	• Funding proposals
• Efficiency	Families	**IMPACT**
• Instructor qualifications	State	• Publication stature
• Currency/ comprehensiveness of course materials	Employers	• Citation
	Community	• Awards/recognition
• Adequacy of support services	Governing boards	• Editorial roles
	Public at large	• Peer assessments
• Teaching-learning climate		• Funding
	Activity level/contacts	
STUDENT OUTCOMES AND PERCEPTIONS	• Selection for leadership roles	
• Preferences	• Reputation	
• Selectivity	• Meeting perceived needs	
• Involvement		
• Learning outcomes	• Satisfaction levels	
• Satisfaction	• Contributions/ funding	
• Retention	• Preferences	
• Interaction with faculty		
• Involvement with faculty research		

Table 4.1. *(continued)*

Teaching/Learning Indicators (cont.)	Workplace Satisfaction Indicators	Administration and Operations Indicators
• Challenge	• Climate	• Financial measures
• Quality of support services	• Attractiveness	• Capacities and utilization levels
• Time spent studying	• Turnover	• Administrative process effectiveness and efficiency
• Career preparedness	• Compensation	
• Placement	• Satisfaction	
• Capacity for life-long learning	• Morale	• Strategic planning and follow-through
		• Leadership effectiveness

Scholarship and Research

Research and scholarship can be defined by assessments of quality in the areas of *productivity* and *impact*. Both are areas in which colleges and universities generally have well-developed measures of achievement.

Typically, productivity indicators include activity level. Depending on the field, activity level measures encompass frequency of presentations, performances, article and paper submissions, publications, and funding proposals. Impact measures for research and scholarship typically include publication rate, selectivity and stature of journals or publishers, citations, awards and recognition, editorial board membership, peer assessments of scholarly excellence, funding of research, and others (Braskamp and Ory, 1994; Carnegie Foundation for the Advancement of Teaching, 1994). In addition, faculty and research satisfaction with academic and institutional support—for instance, libraries, facilities, computing, and administrative support—can also be included in the dashboard.

Public Service and Outreach

The public service and outreach indicator cluster is composed of quantitative and qualitative measures of the engagement and impact of the department or institution, and the extent to which that engagement addresses the needs and expectations of key external stakeholder groups. As illustrated in Table 4.1, this cluster should include measures for each of the groups whose assessments of the quality and performance of the institution or program have important implications for the unit in terms of mission fulfillment, reputation, recruitment, economic viability, and so on.

The definition of *key* external stakeholder groups depends on the nature of the department or institution and its mission. For academic units, the list of potential candidate groups might include the university (beyond the unit itself), profession or discipline, alumni, potential students, organizations and individuals seeking new knowledge, family members or parents of students, employers, community, state, region, governing boards, friends of the institutions, individual and corporate donors, legislators, and the public at large.

Once the scope of key stakeholders is defined, the measures for each should capture the quality of contributions of the unit on the basis of criteria that have been determined to be significant to the external group. Some general measures that are appropriate for a number of these stakeholder groups are the level of participation by department or institution faculty or staff in external groups, selection for leadership roles, and reputation of the institution within the targeted groups.

In some cases, measures are specific to a particular stakeholder group. For instance, when assessing the standing of a department or program within the larger university community, measures may include promotion and tenure rates, requests to serve on thesis and dissertation committees in other programs, and invitations to serve on and play a leadership role in key university committees and projects, in addition to other general measures of engagement and perceived contributions to university life.

In the case of potential employers, preferences for university graduates as employees and the likelihood of promoting an institution among their employees for continuing education are important measurement considerations. In the case of organizations or individuals seeking new knowledge or the solution to problems, the number of contacts, requests for information, proposals requested, and initiatives funded are among the possible measures.

For alumni, key financial and moral support of the university and its initiatives are key measures, and the extent to which the university is perceived to be an essential state resource is an important indicator of public support. For parents and families, issues of interest include attitude toward having a family member attending the university and the likelihood of recommending the institution to friends and acquaintances.

Although institutional data may be available as input for some indicators, focus groups, surveys, and other systematic approaches for capturing the perceptions and perspectives of these groups may be also required.

Workplace Satisfaction

In addition to indicators associated with instruction, scholarship, and service and outreach, another important indicator is workplace climate and workforce satisfaction. Inputs to indicators for each group include measures of attractiveness of the institution as a workplace, turnover, compensation, assessments of workplace climate, and faculty and staff morale and satisfaction. Measures in this category include a combination of institutional data (analysis of application and retention data); perceptual data from faculty and staff groups; and information derived from sources such as exit interviews, focus groups, and surveys.

Administration and Operations

A final set of indicators captures key operational measures, such as financial soundness, capacities and utilization levels, quality and maintenance of facilities, the effectiveness and efficiency of administrative support processes, strategic planning and follow-through, and leadership effectiveness.

For example, financials might include revenues by source—state appropriations, tuition, donations, endowments, grants, and so on—and expenditures, such as operating budgets, debt service, credit ratings and ratios, deferred maintenance, and expenditures for the institution or unit. Specific measures to be included in this category vary depending on the level and type of unit involved.

The Dashboard Approach Is Not a Panacea

The dashboard approach to performance assessment in higher education does not magically answer the questions "What is excellence?" or "What should be measured?" For a department or institution adopting the model, the fundamental task—and certainly not a simple one—involves clarifying how excellence is to be defined, what criteria are relevant to that concept, what measures best capture these criteria, and what methods are most useful for gathering that information. Though not a panacea, the advantage of this approach is its framework for dialogue and a structure for decision making as to the appropriate evaluative criteria, measures, and methods.

The list of dashboard indicators mentioned in the previous section—and specific measures discussed for each—is meant to be suggestive, not definitive nor prescriptive. Many more indicators and measures are mentioned than any single program, department, or institution is likely to want—or be able to monitor—at least initially.

Depending on the mission and goals of a particular department, the appropriate components of the dashboard might be quite different from those discussed in the previous pages. For instance, if the department in question has an administrative or service mission, the dashboard would be composed of indicator clusters very different from those of an academic unit (Ruben, 2003a). Indicators for instruction and research can be replaced by measures appropriate to the department's mission. The top-row indicators for an administrative department would consist of measures of the quantity and quality of a unit's programs, services and activities, using technical, peer, or professionally accepted standards of measurement. A second cluster of measures would capture the criteria and perspective of those who use or benefit from the work of the unit. Thus physical plant, purchasing, or computing services departments might include measures of work productivity, effectiveness, and efficiency, and also indicators of the satisfaction of those departments for which they provide maintenance, building, or renovation services. An administrative department dashboard might also include indicators of the effectivness of relationships with vendors, suppliers, partners, and collaborators. Individual units might well include indicators that highlight dimensions of particular relevance to their plans and goals.

Comparisons and Benchmarking

Another formidable task is identifying an appropriate group of peer departments or institutions with which to compare and contextualize outcomes. In a number of measurement areas, comparisons (benchmarking) with peer, competitive, or leading institutions or departments are essential to have an appropriate context for interpreting indicator information. For instance, without a broader context of comparison, it is difficult and perhaps impossible to meaningfully interpret data on student learning; scholarly productivity; or retention or level of satisfaction of faculty, staff, or students. In some areas, comparative information is readily available. However, depending on the unit, its mission, and the selected indicators, it may be necessary to create a benchmarking process that involves selecting the appropriate topics of comparison and developing methods for gathering information, perhaps in collaboration with peer departments or institutions that would benefit equally from access to the same information.

Concluding Comments

The task of establishing dashboard indicators is not a simple one, yet having an agreed-upon set of measures that operationally define "excellence" for an institution, department, or program is of great value for assessment, tracking, and communication. Clear evaluative criteria are the basis for a straightforward, accessible, and mobilizing answer to the question "How are we doing?" so as to connect outcomes to goals.

Beyond their value for measurement per se, there is perhaps nearly as great a benefit to be derived from the dialogue and consensus-building process through which dashboard indicators and comparison organizations are determined, and there is great benefit to making the activity as inclusive as possible. It can be a process for reclarifying priorities and goals, refocusing and reenergizing faculty and staff, and broadening responsibility for shared leadership within the unit. The review and decision-making processes create an opportunity to discuss the strengths and limitations of measures that may be in use, and to give consideration to additional or alternative measures. Ideally, the selected indicators include both outcome and predictor measures. Outcome measures are essential for determining the current standing of a program, department, or university. Predictor measures are critical to anticipating and influencing outcomes.

In many ways, the dashboard concept is much more than simply a different approach to measurement. It is, rather, part of a larger paradigm for thinking about how information should be collected and used. The paradigm shift is from one that sees information as an institutional resource to one that sees it as a community resource; from organizing information to serve standardized and routine reporting requirements to one that serves decision makers with a variety of analytic needs; from information that is static and historical to information selected to anticipate new and changing needs; from regarding information as a good to be carefully rationed because it is the basis of power and control to a view that regards it as a shared resource and the appropriate basis for open and collaborative discussion and decision making (Friedman and Hoffman, 2001).

The time is right for demanding greater clarity and precision of ourselves in our approaches to thinking about and measuring excellence—whether in academic, administrative, student affairs, auxiliary services departments, or in the institution as a whole. If we fail to be proactive in this task, definitions and measures are likely to be imposed upon us by external sources, and by those who lack our comprehensive knowledge of our work and its purposes. More important, as models to which others look for examples of premier learning organizations, the academy must embody the highest standards with regard to defining and measuring the criteria of excellence to which we aspire. The dashboard approach offers a college or university a creative approach for meeting this challenge; in so doing, it helps to translate the institution's mission and vision into a comprehensive, coherent, communicable, and mobilizing framework for external constituencies and the organization itself.

Notes

1. The author gratefully acknowledges the contributions of the Cedar Group, which extended encouragement and support for the development of earlier publications on performance measurement in higher education.

2. In 2001, 220,000 students from 320 institutions were surveyed (Kuh, 2001a). See www.indiana.edu/~nsse for additional information.

3. I am grateful to Henry Wiebe of the University of Missouri-Rolla for suggesting this term.

4. This approach was used in research by Joseph Cerny and Maresi Nerad of the Graduate Division, University of California, Berkeley.

Narratives

Becoming More Effective Learning Organizations: Clarifying Goals and Evaluating Outcomes

The clarification of goals and the evaluation of outcomes are among the most fundamental activities of learning organizations. Within the academy, these processes require dialogue on the nature of programmatic, departmental, or institutional excellence, and collaborative decision making on how excellence can best be measured, monitored, and communicated. If issues related to goals and outcomes are not appropriately addressed, discussions of quality, progress, or performance are often quite hollow, and decisions about resource allocation, priorities for improvement, and longer-term goals for the future are less informed than they might otherwise be.

Clarifying goals and measurement approaches can serve other functions as well. It can be a means of reaffirming a common set of purposes, a tool for determining institutional improvement needs, a foundation for strategic planning, and the basis for communication and advocacy—for more persuasively telling the story of the program, department, or institution.

In the first narrative in this section, Mary Sue Coleman, president of the University of Michigan, describes how excellence indicators and targets were used to translate strategic goals into easily captured and communicated measures in support of the institutional planning process at the University of Iowa while she was president there.

Next, Susan Williams, professor of management and former vice president for administration, describes the measurement approach used at Belmont University in Nashville, devoting particular attention to the manner in which academic success and the perspectives of students and other stakeholders were addressed.

The use of the balanced scorecard at a divisional level as a strategy for redefining and pursuing excellence is the topic of the narrative by Ron Coley, assistant vice chancellor for business and administrative services, and Paul Dimond, principal administrative analyst, both of whom are at the University of California, Berkeley.

The final narrative, by Mo Qayoumi, briefly describes the use of benchmarking and measurement comparisons across institutions to address what may be one of the most widely discussed issues within the academy: parking.

The narratives presented in the next section emphasize the challenges of self-assessment, planning, and continuous improvement, while also addressing issues related to the process of clarifying goals and evaluating outcomes.

Implementing a Strategic Plan Using Indicators and Targets

Mary Sue Coleman
President, University of Michigan; Former President,
University of Iowa

Universities are frequently targets of public and political scorn for being inflexible, stodgy, and resistant to change. I believe that this undeserved reputation arises from outside observers' perplexity at the decentralization and power sharing typical of higher education. It is true that a nonhierarchical structure makes moving the mother ship in any one direction, to say the least, a challenge, even though creative innovations bubble up all over campus. Consequently, universities appear more static to external observers than they actually are.

A "Report Card" for the University

An important question for me—and for many of my presidential colleagues—is how to harness the energy, the power to convince all in the university to buy into the big picture and contribute to changes that move the whole institution forward. At Iowa, we have addressed this challenge with several Regents-mandated external audits and three five-year strategic planning cycles; regarding the latter, two cycles were coupled with universitywide measures—or indicators of progress—that would form an annual "report card"

Many thanks to Thomas K. Dean, special assistant to the president, for his superb assistance in crafting this study.

for the university. Community building, enhanced communication, and more focus by both internal and external constituencies on universitywide progress have been positive outcomes of this annual ritual. In addition, we have been spurred to better self-management and have developed a powerful tool for public accountability.

The University of Iowa is a comprehensive public university, the state's first public institution of higher learning, founded in 1847. A member of the Big Ten athletic conference, its annual enrollment is twenty-nine thousand students, with twenty thousand undergraduates and nine thousand graduate and professional students. The university is known widely for many of its programs, particularly in the arts and the health sciences. Iowa is home to the renowned Writers' Workshop, five nationally regarded health science colleges (medicine, nursing, pharmacy, dentistry, and public health), and the largest university-owned teaching hospital in the United States. Iowa is also world-renowned for programs in educational testing and assessment, which have spawned such enterprises as ACT, still headquartered in Iowa City. A growing research enterprise garnered $341 million in external grants in 2001–02, and the university's Oakdale Research Park and Technology Innovation Center help transfer the school's research advances to business and industry, as well as incubate emerging businesses. The University of Iowa is located in Iowa City, a small city of approximately 62,000. Cedar Rapids, Iowa's second-largest city, with a population of 120,000, is about twenty miles away from Iowa City. The burgeoning and increasingly interrelated economic development in the area has earned these cities and the area connecting them the name "the Technology Corridor."

Our fundamental mission at the University of Iowa, as a public research university, is to discover, preserve, and disseminate knowledge in order to enrich the lives of all citizens across our state, as well as throughout the nation and the world. It is true that these profoundly significant products of our work are inherently unquantifiable. But because we wish to be judged as a community of learners by the highest public standards, we have worked toward establishing the objective milestones of our indicators to mark advances in our institutional goals.

At the beginning of my presidency of the University of Iowa, I sought to establish a set of core values to guide our strategic planning. James C. Collins and Jerry I. Porras, scholars of management and organizational behavior, point out that truly visionary organizations both "preserve the core and stimulate progress" (Collins and Porras, 1994, p. 82); hence our interest in complementing our long-range mission with shorter-range strategic planning, and developing stimuli within those strategic plans through specific progress indicators. I believe such methods are necessary to track change over time and are crucial to keeping our aims on a straight course. Certainly spontaneous imagination, even audacious ideas that spill beyond the confines of a strategic plan and its targets and indicators, are important parts of stimulating progress. But we also must keep our hands on the wheel of strategic planning as part of our complement of methods for steering—and stimulating—our progress.

We are now seven years into the process of measuring ourselves and publishing the results annually—two successive plans, each with its own indicator list. We send annual reports to every faculty member, and we also publish the annual strategic plan indicators report on our Web site (www.uiowa.edu/%7Eprovost/plan/ind0001/index.html and www.uiowa.edu/president/strat_plan.html).

Selecting Measures

The first challenge for the university—and an educational exercise in and of itself—was assembling a list of possible measures. Our strategic planning committee's first effort produced about three hundred, far too many to be useful. After extensive consultation with the stakeholders, we narrowed the list to thirty-five, a number broad enough to cover many aspects of our university programs but narrow enough to focus on a reasonable number of areas to which we might devote more attention or resources. Of those thirty-five indicators, twenty were "targeted indicators" and fifteen were "progress indicators." Progress indicators reported data that we wished simply to collect and monitor, and targeted indicators were those quality-related measures that could be associated with time-specific numerical objectives. For our targeted indicators, we set five-year targets so that we could stretch ourselves beyond what we might have thought possible with only the narrow vision of an annual scope. (A number of our targeted indicators also had subtargets, totaling thirty-seven specific measures in all.)

All thirty-five of these targeted and progress indicators were directly tied to the seven overall goals of the strategic plan. For example, "comprehensive strength in undergraduate programs," the first goal, was accompanied by nine targeted indicators ranging from measurement of four-, five-, and six-year graduation rates to undergraduate participation in experience-based education, to senior faculty commitments, to teaching undergraduates. Under goal four, "distinguished research and scholarship," we measured success by external research funding, intellectual property disclosures, and library rankings. Under goal six, "strong ties between the university and external constituencies," we measured contributors to our foundation (development), nondegree enrollments, arts programming on the statewide optical fiber network, patient visits to our health sciences centers, and mean monthly national news citations. Under goal seven, "a high-quality academic and working environment," our targets measured both physical and cultural aspects of our workplace. We aspired to eliminate our deferred maintenance backlog by meeting the national building renewal funding norm of 1 percent of our physical plant value. We set targets for participation in professional development programs for our staff, and we maintained progress indicators to monitor satisfaction of our constituencies by conducting periodic surveys of faculty, staff, students, patients, and visitors.

Setting Appropriate Targets

The most common reaction on campus I received to setting targets was the query, "What would be the consequence of not meeting a particular goal?" I thought that if we set the targets too low and reached or exceeded all of them immediately, the university community, as well as the public, would be pretty skeptical of our intention to push ourselves to reach a new level of excellence. So we had to attempt to reach a balance. I assured everyone that it was perfectly acceptable to have some targets that would be very difficult to achieve.

At the end of the first five-year strategic planning period, we had met, exceeded, or made significant progress on 86 percent of our targets, demonstrating to the community that concentration on a few areas could make a substantial difference to the university.

In a number of areas, we discovered that annual reporting worked in a positive way to alter behaviors across the university. This is perhaps best illustrated in our four-year graduation contract. At the beginning of the time period, fewer than 50 percent of our students were signing the contract on entry, while at the end of planning period more than 70 percent of the entering students were doing so. Academic advisors began to focus on encouraging students to take heavier course loads. The residence hall system developed more special-interest floors, which we have dubbed "learning communities." These residence hall options demonstrably enhanced student retention and academic success. From these efforts, overall four-year and six-year graduation rates rose.

We also learned that some of the indicators we had selected were not useful, or they outlived their usefulness in a few years. We dropped our attempts to quantify campus safety, primarily because in a relatively safe community statistical results varied wildly from year to year. We dropped our measurement of technology-equipped classrooms once we simply reached our goal. We dropped targeting the number of National Merit Scholars and high school valedictorians in our entering freshman class because we decided that we wanted to concentrate our measurements on student achievement once they were enrolled at Iowa.

The Evolving "Report Card"

Given our experience with these indicators and the university community's growing comfort with such measurements, devising a new, smaller set of indicators for our recently adopted strategic plan was relatively straightforward. In the new plan we have devised twenty-four indicators with associated targets, including many fewer sub-targets. We also dispensed with the more cumbersome distinction between targeted and progress indicators. Some indicators that simply mark progress remain, but the majority of our new measures are targeted, since they demonstrate not only our progress but also our ambitions most dramatically.

In addition, for our new strategic plan we required each college to develop its own plans, linked to the overall university plan and holding the colleges accountable for universitywide progress. We asked that deans answer four essential questions in crafting their collegiate strategic plans: (1) How will your initiatives contribute to the goals of the university's strategic plan? (2) How will they contribute to the universitywide indicators? (3) If the university-wide indicators are not relevant to collegiate goals, what other indicators do you suggest? and (4) How will the college fund its initiatives?

What has been the effect of having the ability to revisit and report on the plan every year? Within the university, the report serves to remind everyone about the plan at least once each year. For individual units, focus on particular parts of the plan and the targets has become a regular exercise, and it has helped define their own goals while, reciprocally, assisting the progress of the university as a whole. For example, our recently created College of Public Health, by its very nature, emphasizes public outreach, which dovetails with the university's core value of community and the strategic plan's service elements. At the same time, the College of Public Health's development of a strategic goal to "promote meaningful community service and collaboration" and its attendant measures helps the university as a whole chart its service activities, which are difficult to measure institutionwide and are thus not heavily reflected in our twenty-four indicators. A sampling of our indicator measures included in the University of Iowa report card for our current strategic plan is shown in Figure 4.2.

Although a five-year strategic plan and annual report cards on our indicators make up an effective short-term set of stimuli for progress toward achieving our institutional mission and fulfilling our core values, such limited-scope tools can suffer from the exigencies of the moment. As with many other states, Iowa has experienced significant revenue shortfalls in recent years, resulting in budget cuts to the university. Fulfilling even our five-year goals quickly became an untenable proposition, and we were forced to choose among the twenty-four indicators we had established only two years before to measure our progress. For example, we decided to preserve our four-year graduation plan to best serve our students and continue progress toward our graduation rate goals, necessitating that we drop our goals for building repairs. In preserving the academic core of our mission, we also decided that we could not abandon our commitment to maintain our library system ranking by the Association of Research Libraries in the top fifteen, so we protected our library from budget cuts. Although harsh budget realities did have an impact on our goals and indicators in midstream, those same goals and indicators nevertheless proved invaluable in setting priorities and making decisions throughout the budget-cutting process.

Figure 4.2. University of Iowa Strategic Indicators.

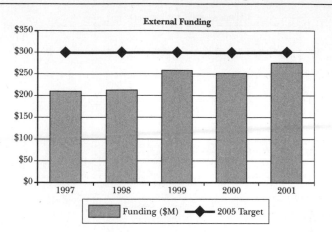

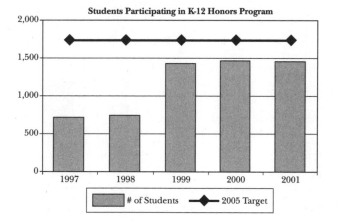

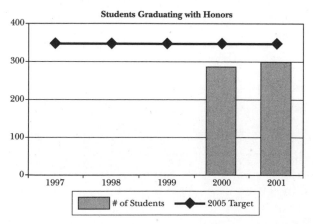

Figure 4.2. *(continued)*

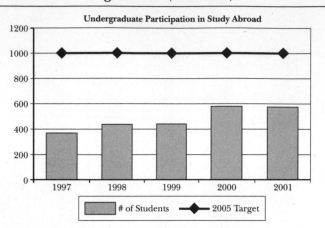

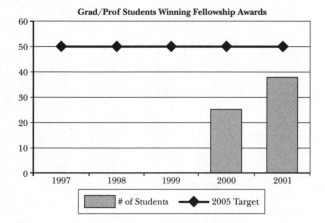

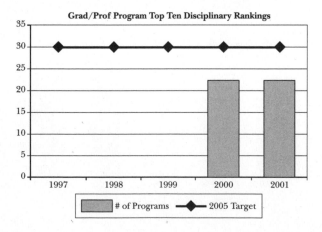

Figure 4.2. *(continued)*

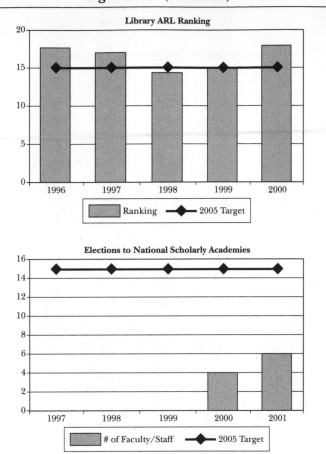

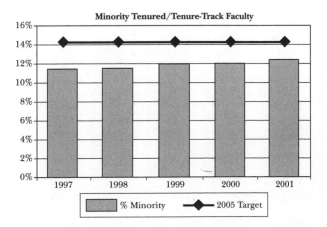

Figure 4.2. *(continued)*

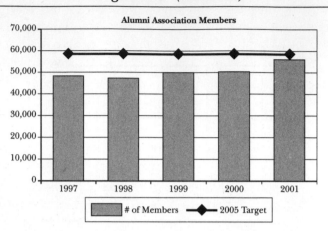

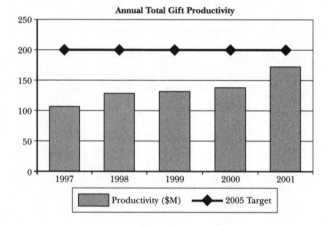

Even in the midst of budget difficulties, our annual report card has greatly increased my ability to communicate more effectively with the university's various constituents and our publics by presenting to them our strategic planning progress. Each year, I make a formal presentation to our governing board, weaving in anecdotes about the people behind the statistics. On occasion, I have used a multimedia show to demonstrate some of the best technology that is available for classroom use. Then I use the same presentation or some slight variant for civic clubs, alumni groups, legislators, faculty, and staff groups. Such a clear and effective presentation helps increase public confidence in the university's activities and accomplishments, sparks enthusiasm for academic accomplishments that are so often overshadowed by athletics, and awakens pride and a sense of ownership in the university as a resource for all Iowans.

Measuring Excellence from a Stakeholder Perspective

Susan G. Williams
Professor of Management, Jack C. Massey Graduate
School of Business, Belmont University

When a university commits itself to the difficult and often humbling process of listening to students and other stakeholders with improvement as the overall goal, good things can happen. The result is an agile approach and a keen awareness of the marketplace where the campus community achieves strong continuous performance assessment, strategic planning, and system redesign.

Belmont University in Nashville, Tennessee, began its improvement initiative in 1990. Since then, the university has been recognized nationally for its work in student-centered teaching and learning. Belmont is a private, coeducational, comprehensive university; it sits in the heart of Nashville, in a quiet area convenient to downtown and adjacent to Music Row. Belmont is home to more than thirty-three hundred undergraduate and graduate students. The university offers undergraduate degrees in more than fifty major areas of study through our six undergraduate colleges and schools. In addition, master's degrees are available in accountancy, business administration, education, English, music, occupational therapy, nursing, and sport administration. The School of Occupational Therapy also offers a clinical doctor of occupational therapy degree, and the School of Physical Therapy offers the doctor of physical therapy degree.

Our faculty comprises two hundred full-time professors. The student-to-teacher ratio is 11:1. Eighty-five percent of Belmont classes enroll fewer than twenty students. Belmont consistently receives national recognition for its commitment to personal interaction between students and faculty.

The Commitment to Stakeholder Data Gathering

Early in the 1990s, the senior leadership group conducted a census of students, asking them what delighted them and disappointed them about all aspects of the university. The president and senior leaders read every comment. At the end of the census, student comments were categorized, and teams began work on those improvements most important to students. Changes included centralized student services through Belmont Central, a one-stop place for students to do business with the university, and a focus on teaching excellence through a Teaching Center. Both initiatives are evidence of the result of listening carefully to students and translating their words into redesigned practices.

Stakeholder Expectations and Requirements

Assessing student and stakeholder needs means determining exactly who those stakeholders are and researching their key requirements. Belmont University spent almost a year in this process. Table 4.2 illustrates stakeholders and their key requirements identified through the research process. Although many of those requirements may seem intuitive, getting consensus on their importance is a helpful activity for campus and community members. Note that most of the dimensions are measurable. The university established a balanced scorecard approach that resulted in measures and "benchmarks" for the most important requirements (Kaplan and Norton, 1996a). Belmont holds membership in the Associated New American Colleges (ANAC), small to midsize comprehensive colleges and universities dedicated to the integration of liberal and professional studies. These colleges meet regularly and share virtually all operational and teaching and learning results. Examples of benchmarking information include salaries, student satisfaction, residence life and housing figures, placement rates, library holdings, and academic structure. When Belmont changed its system of schools to one of colleges within the university, the change was informed by data from other ANAC institutions.

Table 4.2. Belmont University Stakeholder Requirements.

Stakeholder	Key Requirements
Students	Excellent learning opportunities related to programs of study
	Highly qualified, motivated faculty who are accessible both inside and out of classrooms; good advising from those faculty
	Authentic, practical learning experiences, particularly in major fields
	Small classes
	Physical safety; good campus amenities
	Extraordinary student service
	Tolerant environment to explore new ideas; emotional safety in learning environment
	Cutting-edge technology for learning, research, service
	Opportunities to give feedback on their learning and on service
	Diverse cultural experiences
Adult students; Graduate students	(in addition to above) Courses offered at convenient times
	Expedited, prompt services
	Financial assistance
Faculty	Academic freedom
	Competitive compensation
	Faculty development resources
	Classrooms and offices equipped and designed for multiple uses; technology to better serve the learning process
	Reasonable workload shared equitably by all colleagues
Staff	Fair and equitable pay and benefits; job stability
	Relationships with coworkers and supervisors
	Recognition
Alumni	Consistent, positive institutional reputation
	Interaction with other alumni

Table 4.2. *(continued)*

Stakeholder	Key Requirements
	Safety from excessive solicitation
	Information on current life and work in their alma mater
	Inclusion in momentous occasions at Belmont
Parents, families	Safe environment for students
	Hirable skill levels for graduates
	Strong academic reputation
	Attractive, affordable school
	Caring, encouraging staff and faculty
Donors	Thanks and recognition
	Accurate and timely response to gifts
	Opportunities to participate, influence, and develop relationships
Employers	Students who have workplace 2000 skillsets
	Opportunities to present their businesses to students
	Students who have both personally and professionally ethical behavior
Community, society	Well-educated workers
	Service and involvement
	Leadership, community service

The focus of this narrative is on stakeholder measures, but it is important to note that Belmont is also concerned with assessing teaching and learning outcomes that cannot necessarily be effectively assessed by listening to stakeholders. Formal measures and indicators include first-year retention rate, graduation rate by college and program, placement rate by college and program, certification examination pass rates, number of faculty accessing teaching-improvement activities, peer teaching reviews, peer midcourse assessments, general education peer audits, and activities of faculty improvement groups. The university has a teaching center whose entire focus is helping faculty become better teachers, creating a collegial ethos that is student- and values-centered. In addition to within-course assessments, the university recognizes other results as outcome measures. Placement rate, licensure examination pass rate, retention, graduation rate, and students' satisfaction with their learning environment are among the measures that are tracked, and results in these areas have also improved dramatically in the past ten years.

Accrediting agencies, university faculty, and administration all monitor end measures, as well as in-process learning measures. Several indicators are monitored and compared to peer institutions as evidence of student learning. Since 1995, retention from first year to second year has risen from 70 to 78 percent, and placement rate overall is well over 90 percent within six months of graduation. In the largest university program, music business, the placement rate is 97 percent after one year. In the School of Nursing, the state examination pass rate for 2000–01 graduates is 100 percent, up from 93.2 percent over the last five years. The licensure examination pass rate for doctoral graduates in physical therapy is 98 percent for the first two graduating classes. In occupational therapy (another new program), of the eighty-two graduates the placement rate is 100 percent upon graduation with a 98 percent first-time pass rate on licensure examinations. Finding comparative information required research as well as collaboration with other institutions. Belmont's memberships in the National Consortium for Continuous Improvement in Higher Education and ANAC gave us venues for obtaining comparisons and benchmarks.

The Baldrige Framework: Another Measurement Tool

A commitment to continuous improvement as a strategic management construct encouraged leaders to assess the university using the 2000 Malcolm Baldrige National Quality Program criteria for performance excellence. Using first the criteria designed for business and later the *Criteria for Performance Excellence in Education* (2000), Belmont completed three comprehensive assessments in the 1990s, two as part of the Tennessee Quality Award and one nationally as part of the Malcolm Baldrige Pilot Program for Education in 1995. These assessments brought outside evaluator feedback from business and education leaders who were part of site visits and application review teams. As a result of those assessments, many Belmont teams made improvements in areas of importance to the university. In 2000, Belmont University requested permission from its regional accreditor, the Southern Association of Colleges and Schools (SACS), to use the Baldrige National Quality Program *Criteria for Performance Excellence in Education* (2000) for its ten-year reaccreditation study. The results of that self-study served to inform the strategic planning initiatives of 2000. There was a consensus on campus that assessing ourselves in that way would be more helpful than traditional assessment, and our expectation was that the resulting feedback report and reaccreditation documents would lead to more innovation and improved learning systems. Both the accreditation report from SACS and the site visit report commended the university for using these approaches ("Belmont University Alternate Self-Study," 2000).

Belmont University is committed to the premise of "student-centered education," and this commitment drives every aspect of a student's academic, social, and administrative experience. The university collects information through a variety of methods and has done so since the early 1990s. Through demographic and market research, student and faculty and staff surveys, focus groups, academic unit surveys, graduating student measures, and student advisory groups, the university determines and anticipates the changing needs and expectations of current and future students. Such a focus results in consistently high student satisfaction with their learning environment, service, and faculty teaching. In several of these areas, Belmont sets the benchmark for student satisfaction among peer institutions. These universitywide measures and results, based on stakeholder and internal requirements, are shared with campus units through the budgeting process and various teams and committees:

- Student satisfaction (four key areas)
- Faculty satisfaction
- Staff satisfaction
- Student learning (four key areas)
- Financial health
- Enrollment

Measuring the Effectiveness of Internal Partnerships

The university has an extensive network of processes designed to support the teaching and learning process. One of the most noteworthy aspects of these support processes is that we consider them part of a good learning environment for the entire campus community; as such, they are also assessed and improved for excellence. Many support areas have what they call "partnership agreements," which are negotiated internally between and among work units. Work units assess each other on attributes of processes that are shared among them. Figure 4.3 is an example of a check sheet that internal partners use to indicate key process attributes and negotiate those that are important to their areas.

In the design of support processes, the university meets regularly with key suppliers and business partners—food service, technology vendors, high schools and community colleges, book suppliers, building contractors, and others—to take their needs into account. We call our key vendors partners, and at various stages in our relationships we have partner meetings to discuss our mutual expectations and needs. Belmont has defined these key partners, as well as their and our principal requirements. The university uses a set of measures to determine the health of the relationships and to assess whether we and our partners are meeting each other's needs.

Figure 4.3. Partnership Agreement Check Sheet.

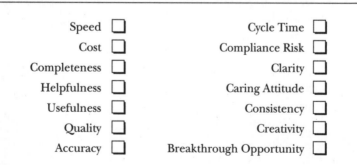

Speed	☐	Cycle Time	☐
Cost	☐	Compliance Risk	☐
Completeness	☐	Clarity	☐
Helpfulness	☐	Caring Attitude	☐
Usefulness	☐	Consistency	☐
Quality	☐	Creativity	☐
Accuracy	☐	Breakthrough Opportunity	☐

Challenges

Ultimately, any assessment initiative's success depends upon the organization's culture for change, resources, people, tools, and processes. Belmont's struggle to assess itself, with improvement as the goal, has been and continues to be a difficult one. The reluctance of people to hear bad news or see figures that are disconfirming impedes trust in assessment processes. People often search for excuses rather than ways to change. The role of leadership and of the larger faculty in assessment cannot be overstated. Strong leaders, both in the faculty and the administration, who ask the right questions, listen with understanding, and plan change with colleagues are the foundation for improvement. Effective measurement and improvement systems ultimately lead to a place where stakeholders value the organization and are willing to help it succeed. Belmont University seeks to be such a place.

A Balanced Scorecard for Business and Administrative Services at the University of California, Berkeley

Ron Coley
Associate Vice Chancellor of Business and Administrative Services

Paul K. Dimond
Principal Administrative Analyst

The University of California, Berkeley, is a member of the ten-campus University of California system and is the largest public research university in the world. On a hillside overlooking San Francisco Bay and the Golden Gate, the Berkeley campus serves a student population of thirty-three thousand, employing nineteen hundred faculty and twenty thousand staff (full-time and part-time). As the original campus of the UC system (1868), UC Berkeley is often referred to simply as "Berkeley" or as "Cal." Its tripartite mission of teaching, research, and public service follows the vision of California's founders, who dreamed of a university that eventually, "if properly organized and conducted, would contribute even more than California's gold to the glory and happiness of advancing generations."

Berkeley's long-solid reputation in agriculture, the humanities, and engineering took on a new dimension in the 1930s with physicist Ernest O. Lawrence's development of the cyclotron, turning Berkeley into the home of "big science." Beginning with Lawrence, eighteen Berkeley faculty have won Nobel Prizes, in physics, chemistry, literature, and economics. In recent decades, Berkeley's faculty has gained the campus a world-class reputation in the biological sciences as well.

Student culture is another distinguishing hallmark of the campus. The Free Speech Movement of the 1960s paralyzed the campus as students fought for the right to advocate for political and social causes. Since then, Berkeley's student body has become known for passionate advocacy around issues of racial, ethnic, and gender equity, and other forms of social and political fairness. Led by the student body, faculty and staff have also embedded diversity and social equity into Berkeley's campus culture.

Berkeley's Business and Administrative Services (BAS) Division provides support services to the academic enterprise. The division encompasses eighteen departments with a total staff of nineteen hundred. Its services range from back-office business functions to physical plant, human resources, environmental protection, police, student health services, intercollegiate athletics, and recreational sports.

In the mid-1990s, the BAS Division was in dire need of resources, and its service level was suffering. The early years of the decade had seen a fiscal crisis in the state that adversely affected the budgets of all public services, including UC Berkeley. Administrative divisions of the campus were allocated a disproportionate share of the cuts, as campus leadership did its best to shelter the core of the enterprise: the academic and research programs.

In 1995, Vice Chancellor Horace Mitchell assumed the leadership of BAS and began a series of administrative improvement efforts that continue to develop through the present. His goal was to improve BAS services to a level of quality commensurate with the stature of the institution. This meant two things: sharply focusing BAS services to support the campus mission of teaching, research, and public service; and achieving a level of service excellence that would enable and facilitate faculty and students in their own quests for excellence.

The intended result would be a corps of support staff—accountants, custodians, plumbers, administrative assistants, police officers, and others—energized, skilled, and viewing their own job as helping students to learn and faculty to expand the frontiers of knowledge.

Recognizing that the campus's academic programs and capital infrastructure needs would limit BAS funding indefinitely, Vice

Chancellor Mitchell determined that it would be necessary to find new methods for increasing the effectiveness of BAS.

The Foundation for Improvement: Core Competencies and Administrative Vision (1996–97)

Beginning with the fundamentals, Mitchell formed a campuswide committee to identify and describe management core competencies—the behaviors and skills needed by all campus managers to meet the needs of a constantly changing work environment. The results of the committee's work can be viewed online (http:// partnership.chance.berkeley.edu/ManageCoreComp/index.html).

Next, another team was formed from all sectors of the campus to articulate the "Berkeley administrative vision," a comprehensive statement of the role and nature of administration in an academic institution (http://partnership.chance.berkeley.edu/vision.html). Together with the core competencies, the administrative vision was a foundation for the needed improvements that were to follow. The impact derived in part from the fact that all sectors of campus administration, both academic and nonacademic, collaborated in their birth.

The Added Vigor of New Campus Leadership: CECCI (1997–1999)

Chancellor Robert M. Berdahl arrived on the Berkeley campus in 1997, charted a course of improved strategic planning, and laid the groundwork for a campuswide culture of continuous improvement.

To secure the commitment of top leadership in his improvement effort, Berdahl selected a group of key campus leaders to make up the Chancellor's Exploratory Committee on Continuous Improvement (CECCI). The committee defined a four-tiered approach to continuous improvement:

1. Strategic leadership and vision
2. Organizational assessment
3. Process improvement
4. Staff engagement

These four categories have been the focus for a host of subsequent academic and administrative improvement initiatives in virtually all segments of the Berkeley campus.

The BAS Balanced Scorecard (1999–2002)

BAS looked for an improvement model to embed in its own operations the four-tiered approach defined by CECCI. The model had to address the fundamental challenges faced by the BAS Division:

- A minimally trained management corps
- Difficult communication throughout its far-flung departments
- Scarcity of collaboration, and untapped synergies, among its departments ("eighteen silos")
- Lack of alignment to an organizational strategy ("1,000 staff, 1,000 strategies")
- A talented but demoralized workforce
- A staff culture in which personal values sometimes superseded organizational values
- A lack of adequate measurement systems, in some units, to track performance
- Scarce resources

In 1999, BAS adopted the Balanced Scorecard model of Kaplan and Norton (1996a, 1996b, 2001) as its framework for meeting these challenges. The scorecard was seen as a vehicle for all four tiers of the CECCI approach:

1. Strategic leadership: by articulating core values and strategic goals, aligning the organization around those values and goals, and giving managers a common language for their leadership efforts
2. Organizational assessment: by developing a system of metrics to track performance toward strategic goals
3. Process improvement: by using the metrics to feed cycles of continuous improvement
4. Staff engagement: by showing staff their connection to the organizational mission, by providing ways to demonstrate accomplishments, and by putting staff into major feedback loops

In sum, the balanced scorecard appeared to provide what BAS needed most: a multifaceted communication vehicle whose aim was alignment of daily operations to the overall mission. A pilot was begun in seven of the eighteen BAS departments.

The Balanced Scorecard Pilot

In tailoring the Kaplan-Norton model to the BAS pilot, a number of adaptations were decided on.

Focus on Frontline Units

Rather than installing an organizationwide balanced scorecard, with goals and measures cascading from the "corporate" level to the work-unit level, the pilot consisted of separate balanced scorecards for each of the fifty frontline work units (termed "strategic business units," or SBUs) in the seven pilot departments. This approach was intended to have a direct and immediate impact on a frontline staff that felt disenfranchised. In addition, it was hoped that the success of these frontline balanced scorecards would win the commitment of senior and midlevel managers who at first showed only marginal willingness to invest in this new structured measurement system.

Critical Goals Instead of Organizational Strategy

The Kaplan-Norton model begins with an overall organizational strategy and aligns goals and metrics to that strategy. The BAS Division, however, lacked a clearly articulated divisional strategy. In tune with the decision to focus on frontline SBUs, managers and supervisors were engaged in an active process to identify "critical goals" for each of their frontline units. Metrics were then identified to track each SBU's performance toward its critical goals.

Values Instead of Perspectives

A final and most critical deviation from the Kaplan-Norton model was the recasting of the model in terms of BAS's core organizational values. Kaplan and Norton defined four "perspectives": learning and growth, internal process, customer, and financial. Hoping to infuse its own organizational spirit into the framework, BAS decided to balance its scorecards around four "core values" that parallel the Kaplan-Norton perspectives:

1. People ("We enable and develop our people for progress")
2. Processes ("We continuously improve our processes")

3. Resources ("We use our resources wisely")
4. Service ("We anticipate and respond to the needs of our customers")

Exceptionally high-quality service is the ultimate value and the ultimate goal. BAS leadership felt that the "value" language offered greater potential for motivating staff and was more aligned with top BAS management's own value-driven leadership style. See Figure 4.4.

The Balanced Scorecards that resulted from these adaptations can be viewed at http://bas.berkeley.edu/BalancedScorecard/.

Figure 4.4. The Logo of the BAS Balanced Scorecard Pilot, University of California, Berkeley.

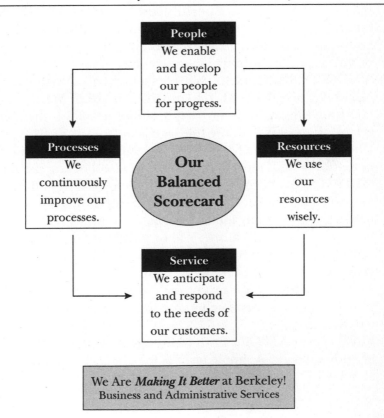

Balanced Scorecard Metrics: Selection Process

Two things proved especially valuable in BAS's metric-selection process: (1) a "coach" with broad organizational experience (the balanced scorecard coordinator) to assist managers in identifying good metrics, and (2) a clear set of guidelines. The BAS guidelines for metric-selection are shown in Exhibit 4.1.

Exhibit 4.1. BAS's Guidelines for Selecting Good Metrics.

---

1. CRITICAL GOALS: Every metric relates to a critical goal. The metric tracks progress toward that goal.
2. GOALS BEFORE METRICS: Critical goals should be identified before metrics, not vice-versa.
3. NEED TWO TYPES OF METRICS: There are two types: those that measure *outcomes* of performance (such as financial performance or customer satisfaction) and those that measure *factors that drive* performance (such as cycle time, staff skill level, or staff morale). Both types are needed.
4. A METRIC IS A NUMBER: If it's not a number, it's not a metric.
5. METRICS SHOULD BE UNDERSTANDABLE: Metrics communicate the organization's expectations to staff. If the metric is hard to understand, the message is lost.
6. USE EXISTING DATA WHERE POSSIBLE: In all cases, the potential benefit must exceed the cost of collecting the data.
7. METRICS MOTIVATE BEHAVIOR: A well-designed metric motivates desired behavior; a poor metric motivates adverse behavior. Almost any metric is capable of motivating adverse behavior if it stands alone; use of multiple metrics ("scorecards") counteracts this.
8. BALANCE YOUR SCORECARD: Strive for several metrics in each of the four quadrants of the scorecard. This encourages your managers to manage to an entire scorecard, not individual metrics.
9. KEEP IT STRATEGIC: Both critical goals and metrics should be truly strategic. A simple test: "Is the chancellor likely to care about this?"

10. A SCORECARD SHOULD TELL A STORY: A good balanced scorecard will *tell the story of your unit's strategy:* What are your critical goals? How will you measure your success in reaching these goals?

Introduction of the Pilot: A Calculated Strategy

The introduction of the balanced scorecard pilot was an exercise in strategic communication. The communication plan included all the usual elements: meetings, newsletters, posters, training sessions. More effective than any of these, however, was the decision to let the tool acquire its own voice through high initial impact. The first element introduced was an organizational climate metric in the form of a staff survey. All eleven hundred staff in the pilot units were asked to fill out a probing 128-question survey titled "Let's Hear It!" asking how they felt about virtually every aspect of working at Berkeley. They replied with gusto, adding reams of detailed comments, and the balanced scorecard was launched.

The "Let's Hear It!" survey brought many telling moments:

• Six supervisors, in a particularly troubled wing of the organization, refused to take the survey so long as their common manager was in the room (they were given a separate room and wrote with great relish).

• About seventy staff took the survey in one of five languages other than English. These staff, for whom English was a second (or fourth) language, showed remarkable enthusiasm for the survey; it was the first time ever that they had been invited to communicate in the workplace in their native language.

• There were expressions of shock by some managers and supervisors when the survey results reported how their staff really felt about their jobs and work environment.

• The five-hundred-person Physical Plant Department decided to use the survey results as one basis on which to design a major reorganization.

Evaluation of the Pilot

BAS leadership originally estimated a three-year time frame (1999–2002) to fully embed the balanced scorecard pilot into operations. Results to date (late 2002) have been encouraging:

- The first annual "Let's Hear It!" survey displayed in dramatic fashion that BAS's workplace climate fell far short of staff expectations. A round of staff-generated improvement initiatives has followed each year's survey, and the second and third annual surveys showed changes in staff opinions that roughly reflected the effectiveness of those initiatives. Management has come to accept this as confirmation that climate and culture can indeed be managed and improved.
- The common language and increased focus of the balanced scorecard evolved into a series of interdepartmental committees charged with managing various dimensions of strategy: safety, communications, human resources, customer advocacy, and others. Collaboration among departments took tangible shape.
- A balanced set of ten to fifteen metrics was developed for each of the fifty frontline units. Each unit's set held two types of metrics: a few common ones (used by all or most units) and some specific (unique to that unit). The configuration, including the common metrics, is shown in Exhibit 4.2.
- Strategy review using the accumulated data began in May 2002. The leadership team of the pilot (associate vice-chancellor plus departmental directors) conduct a biweekly review session at which the managers of two SBUs present their goals, metrics, and results. The leadership team examines each SBU's strategy and makes suggestions for improvement. These sessions are becoming an important vehicle for the "communication that brings alignment." Managers are showing increased focus on what really matters.

One of the strengths of the balanced scorecard approach is its reliance on hard data to measure results. The data are showing positive trends in many areas:

- Customer satisfaction: based on recent survey data from key campus customers, plus reduced frequency and severity of complaints

Exhibit 4.2. Metrics Template Used in
BAS Balanced Scorecard Pilot.

PEOPLE

CRITICAL GOAL	*METRIC*
Excellent workplace climate	Let's hear it! staff survey (annual)
Skilled, knowledgeable, learning-oriented staff	Average percentage completion of individual learning plans (an annually revised plan for each staff member)
Safe and healthful working environment	IIPP performance ranking (a composite metric evaluating the unit's performance on the six major parts of its Illness and Injury Prevention Plan)
Healthy staff	Injury and illness rate (work-related recordable incidents)

RESOURCES

CRITICAL GOAL	*METRIC*
Sound financial performance	Revenue less expense, or budget less expense
Productive use of resources	(Metric specific to unit)
(Other specific goals and metrics)	

PROCESSES

CRITICAL GOAL	*METRIC*
(Specific goals and metrics)	

SERVICE

CRITICAL GOAL	*METRIC*
Satisfied customers	Customer survey
Knowledgeable, collaborative customers	(Customer education metric where appropriate)
Timely service	(Specific metric where appropriate)
(Other specific goals and metrics)	

- Productivity and efficiency: reorganizations in several sectors producing improved outcomes using fewer organizational resources
- Staff knowledge of organizational core values: tracked on the annual staff survey
- Staff training and safety practices: tracked by quarterly training and safety metrics

Other indicators of organizational improvement are also strong. Discussions of strategy are appearing on meeting agendas at every level. The metrics are focusing attention on factors that "drive success" (the past two years have seen a large increase in time allocated to leadership training, supervisory training, customer advocacy training, individual career-development activities, and proactive safety planning). The primacy of improving service to customer groups is being recognized; more service-oriented workshops are being held, their effectiveness is being assessed, and a Web-based survey system to track customer satisfaction has been piloted.

A Balanced Scorecard Framework
for the Entire BAS Division (2001–2003)

Late in 2001, a review of the progress of the balanced scorecard pilot led to the decision to expand the approach to the remainder of the BAS Division. In addition, Vice Chancellor Mitchell perceived that there was a further benefit to be gained: clear articulation, for the first time, of a BAS strategy. This thinking paralleled the evolution of Kaplan and Norton's own view (1996a, 1996b, 2001) of the balanced scorecard tool, from their earlier conception of the balanced scorecard as a "balanced measurement system" into a broadened view of the model as the basis for a "strategic management system." In other words, this tool for measuring organizational performance, if properly crafted, could achieve greater impact as a tool for managing implementation of organizational strategy.

To make the larger BAS implementation truly strategy-centered, Mitchell and his senior leadership team adopted the approach described by Kaplan and Norton in their latest book, *The Strategy-Focused Organization* (2001). The BAS leaders first articulated their divisional strategy in the cause-and-effect language of a Kaplan-Norton strategy map. During the summer of 2002, a select task force created a division-level balanced scorecard by devising metrics and initiatives relating to the strategic objectives on the map. In 2003, the balanced scorecard framework will be cascaded to all the BAS departments and to the strategic business units within each department. Where the "critical goals" identified by the SBUs of the pilot departments align well with BAS strategy, they will be incorporated (see Exhibit 4.2). Where this is not the case, new goals and metrics will be identified.

Ideally, every BAS employee will have a personal balanced scorecard that links to the larger framework. The result, it is anticipated, will be an implementation-and-feedback system without precedent in BAS, and an ever-increasing level of excellence by BAS in support of Berkeley's academic mission.

Comparing Solutions to Campus Parking Problems

Mo Qayoumi
Vice President for Administration and Finance and
CFO, California State University Northridge

As the largest university system in the United States, California State University (CSU) consists of twenty-three campuses with a student body of more than 407,000 and a faculty and staff of 45,000. CSU serves as the gateway for many students who are seeking a college education in California. As such, CSU is awarding more than half of the bachelor's degrees and roughly 30 percent of the master's degrees in California. The system was created by the Donahoe Higher Education Act of 1960, which brought together individual California colleges and universities. The oldest CSU campus, San Jose State University, was founded in 1857; the newest campus, California State University Channel Island, was opened in 2002. CSU offers more than eighteen hundred bachelor's and master's degree programs in roughly 240 subject areas. Since 1961, CSU has awarded approximately two million bachelor's, master's, and joint doctoral programs.

The majority of students are commuters. Similar to most other campuses in the country, parking is an issue and a potential source of dissatisfaction for many students, faculty, staff, and visitors at CSU—a fact that was underscored in the 1999 CSU Student Needs and Priority (SNAP) survey report. One especially important matter for commuting students on any campus is the ease or difficulty in securing and paying for a parking decal. Satisfaction surveys conducted in spring 2001 at many CSU campuses indicated that 36 percent of the students were dissatisfied or very dissatisfied with the long lines and wait time and other problems associated with the existing procedures for securing permits. Because of the importance of this issue for most students, CSU decided to examine the process of decal issuance in some detail in an effort to identify potential improvements.

Decal issuance was also seen as a major problem from the perspective of the institutions involved. The Student Financial Services (SFS) offices at CSU campuses, which include cashiers, student accounts, and bursars' offices, are responsible for processing student requests and payments for parking decals (among many other student financial transactions). Most SFS offices also issue parking decals to employees. Both SFS and the CSU parking offices had identified the issuance of parking decals as a matter in need of study for potential process streamlining.

Our Approach

To address this goal, CSU initiated a benchmarking study to compare performance among CSU campuses as well as other leaders in higher education and other sectors. The study was conducted in 2001, and the report—which serves as the basis for this narrative—was published by the participating team in early 2002.

Benchmarking is an action-biased approach for obtaining information to enhance performance. It begins with the premise that an organization should be humble enough to admit that there can be others who are better in accomplishing a particular task, and that it makes good sense to learn from them rather than reinventing the wheel.

The need for this study became obvious when the CSU Student Account Receivable (SAR) group determined that most campuses used the same methods of decal issuance and were all experiencing similar problems. The first and obvious issue was that at many institutions the largest number of faculty and students were purchasing their decals in person at the cashier's office immediately before and after the beginning of the semester. Long lines were created at most cashier's locations as a result. The challenge was to identify alternative methods that would improve the efficiency and effectiveness of the decal issuance process.

Participating CSU campuses in the study were Chico, Fresno, Fullerton, Hayward, Northridge, San Bernardino, San Jose, San Luis Obispo, and San Marcos. Dolores Basilio, from Quality Improvement Programs of the CSU chancellor's office, facilitated the study. The study was sponsored by William Barrett, associate vice president at CSU Fullerton (acting vice president, administration, in 2001) and myself as vice president of administration and finance at Northridge. John Darakjy, assistant director of financial services at CSU Northridge, led the study. In addition, there were about twenty-five other individuals from the aforementioned campuses that served as team members in the study. The stated goal of the study was to develop a model practice that CSU campuses could adopt to improve service; better meet the needs of students, faculty, staff, and other stakeholders; and increase productivity in the issuance of decals.

Current Practice of Decal Issuance

Most CSU campuses did offer students and faculty advance purchase options. Students options included ordering by phone, Web, mail-in, or drop-box. Faculty and staff had the option of paying parking fees through automatic payroll deduction, eliminating the need for them to wait in line. Where they were widely used, these options greatly eased the workload of cashiering staff and the inconvenience and dissatisfaction associated with a long wait in line.

Although many CSU campuses allow students to request parking decals months before classes begin, thousands of students do not take advantage of advance purchase options. Northridge reported that approximately 33 percent (fifty-five hundred) of student parking decals for the fall 2001 semester were purchased in person, with twenty-five hundred purchased the week before and during the first few days of classes. Fullerton reported that 60 percent (thirteen thousand) of their decals were purchased in person, and Sacramento reported about 40 percent (almost six thousand of their fourteen thousand decals) were sold in person. About half of the campuses surveyed mail the decal to students, and the balance required in-person pickup.

Specific Tools and Methods

The study used a number of tools and methods. A first step was to analyze the various processes and subprocesses involved in decal issuance:

- A flowchart describing the incremental steps from purchase to delivery
- A hand-off map indicating key inputs (among them student request, vendor supplies, payments, regulations) and outputs (permits issued, revenues, and so forth)
- An "as-is" map describing the current step-by-step process as the paperwork moved within and between functions and departments

The next step was analyzing the process using fit/gap analysis and Pareto diagrams. A number of measures such as quality of service, cost of implementing alternatives, timing, and validity period for the decal were identified. The needed information was gathered using student surveys and site visits in other organizations. The student surveys collected data on:

- Preferred method of payment
- Preferred method of applying for a decal
- Satisfaction or dissatisfaction with length of line and wait time
- Reasons for purchasing a decal in person

Clarifying Dimensions of the Problem

Using the knowledge obtained by staff from their interaction with students, faculty, and staff as well as a survey, these root causes for the three key issues were determined:

- *Long lines of students.* The common reasons students purchase decals in person were campus policy, lack of knowledge about advance or electronic purchase options, not receiving the decal, lack of confidence in the decal delivery system, personal choice, procrastination, financial aid issues, and no desire to part with money until necessary.

- *Missing or incorrect information or payments.* Other reasons for avoiding advance purchase options that were common to all categories of purchasers (faculty, staff, and students) were missing request forms, concern about payment getting lost in the mail, lack of proper identification to purchase a decal, or lack of required information.
- *Untimely or nonreceipt of the parking decal.* Students who used advance purchase options reported that they sometimes receive their decals after classes begin—or not at all—thanks to incorrect address, mailing the decal too close to the start of term, postal delays, being unaware of the receipt, and fraud.

The Model Practice

A model practice was developed through using tools for process improvement, referencing survey and research data including the Customer Satisfaction Survey 2001, Performance Measurement 2000, and a process survey of CSU campuses conducted in fall 2001, as well as conducting site visits to USC, UCLA, and the Oakland Stadium to identify best practices. Given this input, the recommended model practice encompasses three key facets.

The first is Web-based service. The primary channel for the issues of parking decals should be the Web. The survey found that this is the most preferred option for students. Self-service for the students, faculty, and staff would resolve many of the problems with the current processes. Other electronic options could be considered, such as phone or kiosk, but would not be as effective as the Web. It was determined that to ensure that the Web is fully used, some procedural changes and new communication strategies (mentioned in the following sections) were needed to highlight the benefits of the approach for students, faculty, and staff.

Second, other strategies can be used to increase effectiveness and efficiency. The model practice recommendations achieve effective utilization of resources for both labor and material costs by significantly reducing or eliminating transaction processing and staffing for long lines of students. This is accomplished through:

- Automation with Web-based parking decal programs and services
- Applying financial aid awards (with student approval) toward the cost of parking

- Sale and distribution of *annual* decals to students instead of *term* decals
- Stronger student accountability for decals
- Long-term decals for faculty and staff
- Human Resources issuing decals to new employees
- Group reissuance of parking decals to permanent faculty and staff
- Outsourcing the mailing of decals to a third-party vendor
- Mailing decals no later than two weeks prior to the start of the term

The third key is increased and proactive communication. It was determined that improved communications will be needed to increase utilization of advance purchase options. Here are some of the communication channels to be used:

- Student venues such as orientation
- Information included in registration and financial aid packets
- Cyber voice technology, if available, by contacting students who have not purchased a decal a month before the start of the term

Impact of the Study

Of the six campuses that participated in the study, three have already adopted the model framework. Two of the campuses have indicated they will be implementing most of the recommendations, and one campus has decided not to implement the recommendations at this time.

Participating campuses learned a great deal from each other as well as the site visits, and exchange of policy and procedural information among participating CSU campuses resulted in campuses reexamining their own practices. There are immediate opportunities under current consideration: increasing communication with the student population through various venues, reviewing reasons for requiring vehicle information and other personal data, rethinking replacement decal fees, implementing more types of electronic payment, improving already available electronic systems, and outsourcing mailing of decals. The introduction of systemwide master enabling agreements to parking offices is already benefiting CSU campuses.

Benchmarking studies such as this one are not per se a silver bullet that can magically transform work processes or eliminate inefficiency or dissatisfaction. They can, however, bring greater clarity and rigor to problem definition and problem solving. The approach can also contribute significantly to changing the cultural fabric of an organization, giving greater emphasis to systematic information gathering and comparisons in institutional assessment and improvement efforts.

Chapter Five

Integrating Organizational Assessment, Planning, and Improvement
Making Organizational Self-Study and Change Everyday Activities

The need for more effective organizational assessment, better synchronization between assessment and planning, and the appropriate linkage of these activities with organizational improvement efforts is a significant one. The Malcolm Baldrige National Quality Award program (MBNQA), established in 1987 by Congress through passage of Public Law 100–107, constitutes a framework that helps address these issues.[1] Named after Secretary of Commerce Malcolm Baldrige, who served from 1981 until his death in 1987, the intent of the program created by this legislation was to promote U.S. business effectiveness for the advancement of the national economy (Baldrige National Quality Program, 2003a) by providing a systems approach for organizational assessment and improvement. The program, which is administered by the National Institute for Standards and Technology (NIST), has also been an influential contributor in national and international efforts to identify and encourage the application of core principles of organizational excellence.

Essentially, the goals of the Baldrige program are to:

- Identify the essential components of organizational excellence
- Recognize organizations that demonstrate these characteristics

- Promote information sharing by exemplary organizations
- Encourage the adoption of effective organizational principles and practices

The recognition aspects of the Baldrige program are well known, but its more fundamental contributions are those related to research, communication, and education. In these respects, the Baldrige program has done a great deal to articulate standards of organizational excellence that transcend particular types of organizations and sectors, and to facilitate dialogue on how principles and practices from one organizational context can be applied in others. The Baldrige process also emphasizes an integrated approach to assessment, planning, and improvement that has been most valuable.

For those of us in higher education, the Baldrige approach has considerable potential. It presents a systematic framework for assessing colleges and universities—and their constituent departments—from an organizational perspective. As such, the framework helps us inquire about the effectiveness and efficiency of our departments and institutions as organizations, and it facilitates efforts to compare ourselves with and translate insights from other higher education institutions, and also from organizations in other sectors that may be grappling with similar generic concerns.

In general terms, the framework suggests that organizational excellence requires:

1. Effective leadership that provides guidance and ensures a clear and shared sense of organizational mission and future vision, a commitment to continuous review and improvement of leadership practice, and social and environmental consciousness

2. An inclusive planning process and coherent plans that translate the organization's mission, vision, and values into clear, aggressive, and measurable goals understood and effectively implemented throughout the organization

3. Knowledge of the needs, expectations, and level of satisfaction or dissatisfaction of the groups served by the organization; operating practices that are responsive to these needs and expectations; and assessment processes in place to stay current with and anticipate the thinking of these groups

4. Development and use of indicators of organizational performance that capture the organization's mission, vision, values, and goals and that permit data-based comparisons with peer and leading organizations, widely sharing this information within the organization to focus and motivate improvement

5. A workplace culture that encourages, recognizes, and rewards excellence; promotes engagement, professional development, commitment, and pride; and synchronizes individual and organizational goals

6. Focus on mission-critical and support work processes to ensure effectiveness, efficiency, appropriate standardization and documentation, and regular evaluation and improvement

7. Documented, sustained positive outcomes relative to organizational mission, vision, goals, the perspectives of groups served, and employees, considered in light of comparisons with the accomplishments of peers, competitors, and leaders

From its inception, the Baldrige program has proven to be an extremely pervasive influence in organizational improvement efforts. Since 1988, nearly eight hundred organizations have submitted applications for awards, and nearly sixty have received recognition for their accomplishments (Baldrige, 2002d; Broadhead, 2000). Not surprisingly, the primary influence in the early years of the program was within the business community. Among the companies selected as recipients of the national Baldrige awards in recent years are divisions of such large and well-known corporations as Motorola (2002), Ritz-Carlton Hotel (1999), STMicroelectronics (1999), Boeing (1998), 3M (1997), Xerox (1997), Merrill Lynch (1997), Armstrong (1995), Corning (1995), and smaller companies such as Pal's Sudden Service (2001) and Sunny Fresh Foods (1999). A complete listing of winning organizations is available at the Baldrige National Quality Program Website (www.nist.gov/public_affairs/factsheet/mbnqa.htm).

The impact of the Baldrige program has been quite remarkable. Each year, approximately 250,000 Baldrige guidebooks are distributed by NIST[2]; in the years since the program was initiated, almost two million copies have been distributed, and reproduction by organizations and agencies has greatly expanded this number (Baldrige, 2002a). The Baldrige Website also receives an average of

150,000 hits each month (H. Hertz, personal communication, Nov. 2000). In addition, the Baldrige framework serves as the prototype for award programs in forty-three states and ten regional or local programs (Baldrige, 2002d). Moreover, many leading companies and a number of governmental organizations have adapted the award criteria to their own needs. Above all else, the pervasive influence of the Baldrige results from the value of the framework as a clear and coherent way of conceptualizing and assessing organizational excellence, and as a guide to leaders pursuing these goals.

The Baldrige in Higher Education

With the goal of extending to other sectors the benefits realized by business, "health care" and "education" versions of the Baldrige were developed and pilot-tested in 1995, and in that first year forty-six health-care organizations and nineteen educational institutions submitted applications (Baldrige, 2002b). The programs and assessment criteria generally paralleled the "business Baldrige" and, like the original version, were designed to foster organizational improvement, recognition for excellence, and the sharing of best practices. NIST provided leadership for this effort with advice and counsel from academicians and practitioners. The pilot involved translating and adapting core concepts and principles of organizational excellence to the contexts of health care and education. The health care version was intended for use by health organizations of all kinds, including hospitals, HMOs, and emergency care centers. The education Baldrige was created for use by educational units at all levels and of all types, public and private. The education version was intended to be expansive enough to include K–12 systems, community and junior colleges, four-year colleges and universities, and even corporate educational programs or centers. Legislative and budgetary limitations in 1996 slowed plans to introduce these new programs on a broader scale, but in 1998 the two new Baldrige programs received the necessary approvals and funding. The programs have now been fully implemented on a national level, with many states also adopting these new awards. Since its inception, there have been more than fifty applicants to the national program in education and three award winners (Baldrige, 2002b).

Within higher education, Belmont University, Northwest Missouri State University, and the University of Missouri–Rolla played an early and visible leadership role in applying the Baldrige framework to institutional assessment and in achieving state recognition, and in 2001 the University of Wisconsin-Stout became the first university to win a national Baldrige award (Baldrige, 2002h). The Baldrige approach is also having a significant impact on professional school and regional accreditation models.

The value of the Baldrige model has been apparent in business, engineering, and the health sciences for several years. More recently, the framework has also begun to have a significant influence on the approaches used by the regional accrediting associations. The North Central Association[3] has introduced an optional accreditation process called the Academic Quality Improvement Project (AQIP), which mirrors the Baldrige approach in a number of respects (Biemiller, 2000). By early 2002, more than two hundred schools had shown interest in this approach and sixty institutions were participating in the program (Spangehl, 2000, 2003). The 2002 *Characteristics of Excellence in Higher Education: Eligibility Requirements and Standards for Accreditation,* published by the Middle States Commission, also reflects the Baldrige criteria in many regards (Middle States, 2002).

For higher education, the potential contribution of the Baldrige approach is substantial. It incorporates many of the best features of the methodologies—such as self-studies, external reviews, management audits, accreditation reviews, and strategic planning—that are familiar to faculty and staff. In so doing, it provides:

- A method for systematic, high-level, and comprehensive examination of an organization or institution
- A framework for high-level analysis of *what* the organization or institution does, *why,* and *how*
- Widely accepted standards of organizational excellence
- An integrated examination of approaches, implementation strategies, and outcomes
- Guidance on the establishment of comparisons within and across institutions
- Input for strategic planning, organizational change, and improvement efforts

- An assessment of current organizational or institutional directions, and a blueprint for the future
- A method for monitoring progress and advancement
- A conceptual and practical guide for leaders

Adapting the Baldrige Framework: The *Excellence in Higher Education* Model

As was recognized with the "business Baldrige," there can be value in customizing the Baldrige framework for the specialized needs of an institution or sector. The President's Quality Award, introduced in 1989, for example, adapted the Baldrige to the context of the federal government. The RIT/*USA Today* Quality Cup, sponsored by the Rochester Institute of Technology, recognizes organizations that provide exemplary customer service. The Johnson and Johnson Signature of Quality Award adapts the Baldrige to the particular needs of its international health care businesses.

Paralleling these efforts is *Excellence in Higher Education* (*EHE*), developed to adapt the Baldrige to the particular needs of colleges and universities (Ruben, 1995c, 2000b, 2001a, 2003a, 2003c; Ruben and Lehr, 1997a). The *EHE* framework uses language of higher education and is designed to be adaptable to the mission of any institution—or of any academic or administrative department within an institution. Because the education Baldrige was intended to be broadly inclusive and appropriate for school systems of all kinds and at all levels, the primary focus of the framework is instructional activities and outcomes. However, unlike K–12 systems, many higher education institutions have missions that also emphasize scholarship and research, public service, and other functions. Additionally, there are a number of departments within colleges and universities that are not directly involved in teaching but rather provide student services of various kinds, or support for research, public service, and outreach activities of an institution. Although such units are not directly involved in instruction—as the term is traditionally defined—the work of these departments *is* vital to the institution, and to students, alumni, faculty, staff, and the broader community; issues of assessment, planning, and improvement are of no less importance in these areas than others. The *EHE* model was constructed to be applicable in these administrative and internal service areas, as well as in traditional academic departments—and more generally to be appropriate for any institution or department, regardless of its mission.

Like the Baldrige framework on which it is based, *EHE* consists of seven categories. Each of the first six categories—leadership, planning, external focus, measurement and knowledge utilization, faculty/staff and workplace focus, and process effectiveness—corresponds to what is viewed as a critical component of, and a contributor to, the excellence of an educational organization. Organizational accomplishments, trends, and comparisons with peer and leading institutions are the focus of category seven, outcomes and achievements. Collectively, the categories and the many interactions between them define a systems framework that can be used to conceptualize and analyze the workings, effectiveness, strengths, and improvement needs of a higher education department, program, or institution (see Figure 5.1).

Each of the categories has a number of elements or subthemes that help to operationally define the area. These are detailed in the *EHE Guidebook,* the *Workbook,* and the *Facilitator's Guide* (Ruben, 2003a, 2003b, 2003c) and briefly summarized in a question format in Exhibit 5.1.

Figure 5.1. *Excellence in Higher Education 2003–04* **Framework and Categories.**

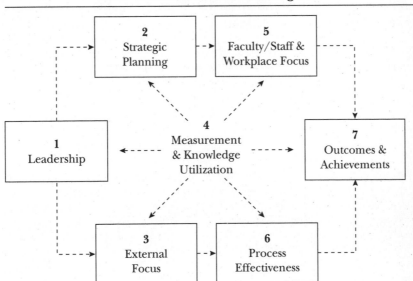

The *EHE* Process

The *EHE* process, as it has most often been implemented, consists of four basic steps: (1) self-assessment; (2) improvement prioritization; (3) project planning; and (4) implementation, report out, and recognition, as illustrated in Figure 5.2. The process described here uses the *EHE* framework as an integrated self-assessment, priority-setting, and action-planning program that has most often been used in an interactive workshop or retreat mode with follow-up sessions. However, it can also be used as a leader's guide to institutional effectiveness, or form the basis of departmental or institutional self-study, or third-party reviews, in a more traditional manner as descriptive criteria for review and assessment.

A brief explanation of each phase of the integrated self-assessment, priority-setting, and action-planning program follows.

Step One: Self-Assessment

Typically, the *EHE* self-assessment process is completed in a workshop attended by administrators, the faculty, or staff from a participating program, department, school, or institution. Depending on the size of the unit and the purposes at hand, the leadership and all members of the unit may attend, or participation may be limited to the leadership group along with selected representatives from a cross section of functions and roles. In any case, senior leadership participation is essential.

Figure 5.2. Steps in the *Excellence in Higher Education* Process.

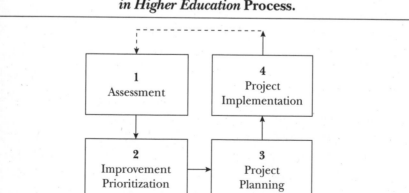

Exhibit 5.1. *Excellence in Higher Education* **Categories.**

Category 1: Leadership
- Does your unit have a clearly defined, documented and shared view of your mission, vision, values, plans, and goals?
- How do leaders guide your unit, and clarify, build, and sustain consensus on your directions and priorities?
- How do leaders focus your unit on understanding and addressing the needs and expectations of stakeholders?
- How do leaders use communication, leadership performance reviews, and other approaches to foster effective leadership systems and practices throughout the organization?

Category 2: Strategic Planning
- How does your unit translate its mission, vision, and values into priorities, goals and action steps?
- Does your unit have a formal planning process and a plan?
- How do you implement and evaluate your plans and goals?
- How do you engage faculty and staff from your unit in the planning and implementation process?

Category 3: External Focus
- For which groups or organizations does your unit provide programs and services?
- How does your unit learn about the needs and expectations of these external stakeholder groups?
- How do you build and enhance your relationships, communication, and reputation with stakeholders?
- How do you assess the satisfaction levels of your major stakeholder groups?

Category 4: Measurement and Knowledge Utilization
- How do you select and use data and information to assess outcomes, achievements, and improvement trends for your unit?
- How do you disseminate and use information to coordinate and improve all aspects of the organization?
- How does your unit select and use comparison information from peers, competitor, and leading organizations?

continued

Exhibit 5.1. *(continued)*

Category 5: Faculty/Staff and Workplace Focus
- How are the faculty and staff encouraged to develop their full potential and to link their efforts with the priorities of the unit and institution?
- How does your unit build and maintain an environment that is conducive to excellence, engagement, appreciation of diversity, and personal and organizational development?
- How do you assess and monitor workplace climate and the satisfaction of faculty and staff?

Category 6: Process Effectiveness
- How does your unit identify, monitor, and ensure the effectiveness and efficiency of your mission-critical work processes?
- How are support processes—those necessary to mission-critical processes—monitored and improved?
- How does the unit regularly review and improve mission-critical and support processes?
- How are comparisons with other organizations used for process improvement?

Category 7: Outcomes and Achievements
- How successful is your unit overall in achieving its mission, vision, plans, and goals?
- How successful are specific programs and services in achieving their goals?
- How satisfied are your major stakeholders and faculty and staff?
- How successful is your unit in terms of organizational effectiveness and efficiency?
- What are your current and overtime outcomes and achievement levels in each of these areas?
- How do these patterns compare to peers, competitors, and other leading organizations?

The workshop consists of a sequential and detailed category-by-category review and self-assessment. Each category is introduced and its elements are explained and discussed. Examples of best practices in other departments or institutions (and other sectors) are provided to help clarify a category and its implications. The focus then shifts to the participating organization, and specific examples of strengths and areas for improvement for the institution, department, or program in the category are identified and recorded.

Scoring is next. Participants individually and anonymously rate the institution or unit on a 0 percent to 100 percent scale, following detailed instructions in the *Guide* and thoroughly reviewed in the session. A 0 percent would be the appropriate rating for an organization that has no activities and accomplishments in a particular category (a highly unlikely circumstance). Ratings in the 10–20 percent range would indicate that "a few" of the criteria and elements associated with a category are being addressed by the organization; 30–40 percent would be appropriate if "some" of the criteria and elements associated with the category apply; 50–60 percent indicates that "many" of the criteria and themes are being addressed; 70–80 percent indicates that "most" of the criteria and themes for a category are being met; and 90–100 percent indicates that "all" of the criteria for the category apply. Ratings are submitted by participants, and the average rating assigned by the group is calculated and displayed.

In addition to percentage ratings, the Baldrige and *EHE* scoring systems also attach a specific number of points to each category, such that the total points possible across all categories is 1,000. Following the Baldrige, here are the possible number of points associated with each *EHE* category: leadership 120; strategic planning 85; external focus 85; measurement and knowledge utilization 90; faculty/staff and workplace focus 85; process effectiveness 85; outcomes and achievements 450. Categories one through six are concerned with factors that contribute to organizational excellence; category seven focuses on outcomes. The effect of the point system is to apply a differential weighting to the leadership, measurement and knowledge utilization, and outcomes and achievements categories. In essence, this scoring results in attaching considerably more significance to outcomes and achievements, and somewhat more to leadership and measurement and knowledge utilization, reflecting the view that these three components are most essential to organizational effectiveness.[4]

The scoring process is repeated for each category, until all seven are completed. The final activities of the self-assessment phase of the workshop involve (1) calculating an overall score that can be used as a reference point against which to measure progress in the future; and (2) reviewing and discussing the overall scoring profile.

The self-assessment rating profiles vary considerably from one institution, department, or program to another, reflecting their unique pattern of strengths and areas in need of improvement. The ratings from the *EHE* assessment process are "the property" of the participating organization and are generally not reported elsewhere unless the unit chooses to do so.

Figure 5.3 is an illustration of a rather typical profile of the percentage ratings resulting from self-assessment. As noted, the standard set by the Baldrige and *EHE* is a very high one. To illustrate this point, see Figure 5.4, a summary of the assessment percentage ratings for national Baldrige applicants in the service, health care, and education sectors in 2000.

Given these rigorous standards, it is not surprising that, as shown in Figure 5.5, on average departments and institutions participating in the *EHE* assessment fall in the 30–40 percent category, indicating that they are meeting some—but not many, most, or all—of the standards set forth by *EHE*/Baldrige.

Step Two: Improvement Prioritization

The next step involves scheduling a second workshop session to review and prioritize potential improvement needs. Multivoting is used to determine priorities for improvement. The top ten items are identified, and generally three to five items are selected as the initial action items. The number selected for immediate attention depends on the scope of the priority projects and available resources.

Step Three: Project Planning

Discussion then shifts to translating the selected priority areas into action plans. The group drafts a preliminary plan for each of the

Figure 5.3. *EHE* Self-Assessment Sample Profile.

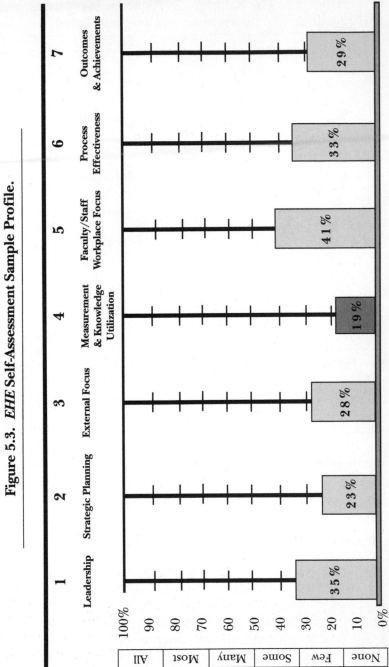

Figure 5.4. The Baldrige—A Rigorous Standard: Baldrige Applicant Average Category Scores.

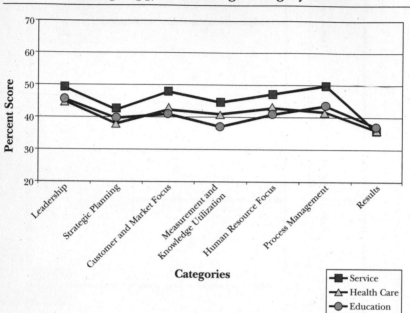

Provided by the Malcolm Baldridge Program, National Institutes of Standards and Technology. Means are calculated based on the 11 applicants in Service, 16 in Education, and 9 in Health Care.

selected projects, including a brief "charge" or mission statement for the project, a list of appropriate individuals and roles to serve on the project team, a recommended team leader, important considerations and suggested procedures, a delineation of the team's "deliverables," and a recommended time line.

Step Four: Implementation

Selected project team leaders are charged with convening the designated teams subsequent to the session, refining the action plan outline, and leading the improvement effort with regular communication and collaboration with the organization's leadership, members of the participant group, and other designated individuals.

As projects are completed, the group returns to select additional projects from the list of priorities that were not addressed in the first

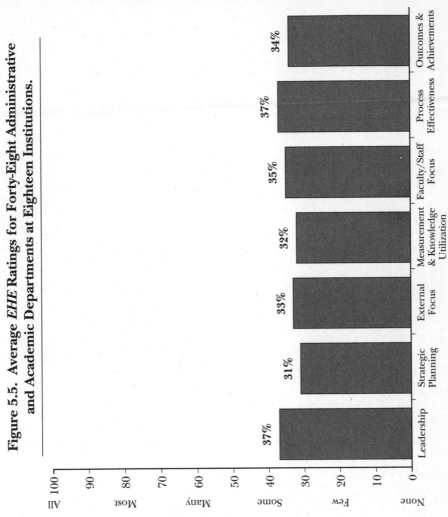

Figure 5.5. Average *EHE* Ratings for Forty-Eight Administrative and Academic Departments at Eighteen Institutions.

round of projects. Annually or biannually, a full reassessment and scoring process can be conducted to gain a sense of progress and to reformulate strategic and action plans for the period ahead.

EHE Case Profiles

The *EHE* framework has been implemented in both academic and administrative departments, and brief case study descriptions of one unit in each category are presented in this section. The profiles that follow are not intended to be comprehensive but rather to give examples of how the process operates, and to convey a sense of the kind of improvement recommendations, priorities, and outcomes that are typical with the *EHE* model.

An Administrative Services Division

The division consisted of fifteen major departments, among them financial planning and accounting, budget management, parking, human resources, facilities management, police, health services, public safety, and athletics. The senior administration of the division determined that the *EHE* process would be a useful tool for obtaining a realistic assessment of department and division strengths and priorities for improvement, heightening dialogue and networking among the leaders of various units, encouraging information sharing on best practices across departments, and fostering a greater sense of division cohesiveness and identity.

The vice president, all department directors, several assistant directors, and key administrative support personnel participated in an *EHE* retreat workshop.

The unit completed the self-assessment scoring and developed a long list of strengths and areas for improvement across all of the *EHE* categories. What follows is a representative sample of the areas for improvement identified by the group for each of the seven categories.

Category 1.0: Leadership, Areas for Improvement

- Create and communicate a unifying vision, theme, and goals.
- Improve cross-unit communication and cooperation among department leaders.
- Increase candid, honest feedback with the senior leadership group.

- Establish a systematic approach to performance review of division and department leaders (including peer and subordinate input).

Category 2.0: Strategic Planning, Areas for Improvement

- Revise the planning process so that it is less cumbersome and more inspirational.
- Revise the strategic planning process so that it heightens the involvement of more individuals within the division and, as a result, strengthens group identity or integration.
- Coordinate and communicate action plans more effectively.
- Improve follow-up on project goals to determine whether they are fully met.

Category 3.0: External Focus, Areas for Improvement

- Communicate more proactively with central administration.
- Develop a method for determining our image and reputation with external groups—on and off campus.
- Improve our collaboration and bundling or integration of services for seamless delivery (in some cases, cross-departmental).
- Establish and monitor service standards.
- Enhance face-to-face contact or service orientation of our units.

Category 4.0: Measurement and Knowledge Utilization, Areas for Improvement

- Review and broaden performance indicators to ensure that we are using meaningful, relevant measures—for example, operational areas, staff satisfaction, user satisfaction, and professional development.
- Consult with a broader audience (including those for whom we provide services) in determining the appropriate indicators for excellence for the division and departments.
- Develop a system for regular review of the measures we use to assess the quality of the division's work.
- Establish appropriate peer and benchmark institutions for assessing how well the division and its departments are operating relative to others.

Category 5.0: Faculty/Staff and Workplace Focus, Areas for Improvement

- Develop methods for assessing and monitoring workplace climate and morale.
- Promote a culture that values and rewards innovation.
- Develop cross-department work assignments to break down organizational boundaries.
- Develop methods for emphasizing the importance of continuous improvement to new employees.
- Design programs for core competency training.
- Reinforce the value of professional development and training.

Category 6.0: Process Effectiveness, Areas for Improvement

- Review, document, and communicate core processes of the division.
- Conduct a needs assessment to identify which processes to improve; focus on improvements to processes that address user needs.
- Analyze, document, and improve vendor relations.
- Take steps to assure that process documentation is "user-friendly."
- Convince middle management of the importance of process analysis, documentation, and improvement.
- Promote innovation as a theme in process review.

Category 7.0: Outcomes and Achievements, Areas for Improvement

- Become more systematic about documenting achievements and progress over time.
- Consolidate ideas and arrive at consensus about important indicators of excellence.
- Become more systematic about assessing and using information for peers and benchmark organizations to assess our excellence levels and trends.
- Disseminate information about our accomplishments and improvements outside as well as inside the division.

Through consolidation and voting, the long list of improvement needs was narrowed, and the top five specific improvement priorities were identified. Project teams were formed to develop and implement action plans for each priority. Reports of progress and consultation with others in the leadership team were included as a regular part of monthly division head meetings.

A Professional School

The dean of the school retired after ten years of service. An acting dean was appointed from within the unit while the search for a new dean was under way. The acting dean and senior leaders in the school felt that it was important for the unit to assess the school's current status, to identify strengths and areas in need of improvement, and to begin to chart new directions for the unit. It was also determined that the self-assessment and planning process would yield useful information for candidates to be interviewed for the deanship. A decision was made to use the *EHE* framework for this purpose.

The school had approximately fifty-five full-time faculty and staff, of which twenty participated in the *EHE* process. The school is composed of four departments; two master's programs; a doctoral program; and several research and professional centers, institutions, and programs. The participating group included the acting dean, associate deans, department chairs, program directors, faculty committee chairs, and a cross section of faculty and staff from various units and ranks.

The self-assessment workshop covering all seven *EHE* categories resulted in the identification of about fifty-five strengths and fifty areas for improvement. A follow-up workshop, a half day in length, was held for the purpose of reviewing and prioritizing suggested improvement areas. Through multivoting, the list was narrowed to the top ten broad priorities:

1. Synchronizing university, school, and department accountability measures
2. Identifying key processes, measures, and process owners
3. Promoting sharing and distributed management responsibilities
4. Formulating more specific and measurable goals
5. Improving, organizing, streamlining, and disseminating existing documents
6. Promoting leadership at all levels
7. Including more faculty and staff in planning
8. Reviewing and updating strategic plans while increasing stakeholder involvement

9. Benchmarking key processes and excellence indicators
10. Synchronizing personal and institutional goals and plans

The workshop also included a strategic and action planning stage, and the acting dean and school leaders began working on a number of the improvement priorities during the year. The results were also provided to the new dean of the school when he was appointed the following fall; efforts to address the identified improvement priorities have proceeded under his leadership.

A number of specific projects were undertaken and completed to address improvement priorities identified in the *EHE* process:

- To form advisory councils to facilitate additional interaction with external stakeholders
- To create a faculty council to broaden engagement in school leadership
- To encourage and facilitate the start-up of new research programs and centers to leverage individual and department strengths
- To review and consider reorganizing administrative and support roles and responsibilities at the school level and within departments
- To review and clarify department mission and goal statements
- To decentralize management functions from the dean's office to departments wherever possible
- To disseminate information on the school and its departments and programs on campus and more broadly
- To develop faculty handbooks to document school policies and procedures for new faculty
- To inventory and streamline a number of critical support processes within the school
- To begin e-mail dissemination of minutes from all school executive meetings
- To review and revise the school, department, and program Web page

To date, the *EHE* program has been implemented by approximately fifty academic and administrative departments at twenty colleges and universities, including the University of Wisconsin, Madison; University of California, Berkeley; State University of New York, Buffalo; Howard University; University of Illinois; University of

Massachusetts; University of Texas, Austin; Penn State University; California State University, Fullerton; the University of Pennsylvania; Marygrove College; Raritan Valley Community College; Seton Hall University, State University of New York, Binghamton; Excelsior College; University of Cincinnati; University of San Diego; Miami University; MIT; Princeton; and Rutgers. Participating academic units have included law, nursing, business, engineering, education, liberal arts, communication, public policy, information and library studies, environmental and life sciences, provost's executive councils, and graduate schools, among others. Student life and support organizations that have participated include residential colleges, housing and residence life, student campus centers, continuing education, and student learning centers. A number of senior leadership groups have participated, as have administrative, business, and service department heads from computing services, facilities and maintenance, research and sponsored programs, human resources, police and public safety, and other areas.

Concluding Comments

The successful integration of assessment, planning, and improvement is a significant leadership challenge within higher education, both at the institutional level and within academic and administrative departments. Equally formidable is the task of making these integrated tasks a regular aspect of a unit's work. The Baldrige framework offers a well-tested approach for addressing these goals. Rather than regarding assessment, planning, and improvement as episodic activities associated with external reviews, accreditation visits, or externally imposed reporting requirements—or the responsibility of a centralized institutional research, planning, or organizational development department—the Baldrige approach positions these activities as a regular and ongoing facet of each department's or institution's mission-critical work.

A limited number of colleges and universities will engage in a formalized Baldrige awards review process, and a far smaller number will win these awards, but all can benefit by applying aspects of the framework and process. This is as it should be, because fundamentally the Baldrige approach is much less important as an award and source of recognition than it is as a guide to conceptualizing and systematically pursuing institutional effectiveness and organizational excellence.

The Baldrige framework enables an institution to dissect and analyze its components and internal interactions, identify strengths and areas for improvement, and focus on strategies for translating visions and aspirations into accounts and outcomes. The approach constitutes a baseline measure using accepted organizational assessment criteria and methods. It is also a guide to leaders that encourages methodical attention to defining appropriate comparison organizations, to gathering information by which to contextualize one's own progress and accomplishments, and to establishing criteria for assessing organizational effectiveness. In the process, it creates a common language for organizational discourse and engages members of the department in developing a shared agenda for change.

There are any number of ways to make use of the Baldrige criteria and methodology. One approach is the model in the *Excellence in Higher Education* program; there are many others. Ultimately, the great strength of Baldrige-based frameworks is that they offer programs, departments, and institutions a systematic, integrated, and effective approach to addressing the challenges of the day in a way that helps to make assessment, planning, and improvement an ongoing process and a responsibility that is understood and shared by all.

Notes

1. The author gratefully acknowledges the contributions of the Cedar Group, which provided encouragement and support for the development of earlier publications on the Malcolm Baldrige program, and the Excellence in Higher Education program.
2. Approximately 160,000 copies are distributed by the Baldrige Program, and 90,000 by state programs.
3. The North Central Association accredits colleges and universities in Arizona, Arkansas, Colorado, Illinois, Indiana, Iowa, Kansas, Michigan, Minnesota, Missouri, Nebraska, New Mexico, North Dakota, Ohio, Oklahoma, South Dakota, West Virginia, Wisconsin, and Wyoming.
4. For each category, the category point score is derived by multiplying the average percentage rating that results from self-assessment by total number of possible points available for a category. In the EHE self-assessment programs, emphasis is placed on the percentage rating for each category rather than points. Point scores would be the focus if an institution were applying for a state or national award (Ruben, 2003c).

Narratives

Integrating Organizational Assessment, Planning, and Improvement: Making Organizational Self-Study and Change Everyday Activities

To be most effective, assessment, planning, and improvement need to be ongoing and integrated into the work of each department or institution, not solely the responsibility of a centralized administrative office, nor episodic activities triggered by external requests, the prospect of external reviews, or upcoming accreditation. The Baldrige program is a well-tested approach for achieving this goal. The primary value of the Baldrige is not to be found in the awards or recognition it bestows, but rather in the guidance it offers for understanding and pursuing institutional effectiveness and organizational excellence. When adapted to the culture and language of higher education, the approach can be extremely useful.

As noted previously, the Baldrige principles and process have become increasingly central to accreditation of such professional disciplines as engineering, health care, and business; more recently they have had considerable influence on the criteria and methods used in regional accreditation. The North Central Association of Colleges and Schools has played a leadership role in this regard through its Academic Quality and Improvement Project (AQIP). In this section, Stephen Spangehl, director of the project, offers a description of the rationale for the AQIP initiative, an overview of some key issues and challenges, and a brief progress report.

The *Excellence in Higher Education* model has been applied in a number of academic and administrative areas using a variety of approaches. In some cases, the program is introduced as part of a formalized, institution-wide, continuous-improvement or organizational-development effort. In other cases, it is introduced within a particular college or university division more informally. This latter strategy was used by Finance and Administrative Services at Miami University in Oxford, Ohio; Vice President for Finance and Business Services Richard Norman, Associate Vice President for Facilities W. James Haley, and Senior Associate Vice President for Auxiliary Services Adolph Haislar describe the approach and highlight some noteworthy outcomes.

Pursuing the external review and validation of the Baldrige program, and being selected as the first higher education winner of a Baldrige award, is the University of Wisconsin-Stout. Chancellor Charles W. Sorenson and Vice Chancellor for Administrative and Student Life Services Diane Moen describe the process and outcomes in the final narrative in this section.

The Baldridge framework, as it has been used at the University of Alabama and Belmont University, was discussed in "Formalizing Corporate Engagement" in Chapter Three and "Measuring Excellence from a Stakeholder Perspective" in Chapter Four. In "Organizational Change at Berkeley: A Work in Progress" in Chapter Nine, the implementation of the Excellence in Higher Education Program will be summarized.

The North Central Association of Colleges and Schools Academic Quality Improvement Project (AQIP)

Stephen D. Spangehl
Director, AQIP

Roses would smell just as sweet if they were called skunk cabbages, but poets and lovers would shun them shamelessly. What's in a name? Lots—people's feelings, prejudices, and reactions. Using language as precisely as they do, academics are more sensitive to words than most people. What will make higher educators in the United States think seriously about adopting quality improvement ideas and techniques? Preaching about quality in the language of manufacturing and sales won't work, but rational discussion using the familiar language of the academy does succeed.

With the support of a three-year grant from the Pew Charitable Trusts in 1999, the Higher Learning Commission of the North Central Association of Colleges and Schools (NCA) has developed and launched a new alternative accrediting process that supports institutions using continuous quality improvement thinking and tools to strengthen the education they provide their students. Named the Academic Quality Improvement Project (AQIP), this effort has faced serious challenges and employed strategies to overcome them. Others intent on assisting higher education to adapt the "quality principles" that underlie TQM, CQI, the Malcolm Baldrige National Quality Award (MBNQA) program, ISO 9000, state quality programs, and similar efforts will find AQIP's experience and tactics valuable.

Traditionally, both higher education and accreditation have focused on resources—inputs such as faculty reputation, endowment, physical plant, or the test scores of entering students—as indices of quality. AQIP shifts the emphasis to performance, to how well an institution meets the long-term needs of students and other stakeholders, and to the improvement of processes that produce performance. Using a quality framework but avoiding business or manufacturing jargon, AQIP helps institutions analyze and improve the key processes responsible for producing their current performance.

For survival, legitimate colleges and universities need to be accredited. Accreditation confers national status, inspires students' and employers' trust, ensures transferability of credits earned, and qualifies an institution's students to receive federal financial aid. Critically, accreditation attracts internal respect: it drives faculty and staff to consider initiatives they would normally resist. AQIP provides accreditation restructured to champion continuous, systematic improvement in the tradition-bound and contented world of academe.

To restructure accreditation, AQIP did not merely substitute a set of output indices for the input requirements traditional in earlier days. Instead, it followed Baldrige's approach of delineating organizational subsystems groups of processes that strive for related goals, and asking institutions to identify their own performance measure within each of these subsystems. American higher education is a diverse affair, with a spectrum of institutions serving myriad student needs. Dictating specific measures for quality would homogenize this vigorous system and diminish the diversity that gives it strength. AQIP uses peer review processes to keep an institution focused on improving its performance on the distinctive goals chosen by the institution itself—not by outside regulators.

Moreover, although it incorporates a paper review and feedback process, like Baldrige's, AQIP has innovated by creating a far more intensive relationship between participating institutions and the Higher Learning Commission. Through an interactive peer process, participants formulate and commit to three or four public action projects that drive systematic improvement, and, on a four-year cycle, undergo a "systems appraisal" examining the performance and underlying processes for each of the AQIP criteria. This combination of action and review makes AQIP a radical departure from traditional accreditation.

Addressing Skepticism and Resistance

When it began, AQIP faced skepticism and resistance from many in the higher education community and from many in accreditation. The American Association of Higher Education (AAHE) had championed TQM's value for higher education a decade earlier, strongly advocating the use of the Baldrige program by colleges and universities, but little came of the sincere efforts of this important organization. When NCA first approached the Pew Charitable Trusts for support of a new quality initiative, the initial response was an understandable "It's been tried, and it's failed" pessimism.

At the Higher Learning Commission, however, we discovered islands of enthusiasm for continuous improvement within the sea of institutions we accredit, and we even allowed a few institutions to use state quality award applications as self-study experiments. These experiences gave us confidence that quality thinking could flourish in the academy if it were effectively explained and combined with the needs and traditions of accreditation. When Pew made clear its willingness to fund accreditation reform efforts, the commission drew upon these earlier experiments in continuous improvement to envision a new alternative accrediting process, a reconstruction of accreditation built upon the foundation supplied by quality thinking and principles. To make certain that our efforts would highlight the educational foci of institutions over their business affairs, and to communicate specifically that our initiative concentrated on higher education, we selected the word *academic* (rather than *educational*), and we called our initiative a *project* (rather than a *program*) to capture its "launch and learn" spirit and our intention to employ continuous improvement principles in our design and operations. We selected *quality improvement* to signal both the goal of the program and its underlying set of principles. Thus we came to launch our Academic Quality Improvement Project.

AQIP's effort to introduce this new alternative began at a perilous period in higher education. Complex dynamics—increased competition, new technology, new economic forces, changing societal perceptions of the role of higher education—threaten academia's traditional structures and standards and are forcing it to find new tools for managing its operations and for increasing the value a college or university can deliver to those who look to it for services. By aligning accreditation and the quest for ever-improving quality, AQIP believes it can help the commission's member institutions better face these challenges and thrive in a rapidly changing environment. Yet in spite of our sincere desire to provide an accrediting service that would deliver more value to the institutions using it, we quickly discovered that language presents serious obstacles to communicating this intention. AQIP has faced and addressed many challenges in its first few years. An account of its approaches to linguistic issues is instructive.

Engaging institutions in a serious discussion about quality was our most fundamental challenge. Many higher educators use the word loosely, to refer to an unelaborated Platonic vision of the archetypal academy (another of Plato's contributions to the academic mind-set), and consequently base their judgments of various real colleges and universities on the difference between what they actually perceive and experience and their unspoken ideal. One person may say that a college is of high quality because its faculty members do reduced teaching and can devote themselves to research—a reflection of his notion of the ideal college. Another makes the reverse judgment because her ideal college includes a focus on serving students. It is unlikely that the mental models of any two people who argue about a higher education institution's quality in this way will ever match. Since we cannot easily enter Plato's cave and compare these mental ideals directly, nor can we be certain that we have forced everyone to adopt a single ideal, debates about quality carried out with this structure are generally unrevealing. Without a common framework, arguments over differing individual judgments of quality do not lead to consensus; nor do they build a solid foundation for talking about improvement.

The "quality movement" takes a different approach, focusing on an institution's *performance* in satisfying its students' and other stakeholders' needs as the determinant of its quality. In education, these requirements are often hard to determine, and educators are rightly concerned with long-term rather than immediate satisfaction of students' needs. Finally, identifying stakeholders—those who rightfully have a stake in the institution's success or failure because it affects them directly—is no simple task, and the expectations of parents, employers, faculty, and other groups must be weighed. In this way of thinking about quality, there exists no ideal college or university against which all real ones can be measured;

nor is it possible, ever, for an institution to reach perfection, since that would imply that a single ideal does in fact exist. Instead, quality describes a journey, a search for better ways to understand and meet the needs of students and others who have a stake in an institution's performance. Insofar as one can measure the deep satisfaction of these needs and measure the performance of the processes that an organization employs to perform the services by which it meets those needs, improvement is measurable—although absolute quality itself is not—and the size and regularity of those improvements are evidence that an organization has a "quality culture." In this sense, *quality* is an adjective, never a noun; it describes an institution that behaves in certain ways, focusing upon processes, basing decisions on facts and measurements, and looking at itself as a system of processes designed to achieve its ultimate mission and goals, serving its students and other stakeholders.

From the outset, AQIP has used *quality* in this sense alone, making clear that quality judgments have meaning only in light of the purpose a product or service performs. Since an education can serve many purposes, the purpose it plays in the lives of those students who seek it must form the primary basis of qualitative judgments. The goals and needs of other stakeholders (parents, employers) also lead to judgments of quality, often quite different from those made by students. AQIP gives these other judgments critical attention but focuses first on student needs. If students want an education to prepare for specific jobs, then the quality of that education is its effectiveness in preparing them for those jobs. If the purpose is to help students mature and become responsible citizens, then education must be judged in terms of how well it accomplishes those purposes. If an education has multiple purposes—or if an institution's students have multiple goals—then it is incumbent on educators to prioritize the purposes, to decide which are essential and which are merely desirable, to segment the students according to their needs and goals, and to evaluate carefully how well the education they offer achieves each of the purposes for which it was designed.

Consequently, bald evaluations announcing that one institution is of higher quality than another are generally worthless. Judgments of quality cannot be separated from the understanding of purposes. The illogic behind simplistic quality judgments is what makes the *U.S. News and World Reports* collegiate ratings so offensive to most educators, even if they cannot accurately articulate the reasons for their discomfort. AQIP's use of quality effectively bypasses these pitfalls by recognizing that an institution's mission and purposes shape its evaluation. It would be absurd to assume that the type of degrees an institution offers or the type of students it targets determines the quality of the education it provides. A specialized two-year institute can offer programs of high (or low) quality for its students, and so can a graduate school. Except for occasional resistance at research universities, AQIP's experience has been that educators are comfortable with quality explained this way. But it does take explaining.

Improvement is another term that can cause anxiety. Higher education long ago decided that a systematic approach to improving teaching would offend faculty by implying that teaching needed improvement, and so it substituted the term *faculty development*. With AQIP, we made the decision that the concept of continuous improvement was so fundamental to our effort that any softening of the language we used would be counterproductive and deceptive. Thus we decided to use *improvement* prominently, stressing the idea that any process or performance result, no matter how good, could always be made better. Nevertheless, presenting improvement as an opportunity, not as a criticism of what an institution achieved in its past, is a continuing challenge. AQIP holds that an institution must acknowledge the possibility of its improving and then undertake a program that fosters improvement, and that avoiding the word *improvement* signals either a lack of realism or a lack of commitment. Though we undoubtedly have driven away some institutions unwilling to admit they are not as uniformly good as they could be, we believe our use of *quality improvement* captures accurately what we are helping institutions do.

The Decision to Avoid Comparing
Higher Education to Other Sectors

Other words also present problems. Educators are particularly sensitive to language, and we realized early that some of the language used by quality enthusiasts undermined adoption of their ideas by the academy. Reactions to language undoubtedly have reduced the willingness of educators to use the Baldrige program, which uses generalized business terminology to describe all applicants. Terms such as *customer* are particularly offensive, especially in senior colleges and universities, although many two-year colleges appear able to endure that term, perhaps because they work so closely with employers in preparing students by way of occupational programs. Although AQIP held fast on *quality* and *improvement,* we decided early that an effort that tried to get the academy to talk about itself in the language of business would face insurmountable barriers. We discovered that many faculty members stopped listening and began arguing when words such as *customer* entered the conversation, and that finding synonyms for such shibboleths in no way distorted the principles we were trying to communicate or the tools whose use we were encouraging. We made a conscious decision to communicate to higher educators solely in language traditionally used in higher education, without comparing higher education to other fields of enterprise. AQIP therefore contains no exhortations to "run your college like a business or factory." Although this has consistently taxed us creatively, we believe it was a wise decision, one that other proponents of continuous improvement would be prudent to emulate. As one would expect from an enterprise that is predominately nonprofit and populated with underpaid altruists, higher education resists seeing itself as a business, or even being compared with business by outsiders. There is logic behind this aversion; understanding it is critical to showing educators why continuous improvement makes sense.

Higher education does shares features with businesses—employees, rent and utility bills, advertising, boom and bust times, surpluses and shortfalls—but it is *not* a business in the usual sense. Although students often pay their own money for the services an institution provides, the relationship is far less direct than in business. Tuition may cover only a portion of the cost of services received, and it often comes from a third party—employers, parents, or government—rather than from the student receiving the services. Unlike products or services that customers typically buy from businesses, education is not purchased repeatedly; once done, it is not easily redone. The unsatisfied buyer of a car, a restaurant meal, or a haircut can shop elsewhere next time, and the satisfied can become repeat purchasers, but the student who receives a defective education most likely lives with it shaping his or her entire life. Even *satisfaction* has a different meaning in education: whether an education really met a student's needs can't be gauged accurately until years later and may have little relation to whether the student found the educational experience pleasurable. Society can endure *caveat emptor* as the guide for most business dealings, but it carefully regulates educational providers (either through governmental controls or accreditation, or both) because what educators do leaves permanent marks on people's lives and on the common good. Since AQIP's goal is to keep open the lines of communication about quality with the educational community, we have taken seriously educators' prejudice against business language. Even when we select a quotation to illustrate a quality principle, we find one from a poet, scientist, or philosopher, rather than using one from an industrialist or management theorist. It matters.

Accreditation and Quality

Since 1895, when institutional accrediting agencies first appeared on the scene in U.S. higher education, people have been remarkably willing to trust their educational investments and futures to a unique and little-understood mechanism. Today, with new and unfamiliar educational providers appearing—including for-profit universities, distance-delivery colleges, higher-education chains, and transnational organizations—it is critical that both higher educators and the public appreciate what quality really means in education, and how accreditation can help to promote it.

As it evolved historically in American higher education, accreditation focused on ensuring quality by demanding compliance with a set of minimum expectations. These expectations came in the form of prerequisites, requirements that an institution or program must possess before it was eligible to join the circle of members of a regional accrediting association, those who already demonstrated they met the standards. However, the variety and vitality of higher education now existing in the United States dictates that, at the institutional level, these standards cannot do what they typically do in other situations: impose standardization. Our education system's strength lies in its diversity, its willingness to experiment, and its ability to customize education to the needs of specific groups. U.S. citizens and residents enjoy the greatest access to higher education in the world because our system spawns and maintains a variety of institutions that cater to the needs of numerous segments of the educational market. We have broad research universities, large and small technical colleges, entrepreneurial distance-delivery universities, and both public and private comprehensive institutions, as well as focused colleges offering specialized programs in teaching, law, business, chiropractic, nursing, medicine, engineering, osteopathy, mortuary science, theology, art, pharmacy, Bible studies, and many other fields. The vitality and diversity of our system is the envy of the world, and students from around the globe choose the United States as the place they come to receive a higher education. The quality assurance process that has evolved for this massive educational system is accreditation, a uniquely American phenomenon; it is the harnessing of this mechanism to drive quality improvement that AQIP set as its target.

The Response to the AQIP Project

Since July 1999, when the Pew Charitable Trusts announced their support of the Higher Learning Commission's attempt to bond quality principles and accreditation, more than sixty colleges and universities have elected the AQIP path to reaccreditation. More than two hundred others have demonstrated interest by attending seminars or other programs offered by AQIP to acquaint institutions with quality thinking and with our accreditation alternative. Approximately one-third of the eighty-two that have joined (as of early 2002) are institutions where a quality approach was already under way—or had been started, perhaps stalling after a promising beginning. Institutions such as Fox Valley Technical College (Wisconsin), San Juan College (New Mexico), Jackson Community College (Michigan), Western Wisconsin Technical College, and Lansing Community College (Michigan) saw AQIP as a means of continuing or reinvigorating what they had already begun. The majority, however, had not yet formally launched institutional quality initiatives, although some had continuous improvement programs in specific units or departments. Many institutions viewed AQIP as a more cost-effective approach to accreditation; knowing they easily met minimum requirements for continuing accreditation yet were required to undergo the standard self-study and peer visitation process anyway, they saw in AQIP a process that would give them continued accreditation and "something more": a continuing external stimulus driving desirable institutional change, and perhaps external recognition for their improvement efforts.

AQIP requires participating institutions to undergo a four-year cycle consisting of (1) a comprehensive Baldrige-like evaluation review and feedback report, without a site visit; (2) a series of ongoing action projects that keep the institution focused on real improvement endeavors; and (3) annual updates of activities and progress. In return, AQIP gives institutions visits from consultants when requested, a networking structure that allows an institution to work with peers on common challenges, and mechanisms for recognizing and disseminating best practices developed within an institution. For institutions acutely aware of the competition and challenges that higher education faces, AQIP seems to many to produce—in peer advice, external motivation and recognition, and networking possibilities—a higher return on their investment in accreditation than does a standard process that merely confirms their compliance with minimum requirements.

The institutions first attracted to AQIP were predominantly two-year colleges, private bachelor's- and master's-level institutions with an entrepreneurial bent (such as Capella University, Minnesota, a for-profit, distance-delivery institution; and Bellevue University, Nebraska), faith-based private institutions (Concordia University, Illinois; Benedictine University, Illinois; Maranatha Baptist Bible College, Wisconsin; Central College, Iowa), and regional state universities (Kent State University, Ohio; Ohio University; Northern Michigan University; Fort Hays State University, Kansas; and Southern Illinois University at Edwardsville). Flagship and research universities showed interest but adopted a wait-and-watch approach. (A complete, current list of participants can be found on the AQIP Website, www.AQIP.org.) The reasons for this pattern are not difficult to understand. Compared with public universities, two-year and private colleges have clearer, more focused missions, fewer independent subunits (or silos), and quicker decision-making processes. Moreover, the businesslike thinking some educators perceive in quality approaches is often less offensive to two-year institutions, many of which have patently vocational programs and close relationships with local businesses. In contrast, the large, complex university that wants to use a quality approach to maintain its regional accreditation must first build acceptance among as many as a dozen schools and colleges, academic units whose faculties often have greatly differing operational traditions and ambitions. Unless they all reach consensus, unless the entire institution embarks on a quality journey together, AQIP is not available to the institution as its means of maintaining regional accreditation. AQIP is confident that such institutions can and will take on the challenges of continuous improvement, but building the required campuswide consensus takes time.

Conclusion

Moving our higher education accreditation process toward a quality approach requires a major shift in mindset. AQIP attempts to move educators' thinking away from inspections that guarantee compliance with minimal standards to an understanding that continual attention to the performance and improvement of systems yields a far stronger form of quality assurance. It is crucial that we choose our words carefully if we want to be effective in talking educators through this necessary and beneficial change. AQIP's success proves that this strategy works.

Applying *Excellence in Higher Education* in Finance and Administrative Services

Richard M. Norman
Vice President for Finance and Business
Services, Miami University, Oxford, Ohio

W. James Haley
Associate Vice President for Facilities,
Miami University

Adolph Haislar
Senior Associate Vice President for Auxiliary Services
and the Excellence in Higher Education Executive
Initiative, Miami University

Miami University, in Oxford, Ohio, was founded in 1809 and is the seventh oldest state-assisted university in the nation. With forty-one hundred faculty and staff, and an enrollment of more than twenty thousand undergraduate students and fourteen hundred graduate students, the university's primary focus is on undergraduate liberal arts education. Richard Moll (1985), a recognized higher education admissions specialist, classified Miami University as one of the eight "public ivies" in the United States; in 2001, Miami was again listed as a "public ivy" in *The Public Ivies: America's Flagship Universities* by Howard Greene and Matthew Greene (2001). The university has received high rankings in *U.S. News and World Report,* and the *Fiske Guide to Colleges 2002* and other rating publications.

One of the central themes in all Miami University projects and programs is "First in 2009," the title of President James C. Garland's vision statement for Miami University adopted in preparation for the university's bicentennial in 2009. In his words, "To become the leader in the nation, Miami University must be a vibrant, energetic, forward-looking institution which seeks continuously to enhance its academic and intellectual vitality." This will be achieved by meeting these eight goals:

1. Strengthening the academic profile of entering students
2. Strengthening the academic profile of new faculty and academic support for existing faculty
3. Developing a curriculum for the twenty-first century at both undergraduate and graduate levels
4. Strengthening academic standards and enriching campus intellectual and cultural life
5. Increasing diversity of the faculty, staff, and student body
6. Enhancing campus facilities, buildings, systems, and technology
7. Strengthening the university revenue base
8. Developing improved benchmarking with peer institutions

In response to the president's "First in 2009" vision statement, the Miami University board of trustees in 1999 asked that a comprehensive benchmarking process be established for the university. Each major division of the university maintains a comprehensive list of performance goals that are benchmarked against peer and aspirational institutions, as well as internal measures. Benchmarking comparisons of one's own activities with those of others has proven highly beneficial and leads to an ongoing process of self-assessment, reevaluation, and adjustment of goals. For example, the university has only recently implemented an enrollment management process that established the University of North Carolina and the College of William and Mary as benchmark institutions. This is a good example of an activity that is continually adjusted but can be measured explicitly. On the operations side of the university, a goal of increasing minority staff is benchmarked against local and regional data regarding the availability of potential personnel.

The Division of Finance and Business Services has pursued the challenge of continuous improvement by using the *Excellence in Higher Education (EHE)* model (Ruben, 2003a, 2003c). The senior leadership from the division participated in an *EHE* assessment and planning retreat, from which division strengths, areas for improvement, and priority action items were identified. The division's staff determined that enhanced communication was the highest priority for improvement. As a result, we decided to emphasize one-on-one meetings with direct reports and improved communication of university priorities at regular staff meetings; we also established a staff listserv for rapid distribution of information. The second priority identified was creation of a common mission statement for the division. The statement was developed by Finance and Business Services staff after a thorough review of divisional goals and objectives. To further respond to the excellence initiative, the division has adopted a leadership primer, *The Leadership Secrets of Colin Powell* (Harari, 2002), to be read and discussed at staff meetings by all primary staff within the division. Using a single work permits a common point of discussion and a regularly scheduled review and measurement of leadership responsibilities.

The *EHE* process is being used in purchasing, accounts payable, the recreational sports center, the Marcum Conference Center and Inn, and various other support offices within the Finance and Business Services Division. The narrative presented here is limited to a brief description of how the *EHE* framework has been implemented in two major units within the division: the Physical Facilities Department and Housing, Dining, and Guest Services.

Long-Range Facility Master Planning at Miami University

Traditionally, facility planning at Miami University was a coincidental byproduct of the submission of a biennial capital appropriation request to the state of Ohio. The planning process was for six years, which conformed with the state's appropriation planning process. Generally, locally funded projects were decided on their own merits, and planning associated with those projects focused on the best solution of the moment. Comprehensive planning was neither mandated nor deemed necessary beyond the state's six-year planning horizon. Miami University, like most public universities in this country, is now confronted by the need to renovate the facilities built to respond to the burgeoning enrollments of the postwar baby boom in the 1960s and 1970s. A simple update of the biennial capital budget was clearly not adequate, and a new comprehensive planning process was initiated. Figure 5.6 is a time line showing the growth in square footage of the Miami University

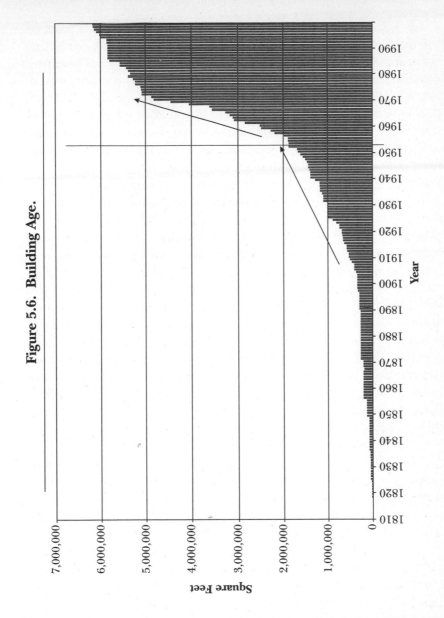

Figure 5.6. Building Age.

campus. The vertical bar represents the "renovate, replace, or reprogram" time line. On average, when a building is forty-three years old, the university must make a significant investment in its infrastructure or risk a serious deterioration in academic quality.

In early 2000, the board of trustees directed that a plan be formulated to address upcoming building renovations, including recommendations concerning resource requirements and proposed sources of funding. In September 2002, the management team of the Miami University Physical Facilities Department participated in a three-day *EHE* workshop that resulted in the identification of seven action plans. Action plan number four, "Develop and implement regular review and revision of the strategic planning process," and plan number six, "Establish a commitment to the strategic planning process and continual improvement," were in recognition of the shortcomings of the traditional planning process and a desire to change the university's facility planning process. Although the *EHE* workshop was not specifically intended to respond to the board of trustees' task to formulate a facilities plan, the workshop led to examination of and change in the planning process, such that in the spring of 2001 a universitywide facilities planning team was formed. Rather than identify the planned actions explicitly as a formal continuous improvement process, a representative from each of the campus stakeholder groups was invited to a series of meetings for the purpose of "examining the facility needs of the campus" in support of the state capital appropriation request due that fall. Supported by the university's Planning and Construction Office, the campuswide planning group identified needs, examined a large number of possible alternatives, and developed a twenty-year campus plan.

The plan was then shared with the university community, both internal and external to the campus. Those groups contributed a number of thoughtful responses that led to minor revisions of the plan and confirmed that the plan would have broad community support. Late in 2001, a preliminary recommendation of the plan was sent to and accepted by the board of trustees. With board support, each project was then refined with a program of requirements, cost estimates, and a construction sequence plan. After determining the time line for the projects, a general funding plan was developed using all possible sources of support. All elements of the plan were then merged with the overall university programmatic planning to establish a long-range financial plan for the university. The plan was presented to the board in the fall of 2002, and the board approved the implementation of the first part of the plan.

Although not identified as such, the action of the board and its engagement with the subject was structured somewhat similarly to that of a quality council or sponsor. The board initiated the process, supported the team, and is in the process of implementing the recommendations. Although the change in the planning process resulted from an *EHE* workshop, contained all the elements of a classic quality improvement process, and represented a major change in the method of facility planning at Miami University, it was done without having been identified as a "quality" effort. The team stayed focused on the output of the process rather than on the process itself. As a first major campus-wide *EHE* continuous quality improvement initiative, it has proved a resounding success. It is expected that with this success as an example additional improvements will be possible, and the community as a whole will recognize the value of this approach for the university at large.

Evaluation, Planning, and Improvement Within Housing, Dining and Guest Services

For at least the last twenty-five years, Housing, Dining, and Guest Services (HDGS) at Miami University has used a number of evaluation tools to assess quality and measure the level of customer service. These efforts were periodic and not well coordinated within the division. An integrated approach to evaluation and planning was needed, and the *Excellence in Higher Education* model (Ruben, 2003a, 2003c) seemed well suited to this purpose. Using the *EHE* framework, HDGS has systematically and strategically evaluated all of its operating units. Every HDGS manager and administrator attended sessions to learn about the *EHE* process and identify organizational strengths, weaknesses, and opportunities. From each session, unit goals were identified and aligned with the department's broad strategic goals, which support President Garland's "First in 2009" vision statement.

Overwhelmingly, *EHE* participants identified "customer focus" as the primary departmental strength. Several groups acknowledged that serving customers with care, professionalism, and efficiency is an integral part of the departmental culture. All HDGS units shared the same opinion of a strong heritage of excellent customer service. Participants indicated that HDGS consistently focuses on quality.

The *EHE* groups also identified several areas for improvement, including a need to improve internal communication and feedback. Communication was viewed as being "spotty" and inconsistent. Both formal and informal communication were discussed, as well as how to improve each. Lastly, reduction of staff turnover through improved retention was identified as a division goal. All managers were requested to formulate individual goals for the upcoming year that would address organizational weaknesses identified during the *EHE* process.

With a focus on service as a departmental strength to be maintained and improved, we felt it was important for all staff members to understand how their individual performance affected other employees, faculty, staff, and most important the students. Staff development became a top priority; new team member orientation was identified as an important part of the HDGS training and development program. The goal was for all staff members to be well trained to deliver excellent service and create superior products. Because HDGS is such a large department, a primary goal is to make new team members' first few weeks more personal. Training begins with orientation, consisting of four four-hour sessions. HDGS continues to refine the program so that new team members are given accurate and helpful information as they enter the departmental workforce.

HDGS also runs the Job Enrichment Program, a voluntary program in which staff members can select the training program they feel is most important to their future success. The program has three phases for each job classification within HDGS, and each phase has four parts, from learning sign language to basic plumbing skills. To offer an incentive, each participant receives a 4 percent raise when he or she completes one of the four parts. As a result, the staff member's annual compensation grows, as does his or her knowledge base, job-related skills, and understanding of user expectations and overall satisfaction.

In HDGS, training is viewed as a lifelong process. We strongly endorse the philosophy of training and performance rewards, and we promote professional development throughout all levels of the organization. The underlying objective is to reward personal growth and achievement while encouraging on-the-job service excellence.

The development of a systematic method for assessing organizational climate was another identified improvement need within HDGS. An annual staff climate survey was initiated in conjunction with HDGS's orientation and Job Enrichment Program to give senior leadership information about how nearly eight hundred team members feel about working conditions and overall job satisfaction. Employees are asked about how safe they feel at work, how they feel about teamwork in their work unit, how they feel about communication within the organization, and other related questions. By monitoring staff opinion, the goal is to reduce turnover, improve service and quality, reduce operating costs, generate new revenues, improve productivity, reduce absenteeism, and improve overall organizational effectiveness.

A systematic analysis and review of the employee climate survey is done annually to determine progress. Results are shared with all employees. Bar charts and graphs are displayed prominently on employee bulletin boards so the staff can easily see how their unit is doing and in what areas they have improved, compared with the previous year's survey.

Benchmarking was identified as another component for continuous improvement. As HDGS strives to improve operations, one of the most useful measurements is to compare performance with that of peers. It is also helpful to know what are considered to be best practices. Through the Association of College and University Housing Officers–International, and Educational Benchmarking, Inc., HDGS has recently begun participating in a benchmarking project for residence and dining halls. Thousands of students from 183 major universities participate in the study. From that group, six selective-admission peer institutions are chosen to directly compare results. Miami ranked very high among the 183 universities on these questions:

- How satisfied are you with the cleanliness of residence halls?
- How satisfied are you with the attitude of the cleaning staff?
- How satisfied are you with the timeliness of repairs?
- How satisfied are you with the cleanliness of bathroom facilities?
- How satisfied are you with study facilities in your residence hall?

In the past year, Housing Services ranked in the top 5 percent on five of the thirty-six total questions and was in the top 20 percent on twenty-two of the thirty-six total questions. Dining services also received similar results. Among the six selected institutions, Miami ranked in the top 5 percent on seven of the total of eleven dining questions:

- How satisfied are you with the quality of dining hall food?
- How satisfied are you with the cleanliness of the dining hall facilities?
- How satisfied are you with the dining room environment?
- How satisfied are you with the service provided by dining hall staff?
- How satisfied are you with the dining facility hours?
- How satisfied are you with the variety of food plan options?
- How satisfied are you with the value of the meal plan?

For the last twenty-eight years, HDGS has completed an internal survey of students to determine their level of satisfaction. Scores have traditionally indicated a high level of satisfaction with services provided. Generally, 50–60 percent of the students living on campus respond to the survey. Over the last three years, HDGS has received ratings consistently in excess of 95 percent in response to questions about cleanliness, staff attitude, speed of service, and quality of services and products.

The results from external stakeholder surveys are used to assess how service is being perceived, to recognize team members who are making positive contributions to the organization, to determine where changes in services and products are needed, and to identify future training programs. In addition to the comprehensive survey, reply cards, monthly minisurveys, electronic surveys, and paper-and-pencil surveys are now included in individual client billings. All survey results are monitored, recorded, and compared with past results. Feedback from these various methods is used in decision making, which allows the organization to take effective action on the basis of external stakeholder measurements.

In the dining operations for any university, it can be said that students vote with their feet on the success of the program. One of the key indicators of service and quality is the level of complaints and the ability to attract new customers. The Oxford campus of Miami University houses only about 50 percent of the students on campus, with the remainder living in apartments and homes in the city. Figure 5.7 illustrates the three-year history of dining contracts for on-campus and off-campus students. The surprising statistic in the figure is the steady increase in the number of students who live off campus yet choose to purchase a campus meal plan. Food service is the recipient of many compliments and notes of appreciation for excellent service.

Figure 5.7. Meal Plan Contracts, On- and Off-Campus.

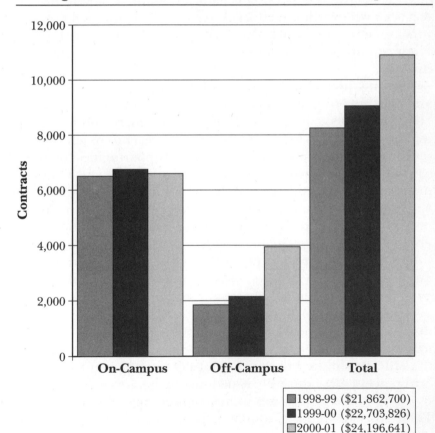

As has been described, there are various benchmarking activities under way within Housing, Dining, and Guest Services. *EHE* benchmarking indicators in place include levels of student/client satisfaction, levels of staff satisfaction, staff turnover ratios, staffing levels per student, revenue per student/client, energy (electric, water, steam) usage per student, food cost per student, supply cost per student, maintenance and repair cost per student, food and labor cost per student food-service contract, and year-to-date financial results.

Indicators are being used for comparisons with the department's past performance, as well as with other universities and organizations. Although it can be difficult and time-consuming to collect data from these other organizations, the resultant insight has been well worth the effort. Additional benchmarking indicators are being developed and refined as more areas within the Finance and Business Services Division progress in the *EHE* process.

During the fall of 2002, all staff members of the purchasing and accounts payable offices were brought together by several HDGS directors to initiate an *EHE* process. The reason for bringing these two offices together is that they have a prominent service profile within the university and constitute opportunities for quick wins in terms of service improvements. Since these two departments are interdependent, an *EHE* application was a natural fit. In a daylong session, an overview of *EHE* was conducted. Participants discussed the importance of obtaining feedback from stakeholders and using this information to identify areas for improvement. Interestingly, the directors of each office said that after the meeting communication between offices improved noticeably. Moreover, they felt staff members were motivated to identify specific processes to improve. For instance, the office of purchasing immediately began to review LPOs (limited purchase orders) and look for ways to streamline this cumbersome paper process. As a result, the office has started to switch the LPO process over to a credit card process. All offices were issued new MasterCards and received training on the procedures to be followed for the campus card. This change has reduced substantially the use and cost of the LPO process, the check-issuing process, and the staff time it takes to get the purchase data into the financial system.

Accounts payable identified the travel reimbursement process as an area for improvement. The office assigned a staff member as a "problem solver" and reduced the reimbursement time to travelers (what used to take seven to twenty days now takes two to three days).

Both departments were asked to develop customer satisfaction surveys to regularly solicit client feedback. They were also encouraged to identify the external organization(s) with best practices and to begin to benchmark against these organizations to further improve their department's services. We anticipate that in the coming year many other areas of the Finance and Business Service Division will benefit from adopting the *EHE* process for their unique operations.

The use of *EHE* within HDGS has helped a division that already enjoyed an excellent reputation reach a higher level of service through better communication, improved employee retention, and an emphasis on professional development. At all levels, HDGS is preparing to be "First in 2009."

Conclusion

An exemplary stakeholder service focus and tone is set by the senior administration of a university division. However, it is the frontline team members who, through their daily work, implement the philosophy and make it real. Continuous improvement programs are designed to encourage organizational self-reflection and improvement, and to sustain enthusiasm and good employee relations. Sincere, day-to-day human caring, complemented by excellent service, is the first goal of quality leadership. A systematic approach to assessing current organizational strengths and needs, and developing plans for improvement—using a framework such as that of *Excellence in Higher Education*/Baldrige—is critical in ensuring these outcomes.

During turbulent times in higher education, it is important for each institution to devote extra attention to the needs of its team members, so they in turn will pay more attention to the needs of external stakeholders. At Miami University, we are excited about the future and are committed to these goals.

Winning the Baldrige National Quality Award

Charles W. Sorensen
Chancellor, Administrative and Student Life Services,
University of Wisconsin–Stout

Diane Moen
Vice Chancellor, Administrative and Student Life
Services, University of Wisconsin–Stout

The University of Wisconsin–Stout, located in Menomonie (seventy miles east of Minneapolis, Minnesota), is one of thirteen publicly supported institutions in the University of Wisconsin system, which collectively serve more than 155,000 students and has an annual operating budget of $3.1 billion. The university was founded as a private institution in 1891 by James Huff Stout, a Menomonie industrialist and state senator.

For nearly two decades, the school remained a private institute, developing two-year certificates for manual training as well as preparing kindergarten teachers. Upon Senator Stout's death in 1910, it became a publicly supported institution and gradually evolved into a four-year degree-granting school. Stout Institute changed names several times and became part of the Wisconsin state college system in 1955. When a final consolidation of all public schools in Wisconsin took place in 1971, it became the University of Wisconsin–Stout.

The university's annual operating budget is $95 million. Less than half of our support is received from the state, with the remainder of funding from academic student fees; auxiliary enterprises; and private and federal gifts, grants, and contracts. We have twelve hundred employees and serve a student population of eight thousand undergraduate and graduate students. As a special mission institution, UW-Stout holds a unique role in the UW system by specializing in degree programs that lead to professional careers, primarily in the areas of technology and human services. Our degree program inventory is highly focused, with twenty-seven undergraduate and seventeen graduate programs. Our programs have a distinctive, applied focus—consistent with our "hands-on, minds-on" philosophy.

The Baldrige at UW-Stout

Although institutions adopt management models best suited to their unique campus environment, the Malcolm Baldrige National Quality Program (Baldrige, 2003a) offers an excellent approach since it boasts well-developed criteria that are appropriate for higher education. UW-Stout committed to the Baldrige Quality Program values and criteria for several reasons. In the early 1990s, we implemented various quality approaches. Then, in the mid-1990s, severe budget reductions, poor communication between the administration and the faculty, and growing mistrust of how priorities were set developed into a crisis. Significant organizational changes were made in 1996 that began to address the issues, but everyone clearly understood that we needed to do more; we had to change the campus climate and culture. The Baldrige model was a good match for the campus; its criteria are based on quantitative information, and UW-Stout has a long history of gathering and using data systematically for decision making on academic program development, program evaluation, and in general business functions. The very fact that virtually all accreditation bodies (regional as well as specialized) are adopting the Baldrige or similar criteria is a good indication that the continuous improvement framework will become a permanent part of higher education.

In the 1990s, we organized a Quality Council, hired consultants, engaged faculty and staff in training, and set up cross-functional teams in twenty areas. This evolved into a systematic approach to more consistent improvement of processes and functions universitywide. Two additional continuous improvement processes were developed and implemented, along with the ongoing critical academic program review process for degree programs: the educational support unit review for service units, and the process review to review the major processes of the organization. This early work in the quality arena enabled support services to outperform national benchmarks and established consistent and meaningful review of our academic programs.

When the campus experienced the crisis of 1996, we made a conscious decision to use Baldrige Quality Program values and criteria to strengthen the campus. This narrative focuses on the impact of the Baldrige within UW-Stout, specifically:

- How the model created an environment for transformational change by redefining leadership
- How budget planning and strategic planning aided in transforming the campus culture
- How this planning process was applied to meet campus demands for a modern, efficient technology infrastructure

Leadership

Leadership is the first category in the Baldrige framework and the most critical, since it can be used effectively to create a campus environment that promotes, encourages, and in some ways demands clear communication and collaboration in establishing campus priorities and developing strategies to achieve them. Over time, we redefined leadership. Instead of viewing leadership as emerging from a single office, we talk about leadership "systems," believing that shared governance means shared responsibility. So the faculty, academic staff, and students do share leadership authority and responsibility. This commitment to leadership is critical for quality systems, sustained performance improvement, and the achievement of university strategies.

UW-Stout, like most institutions, relies on a traditional administrative model. The Academic and Student Affairs Division is organized around three academic colleges, each headed by a dean. There is also a dean of students. The Division of Administrative and Student Life Services administers auxiliary enterprises, physical plant, and all business functions of the university. The Chancellor's Division includes university development, information technology, university relations, and affirmative action.

This hierarchical structure by itself proved to be inadequate, since it did not facilitate good, consistent communication throughout the campus. This became painfully clear when large budget reductions were forced on the UW system in the 1993–1995 biennium. The faculty lost faith in how budget cuts and priorities were established; they demanded more consistent and open communication and said so very clearly. In other words, the structure had failed, and we had to act quickly to solve the crisis.

Actions were taken that set in motion both short- and long-term resolutions. First, the chancellor met frequently with the Faculty Senate, asking for formal and informal discussion to improve communication throughout the campus and strengthen the role of shared governance. Meetings were held with each of the twenty-six departments, and all the faculty, academic staff, and classified staff had the opportunity for face-to-face discussion on how to improve campus conditions. With agreement, further discussions were held, and the senior administrators began to meet with the Faculty Senate weekly.

Next, through close consultation with the faculty, we established the Chancellor's Advisory Council (CAC) to promote horizontal integration of the organizational structure and a means to strengthen collaborative decision making. In a sense, it is an overlay on the traditional, hierarchical management structure and actually flattens the structure. CAC includes twenty members representing senior leadership, governance groups, and other internal stakeholders. It has many roles, notably:

- Setting and deploying organizational direction and expectations
- Maintaining communication with and among all units of the university
- Providing a forum for leadership personnel to bring forth issues and priorities that support the mission and goals of the university

The Chancellor's Advisory Council operates within an open, collaborative environment by embracing governance groups; it actually serves to strengthen the general concept of shared governance on campus.

Planning

A third and critical decision was also structural in nature: the creation of the Office of Budget, Planning, and Analysis (BPA). All of the elements needed for both short- and long-term planning reside in this office. Charged with creating a new budget process that was open and democratic and that allowed everyone a chance to be heard, the director took immediate action and within months had implemented what has become a planning process that is ongoing, inclusive, and participatory. This produced substantial outcomes, including the identification of critical university priorities. It developed a commitment to emerging priorities. The quality of resource decisions was improved through meaningful recommendations from faculty, staff, and students, either as individuals or through the formal governance and administrative structure. The planning processes increased communication, understanding, and trust between the administration, faculty, and students. Participation reinforced campus focus and buy-in with regard to allocation of resources and the strategic plan, and perhaps most important it clarified university goals, priorities, and strategies. This planning model includes the development of mission, values, vision, situational analysis, five-year goals, action plans, and periodic reviews.

Multidirectional communication is critical to quality at UW-Stout, and these two important structural changes—CAC and BPA—were the means to develop a flat, open, communicative structure; they also generated direct lines from faculty, staff, and students to the administration. Widespread distribution of information became the norm. Open communication and open information took the mystique out of planning and decisions. Communication channels included open forums, regular attendance by senior leaders at weekly governance meetings, meetings of the provost and chancellor with each academic department annually, presentations to college and division councils, posting of data (including analytical reports) and basic information on the UW-Stout Website, and frequent campuswide meetings.

Technology Infrastructure

The establishment of a solid leadership system and a comprehensive planning process established the framework for information technology and other emerging demands to be successfully developed and deployed by the institution. Through these systems, we now have solid IT planning that has produced needed outcomes such as upgrade and maintenance of the campus IT infrastructure, establishment of a computer replacement program, emergence of a digital campus culture, funding for a laboratory renewal plan, and rollout of a laptop initiative for students—in short, the Stout Technology Advantage.

Measuring Institutional Excellence

UW-Stout deploys a four-step process to select, align, use, and improve organizational performance, as illustrated in Figure 5.8. Key indicators are selected that align to and permit assessment of both strategies and annual progress. Next the institution identifies and measures targets, reviews comparative data (best-in-class, peers, competitors, national averages), data segments, and trends. We employ a broad approach to ensure high-quality data integrity, including data scrubbing, data logic cross-checks, single point of entry, and data editing standards. This approach is critical in generating the information necessary for accurate, effective, and timely access.

UW-Stout uses many relevant indicators to evaluate how well the campus is realizing its mission, values, and strategic plan, and to judge performance. Comparisons are made to peer universities, those with similar programs, competitors, national averages, leading organizations, and groups of like universities.

Student Performance Results

UW-Stout tracks a student's career from the time he or she enters the university through graduation, placement in a professional career, and as alumni. We also track employers' assessment of our graduates. The performance results are directly related to the university's clearly defined mission of educating students in applied programs leading to successful careers in industry, commerce, education, and human services.

ACT Composite Scores
ACT scores are not themselves a measure of performance, but they constitute the foundation for an examination of performance results.

Figure 5.8. Measuring Institutional Excellence.

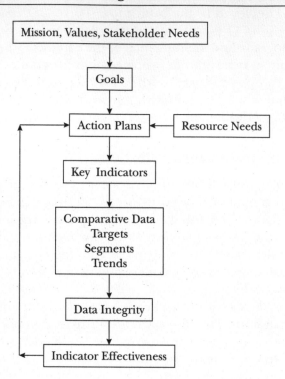

Active Learning

UW-Stout assesses students' active learning throughout their academic careers through external benchmarking surveys, and by evaluating computer competency. These results permit assessment of UW-Stout's goal to "preserve and enhance . . . the application of active learning principles."

Table 5.1 demonstrates that UW-Stout students rate higher on active learning factors than a peer composite of 157 master's colleges and universities that participated in the National Survey of Student Engagement (NSSE), and a national composite of 366 four-year colleges and universities that participated in the NSSE survey.

Table 5.1. Active Learning Factors, with UW-Stout Seniors Scoring Significantly Higher Than Peer and National Composites.

UW-Stout Trend		Comparisons	
Active Learning Philosophy Items	2002	Mast I & II 2002	Nat'l Avg. 2002
Working with other students on projects in class	2.84	2.54*	2.45*
Working with classmates outside of class on assignments	2.93	2.69*	2.72*
Working effectively with others	3.29	3.13*	3.13*

Note: 1–4 scale; * statistically lower than UW-Stout 2002.

Source: NSSE Survey (2002).

Student Placement Success

Student placement success is a primary student requirement and a UW-Stout imperative. Consistently, more than 97 percent of graduates are placed into career positions. This rate is due to the campus's focus on achieving its mission and a program director process that ensures the programs offered correspond closely with career demands and employer stakeholder needs.

Student and Stakeholder Satisfaction Results

Key indicators are also used to evaluate UW-Stout's value of building "collaborative relationships." Results demonstrate that noteworthy improvements have been made in student and stakeholder satisfaction relative to key requirements. UW-Stout students are surveyed extensively, beginning at freshman orientation, continuing throughout their academic careers, and into their careers beyond the campus by means of follow-up studies, alumni relationships, and as employers or business and industry partners.

Would Attend Again

First-year students, seniors, and alumni segments are surveyed and asked whether "they would attend UW-Stout again." Our results indicate that most students say that if they had to decide again they would choose to attend UW-Stout.

Employer Satisfaction with Graduates

UW-Stout's approach of hands-on, minds-on experiential learning has prepared graduates well for the job market. *Measuring Up 2000*, a state-by-state report card for higher education, recently surveyed employers for satisfaction with how colleges and universities in their state are preparing students for work. Graduates in Rhode Island were identified as best in class on this measure, with 83 percent of employers indicating satisfaction. Employers rate UW-Stout students as more prepared than this comparative best-in-class group, demonstrating leadership in effectively meeting needs and expectations of this key university stakeholder group.

Budgetary and Financial Results

Key indicators of budgetary and financial performance are used to ensure performance acceptable to its students and key stakeholders.

Affordable Tuition

UW-Stout's tuition, like that of the other comprehensive institutions in the UW system, is affordable. Legislative goals to give Wisconsin residents affordable undergraduate tuition are affirmed by the current tuition structure.

Affordable On-Campus Room and Board

UW-Stout's room and board is lower than comparative institutions, yet students are satisfied with dining services and residence life. These findings indicate that UW-Stout uses its on-campus room and board fees effectively (Table 5.2).

Organizational Effectiveness Results

Key indicators in this section demonstrate performance contributing to enhanced learning and operational effectiveness.

Table 5.2. On-Campus Room and Board, with UW-Stout Ranking Number One for All Four Years.

Comparisons	1998–99	1999–2000	2000–2001	2001–2002
UW-Stout	$3,156	$3,284	$3,870	$3,681
Peer 1	$4,966	$5,110	$5,258	$5,628
Peer 2	$5,355	$5,554	$6,246	$6,588
Peer 3	$6,595	$7,050	$7,300	$7,490

Source: IPEDS Peer Analysis System.

Distinctive Array of Programs

UW-Stout's array of programs is evidence of its strong focus on mission. As compared to the forty to sixty undergraduate programs typical of other comprehensive universities, UW-Stout offers a small and discrete set of degree programs. The campus's twenty-seven undergraduate programs are the fewest offered in the UW system, and several are unique in the nation. Even degree programs that appear to be similar to programs elsewhere have an applied focus that sets them apart (Figure 5.9).

Percentage of Lab-Based Instruction

Our active learning approach sets us apart from other universities. One material measure of this is laboratory-based instruction. Laboratories foster involvement and inquiry and allow students to combine theory, practice, and experimentation. For the fall terms of the last four years, 27–30 percent of our total group instruction has taken place in laboratories, compared to a 16–19 percent average at other UW system comprehensive universities. Additionally, UW-Stout's juniors and seniors have received the most laboratory-based instruction of any of the UW comprehensives in the past five years (Figure 5.10).

Support Service Performance

Surveys administered to both current students and alumni show greater satisfaction with support services than comparative groups, demonstrating a commitment to continuous improvement of facilities and services.

Figure 5.9. UW-Stout's Distinctive Array of Programs.

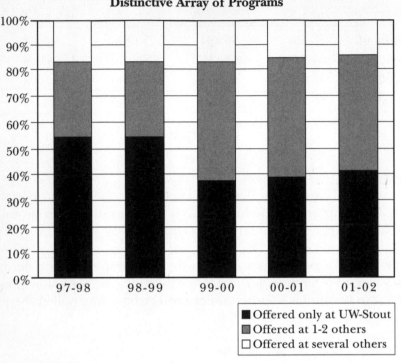

Source: University of Wisconsin System, 2003.

Faculty and Staff Results

UW-Stout faculty and staff results address faculty and staff well-being, satisfaction, and development.

Faculty Diversity

"Diversity of people, ideas, and experiences" is a UW-Stout core value. UW-Stout has been deploying initiatives to increase the number of women and minority faculty members. For example, universitywide advertisements have been placed in targeted female and minority journals for the past three years (Table 5.3).

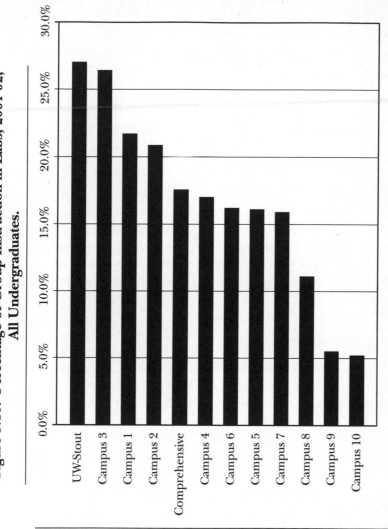

Figure 5.10. Percentage of Group Instruction in Labs, 2001-02, All Undergraduates.

Source: PMIS Section Size Analysis.

Table 5.3. Percentage of Women Faculty.

Comparison	1995	1997	1999	2001
UW-Stout	32.5%	34.4%	33.4%	39.6%
Peer 1	24.7%	23.6%	25.5%	37.1%
Peer 2	17.4%	20.0%	21.1%	29.8%
Peer 3	11.8%	14.5%	16.4%	16.7%

Note: 2001 was calculated differently from previous years because of changes in IPEDS.

Source: IPEDS Peer Analysis System, 1995, 1997, 1999, 2001.

Employee Safety

UW-Stout initiated action in recent years to reduce the number of worker's compensation claims filed and premiums paid through proactive implementation of workplace safety programs and accident prevention procedures. The effectiveness of this approach is demonstrated in the decline of the number of claims filed and premiums paid.

UW-Stout Today

Over the past decade, UW-Stout has seen many positive and needed outcomes as a result of using the Baldrige model. It is apparent that higher education fits well with the Baldrige criteria, and that quality is most appropriately measured by sustained improvement and performance outcomes. Accountability is no longer an option; using the Baldrige criteria prompts responsiveness to students and stakeholders and clarity in identifying their requirements, along with a highly refined approach to the university as a system.

Breakthrough change is possible. Having solid leadership and planning systems has allowed us to be agile, which in turn enables focused change and improved decisions and buy-in. For most, this is a significant cultural change.

University governance and administration can work together effectively. Participatory and collaborative practices promote an environment of trust and respect. Identification of priorities, allocation of resources, and identification of outcome measures are reached together—thereby sending a consistent message to faculty, staff, and students.

The Baldrige criteria underscore the idea that visionary leadership is critical. Commitment and involvement from the senior leadership team are the basis for effective multidirectional communication systems, participatory processes, and performance outcomes.

Most important, the Baldrige criteria focus on learning-centered education. UW-Stout has excelled in this arena for decades, being one of the first to apply active learning principles, to focus on hands-on, minds-on education that is responsive to the needs of employers and to the unique needs of students.

The Baldrige Award

In 2001, UW-Stout was honored by being selected as the first higher-education recipient of the national Baldrige performance excellence award. The Baldrige Award is a demonstration of dedication to hard work, focus, and commitment to excellence. Winning the award has had a profound impact on UW-Stout. First, there is simply the prestige that comes with such an award. We have had requests from numerous colleges and universities (nine from other countries) to visit our campus to learn more about our quality improvement initiative. Our speaking and consulting engagements are numerous. Second, we have historically had strong relationships with companies and corporations, and this has been strengthened. Because of the award, more nationally known companies want to visit our campus, review our programs, and establish a relationship with us. Third, we have changed in some fundamentally important ways. We are clearly more proactive, much more sensitive to looking at our internal measurements more frequently, and focused on outcomes. Finally, the greatest benefit is the recognition of a quality, dedicated faculty, academic staff, and clerical and service staff who made this possible. The beneficiaries are the eight thousand students UW-Stout serves annually.

Chapter Six

Enhancing Collaboration and Community

Aligning the Rhetoric and Reality of Campus Culture

Respect for individual differences, collegiality, and collaboration are core values in higher education. Indeed, many of us have chosen careers in higher education precisely because we understood these to be among the defining principles of the academy.

On campuses throughout the country, vision statements proclaim dedication to a climate of mutual respect, cooperation, and community. Variously phrased, these commitments pledge to create a culture that welcomes and values all members of the campus community, regardless of gender, race, religion, color, ancestry, age, national origin, sexual orientation, or disability or ability. There is much evidence that the commitment to these purposes is real. On every campus there are advances in these areas to point to with pride each year, and the academy serves as a leader for society in advancing these goals (Antonio, 2001; Astin, 1993; "Women Faculty Members . . . ," 2002; Chang, 2002; Hurtado, Milem, Clayton-Pedersen, and Allen, 1998; King, 1999; Light, 2001; McDonald, 2002; Wall and Evans, 2000). Nonetheless, there are notable gaps between rhetoric and reality in some important areas. Where they exist, they stand as barriers to the model of institutional excellence we seek to become.

Campus Cultures Based on Occupation and Role

The relationships among various occupational groups within the academy—particularly between faculty and staff—are one area where we face significant challenges. Although faculty, staff, and administrators all perform indispensable functions within colleges and universities, there are obvious and significant differences in the work, work styles, and perspectives of these groups, and these differences often create obstacles to mutual respect and satisfying collaboration. These barriers frequently interfere with the practice of excellence within colleges and universities and stand in marked contrast to our ideals.

The distinctive nature of the faculty culture—and perceived contrasts with other cultures on campus—is a central issue. The work of the faculty contributes directly and visibly to instruction, scholarship, and public service. These activities define the core mission of a college or university, and they are the basis upon which institutional excellence has traditionally been judged. Thus faculty members are socialized into a culture that prizes their contributions and places them and their work at the center of the institution. This privileged role can lead quite naturally to a view that one hears frequently: that "the faculty are the university." Although the cultural origins of such an assertion are understandable, this way of talking—and thinking—can be very troublesome to other professional and support staff if it signals a climate where their contributions are overlooked or marginalized as a consequence.

Highly visible trappings of the faculty culture are numerous, and differences between the faculty culture and those of administrative and staff groups are often quite striking. In managing time, for instance, faculty members operate in what staff groups perceive to be a highly autonomous manner. As faculty members, we often appear to be following the same calendar as students, complete with holiday and seasonal breaks. We often seem to be able to decide which days to "come to work," and which classes we want to teach, and at what time of the day we want to teach them. Our autonomy is even seen as extending to decisions about whether to keep "office hour" commitments, respond to e-mails or phone messages, attend department or college meetings, or comply with requests to serve on university or student committees. In sum, it is a commonly held view that faculty autonomy permits wide variation in definitions and behaviors regarding enactment of "institutional responsibilities." Even those of us who would see this perception as inaccurate or exaggerated can recognize how such a view might develop (Bennett, 1998).

When confronted with these perceptions, we faculty members are quick to point out that our autonomy is coupled with a substantial degree of accountability. We undergo regular review of teaching effectiveness, scholarship, and professional and service contributions to our disciplines, departments, and institutions. We see ourselves as struggling to balance our many responsibilities to students, our disciplines, and our institutions. Moreover, as faculty members we can seldom leave our work "at the office." Faculty also point out that it is not unusual to spend evenings, weekends, and holidays occupied by reading students' papers, preparing lectures, engaging in university committee work, attending to professional association activities, or writing articles or books, though it is also recognized that this characterization does not apply equally to all faculty members.

In contrast to the world of the faculty, most administrative and support staff have considerably less autonomy in the enactment of institutional responsibilities. The expectation is that staff come to work every day of the week, work regular hours, seek permission for vacation days, take lunch at prescribed times, answer all e-mails, attend scheduled meetings, serve on committees when asked, and so on. Unlike the faculty, staff members are expected to do these things whether they would like to or not, and without regard to the value they personally perceive the activities to have—for the institution or their own professional advancement. Even for the most senior administrators or technical staff—most of whom may also have advanced degrees and significant disciplinary and professional responsibilities—there are typically no sabbaticals, no spring break weeks to regroup and catch up, no days to work at home to focus on particular writing projects, and far less job security than faculty enjoy. Given these contrasts, whatever knowledge administrators and staff members may have about nuances of faculty accountability is easily overshadowed by patterns of behavior that confront them daily in the workplace—patterns that can foster frustration and resentment.

On the other hand, viewed from the perspective of the faculty culture—with its emphasis on measurable teaching, scholarship, and professional productivity—it may appear that the culture of administrative and support staff lacks mechanisms for meaningful review and accountability. At many institutions, midlevel and lower-level administrative and staff positions seem quite secure, a kind of functional equivalent to tenure as viewed from the perspective of the faculty culture. Moreover, the staff review and reward processes that exist are often perceived to have little impact on performance.

The cultural differences and attendant sensitivities are most striking in aggregate comparisons *between* faculty and staff roles, but it is obviously an oversimplification to imply that there is a single faculty or staff culture; indeed, on any campus there are many (Berquist, 1992; Snow, 1993; Tierney, 1990). Some of these same contrasts, and the same consequences, can be seen *within* the faculty culture (as in, for instance, differences between untenured and tenured faculty) and staff cultures, as well. In some nonacademic departments, the mere use of terms such as "professional" and "support" staff to differentiate work positions can trigger strong reactions and resentment. Additionally, there are numerous and diverse student cultures (Whitt, 1996). On most campuses throughout the country, the increasingly complex student body makes the mix of belief and value systems richer and potentially beneficial in terms of learning, but it also adds another dimension of cultural complexity and challenge from the perspective of establishing the sense and reality of community.

It is also well known that cultural divides emerge that are based on one's area of specialization. Within academic or administrative departments, for instance, distinct cultures often develop among faculty or staff with particular subspecialties or methodological expertise, and it is well known that still more dramatic cultural cleavages emerge *between* disciplines. It is, of course, quite natural for members of a specialty or department to highly value their own contributions to the institution and the academy. Moreover, one would expect individuals within a discipline or administrative unit to be informed about their own work, their own department, and the role the unit plays in campus affairs. Unfortunately, the same dynamics that lead to differential knowledge and valuing of one's own role or specialty can lead also to a climate that undermines mutual respect across employee groups, disciplines, and administrative departments.

Cultural Differentiation and Organizational Excellence

There is nothing unique about the existence of multiple and diverse cultures within an institution. Even the wide range of occupational and disciplinary subcultures that characterize the academy occurs in other organizational settings. Obvious parallels exist, for example in health care institutions, where the excellence of the institution depends upon effective collaboration among physicians, nurses, allied health care workers, administrators, and support staff.

The community orchestra is another interesting, if unlikely, parallel to higher education, and an analysis of the communication and cultural dynamics in that context helps to clarify some of the challenges faced within the academy. In studies of community orchestras, three distinct and divergent cultures have been identified: the administration, the performers (the musicians), and the board of directors (Ruud, 1995; Ruud, 2000). Studies found that each best understood and most prized the contributions of its own group, believed these contributions to be the most critical to the success of the enterprise, and tended to marginalize and misunderstand the perspectives and contributions of the others. Intensive study of the core values of these three cultures led to identification of symbols and ways of communicating, in addition to obvious differences regarding the nature of their roles and responsibilities. The performers were dedicated to a high level of artistic excellence and to ensuring the quality of the music as their first priority. From the performers' perspective, excellence required an organizational environment that was dedicated to challenging the musicians artistically. Their emphasis therefore was on creating a strong artistic foundation for the organization. The administrative culture and that of the board tended to place much greater emphasis on audience expectations and marketplace economics than on artistic standards (Ruud, 2000).

Over the years, cultural differences among the groups were significant and resulted in threats, acrimonious contract negotiations, canceled concerts, strikes, and lock-outs (Ruud, 2000). As described by researcher Gary Ruud: "It was evident that the symphony, like many organizations, was beset by internal differences that made coordinated action difficult to achieve. Moreover, organization members failed to reflect, at least in any systematic way, on the underlying ideologies that were so prevalent in symphony interactions" (Ruud, 2000, p. 138).

The cultural patterns and attendant consequences observed by Ruud in the symphony certainly have parallels within higher education (Becher and Trowler, 2001; Caplow and McGee, 2001; Noble, 2001; Ramsden, 1998; Weinstein, 1993). Whether in health care, community orchestras, or higher education, when organizational subcultures become too differentiated and disconnected, core values, operational effectiveness, and ultimately institutional excellence are all at risk.

Enhancing Collaboration and Community

A great many factors play a role in creating—and overcoming—divided and sometimes divisive cultures within organizations. Among the factors that are particularly critical in the case of higher education are formal education and socialization, organizational structure, and incentives and rewards.

Education and Socialization

Clearly, socialization and formal education are critical contributors to the creation of cultural differences, and to the barriers that sometimes become problematic within the academy. From our early days in school, the value of competition and individual accomplishment is well engrained in our thinking, and these values are reinforced in any number of ways. The message is quite clear: "Working on one's own is the right thing to do." "Seeking help from others is a sign of weakness and inadequacy at best, and 'cheating' at worst."[1] The pattern may be changing somewhat today, but for most of us some twenty years of encouragement to "do your *own* work" has left an indelible imprint on our psyches.

The significance of individual accomplishment and competitiveness reaches new heights in the college application process. For a time, at least, class rank and scores on standardized tests seem to become the major indicators of personal worth for students and their parents.

The graduate education of college and university faculty and staff tends to exacerbate these values. For those who have pursued school beyond a bachelor's degree, especially for those who have chosen the life of scholarship in the academy—these themes are further reinforced as we learn to become *independent* scholars. At the same time, our advanced education and training equip us with specialized disciplinary and technical expertise, language, and methodological capability. This preparation facilitates information sharing with others who share our linguistic and conceptual facility and disciplinary background, but it creates special challenges when it comes to interacting with individuals who have differing experiences, capabilities, and frames of reference. Through our graduate education, we also learn the values and skills necessary to critique and aggressively challenge others' ideas, and to defend and persuasively argue our own positions. Confrontation and combativeness become quite a natural style. Ironically, or perhaps not, when one completes a master's or doctoral thesis, the presentation of the completed work is termed a "defense."

In the academy's efforts to advance knowledge, the values of individualism, disciplinarity, and competition serve us well. They are particularly helpful to the extent that success in the academy is dependent upon operating as an independent thinker, holding one's own in scholarly debates and presentations, and disseminating one's ideas through competitively reviewed publications in which one's unique contributions can be easily discerned.

Faculty socialization and training in these values and skills, however, also serve to limit and constrain us in other ways. We are often not well prepared to value or engage in collective endeavors that require teamwork, negotiation, or collaborative problem solving—competencies that are called for in a great many higher education roles and circumstances. Whether it is working effectively with students and colleagues, serving on committees, participating in meetings, contributing to shared governance, working on group projects, or facilitating interdepartmental initiatives, collaborative skills are absolutely essential. In such settings, the behaviors associated with individuality and competition are generally not helpful and are often counterproductive. At a time of increased interdisciplinary initiatives, these limitations are particularly troublesome. In so many of our collective endeavors within higher education, excellence requires that the *whole* must be something more than the simple sum of the distinguished parts.

Collaborative values and competencies are also important themes in our courses. As one Harvard student noted in interviews conducted by Richard Light (2001):

> The biggest message I want to share is that teamwork ultimately depends almost entirely on human connections . . . some adults who do this all the time don't realize, or maybe forget, how hard this is to learn. Look at what I had to learn, in addition to all the substantive economics and methods of analysis, in order to become an effective member of this small working group. I had to learn how to criticize constructively. I had to learn how to argue constructively. I had to learn how to say I disagree with someone else's idea constructively, even if I secretly think the idea is idiotic [p. 50].

In recent years, there has been a growing awareness that graduate students who anticipate a career in the academy need to be equipped with teaching as well as research skills as a part of their graduate education experience, and a growing number of programs have been designed to address this goal—including the Rutgers program described in a narrative by Barbara Bender (Chapter Seven).

It is becoming increasingly clear that interpersonal communication and socioemotional competencies are also components for effective training of faculty members and professional staff (Applegate, 2001; Nyquist, 2001). In fact, Goleman (1995, 1998a, 1998b) and others have pointed out that capabilities such as self-awareness, self-control, political savvy, cooperation, and communication competence are frequently at least as significant to occupational and personal outcomes as academic or technical capability (Daly and Wiemann, 1994; Kealey and Ruben, 1983; Mayer and Salovey, 1997; McClelland, 1976; O'Hair, Friedrich, Wiemann, and Wiemann, 1997; Ruben, 1976, 1978; Ruben and Kealey, 1979; and Spitzberg and Cupach, 1984).

Although many of the critical psychological, social, and communicative capabilities do not naturally or necessarily accompany mastery of a subject matter or advanced degrees, they do involve concepts, attitudes, and skills that can be taught and learned as a part of one's graduate work. For example, graduate study could include readings, seminars, colloquia, and case studies to highlight the nature and importance of collaboration. Course assignments could be created that encourage students to work together on the design, conduct, presentation, and evaluation of research or scholarly projects, and include a requirement that they analyze their own interpersonal and group dynamics as the project progresses. Or one could use any number of other hands-on instructional approaches typically used for teaching research concepts and methodologies—another domain where there are both concepts and competencies to be mastered. There are many other possibilities. Using a combination of approaches, the goal should be to effectively integrate collaborative values and skill training throughout the graduate curriculum, to help prepare future academics and professionals for the many situations where these capabilities are indispensable.

Organizational Structure

Within the academy, as elsewhere, people with similar disciplinary expertise or functional responsibility are generally grouped together structurally and physically in the workplace. The admissions staff works together in one department, the English faculty are in another department, and computing services personnel are housed in yet another department. This practice encourages the emergence of well-defined and tightly bounded work groups—what are often referred to as work group "silos"—throughout an institution. Clear identities, strong loyalties, and sometimes a high level of productivity develop *within* these work groups, but unfortunately this cohesiveness and solidarity often creates barriers to collaborating *across* departmental boundaries.

The difficulties of traditional organizational structures have been a concern in other sectors for some time (Hammer and Champy, 1993; Lathrop, 1993; Marszalek-Gaucher and Coffey, 1990; Merwick, Godfrey, and Roessner, 1990; Federal Quality Institute, 1994; Rummler and Brache, 1995). Classical manufacturing companies, for example, have divisions or departments of production, sales, operations, marketing, finance, and research and development. Experience teaches that when the research and development division of a corporation designs a product without the benefit of collaboration with manufacturing, operations, and marketing, any number of unfortunate outcomes can occur, such as creating a wonderfully designed product that the company cannot easily manufacture, and for which there is no market. Analogous concerns have been raised in health care, where it is recognized that departmental insularity impedes organizational effectiveness and the rendering of quality service to patients (Ulschak, 1994; Zeithaml, Parasuraman, and Berry, 1990).

Simpler, "flatter," better-integrated organizations that facilitate cross-functional and cross-divisional coordination have been suggested as a means for improving organizational effectiveness in business and health care (Ashkenas, Ulrich, Jick, and Kerr, 2002; Hammer and Champy, 1993; Lathrop, 1993; Marszalek-Gaucher and Coffey, 1990). For example, in the case of manufacturing, cross-functional structures and work processes that integrate functions—research and development, operations, marketing, and sales, as shown in Figure 6.1—have the potential to overcome problems that arise from homogeneous-function structuring.

Figure 6.1. Cross-Functional Approach to Basic Business Processes.

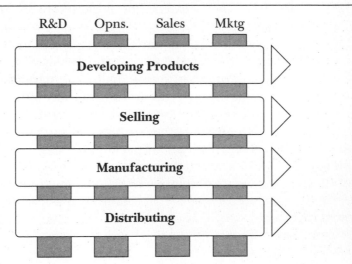

In government, the integration of various agencies and organizations concerned with facets of homeland security also offers a vivid example of an effort to overcome problems posed by traditional organizational structures.

How do the models of cross-department and cross-functional structure apply to higher education? In some areas, higher education has always been organized cross-functionally. In academic departments within research institutions, for example, instructional, research, and service or outreach activities are performed by each member of the faculty. Looking more broadly at colleges and universities, however, it is apparent that our institutions suffer from the same problems that plague organizations in other sectors. Individual academic units often operate in relative isolation from one another, and in some instances the relationships are even adversarial, as units perceive themselves to be in competition for students, faculty and staff lines, operating funds, physical facilities, and visibility and prestige within the institution.

The Kellogg Commission described the academic implications of these issues this way: "It is easy for many outside the academy to conclude that we are uninterested in the need for change. They are wrong. The issue is not the lack of interest; it is that we are poorly organized. . . . As the nature of knowledge changes, our departmental structure has difficulty responding. As the challenges facing our communities multiply, we find it hard to break out of the silos our disciplines created. The world has problems; universities have departments" (Kellogg Commission, 1997, p. 7).

Structural isolation also contributes to disconnects between occupational and role-based cultures, and to a lack of integration and functional coordination across faculty and staff lines, as mentioned earlier. In the area of undergraduate education, for instance, most faculty members in large institutions have little operational involvement in areas such as recruitment, admissions, housing, student life, facilities, or personnel training, as suggested in Figure 6.2. Similarly, staff members are seldom systematically involved in curriculum development or classroom instruction, even in areas where their expertise or experience would suggest they could make a substantial contribution. It could be otherwise, even in larger institutions.

Figure 6.2. Traditional Silo Structures in Higher Education.

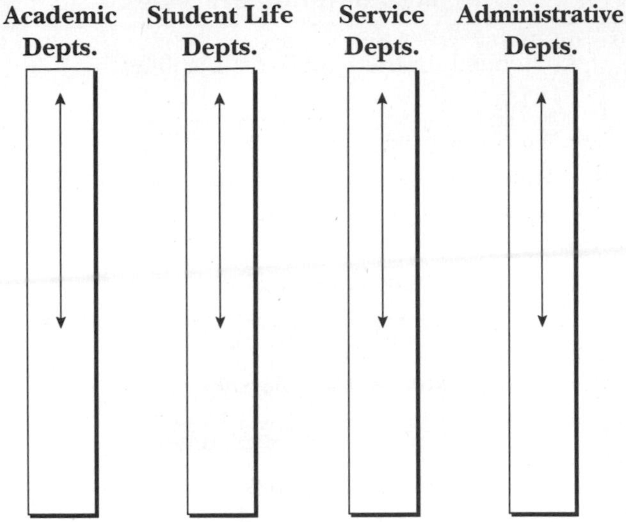

Academic Depts.	Student Life Depts.	Service Depts.	Administrative Depts.

From the perspective of constituencies for which we provide programs and services, institutional roles and structures are of little consequence in and of themselves. What matters is how the work of individuals and departments comes together. As defined from the perspective of our beneficiaries, institutional excellence requires a coordinated effort in recruiting (students and faculty), admissions, advising, teaching, scheduling, housing, dining, student services, the library, transportation, classroom and study facilities, and many other areas, as illustrated in Figure 6.3. The reputation of the institution as a whole is affected by any and all of the individuals or departments with which constituents interact in these processes. In the case of instruction—as in examples one might select relative to research and scholarship or service and outreach—most of the difficulties we face require cross-functional solutions. Few service or quality gaps are solely academic or administrative, or exclusively the responsibility of a faculty or staff group. Similarly, few of these gaps can be eliminated by one department alone; typically they require a more seamless integration, coordination, and cooperation across functional units.

**Figure 6.3. Cross-Functional Approach
to Higher Education Processes.**

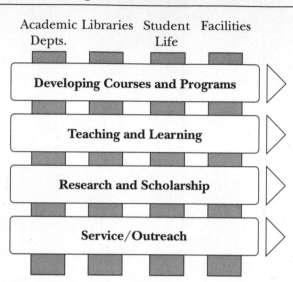

One can conceive of organizational structures that would promote far more collaboration among faculty and staff from various departments working on the critical issues facing the institution. For instance, one approach is to create interfunctional, interdepartmental, and interdisciplinary structures that overlay and supplement the work of the traditional organizational structures. We do this when we form collegewide or universitywide committees, councils, or senates, and we might well look for additional opportunities to expand this approach. These structures make available broadened expertise for the topic at hand and presumably lead to better decisions or recommendations. They also have the potential to bring together faculty and staff from quite divergent specialties in a context that can help to increase mutual understanding, respect, and a sense of community.

Another advantage of transitory or virtual organizations is that they do not require physical structures, bylaws, or continuing support. Once the goals of a particular problem-solving group have been achieved, the structure can be dissolved, and these resources can be directed toward other endeavors. Many such areas of opportunity come to mind where transitory collaborative structures can be created to engage both faculty and staff from a variety of relevant departments. Examples include efforts to plan and implement welcome and orientation programs and recruitment efforts; interdisciplinary courses and programs; recognition committees and events; campuswide planning activities; improvement in priority setting; and new curricular and administrative projects.

There are also instances where similar approaches can be used to facilitate collaboration and expertise sharing across institutions. Professional organizations and entities such as the Kellogg Commission have promoted ventures of this kind, but the potential for benefit from such models has only begun to be realized.[2]

Rewards and Incentives

Collaborative, team, departmental, and community endeavors *could* be encouraged and rewarded through financial and other incentives, but in most cases incentive structures reinforce the emphasis on individual accomplishment. Greater verbal encouragement given to team-based innovations in instruction, interdisciplinary and interdepartmental research, and outreach and public service is helping to address this issue, but all too often there are few incentives to sustain these efforts.

Eliminating disincentives to collaboration wherever possible would be a significant step forward. In faculty promotion and merit reviews, for example, considerable effort is expended to identify and document one's *unique* contribution to scholarly research and publications. Discouragement of collaborative endeavors is often an unintended consequence. Similarly, for staff, performance review systems typically seek to identify, document, and recognize *individual* contributions. In these contexts, it would also be possible to recognize and reward collaborative performance by individuals, or outstanding performance by groups or departments. As in other areas, society should be able to look to higher education to be the leader in developing and testing new models of organizations—models that offer incentives for both individual and collective accomplishment (Clifton and Rubenstein, 2000; Harrison and Brodeth, 1999; "Enhancing Faculty Performance . . . ," 2002).

Concluding Comments

In practice, colleges and universities are seldom the fully integrated systems we wish them to be. As Jim Carey (2000, p. 12) notes: "borders . . . are . . . firmly entrenched between departments around the university, they are more firmly entrenched between departments and disciplines, students and teachers, administrators, researchers and faculty and above all, between types of faculty: adjunctions, assistants, part time, tenured, and tenure track."[3] Boundaries not only separate academic units and personnel from one another, as Carey indicates, but also business and administrative departments and staff from each other, and even more so from the employees in academic areas.

Despite rhetoric endorsing collaboration, mutual respect, teamwork, and community, significant gaps exist, and some are yet to be widely recognized as problems. As noted, there *are* similarities between higher education institutions and other organizations in this regard. However, for those of us in the academy, the rhetoric-reality paradox is particularly troublesome as we find ourselves confronted with role-based and discipline-based profiling and prejudices that are so at odds with our core values. As Rhodes (2001, p. 47) comments, "The loss of community is not a mere misfortune; it is a catastrophe, for it undermines the very foundation on which the universities were established."

Within the academy, as within comparable institutions, the existence of diverse organizational cultures is not per se the problem. In fact, what Tierney (1993) has termed a culture of difference is both a necessity given the complex functions performed by the organization and an opportunity in terms of the potential enrichment of experiences that result in learning for all involved. As Rhodes (2001, p. 31) states so articulately, "The challenges of life and the needs of society defy traditional disciplinary boundaries, and the collective expertise of the campus is an asset of growing value that is widely acknowledged, though not yet fully utilized."

Unfortunately, these benefits derive for the academy only to the extent that cultural barriers that separate and disconnect groups from one another and the overall purposes of the organization can be transcended to create a coordinated community that enacts the values we espouse and furnishes a model of excellence to which others can aspire.

Notes

1. See discussion in Light (2001), pp. 51–53.
2. See, for instance, the Kellogg Foundation FIPSE and Leadership for Institutional Change (LINC) Programs Websites (www.leadership onlinewkkf.org; http://cuinfo.cornell.edu/LINC; http://www.fspe. org/linc).
3. It should be noted that Carey attributes the emergence of these internal boundaries to the engagement by the academy and to the corresponding deterioration of boundaries between the university and its external constituencies. The position taken here is that formidable internal boundaries and disengagement have existed for some time, and that they are more likely causes than effects of current circumstances.

Narratives

Enhancing Collaboration and Community: Aligning the Rhetoric and Reality of Campus Culture

Respect for individual differences, collegiality, and collaboration are defining values within higher education. We pride ourselves on setting a high standard of excellence in these areas, providing leadership for other organizations and other sectors. However, we too face challenges. Distinct cultures define and sometimes create divides between faculty and staff, and among various academic and administrative units; in so doing they erect barriers to institutional excellence and a shared sense of purpose. The narratives in this section summarize efforts to overcome cultural and structural barriers within and between institutions.

In the first narrative, Francis Lawrence, Rutgers president emeritus, and former vice president Christine Haska Cermak describe a major strategic planning effort designed to heighten academic collaboration across disciplines and campuses, and ultimately to identify new academic priorities for the university.

An innovative interinstitutional initiative undertaken by the Big Ten universities is the topic of the second narrative. Robert Secor, coordinator of the Committee on Institutional Cooperation, describes this collaborative effort, which is dedicated to fostering enhanced leadership development opportunities for all the institutions involved.

Many other narratives in this book address the theme of collaboration. For instance, the one by Stacey Connaughton and Michael Quinlan following Chapter Three is an excellent example of collaborative effort between academic and administrative departments to address a campus problem in a manner that also created a useful learning opportunity for students. The Chapter Nine narrative by Louise Sandmeyer and Carol Lindborg Everett describes a campus Quality Expo that promotes and celebrates collaboration and encourages a sense of community among administrators, faculty, and staff. In that same chapter's narratives, John Byrne, who served as executive director of the Kellogg Foundation Commission on the Future of State and Land-Grant Institutions, describes the unique and highly significant collaborative effort involving presidents from twenty-five colleges and universities in reaffirming their common purposes and aspirations.

Advancing Academic Excellence and Collaboration Through Strategic Planning

Francis L. Lawrence
President Emeritus, Rutgers, State
University of New Jersey

Christine Haska Cermak
Associate Provost, Naval Postgraduate School; Former
Vice President for Planning, Rutgers University

Rutgers, the State University of New Jersey, was chartered in 1766 as Queens College. One of the nine colonial colleges, it had a long and often financially precarious existence as a private college before becoming the state's land-grant college in 1864 and the official state university through legislative acts in 1945 and 1956. New Jersey was the last of the fifty states to designate a state university. Some older Rutgers alumni and faculty members still look back with nostalgia to what they remember as a golden age of semi-Ivy-League status. Some nurture ambitions to return to that genteel existence.

Divided Perceptions

From colonial days to the present, New Jersey too has suffered from a divided sense of itself, attracted by two magnetic poles: New York City in the north and Philadelphia in the south. Ben Franklin called it "a tunne [cask] tapped at both ends." The opening scene of the popular television program *The Sopranos*, in which mobster Tony Soprano drives the first few miles of the New Jersey Turnpike, cleverly manipulates the archetypal images of the state as an industrial wasteland and a haven for organized crime as effective framing devices for the series. But, to borrow a few phrases from President Kennedy's memorable rhetoric (in a commencement address at Yale University in 1962), "Mythology distracts us everywhere. For the great enemy of the truth is very often not the lie—deliberate, contrived, and dishonest—but the myth: persistent, persuasive, and unrealistic." This is true of both New Jersey and Rutgers.

Contemporary Realities

The New Jersey of today is a high-technology powerhouse; its central counties are as great a force in biotechnology and the pharmaceutical industry as Silicon Valley has been in the computer industry, and its family income is now the second highest in the nation (U.S. Census Bureau, 2001). Rutgers has grown to be one of America's largest, most distinguished, and most diverse major public research universities. More than 150 Rutgers research and policy centers and institutes contribute to academic programs and serve the public and private sectors at the regional, state, national, and international levels. With a budget that totals $1.4 billion, it educates fifty thousand students working for degrees in its one hundred distinct bachelor's programs, one hundred master's programs, and eighty doctoral and professional degree programs. In 1989, the university's New Brunswick campus accepted an invitation to join the ranks of the country's most prestigious public and private research institutions as a member of the Association of American Universities (AAU). In New Brunswick, it has initiated and carried through a long list of projects to improve the schools in areas ranging from reading skills to science and math. It has also been one of the prime movers in the renewal of its urban area over several decades. Rutgers's Newark campus, which has become a Research University I during the last decade, takes pride in its reputation as being the most diverse campus in the nation, and in the fact that it has been an important partner in the city's renaissance. Finally, its Camden campus has been recognized among the best regional universities in the country and is participating in a growing number of city improvement efforts, ranging from a minor league ballpark that doubles as a Rutgers facility to a campaign for children's literacy and a charter school that has recently added a high school.

In 1990, New Jersey entered an economic downturn that began earlier there and lasted longer than it did in the rest of the nation. State aid was cut drastically, $20 million in FY1990 alone, a total of $96 million over a four-year period. At the same time, the state limited tuition increases by linking funding to tuition caps. The effects of such draconian budget cuts were devastating to the academic community. Hard-earned progress in academic quality was jeopardized, and everyone felt uncertain about the future of their own programs specifically and the university's vitality in general.

Building a Vision

Rutgers chose a bold, counterintuitive way of raising universitywide morale and mustering resolve to make progress in a time of increasingly straitened financial circumstances. We initiated a universitywide strategic planning process to meet our challenges by setting ambitious goals:

- To enhance world-class scholarship by strengthening the core missions of instruction, research, and service
- To unify disparate communities, create supportive administrative structures, and develop a culture of "one university"
- To work as a community to tell the Rutgers story persuasively and effectively, thus positioning the university for a major fundraising effort to help realize its academic aspirations

Constructing a Framework for Change

Our first step in strategic planning was to marshal the resources of our three campuses to produce planning studies. Our process was inclusive: every part of the university was called upon to participate. Our academic units developed planning studies; our major administrative units submitted self-studies and underwent a management audit. The plans from all three campuses were integrated into a universitywide plan, *A New Vision for Excellence*, which was then shared for comment with a variety of groups both inside and outside the university. Advice and suggestions were sought from our own academic community as well as from corporate, political, and higher education leaders. The final version of the plan was approved by the board of governors in June 1995. In that plan, we asserted our core values of commitment to academic excellence in research, teaching, and service. We acknowledged that higher education in New Jersey was facing increasing expectations and demands at the same time as it was experiencing serious economic shortfalls. We pledged renewed partnership with the state to work together on pressing issues. We declared our commitment to interdisciplinary, intercampus, and interinstitutional collaboration. To serve our state and its citizens, we pledged ourselves to foster partnerships with the schools, business and industry, and government, working with the public and private sectors to achieve mutual goals.

Recognizing the liberal arts and sciences as the foundation of our academic enterprise, we also paid tribute to the effects of the information revolution, in which the concept of community and the possibility of engagement are enhanced by computerized communication. We noted that Rutgers's Quality and Communication Improvement program—since renamed the Center for Organizational Development and Leadership—was designed to improve the university's services to students and faculty and to make service orientation an integral part of the culture of the university. We concluded that the continued progress of the strategic planning process, which we envisioned as a living, evolving instrument of progress at Rutgers, would give the community the opportunity to reform and reshape our culture, and to acquire a new, shared perspective about the university as a community committed to excellence and a heightened sense of service.

Building Community

Rutgers's strategic plan, then, was not a volume to be put away on the shelf. Our next step was to go forward with implementation. We identified twelve broad, interdisciplinary academic growth areas based on specific criteria: their excellence, their centrality to our mission, and their responsiveness to emerging needs in our society. The areas chosen for their strength and potential were

liberal arts and sciences, business, cognitive science and neuro-
science, creative arts, education, engineering, environmental studies, information sciences and technology, international studies, life
sciences and agriculture, public policy and the law, and women's
scholarship and leadership.

Again, just as in the initial work of planning, our aim was to
involve as many faculty as possible in a collegial strategic planning
implementation process. More than 250 members, serving on universitywide committees representing the priorities identified in the
strategic plan, worked for a year to solicit and evaluate the
hundreds of proposals that they received from faculty on all three
campuses. Each of the committee reports proposed a vision for the
future and outlined specific priorities for achieving greater excellence in our academic programs. Among the many proposals
sketched in the reports, several common themes figured prominently. Those fundamental to a major student-centered research
university today were undergraduate education, graduate and professional education, program support and development, faculty
development, academic support systems, linking research with public service, diversity in the academic community, and buildings and
facilities.

A respected committee of distinguished faculty, the President's
Committee on Standards and Priorities in Academic Development
(CSPAD), reviewed committee reports and drafted an integrated
document. The president's cabinet then reviewed, edited, and
approved the report and the board of governors endorsed the implementation progress report in June 1996. The hundreds of Rutgers
faculty from all three campuses who worked together on the implementation planning committees were reluctant to dissolve their productive partnerships, so most of the committees resolved to continue
to work together as the implementation plans progressed. Along
with the chair of CSPAD, the head of the Rutgers Foundation, and
the members of the president's cabinet, key faculty members from
the committees were asked to serve on an executive committee, the
Committee for the Future, charged with general oversight responsibility to advise on the plan's implementation.

Still in the grip of a recessionary climate, with annual cuts to the
university budget and continuing caps on tuition increases, Rutgers
undertook what we called a Strategic Resource and Opportunity

Analysis (SROA) to identify administrative savings throughout the university that could be devoted to providing seed funding for some of the projects proposed in the strategic planning implementation process. The $4 million freed by these economies were placed in a revolving account to generate start-up grants from the Committee on the Future for new academic initiatives, with the potential to attract significant external funding.

In addition to the SROA grants made by the Committee for the Future, among the major programs to support strategic plan implementation was the Reinvest in Rutgers initiative, an infusion of more than $35 million into our core academic disciplines that became possible as state funding improved with the revived economy. A third massive universitywide project, RUNet, was undertaken to wire the Rutgers campuses for voice, video, and data; its $100 million cost was financed by a combination of state bond funding, federal grants, student fees for computing, and internal allocation. Significant support from key university offices also played an important role, among them university relations, research and sponsored programs, corporate liaison and technology transfer, federal and state relations, institutional research and planning, organizational development and leadership, and the Rutgers Foundation.

Measuring Outcomes

Since the adoption of the strategic plan in 1995, the university has made impressive strides. By the close of FY2001, the number of full-time Rutgers faculty had risen by 2.5 percent, with more than three hundred faculty hired in just the preceding three years. Undergraduate applications rose by 31 percent, and the academic qualifications of entering students improved markedly; the demand for a Rutgers education was never greater. The enrollment of underrepresented minorities increased 25 percent, making Rutgers second among its public university peers in the Association of American Universities in underrepresented minority enrollment and sixth in total minority enrollment (surpassed only by members of the University of California system). The SROA program, completing its sixth cycle of funding, made available a total in excess of $24 million to support some 125 initiatives that leveraged a total of more than $275 million in external funding. Equally important was the fact that the program's interdisciplinary focus and the ongoing strategic planning process created incentives for cooperation and collaboration, bringing together faculty from related disciplines across the university in a way that had never been done before.

The ambitious RUNet project, launched in 1998, completed wiring in more than one hundred residence halls by the close of FY2001; fifty academic and administrative buildings were being wired. All told, nearly 250 buildings were connected via new wiring. RUNet has made a significant impact on the university by allowing Web-enabled services to better serve its students and by bringing together technology with research and instruction in new ways for innovative teaching and cooperative research efforts. Sixty "smart" classrooms were opened, enabling faculty to use multimedia presentations, including Internet access, on a giant screen controlled from a single console in the front of each room. Rutgers was able to attract such initiatives as the Protein Data Bank, a computer-based, three-dimensional atlas of biological macromolecules accessible on the Internet and funded by a $10 million award from the National Science Foundation. Rutgers's own television network was launched in fall 2000 with sixty-five channels of educational, news, and public affairs programs, all university-produced, as well as commercial programming that goes out to twelve thousand Rutgers students in their dormitories. Instructional technology is being integrated into Rutgers classrooms, enabling more than eight thousand students a year to take enhanced courses in disciplines ranging from music theory to genetics. Perhaps most important was that RUNet was completed on time and within budget, showing the state and the nation that Rutgers worked effectively as a community to manage a $100 million project to successful completion. The project continues as a testament to what can be imagined and implemented through collective Rutgers community effort.

The Rutgers libraries are now offering access to important digital library resources for students and faculty on all three university campuses and sharing resources throughout the state by way of the New Jersey Virtual Academic Library Environment (NJVALE), in which Rutgers plays a leading role. Rutgers was also a primary architect of NJEDge.Net, the state's higher education network, which is designed to extend higher education's outreach

to off-campus learners, K-12 schools, and corporate and community constituents across New Jersey.

Research, education, and public service grants rose in a steep
upward trajectory from $92.8 million in FY1990 to an all-time high
of $222.4 million in FY2001. Rutgers's research and development
expenditures rose by 95 percent in this period, placing it among
the top ten AAU public universities in the rate of growth in this
R&D measure. The emphasis of the strategic plan on productive
relationships with business and industry is reflected in the growth
of the number of U.S. patent applications, from 20 in 1991 to 119
in 2000. During the same period, Rutgers increased its annual roy-
alty income threefold, from $1.7 million in FY1991 to $5.2 million
in FY2000. Even more significant is the total of forty-eight spin-off
companies that the Rutgers faculty has created, among them thirty-
five in New Jersey. Private giving, which provides critical support
for scholarships and fellowships, academic programs, and research
funding, has risen exponentially during the $500 million major
funding campaign *Creating the Future.* Just forty-five months into
the seventy-two-month campaign, the total raised is more than
$400 million.

The Rutgers strategic planning process has uniquely blended
academic and fiscal planning by focusing on multidisciplinary, cutting-edge academic initiatives, creating a cyclical proposal submission and evaluation process that requires multidisciplinary,
multiunit participation and support, and creating administrative
support structures to help the process along. In the future, this
constantly evolving process of planning and resource direction will
produce greater integration of programs across disciplines,
schools, and campuses, continuing to strengthen Rutgers as one
university in which the whole is greater than the sum of its parts.
It will also encourage more partnerships between Rutgers and the
schools, the state and federal governments, and the private sector,
increasing Rutgers's resources and its contributions to New Jersey's
educational quality and economic gains. We may expect increasing success in fundraising from all of the sectors we serve and with
which we are building mutually beneficial partnerships. All of these
efforts will produce enhanced visibility for the university and
increase its well-deserved reputation for distinction in research,
teaching, and service.

The Committee on Institutional Cooperation's Academic Leadership Program

Robert Secor
Program Coordinator and Vice Provost for
Academic Affairs, Pennsylvania State University

In 1956, the presidents of the Big Ten universities met for the twentieth year to discuss their mutual problems. Those problems included such topics as trends of faculty salaries, the growing impulse of state governments and governing boards to become involved with the workings of the university, ways of preserving academic freedom, and support of libraries. It was at this meeting that the idea for the Committee on Institutional Cooperation (CIC) was born. The CIC, presided over by the chief academic officers of the Big Ten institutions (Illinois, Indiana, Iowa, Michigan, Michigan State, Minnesota, Northwestern, Ohio State, Penn State, Purdue, and Wisconsin) and the University of Chicago, came into being in 1958. It has been addressing some of the same problems that the presidents were facing in their yearly meetings when they formed the CIC, along with many other problems that have come up as the years advance into the twenty-first century.

The principle behind CIC programs is that there are opportunities opened to us when we act collectively or in cooperation that are not available when we act simply as individual institutions. Such cooperative efforts offer opportunities for greater educational possibilities and experimentation, for concerted action, and for economic savings by sharing resources and as a result of economies of scale. CIC working groups that involve all of its member institutions include deans of the various disciplinary colleges, affirmative action officers, international student officers, faculty senate leaders, learning technology groups, library directors, purchasing directors, registrars, study abroad directors, university press directors, and many others. These groups have in turn developed a number of collaborative projects. The list includes a Traveling Scholars Program, which facilitates graduate students' spending some time studying with a professor at another CIC institution; participating in partner study abroad programs; a Virtual Electronic Library (VEL) serving all of the CIC institutions; university press collaboration; interinstitutional sharing of online courses; purchasing and licensing coordination; and programs of collaborative professional development.

The Academic Leadership Program: The Need and the Aims

The CIC felt it needed to invest in collaborative professional development programs because human resources are our universities' greatest investment. In particular, higher education was asking the questions "How are we training the academic leaders of tomorrow?" and "How can we ensure that these leaders of tomorrow will bring greater diversity to our institutions than the leaders of today?" In response to these questions, in 1989 the CIC initiated the Academic Leadership Program (ALP), with the idea that it could create a leadership program more efficient and more effective by pooling the resources of its member institutions. These resources are human as well as financial, since by developing strong faculties and academic administrators all of our institutions have earned significant academic reputations. They are always listed among the top third of public universities, with several usually listed among the top ten. None of the other sports conferences have a counterpart to the CIC.

The CIC consortium recognized that academic administrators at research institutions such as ours have dual roles. They must be educational leaders and at the same time act as managers of large, complex organizations. They are challenged by tightening budgets, changing student populations, and increasing pressures from external sources. To find creative, workable solutions to the problems that lie ahead, our universities must pay serious attention to leadership development. Even though agencies, consulting firms, and institutions currently offer many professional development programs that serve the overall higher education community, the CIC members wanted to create a program that would be specifically oriented to the challenges of academic administration at major research universities. (See www.cic.uiuc. edu/programs/alp/ALP.html.)

In designing the program, the CIC set these goals:

- To prepare more individuals for leadership positions in the CIC universities or similar research and teaching institutions, in contrast to leadership programs targeting individuals from the entire range of higher education
- To augment the diversity of individuals prepared for leadership
- To minimize the total cost while maximizing the number of individuals participating in leadership training programs

The Program Design

Three times each year for the past thirteen years, a class of ALP Fellows (about fifty in all, with four to six chosen by each institution) has met at a different CIC campus, from a Thursday afternoon through lunch on Saturday. They learn from experienced administrators and peers from their own and other CIC institutions, and from each other. Participants include academic administrators, such as program directors, department chairs, deans (often assistant and associate deans), and faculty leaders. The programs are designed to enhance and test their leadership skills and make them more aware of the various issues and challenges that are facing higher education, now and in the future.

How the Program Works

The director of the CIC appoints a program coordinator from one of the CIC institutions to a three-year term. At the same time, each campus has a CIC ALP liaison, who, frequently along with the university provost, chooses the year's Fellows and then mentors those Fellows throughout the year. The liaisons as a whole form the planning group for each year's seminars and serve as an advisory group for the program coordinator. The liaison whose campus is hosting the seminar has special responsibility for working with the program coordinator in planning and implementing the program on that campus.

Liaisons meet in the summer at the Big Ten Conference Center in Chicago. They review the previous year's programs and discuss those of the coming academic year. They also meet throughout each seminar to review its progress and plug holes when they arise (as when a presenter is delayed or has to cancel after the seminar begins), and also to anticipate the upcoming seminars. Sometimes our liaisons themselves present, or fill in for presenters, since they are themselves experienced academic leaders, usually from high positions in the administrative structure of their own institutions.

Each seminar draws widely on the major talent that we have in our Big Ten institutions, including deans, vice presidents, provosts, and presidents. In the spirit of cooperation, presenters from our institutions contribute their time and expertise. Demonstrating their commitment to the program, our provosts and presidents are important participants in all of our seminars. They host receptions and dinners and often make major presentations and serve on panels. Each seminar also involves group discussions and activities, through which our Fellows learn from each other and establish strong relationships that build from seminar to seminar. By the third seminar, they all feel that they have a number of new friends and colleagues throughout the Big Ten, whom they can call on for professional advice in the years to come.

Last year, our keynote speakers were Mark G. Yudoff, president of the University of Minnesota, at the Minnesota session; Stanley O. Ikenberry, president emeritus of the University of Illinois at Urbana–Champaign (and immediate past president of the American Council on Education) at the one in Illinois; and Yolanda Moses, president of the American Association for Higher Education at our seminar at Michigan.

Our first seminar, on leadership and human resources, featured a panel called Academic Leadership and Diversity, which included Rodney A. Erickson, Penn State's executive vice president and provost; a workshop "Academic Faculty Development and

Performance"; a presentation "Dealing with Manipulative and Destructive Behaviors"; and special sessions with such subjects as academic and legal issues, the legal climate for diversity in higher education, balancing work/life demands, conflict resolution, and faculty development to improve teaching and learning.

The second seminar, Long-Range Planning and Budgeting, included a panel discussion of sources for funding, including federal, state, self-generated auxiliary, and gift funds. Edward J. Ray, provost at Ohio State, gave a thought-provoking talk, "Building Academic Community Through Strategic Planning." It was followed by a discussion of three approaches to strategic planning, led by a panel that included Richard H. Herman, provost and vice chancellor for Academic Affairs at the University of Illinois at Urbana–Champaign. On the second day, the Fellows divided into small groups to put themselves in the place of the president at the fictional Quality University, as they discussed a case study on university budgeting. The session was led by Weldon Ihrig, executive vice president at the University of Washington. The final morning featured sessions on financing the academic health center, with the senior vice presidents from the health centers at Minnesota and Penn State. We concluded with a panel on planning and budgeting at the department level, consisting of a dean and two department heads, from three different institutions.

Seminar III was the University of the Future and Motivating Change. We structured it on a cover article in the *AAHE Bulletin* written by our keynote speaker, in which she focused on four key areas for the future, which we adapted as "technology and higher education," "the faculty of the future," "accountability," and "motivating and sustaining change." These became the four key topics for our seminar, and after an address by Professor Moses each was introduced by a panel or a speaker. For example, the topic motivating and sustaining change was introduced by a stimulating presentation by Interim President Joseph White. The Fellows were then asked to meet in groups to assimilate what they learned from the presentations, as well as from a good amount of reading sent to them in advance of the meeting, and then to present their views on these topics in our Saturday sessions. By the end of the three-seminar program, we had essentially turned the participants from listeners and questioners into presenters themselves.

Summary of Outcomes

By sharing resources, the Big Ten public institutions have been able to deliver a high-quality, yearlong leadership experience to the Fellows of the consortium. The initiative has been successful by a number of measures:

- *Numbers.* Beginning with thirty-one participants from nine participating institutions in 1989–90, the program has steadily increased its numbers, so that the average number of participants each year is now between fifty-five and sixty from eleven participating CIC institutions. At the completion of this year's program, 635 fellows will have graduated.
- *Costs.* By sharing, the ambitious program has been funded at a fraction of the cost of similar leadership development programs. Excluding the cost of travel to the seminar, but including meals and lodging, the average total cost per Fellow to participate in all three seminars has been less than $2,000 over the past six years. The program has succeeded because administrative leaders from our consortium of institutions have been exceptionally cooperative in sharing their knowledge and contributing their time; some have participated year after year in working with each class of Fellows.
- *Diversity goals.* Reflecting the program's goal of increasing the diversity of those whom we are training for leadership positions, 27 percent of its Fellows over the past three years have been people of color, and 60 percent were women.
- *Participant satisfaction and development.* Each seminar is evaluated every year and receives a consistently high evaluation. On a ten-point scale, the average score per seminar over the past five years has been over 8.6. As one of the fellows wrote in her year-end evaluation last year: "Each weekend program has just been better and better, and I think this is partly due to the developing relationships among the participants." Moreover, our participants have moved to higher administrative positions at a regular rate, with a number moving to positions as deans, and in one case provost at a CIC institution.
- *Other outcomes.* There are also positive outcomes of the ALP that go beyond the three seminars. For one, ALP liaisons have extended leadership development for their Fellows to their home

campuses, while relating those efforts to the ALP. These initiatives are discussed at our summer liaison meeting and are listed and described in our *Liaison's Handbook*. Although campus programs for ALP Fellows vary, they include briefing meetings, at which Fellows learn from top administrators how their own institutions approach issues that will be discussed at the upcoming seminar. These Fellows thereby become more knowledgeable listeners and better participants at the seminar. Debriefing meetings with the university provost allow Fellows to share what they have heard in order to get their own provost's views, and to suggest initiatives that might be tried at their own campuses. One liaison arranges for Fellows to shadow an administrator of their choice for a day; another plans a series of luncheon discussions with key administrators; and another holds a series of events and activities around a particular theme for the Fellowship year.

The success of the ALP has had another consequence—the development of another CIC leadership program for what we call department executive officers (DEO). Modeled on the ALP, and five years old, the DEO program also brings a group of leaders together, from a Thursday afternoon through Saturday morning. The difference is that this program meets only once a year and is more narrowly targeted at chairs and directors who oversee the work of a department faculty and staff.

In addition to hearing major speakers on such subjects as survival tactics for departmental administrators, how to handle the stress of the job, how to mentor and evaluate faculty, and how to do fundraising and budgeting at the department level, chairs and directors have the opportunity to compare notes and experiences with others who oversee similar administrative units at public research-oriented institutions. Several times during the seminar, chairs and directors meet in small groups to present real problems they are facing and to get advice from peer department heads from outside their institutions, with whom they can speak with a frankness that is not possible when everybody knows the players involved. Participants return with new ideas to share with other department heads at their own institutions.

In the ALP and chairs and directors programs, we have all come to appreciate the advantages of partnering in leadership development from a peer group with similar problems and issues, but with a wealth of human resources to draw on as we teach and learn from each other. Our Fellows bring back new ideas and enthusiasms, and they frequently help to develop and shape leadership programs at their campuses on the basis of their experiences. But the most important outcome of the ALP program is that so many of our past ALP Fellows have advanced in leadership positions, either in their own institutions or elsewhere, and have already taken their place in the next generation of academic leaders.

Chapter Seven

Recognizing That Everyone in the Institution Is a Teacher

Focusing on the Student Experience

The topic of undergraduate teaching—its quality, cost, outcomes, and appropriate relationship to research and other institutional activities—occupies a prominent place in nearly every discussion of excellence in higher education. A consequence of this dialogue is a renewed interest in the student perspective on the college experience (Boyer Commission, 1998; Kellogg Commission, 1997; Light, 2001). One of the most interesting insights to emerge from these discussions is a recognition of the importance of distinguishing between *teaching* and *learning*. Conventionally, the words *teaching* and *learning* have been uttered in a single breath, as if they were inseparably linked to one another conceptually and operationally. A more careful analysis of the communication processes involved, however, indicates that this is clearly not the case. This recognition has a number of significant implications for understanding the dynamics of the student experience, and furthering the quality of educational practice generally.

Human Communication, Teaching, and Learning

The communication process has often been described using the $S \rightarrow M \rightarrow C \rightarrow R = E$ model (Ruben and Kim, 1975; Ruben and Stewart, 1998), where S refers to a *source*—the initiator of a communication encounter. Applied in a classroom context, the source

249

would be the teacher. *M* signifies *messages*—the content or information in a lecture, textbook, Website, or lab assignment. *C* denotes *channel*—the print, visual, vocal, or electronic means by which messages are conveyed. Students are *Rs*—*receivers*. The arrows and equal symbol are meant to suggest that the $S \rightarrow M \rightarrow C \rightarrow R$ sequence results in the achievement of particular goals, outcomes, or *effects*—the *E*. As is apparent, this framework can easily be applied to a description of the instructional process in terms of a teacher preparing and delivering messages to students through various channels and bringing about particular learning outcomes.

In this way of thinking about human communication, tremendous power and influence are attributed to a source and to his or her intentions, to messages, and to the channels through which messages are transmitted from a source to intended recipients. It is assumed that the message received will correspond with the message sent: $MS = MR$.

It has become increasingly clear, however, that human communication is not nearly so simple a process as implied by earlier efforts to model its dynamics, and nowhere are the inadequacies of the $S \rightarrow M \rightarrow C \rightarrow R = E$ communication paradigm more apparent than when thinking about education. The model implies that learning is largely controlled by teachers who impart instructional messages to students through lectures, books, and other channels. The perspective further suggests that when lectures, assignments, and other instructional messages are well formed and articulately delivered, the desired learning outcomes naturally follow. This way of thinking also leads to the view that a teacher's primary concern ought be *subject matter content, information,* or *knowledge,* and the construction and delivery of quality messages through appropriate channels: Is the information in lectures, texts, discussions, Websites, and lab protocols correct and up to date? Is the mode of delivery effective and efficient? Is the technology appropriate? Are tests and other evaluative mechanisms valid and reliable?

Systems theories of communication are considerably more helpful for thinking about teaching and learning. They assert that communication and learning are natural and inevitable; they are ongoing and often invisible processes that occur as living beings process messages in the environment to adapt in some small or large way to the challenges and opportunities that present themselves (Miller, 1965; Ruben, 1983, 1993b; Ruben and Kim, 1975; Thayer, 1968). As Spence (2001, p. 15) notes, "Human beings are fantastic learners—mastering millions of details of language, objects, human behavior, and patterns of relations among those details. And they learn all the time."

The dynamics of student *learning* are exceedingly complex and do not align in any lock-step fashion to the dynamics of teaching; MR seldom corresponds well to MS. If we think about education and human communication not so much in terms of teaching but rather in terms of learning, the process begins with a focus on the receivers and their goals, needs, expectations, and environments, and the messages that are likely to become important to them, rather than on information sources—teachers—and on what they intend, what they say or write, how they do it, or the books and materials they use.

Concerns about course content, teacher preparation, delivery, and support technology are certainly vital considerations; it is not the intent here to suggest otherwise. However, systems theories of communication remind us that what is needed is a broadened and enriched view of instruction, one that focuses more on the teacher as being the architect of learning environments and experiences and a guide and mentor in the learning process rather than as a source or conduit of information (Ruben, 1977, 1999; Spence, 2001).

Accessing the Student Experience

Communication systems theories make clear that, as learners, we are surrounded by messages that compete for our attention and that present challenges and opportunities to which we may react. Detecting, prioritizing, interpreting, and acting upon these messages and the interpretations we make of them is a fundamental aspect of communication and life. This view makes it clear that a college education and its consequences are shaped by the interactions that transpire between the learner and the physical and social environment as an individual progresses through the various stages and processes that constitute the college or university experience (Astin, 1993; Boyer, 1997; Kuh, Douglas, Lund, and Ramin-Gyurnek, 1994; Ruben, 1977, 1999). From this perspective, the student experience begins with the first exposure to campus life and continues through graduation and beyond, progressing through a series of adaptation and learning stages illustrated in simplified form in Figure 7.1. Each stage consists of innumerable encounters and interactions with the institution and its representatives, and each generates potential learning demands and opportunities. At every stage, students navigate in a physical and symbolic environment composed of places and spaces, planned and unplanned events. Some are academic and some cocurricular. Some involve faculty, others staff, still others fellow students.

Figure 7.1. A Process View of the Undergraduate Student Experience.

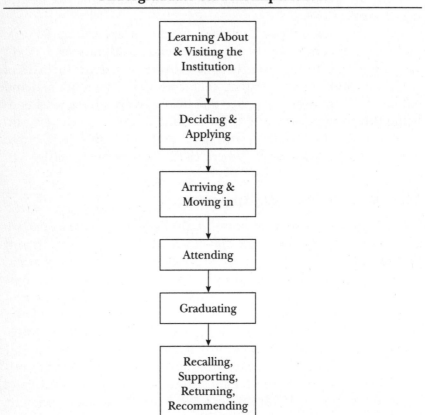

A Study of the Student Experience: What Students Remember

For those of us who work in colleges and universities, there is a natural tendency to think about these and other stages in a learner's experience from the perspective of the institution. We typically conceptualize such events from the viewpoint of our own roles and the outcomes we envision—that is, in terms of the messages and meanings we intend to convey, the channels through which we expect the learning to take place, and the effects we plan and hope for. When we are able to access students' perspectives on these same events, it is often quite astonishing to realize how different the worlds of the educator and the learner can be.

Illustrating the point is a study by the author utilizing a critical-incident method[1] in which students were asked to reflect on their college experiences and to identify and describe particularly memorable positive or negative events (Carson, 1996; Ruben, 1995d). This was the approach used by the author in a study that focused on 165 undergraduate students in an introductory social science course at Rutgers (Ruben, 1995d). The course included students from a variety of majors and colleges. Most were first- and second-year students, but there were also a smaller number of third- and fourth-year students enrolled in the course. Each student in the class was given a sheet of paper with the following question and asked to respond anonymously:

> Think back on all your experiences as an undergraduate student.
> WHAT ONE EXPERIENCE MOST STANDS OUT IN YOUR MIND?
> This can be any experience related to college life involving classes, social activities, students, faculty, or administrators, or any other aspect of your life at the university. (Please describe the experience in several sentences below.)

The resulting narratives were then content-analyzed to identify themes, and patterns were identified.

The students described a total of 205 experiences. These were content-analyzed to identify *themes* and the *roles* of the individuals mentioned[2] (faculty members, staff, other students). Four recurrent themes were identified:

- *Academics:* experiences involving academic aspects of college life such as classes, instruction, exams, library use, lectures, studying, and content learning
- *Policies and procedures:* experiences involving university policies, regulations, rules, and procedures
- *Facilities, accommodations, environment:* experiences involving university facilities, accommodations, or the campus environment
- *Interpersonal relations and communication:* experiences involving interpersonal communication, relationships, or social interaction, including encounters with faculty, teaching assistants, administrators, other students, tour guides, or other individuals on campus

Frequencies were calculated for each thematic category, and a ranking was developed. As shown in Figure 7.2, experiences related to interpersonal communication and relationships accounted for 44.4 percent of all memorable events reported and ranked first. Experiences related to facilities, accommodations, and the physical environment ranked second (25.8 percent); experiences that involved policies and procedures were third (17.1 percent); and experiences related to academics came in last, accounting for only 12.7 percent of experiences reported.

The Findings and Their Significance

The content of the narratives point to the difficulties of adjusting to campus life and new challenges, new surroundings, new freedoms, new colleagues, new rules, and new responsibilities. The personal and emotional baggage that many students today bring with them to their college years exacerbates the challenges of adjustment to college. Student affairs professionals remind us, for instance, that this generation of students struggles with issues of intimacy and involvement, and that students often report having seldom observed successful adult romantic relationships (Levine and Cureton, 1998). Studies in the late 1990s report a rise in eating disorders on 58 percent of the campuses studied, in drug abuse on 42 percent, in alcohol abuse on 35 percent, in gambling on 25 percent, and in suicide attempts on 23 percent of campuses, which gives additional insight into the problems of adjustment and the complexity of the contemporary student experience (Levine and Cureton, 1998).

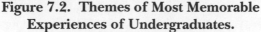

Figure 7.2. Themes of Most Memorable Experiences of Undergraduates.

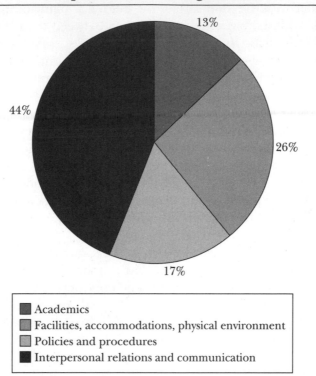

- Academics
- Facilities, accommodations, physical environment
- Policies and procedures
- Interpersonal relations and communication

The study of student narratives illustrates the complexity and diversity of the teaching and learning environment. Their stories also speak to the richness and range of students' experiences at any one institution. The study also suggests that several generic themes are common across students. By implication, the students' stories also inform us about probable sources of satisfaction and dissatisfaction, and they contribute to an understanding of the criteria upon which images of educational institutions are formed.

The Importance of Interpersonal Relations and Communication

It is most interesting to note that the largest group of narratives were *not* concerned with academics or instruction—what the institution regards as its primary mission relative to students. This finding may come as no surprise to those in the student life professions or others familiar with the literature of the field. For many of us without this background, however, the disconnect between the world of the faculty and staff and that of the student is quite surprising—perhaps a bit disconcerting—and an important topic for contemplation. For instance, Richard Light (2001), in discussing the results of interviews with Harvard seniors over a ten-year period, comments: "I had assumed that most important and memorable academic learning goes on inside the classroom, while outside activities provide a useful but modest supplement. The evidence shows that the opposite is true: learning outside of classes, especially in residence settings and extracurricular activities . . . is vital. When we asked students to think of a specific, critical incident or moment that had changed them profoundly, four-fifths of them chose a situation or event outside the classroom" (Light, 2001, p. 8).

The student narratives in the present study (Ruben, 1995d) point to the same conclusion as that reached by Light and colleagues on the basis of the interviews he conducted. Students' most poignant memories seldom related to formal communication in a lecture, discussion, or lab, but rather to a broad range of formal and informal, intended and unintended communication events, only a relatively small number of which involve faculty.

In terms of what students seem to most remember and value, communication and relationships were very important. Encounters with individuals in academic roles accounted for only 7.5 percent of the 160 interpersonal encounters mentioned by students in their narratives. Experiences involving other students were mentioned most often (37.5 percent), followed by collective references to groups (22.5 percent). Members of the staff were mentioned in 20.6 percent of the recollections, while faculty, instructors, and TAs were mentioned in only 7.5 percent of the narratives, and administrators in 4.4 percent of the situations described. Ultimately, these results remind us that much of what is important to student learning experiences occurs outside classes and classrooms, in a manner that does not necessarily conform to institutional logic, and is unrelated to the formalized teaching efforts by the faculty.

Is the perspective that emerges from this study uniquely an undergraduate phenomenon? Perhaps not. When students in one field were asked to respond to the same open-ended question near the completion of the first semester of their doctoral program, the overall results closely paralleled findings for undergraduate students. These results—summarized in Figures 7.3 and 7.4—are based on a small group of students in only one field and may not be applicable to other groups, other disciplines, or other points in students' graduate programs. Nonetheless, it is interesting to note that for this class of first-year doctoral students, 64 percent of their most remembered experiences had to do with interpersonal communication, and a majority of the critical incidents involved program administrators and support staff rather than faculty.

Figure 7.3. Themes of Most Memorable Experiences of Graduate Students.

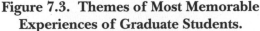

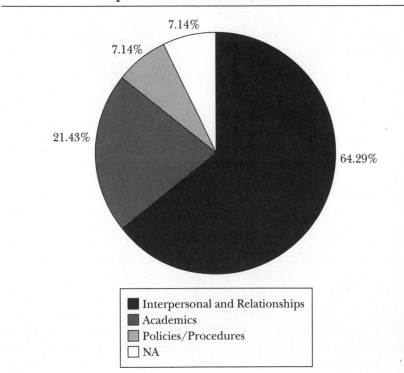

Figure 7.4. Roles Associated with Most Memorable Experiences Among Graduate Students.

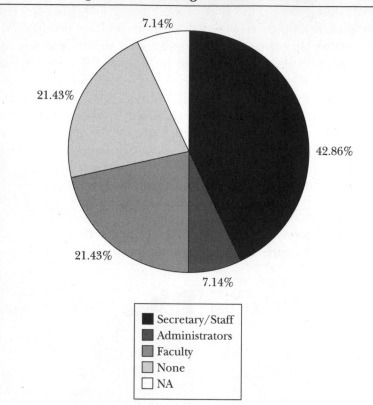

Implications: Teaching in All That We Do[3]

The study summarized in the preceding section is a useful reminder of what many of us know—or knew during our college years—but may easily forget. The student experience is often quite different from that designed by educators. Learning takes place everywhere and anywhere, in a classroom, for credit, and inspired by teachers; but learning also occurs outside a classroom for no credit—from friends in a class, staff in the library, receptionists in an administrative office, campus policies and procedures, even from the appearance and maintenance of buildings on campus. Student learning focuses on the basics of chemistry and the basics of living away from home, on fashioning essays and developing one's identity. It involves lessons on finding research sources and finding friends, on paying attention and paying bills, and on writing papers and righting relationships.

Another important, though perhaps less obvious, insight is that we often think far too narrowly about who the educators are. Every hour, thousands of faculty members enter classrooms at colleges and universities throughout the country to discharge their responsibilities as teachers. Thus the origin of the phrase "the faculty are the university." But there are certainly many other teachers, as well.

Student Affairs Professionals

We know that student affairs professionals play a vital role as educators. Research on student learning outcomes in the 1980s has led to growing recognition of the interplay between the curricular and cocurricular domain. Recognized also is the importance of collaboration between academic affairs and student affairs, following many years of separation of these two areas ("Improve Learning . . . ," 2002): "[Although] colleges traditionally organize their activities into 'academic affairs' and 'student affairs' . . . this dichotomy has little relevance to post-college life [and to] . . . one's job performance, family life, and community activities" (American College Personnel Association, 1994, p. 1). Viewed from the perspective of the student experience, boundaries between academic and student affairs are extremely artificial; every effort should be made to create seamless institutional relationships between these functions (Schroeder, 1999). There are many areas in which effective partnerships between academic and student affairs can enrich the education offered by colleges and universities. As Terenzini and Pascarella (1994) note: "If undergraduate education is to be enhanced, faculty members, joined by academic and student affairs administrators, must devise ways to deliver undergraduate education that are as comprehensive and integrated as the ways that students actually learn. A whole new mindset is needed to capitalize on the interrelatedness of in- and out-of-class influences on student learning and the functional interconnectedness of academic and student affairs divisions" (p. 32).

There are many areas where formalized and explicit collaboration between academic and student affairs is appropriate, among them orientation for new students; first-year programs; advising; and curricular innovations such as service learning, learning communities, leadership development initiatives, special programs for diverse student populations, student experience assessment and evaluation, and retention efforts ("Improve Learning . . . ," 2002; American Association of Higher Education, 1997–2000; American Association for Higher Education, American College Personnel Association, and National Association of Student Personnel Administrators, 1998; Astin, 1993; Kezar, Hirsh, and Burack, 2001; Kuh, 2001b; Zlotkowski, 2001).

The Many Other Teachers

What of other staff? Of course, we are often told that staff throughout colleges and universities *support* the core mission of the institution. But this is a limited and simplistic view of the role played by staff. Indeed, one of the profound implications of a review of communication theory as it relates to teaching-and-learning, and the study of what students most remember discussed previously, is that staff members do considerably more than what is generally implied by the phrase "support the core mission." Like the faculty, they too are teachers. In practice, we are all teachers—the full- and part-time faculty and TAs, and each and every staff member. Faculty members carry out their instructional responsibilities in the classroom, in the laboratory, and during office hours. Support and service staff members teach in libraries, residence halls, buses, health centers, the cashier's office, the bookstore, and the campus police headquarters—in each and every business and administrative office that deals with students.[4]

Concluding Comments

Faculty *and* all members of the administration, professional, and support staff teach through every one of the tens of thousands of interpersonal encounters with students, guests, and one another that transpire daily on our campuses. Undergraduate students typically enter college or university at a critical and formative point in their intellectual, social, and personal development. It is a time when most begin to play a much more central role in managing their own lives. For some, this may well be the first time they have lived away from home and assumed primary responsibility for managing their own health care, finances, priorities, and time. It is also a time when many students find themselves in any number of situations where they are with others with whom they may have little in common. As one student recalls (Magolda, 1999):

> I think the general theme of what I got out of my college career was a chance to work with a lot of different people and see so many different perspectives on life through my male-female relationships, my fraternity brotherhood relationships, through my acquaintance relationships. I look back at college and I say "Wow! That was great." A lot of it was the interaction with people and a chance to see things in different ways and really grow as a person. You'd take up issues like abortion and how your opinions have evolved on that throughout my college years. And dealing with women. When I first came into college it was like the woman should be the subordinate type person. Now from my involvement with people in school I've gotten away from that. . . . A lot of it was dictated by environments I was in—student government, being a Resident Advisor my sophomore year, campaign manager for two years, student credit union, the National College Student Credit Council, my fraternity—dealing with people, taking on leadership roles . . . the personal contacts I had with different people [1999, p. 22].

Clearly, students gain important knowledge and insight inside the classroom. But they are also being taught poignant and enduring lessons outside the classroom as they watch how faculty, administrators, and staff at all levels relate to them and one another, participate in various activities, strive to understand, adapt to campus policies and procedures, and learn how a complex organization functions.

Together, the staff, the faculty, and the administration create the educational experience and the images and the frames through which students come to view courses, the disciplines, departments, colleges and universities, higher education, organizations, and society generally. Together, we are extending a complex and diverse array of lessons—for the next generation of lawyers, doctors, teachers, engineers, artists, corporate managers, health care providers, and civic leaders. What kinds of lessons are we providing? What kinds of organizations, relationships, and environments do we offer as models? Are we teaching the values, ethics, and practices that are needed to create the world we want to exist? Or, by default, are we reinforcing the full range of interpersonal, organizational, and societal systems about which we may so often complain?

Viewed from this broader perspective on teaching and learning, every contact with a student is an encounter that either contributes to or detracts from the educational excellence. In practice, we are all stewards of the student experience, as instructors, architects, tour guides, role models, and mentors; we share responsibility for the quality of the teaching and learning environments we create.

The implications are several. First, we need to devote more attention than we often do to understanding the student learning experience—as distinct from the institutional teaching experience. Second, we must do all that we can to design more integrated and student-centered programs and services that are responsive to the logic of the student experience. Third, of those aspects of the teaching and learning processes over which we have direct and immediate influence, there is nothing more important than our own words and actions. We are sources, channels, and messages. We are the lesson.

Notes

1. The critical-incident method was first described by Flanagan (1954) and popularized through the work of Herzberg, Mauzner, and Snyderman (1959). The approach has subsequently been used in a variety of fields, including intercultural communication (Ruben and Kealey, 1979), health (Ruben, 1993b, 1993c; Bowman and Ruben, 1986), and education (Carson, 1996; Light, 2001; Ruben, 1995b).
2. The valence of the narratives—whether those reported on positive or negative events—was also assessed. See Ruben (1995b).
3. This phrase was first used by W. David Burns in an address to the Rutgers University Health Service staff in the late 1980s.
4. An excellent illustration of how faculty and staff can collaborate in the design and implementation of formalized teaching and learning opportunities is described in the Chapter Three narrative by Connaughton and Quinlan.

Narratives

Recognizing That Everyone in the Institution Is a Teacher: Focusing on the Student Experience

For any number of seemingly logical reasons, colleges and universities are organized in a manner that clearly differentiates between departments and personnel whose work relates to the academic mission and those whose work pertains to administrative, service, and support services. These structural distinctions—and the institutional priorities that they reflect—make good sense in some respects. However, when viewed from the perspective of the experience of students, alumni, the public, and even potential donors and sponsors, these distinctions are often irrelevant, even dysfunctional. Distinctions, for instance, between a tenure-track faculty member, an adjunct faculty member, or a teaching assistant may go undetected by undergraduate students, who simply perceive and perhaps refer to all of them as their "professors" or "instructors." For such students, each member of the instructional staff of an institution plays a critically important role in shaping the perceptions and actualities of teaching excellence, regardless of his or her institutional role and title.

In many research institutions, teaching assistants play a particularly crucial role, both because of the number of such individuals involved in instruction and because they are often among the first academic representatives of the institutions that students encounter when they enter the university. Increasing recognition of the influential role teaching assistants play—particularly for first-year students—has led to the creation of professional development programs for this group. One such initiative, the Teaching Assistant Project at Rutgers, is described by Program Director Barbara Bender in the first narrative in this section.

Another important point in this chapter is that the teaching function of colleges and universities is not exclusively the work of the faculty—or of academic units. Important lessons are taught by staff in all departments. Acknowledgment of the important role of administrative and service units in creating the student experience is a defining theme of the quality service and communication initiative at the University of Cincinnati, described in the second narrative by James Tucker and Marie Sutthoff.

The power of the community as a source of meaningful student learning experiences is the theme of the final narrative in this section, in which Michael Shafer describes the Citizenship and Service Education program at Rutgers.

Enhancing the Quality of Graduate Student Instruction: The Teaching Assistant Project (TAP)

Barbara E. Bender
Associate Dean and Director, Teaching Assistant
Project, Graduate School–New Brunswick, Rutgers
University

Rutgers University in New Brunswick, New Jersey, is a publicly supported doctoral-granting research extensive university. A member of the Association of American Universities, in fall 2002 the campus comprised thirty-six thousand students, including twenty-eight thousand undergraduate and eight thousand graduate students. Similar to many comprehensive research universities, Rutgers is perennially seeking to develop programs that complement and augment the curriculum to enable the university to meet its multifaceted mission of teaching, research, and service.

Under the leadership of the Graduate School–New Brunswick (the Ph.D. unit of Rutgers, New Brunswick), the Teaching Assistant Project (TAP) was developed to enhance the quality of both undergraduate and graduate education. This narrative is an overview of the role of teaching assistants in undergraduate instruction and why Rutgers created TAP; it discusses the confluence of forces that precipitated the growth of programs to prepare graduate students how to teach and describes the specific components and scope of the TA project.

Identifying a Gap

Most college and university faculty members are quick to admit the abject terror they felt at having to stand in front of a class for the first time. They confess that they did not know if they had enough material for the entire class session, were unsure if they were going to be able to speak coherently in front of a group, and were frightened about what to do with the inevitable question for which they did not have the answer.

Although catalogues published by research universities typically enumerate multiple and complementary missions involving teaching and research, those institutions that educate the majority of Ph.D. students have paid little attention to preparing their graduate students to assume their role as today's teaching assistant, and tomorrow's faculty member. It is not a trade secret that most college faculty members, though having well-developed research skills, have had almost no education in the art of teaching and have learned to manage a classroom through a sink-or-swim initiation. Nowhere is the challenge more evident than when doctoral programs socialize their students to consider teaching undergraduates as a secondary, annoying responsibility. Anecdotes abound regarding graduate students who have been cautioned by their advisors to hide their commitment to becoming good teachers because it would hurt their chances of securing an appropriate research appointment after graduation.

Forces of Change

Until recently, the notion of including instruction about student learning and pedagogy would be heresy in any self-respecting Ph.D. program. In the past several years, however, extraordinary changes have begun to occur. There seems to be an almost perfect confluence of academic, financial, and consumer forces that is transforming the professional preparation of Ph.D. students. These forces serve as a catalyst in creating a college teaching movement that will lead to a permanent change in U.S. higher education—a change that will improve the learning experience of hundreds of thousands of undergraduate and graduate students.

Many in this generation of college parents were taught by TAs and now expect more for their tuition dollars than did their own parents. Today's college students have equally high standards and expect their instructors to be knowledgeable in their field and to have the experience and skills to teach effectively. College students also expect that their TAs will have an adequate command of English, an understanding of what it means to be in charge of a class, and the professional demeanor to lead the students in all aspects of the course.

At universities across the country, there are faculty members who are leading the effort to transform a historically institutionalized laissez faire attitude toward teaching (Showalter, 1999). Some are younger faculty who were exposed to pedagogical training in their own doctoral programs, while others are seasoned veterans who have identified serious shortcomings in the quality of undergraduate classroom instruction. These faculty members recognize the critical importance of good teaching in the learning process, and they can make the difference in transforming a culture of indifference to pedagogy to one of commitment to excellence in teaching (Showalter, 1999).

The increasing demands for accountability in higher education by accreditation bodies, legislators, voters, employers, and consumers are also forcing universities to accept responsibility for teaching their doctoral students how to teach, thereby enhancing the quality of both undergraduate and graduate instruction. Although graduate schools have always recruited graduate students who have the best potential to succeed as researchers and scholars, they must now also consider whether or not these same graduate students have the ability to serve successfully as TAs. To ensure that the instructional experiences that are promised to undergraduates in promotional materials and catalogues are actually provided, universities need to create opportunities for graduate students to learn how to teach.

Additionally important is the fact that today's graduate students enter doctoral programs from around the world. To accommodate this diversity of educational preparation, cultural backgrounds, and varying English language skills, TAs must be oriented to the culture of the classroom and the nature of undergraduate education in the United States.

Teaching Assistants Make a Difference

Teaching graduate students to teach makes sense from a range of perspectives. Most important, TAs who know how to teach promote and foster classroom environments that strengthen the quality of the undergraduate learning experience. Typically, undergraduate students are more interested in their courses when the teacher is effective. The greater the student interest, the more likely undergraduates are to do the readings, complete the assignments, and become engaged in the learning process.

Whether they want to be or not, TAs are important role models for undergraduates and often serve as influential mentors for the students in their classes. TAs make a significant difference in the lives of undergraduates. An enthusiastic and committed graduate student can help to transform an undergraduate student not only into a major in the field but into a potential graduate student. The reverse is also true: when graduate students fail in their teaching duties, undergraduate learning suffers. A disorganized, ill-prepared, and ineffective classroom instructor can undermine the hopes of even the most dedicated undergraduate to pursue the discipline in future semesters.

Generations of academic leaders and students have discussed the need to improve the quality of the undergraduate learning experience. After many years of discussion, there are now numerous institutional and grant projects and higher education association initiatives powerfully influencing the development of teaching programs for graduate students at universities across the country (Preparing Future Faculty Program, 2002).

The Rutgers University Teaching Assistant Project

The Graduate School–New Brunswick of Rutgers University instituted a multidimensional professional development program for TAs in 1987. With approximately eight hundred TAs in New Brunswick, TAP provides programming for students in all disciplines. The goals of the program are to (1) facilitate the adjustment of new TAs to their responsibilities as instructors, recitation leaders, and graders; (2) impart specific information to help TAs succeed with their instructional duties; and (3) create opportunities for TAs to explore ways to consider and strengthen their skills as teachers. TAP offers an array of programs and services, including new TA orientations, publications on teaching, classroom video-taping and peer observation, confidential telephone help line services, and interdisciplinary seminars on pedagogy.

TA orientations are presented every August for all newly appointed TAs. The orientations serve as an introduction to Rutgers and an overview of the undergraduate experience. The programs focus on the challenges of serving as a teacher; analyze the roles, rights, ethics, and duties of TAs; and highlight the experiences of senior TAs who discuss how to handle the various pedagogical challenges that new TAs encounter. Specific sessions are also organized for new international TAs, who may face some special challenges having to teach for the first time in an unfamiliar cultural environment.

TAP's publications, both print and electronic, give TAs information pertaining to teaching throughout the year. *TAPTALK,* our monthly newsletter written and edited by an experienced TA and distributed to all TAs, includes such topics as academic integrity, designing and administering tests, and how to motivate students in large classes. The *TA Handbook,* distributed to all new TAs and also available online, is a comprehensive introduction to the myriad issues that new instructors encounter.

TAP's videotaping and peer observation programs are especially useful in helping TAs hone their presentation and organizational skills. The videotaping equipment and technician are provided by TAP and the tape is then reviewed with the TA by a faculty member or someone on the TAP staff. For TAs who are camera-shy, the Peer Observation Program enables instructors to gain feedback on their teaching without the potentially intimidating experience of having a video camera and technician in the classroom. We have found peer observation to be most successful when graduate students from different disciplines view each other's classes. With this approach, students who are not acquainted with the subject matter are able to comment from a similar vantage point to that of an undergraduate who is not familiar with the discipline.

The TA Helpline, a confidential telephone service for TAs, and TAP's midsemester evaluations also serve to assist TAs in improving their instructional skills. The telephone help line enables TAs to ask questions about teaching without risk or embarrassment—questions that they may not want to ask in their own department. Similarly, the midsemester evaluation, a form that is completed anonymously by the students in the class and reviewed only by the TA, gives TAs early and instant feedback to help them learn about students' perceptions of their pedagogical skills before it is too late in the semester to rectify any identified problems.

Throughout the year, TAP convenes interdisciplinary seminars on issues related to teaching, undergraduate education, and pedagogy. We also sponsor a semester-long course entitled Introduction to College Teaching, which covers a range of topics including higher education governance, designing syllabi, and technology in the classroom. These centralized programs provide direct service to TAs and faculty; they foster an institutional ethos of commitment to strengthening the quality of graduate student teaching.

The most important pedagogical programs that we sponsor for TAs, however, are those that occur within the disciplines. Students learn best about teaching in their own field from the faculty in their own department. Monthly seminars, for example, are organized by the undergraduate and graduate directors of the Rutgers Department of Political Science, where graduate students have the opportunity to learn not only about political theory but also how to teach it. By focusing on the theory of the discipline and the pedagogical aspects of enhancing undergraduate student learning, our graduate students in political science have the opportunity to test their ideas with senior faculty and exchange insights about their own successes and challenges in the classroom. When these TAs graduate, they will have the research skills required for success as political scientists, along with the teaching skills, experience, and confidence to succeed as teachers.

An additional outcome of Rutgers's TA training is the anticipatory socialization that is occurring for our faculty-in-training. Campuswide seminars bring students together from all the disciplines, giving them the chance to learn about the nature of graduate study in fields that are not their own. They also have the opportunity to become acquainted with faculty and administrators beyond their department, who can serve as an important influence in their development as future faculty members. Programs on teaching that are sponsored in the disciplines give students a sense of what it means to be professionals in their field.

The Marketplace as a Motivating Force

Doctoral students who have positive experiences in teaching undergraduates, and who have developed the skills to succeed in the classroom, have greater options during a job search and a better likelihood of becoming employed as college faculty members. The number of institutions where undergraduate teaching is the primary institutional mission far outweighs the number of doctoral-extensive and doctoral-intensive institutions. According to the recently revised Carnegie Classification of Institutions of Higher Education (Carnegie Foundation for the Advancement of Teaching, 2002), of the 3,941 institutions that were classified, only 261, or 6.6 percent, are included in the research category of doctorate-granting institutions. Except for some of the specialized institutions in the Carnegie classification (medicine, law, and so on), the majority of the listed colleges and universities focus on undergraduate education. Regrettably, graduate schools have, almost without fail, continued to prepare new Ph.D.s for positions solely in the research arena. This historical lack of emphasis on pedagogical issues in traditional doctoral education is alarming when considering the realities of the job market. Not surprisingly, the preponderance of graduate schools across the country still gear their curricula toward preparing researchers without the recognition that those future Ph.D.s may need, or choose, to work at an institution where teaching is the primary mission.

From an institutional perspective, ensuring the preparedness and effectiveness of graduate teaching assistants is educationally important and makes good economic sense. Administrators should be able to demonstrate to the multiple constituencies they serve that their institutions are working diligently to ensure excellence in instruction. Good teaching helps to recruit and retain students, and it also helps to increase the number of majors in the field to create the next generation of faculty. Sponsoring programs on pedagogy also helps to recruit future graduate students to an institution. Administrators, in both public and independent institutions, must be able to demonstrate that the quality of instruction they offer is not compromised through reliance on TAs. From testing and training nonnative speakers of English before they are assigned instructional duties, to providing all TAs with the skills they need to thrive in the classroom, we must do as much as possible to work with graduate students to prepare them to handle their instructional responsibilities.

Since the inception of the project, we have had more than four thousand new TAs participate in orientation; programs offered during the semester are also well attended. This global participation in programs designed to strengthen the quality of instruction has resulted in a significant change in the teaching culture, for TAs and faculty alike. TAs, who have the opportunity to evaluate all project activities, now expect that they will receive training and professional development opportunities to prepare them for their duties as an instructor.

Many of the faculty, wishing they had had the opportunity to learn about teaching when they were in graduate school, have embraced the importance of preparing graduate students for teaching. Faculty are dedicating time to preparing graduate students for their roles as instructors; undergraduates are receiving higher-quality instruction; and the emphasis on teaching has strengthened our ability to achieve our tripartite mission of teaching, research, and service.

Realistically, we no longer have the luxury of ignoring the quality of instruction provided by graduate students—their role in the classroom is too important. Today's TAs are tomorrow's faculty members.

The University of Cincinnati *Is* Listening: The Quality Service Initiative

James R. Tucker
Vice President for Administrative and Business Services, University of Cincinnati

Marie L. Sutthoff
Coordinator, Special Projects, Administrative and Business Services, University of Cincinnati

The University of Cincinnati is located in the southwest corner of Ohio. It has a total enrollment of approximately thirty-three thousand students, and more than fourteen thousand full-time and part-time employees. It is estimated that between 1999 and 2011 colleges and universities in the Midwest region will experience shrinking freshman enrollment. In Ohio, this will be due in part to an expected 4 percent decline in high school enrollment during that period, compared to significant increases that will be experienced elsewhere in the country, especially in the Western and Southern regions (U.S. Department of Education, 2001). Administrators at the University of Cincinnati, as at many other institutions of higher education in the state, were concerned about how these patterns would affect enrollments in future years.

The University of Cincinnati is located in a dense urban area of institutions of higher education. Competition for freshmen is rigorous. With a shrinking pool of prospective students, declining financial support from the State of Ohio, and the competition created by increasing levels of service at other institutions, it became even more

crucial to enhance our services. To improve the university's quality
and competitiveness, we committed ourselves as an institution to five
imperatives:

1. Academics
2. Open space
3. Connectivity
4. Quality of student life and services
5. Quality service initiative

The first three imperatives dealt with the physical aspects and infrastructure of the campus—facility construction and renovation,
green space development, and access enhancement. The university's Master Plan called for older academic and auxiliary facilities
to be redeveloped; new facilities (designed by eminent, world-class
architects) to be built; and trees, green spaces, fountains, and walkways to be installed to make the campus more attractive and pedes-
trian-friendly in what is otherwise a congested urban setting.

One example of how these initiatives are transforming the way
we provide service is the University of Cincinnati's new University
Pavilion. A one-stop Student Services Center will be located in University Pavilion; it will virtually eliminate the need for students to
visit various campus offices residing within numerous buildings. At
the center, cross-trained service specialists are available to assist
students with their individual enrollment needs.

The fourth imperative, quality of life and services, promotes
programmatic changes to campus life to create a culture and community for an ongoing learning and living environment. By fostering the development of additional on-campus recreational and
social activities, we hope to increase the opportunities for our students to enjoy a variety of on-campus amenities. We want to make
our campus a seven-day-a-week, round-the-clock "happening place,"
not just an eight-to-five academic operation. With this purpose at
its core, we began creating a vibrant corridor of food, entertainment, housing, retail, and recreation venues throughout the heart
of campus—a University of Cincinnati Main Street where students
can interact.

Key to the execution of all of the imperatives is the ability to
develop and foster a set of employee behaviors to support the new

facilities and programmatic changes that are under way. The fifth imperative, the quality service initiative instituted in 2001, enhanced the skills and behaviors of the University of Cincinnati's employees to provide excellent service to attract and retain students.

Quality Service Efforts

At the direction of University of Cincinnati President Joseph A. Steger, a universitywide quality service initiative was established. The lead author of this narrative, James R. Tucker, vice president for administrative and business services, was appointed to take charge of efforts to address the fifth imperative, the quality service initiative.

The initiative's purpose is to transform the University of Cincinnati experience into one in which people choose to live, learn, and work, by communicating openly, working together, valuing one another's contributions, understanding and fulfilling needs and expectations, and being accountable for their work. The effort involves planning and universitywide training, recognition, and reward efforts that reach throughout the organization to further enhance the University of Cincinnati's ability to attract and retain students.

Essentially, the goal of the initiative is to dramatically improve services throughout the organization. Its philosophy maintains that all students, faculty, staff, and visitors should be able to concentrate on the challenge and enjoyment of living, learning, and working at the University of Cincinnati, rather than the challenge of navigating the system.

In mid-2001, the university officially launched the quality service initiative. Approximately seventy-five university administrators and employees were assembled to serve on four committees that focused on the quality aspects surrounding strategies, people, place, and process. Committees met monthly to review and recommend areas for quick wins, as well as intermediate and long-term gains. They focused on cultivating positive attitudes among staff, providing development and training of managers and associates, examining regional competitors, and evaluating critical services.

By January 2002, the strategies, people, place, and process committees concluded their initial reviews. A new group set forth to carry on the work identified by the first four committees. This advisory team is composed of twenty-two volunteer administrators representing the major university service and academic areas. They continue to meet monthly to develop successful inroads on the paths to quality service, including creating a strategic plan and identifying goals and objectives.

At the outset of the quality service initiative, "customer" service training was also a priority. A training council developed educational programs for front-line and management personnel on the main and branch campuses and the medical center. The universitywide phase one training effort began in July 2001 and concluded by the beginning of fall quarter, September 2001. Sessions were held over an eight-week period during daytime, evening, and late-night hours to accommodate the various schedules of our employees.

As a result of the success of these programs, all new employees now receive quality service training as part of their orientation through our Human Resources Department. In addition, our College of Business Administration and the HR department jointly presented additional management training on quality service for more than one hundred administrators and managers in January 2002. Plans are in progress for phase two training, which will also include more in-depth work facilitated with eleven of our academic departments.

The university president and vice presidents made videotaped introductions to convey the importance of this global training effort and to help clarify our quality message. Included in the training were contracted employees who provide shuttle and food services to our university.

Once the fall quarter began, we also conducted specialized sessions designed for our student workers to introduce them to the effort and raise awareness of the importance of providing quality service in all situations. In total, approximately thirty-seven hundred students, administrators, and staff received the benefits of our global training endeavor.

Academic leaders were invited to attend a special workshop planned in conjunction with the university's quality service initiative. The workshop for our academic leadership focused on two topics of special interest: challenges facing the academy (implications for academic leaders), and approaches to identifying priorities and focusing energy in a time of increasing demands and decreasing resources.

New Approaches to Communication

We also instituted a new form of feedback called UC Is Listening (Figure 7.5). Located online at www.feedback.uc.edu, this is a tool that collects information on various key services provided by the university to its major constituents: the students, faculty, and staff. Developed by PlanetFeedback, UC Is Listening queries our students, faculty, staff, and visitors on seventeen internal services, ranging from admissions to libraries to student organizations. Most important, it gives those who use our services direct input to send our administrators compliments, complaints, suggestions, questions, and survey information. Comments are routed directly to assistant or associate vice presidents and directors for service-related issues, and to vice provosts for academic-related issues for their review and reply.

Figure 7.5.   UC Is Listening.

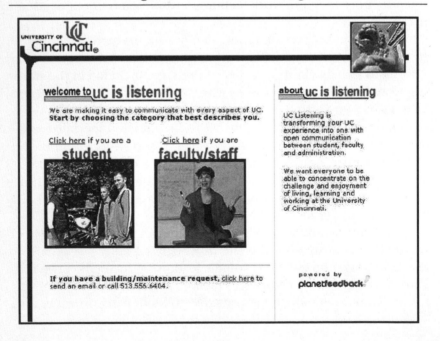

Although UC Is Listening does not replace any existing communications tools, this Web-based feedback mechanism has the potential to enhance our ability to investigate and respond more quickly to student, faculty, and staff issues by virtue of the technology it embraces. We feel that it is one more valuable mode of communication for those who use our services.

Our UC Is Listening program is achieving significant improvements in how we conduct business. Our operations are becoming more transparent to those we serve, and students and other people who provide feedback now know the name and title of the administrator who receives their comments. During the first three quarters of academic year 2002, we received 687 feedback items from our Website, and in each case comments were e-mailed directly to administrators who investigated and responded to the student, faculty, or staff member, generally within three to seven business days.

The program is opening the eyes of our administrators, those individuals who actually have the ability to change process and practice. Our records and registration administrator indicates that results from the feedback include process reviews and improvements that are under way, thanks to a staff member's comment about class standing updates and a student's complaint regarding priority registration practices. Our controller also reports that tuition payment policies are being rewritten to promote clarity for students as a result of feedback received. Complaints from students concerning menu alternatives at a food-vending site also prompted expansion of the entree options from two items to six. Many feedback items include compliments about staff members who have helped students by resolving payment or programming difficulties. Employees have requested and received explanations about various operational and benefits-related programs.

Another initiative introduced to improve communication is our Helping Hands program, a welcoming effort to the new students arriving on campus for fall quarter. Over a three-day period, faculty, administrators (including the university's president and some vice presidents) and employees volunteered to assist the new residence hall occupants by helping them with their belongings as they moved into their accommodations. Residents and parents were overwhelmed by the gracious welcome that awaited them.

We also introduced a new Ask Me Ambassador Program. For the first few days of fall quarter, a group of volunteers are posted at critical areas on campus to give directions and information to our incoming students.

Additionally, we have introduced new user-friendly signage on campus. In the process, we replaced old and unattractive "No Trespassing" signs with new "Welcome" signage on the entrances of all of our buildings. The new signage also included contact numbers for off-hours access and information. Aesthetic improvements were made to a number of the campus drives in time for fall quarter opening. We also used both internal and external "mystery shoppers" to survey our retail and service areas. In an effort to conduct a focused communications effort for the quality service initiative, we have instituted a Website (www.qsi.uc.edu) to continue to educate our community.

Finally, we have introduced new approaches to increasing communication with the faculty. During summer quarter, we conducted an e-mail survey of issues related to process improvements, institutional barriers, and best practices. This information was compiled and reviewed by the provost's office for future discussion. Other plans occurring through the quality service advisory team include a universitywide suggestion program that gives a $50 incentive to faculty, staff, and students, a leave donation program, and a presidential quality award program.

Encouraging effective two-way communication with the students and others through our administrative services is a core objective at the University of Cincinnati. We see administrative services as an important aspect of the learning environment, and we want these services to contribute to positive and productive experiences for those we serve. To do so, we want to better understand the experiences of students and do all we can to improve the quality of the services the university is providing. UC *is* listening.

Community and Service Learning: The Rutgers CASE Program

Michael D. Shafer
Professor of Political Science, Director of Rutgers
Citizenship and Service Education (CASE) Program,
Rutgers University

When President Bill Clinton came to Rutgers in 1993 to announce his national service plan, he recognized the Rutgers Citizenship and Service Education (CASE) Program as a model for colleges and universities across America. Specifically, the president came to recognize Rutgers's effort to make service learning central to the undergraduate curriculum, and to train students to be competent, participatory, democratic citizens possessing the knowledge, skills, and attitudes necessary to flourish in today's complex world. In the years since Clinton's visit, CASE has become part of the fabric of a Rutgers undergraduate education. No less important, CASE has grown as an organization to meet the needs of all of its stakehold-ers—the university, faculty, students, community partner organizations, and citizens of New Jersey—and to ensure its survival by developing autonomous sources of revenue through its own entrepreneurial activities.

The key to CASE's success is the ability to pursue its mission in ways that help Rutgers meet all facets of its mission as a public research university: to produce and propagate knowledge, and serve citizens and taxpayers. On the teaching front, CASE's experiential pedagogy engages professors in exciting ways with their students and ensures that students learn better and retain longer; acquire social, teamwork, and workplace readiness skills that cannot be learned in the classroom; and do what citizens do— engage in the life of the community. CASE therefore speaks directly to parental, taxpayer, and employer concerns about the quality and utility of a Rutgers education. But CASE also conducts research on how participation affects student attitudes and behavior, and it collaborates in national and international assessments of the impact of service learning. Finally, by engaging thousands of students in newsworthy projects across the state, delivering hundreds of thousands of hours of service worth millions of dollars, sharing Rutgers resources with hundreds of nonprofits, and providing direct service to tens of thousands of citizens, CASE not only allows Rutgers to meet its service mission but also helps the university sell itself to legislators, the governor, business, the civic sector, and taxpayers (Table 7.1).

Table 7.1. CASE Stakeholders and What CASE Can Offer Them.

Actor	Benefits CASE Provides to Actor	How CASE Helps Actor Help Others
University	Advances service mission	Engages university and community in common project
	Advances teaching mission	Provides community access to university resources
	Provides community connection and helps overcome town-gown divisions	Helps educate new generation to be active citizens
	Excellent public relations	Provides student volunteer labor
	Great fundraising possibilities	Provides possibility of new fundraising for partners

Table 7.1. *(continued)*

Actor	Benefits CASE Provides to Actor	How CASE Helps Actor Help Others
Faculty	Enhanced capacity to teach subject matter with service-learning-oriented field work placement	Improves students' learning and retention of subject matter
	Enhanced capacity to teach critical thinking, reading, and writing skills	Improves students' acquisition of critical thinking, reading and writing skills
	Enhanced capacity to teach social and teamwork skills for life and work	Improves students' social and teamwork skills; raises students' self-confidence and competence as young adults
	Permits teaching of citizenship and citizenship skills	Gives students an education in citizenship and enhances the community as a result
	Provides opportunity to have a direct community impact	Provides needed volunteers, skills, and resources to community partner organizations and the community
	Adds exciting dynamism to classroom; raises student evaluations of professor	Assists university in meeting criticisms of lack of attention to teaching and innovation
Students	Improves learning and retention of subject matter	Provides needed help to community partner organizations and the community
	Improves learning of critical skills	Provides needed and qualified help to community partner organizations and their clients

continued

Table 7.1. *(continued)*

Actor	Benefits CASE Provides to Actor	How CASE Helps Actor Help Others
	Offers opportunity to learn critical social and teamwork skills and to gain confidence as a young adult, not available in normal courses	Provides critical, personal connection between the school-university and the community
	Offers opportunity to learn about citizenship and to be a citizen of the community	Helps community and nation forge the citizenry of tomorrow
	Offers opportunity to take courses that give real meaning to their education	Helps restore the once commonplace notion that the community as a whole is what makes life worth living, not only the individual's private successes
	Offers opportunity to experiment with career possibilities and to develop resume	Ultimately provides employers with workforce-ready employees better prepared to succeed on the job
Community partners	Brings in badly needed volunteer staff and expands the community volunteer base	Expands the quantity, quality, and nature of services to clients
	Opens door to other university resources and expertise	Provides invaluable learning experience to student volunteers
	Excellent public relations	Provides critical assistance to university's teaching mission
	Great fundraising possibilities	Provides possibility of new fundraising for partners

Table 7.1. *(continued)*

Actor	Benefits CASE Provides to Actor	How CASE Helps Actor Help Others
	Provides opportunity to leverage existing resources at little extra cost	Permits provision of critically needed but underprovided services
	Provides opportunity to socialize a new generation of civic-minded community service volunteers	Expands the quantity, quality, and nature of services to clients
	Provides means to forge new partnerships with the university	Offers university the means to reach the community

CASE began in 1988 with a call to action by the late Edward Bloustein, who was then the university president: "I propose that we look at community service as a necessary component of the learning experiences which constitute a liberal education." The board of governors of the university unanimously endorsed the idea and called for a Rutgers that is dedicated to teaching the fundamentals of citizenship; a lifelong service ethic; an understanding that diversity is the source of America's strength; and the academic, social, and job skills needed to thrive in modern America. In doing so, the board also dedicated Rutgers to meeting three concerns critical to all Americans: concern about the collapse of community, concern about the failure of our educational institutions to prepare young people with the skills to succeed economically and be good citizens, and concern about the growing chasm between have and have-not communities.

Since Bloustein's 1988 call to action, CASE has grown dramatically to become an integral part of the Rutgers curriculum, and an important player in the New Jersey human services system. CASE offered its first service learning courses in the fall of 1989; by the spring of 2002 CASE had become the largest provider of community service volunteers in New Jersey, and an important direct service provider as well. In thirteen years, 12,500 students have taken CASE courses; CASE volunteers have rendered almost

seven hundred thousand hours of service valued conservatively at
$3.75 million. Today, CASE counts almost six hundred New Jersey
nonprofits, faith-based organizations, schools, and government
offices among its community partners. Annually, students in some
sixty-five CASE courses provide fifty thousand hours of service
worth $350,000 dollars. CASE also operates study abroad programs
in Costa Rica and South Africa. Finally, njserves.org, CASE's Internet portal for the New Jersey civic sector, has made CASE *the* source
of online information for New Jerseyans. Operated by CASE student staff, njserves.org offers ten thousand unique visitors per
month access to a searchable database of forty thousand organizations, an online newspaper, statewide events calendar, resource
center, and comprehensive one-click access to disaster resources
for New Jerseyans touched by the events of September 11, 2001.
(To visit, point your browser to www.njserves.org.)

Growing CASE from a Great Idea to a Self-Sustaining Organization

As it has grown, CASE's mission has evolved and its organizational
structure has changed accordingly. CASE began in 1989 as a traditional academic program. It was student-focused and university-
centric, and it departed from preconceived ideas about the
substance of what ought to be taught. CASE focused narrowly on
student learning needs and functioned to support a limited number of specially conceived service learning courses taught on soft
money and outside the regular catalogue offerings of departments.
CASE thus offered such courses as Service and Community, using
active learning to improve student learning outcomes, forging links
between the classroom and the "real world," making citizenship
central to a Rutgers education, and encouraging the development
of a service ethic among Rutgers students. By 1994, this CASE had
stalled.

A review of CASE's mission and method indicated that the
problems resulted from a single, basic flaw: CASE failed to embrace
the needs of all of its real stakeholders and so ignored or even
alienated key constituencies. A new management team therefore
created a master list of stakeholders and asked them what they
liked, disliked, wanted, and needed. The findings suggested that

the CASE mission and way of doing business needed changing, and that once the changes were made CASE had to convince stakeholders that collaboration with CASE was a win-win proposition. Within months, focus groups helped CASE create a crude but effective spreadsheet.

Armed with these findings, the new team modified the CASE mission to include all stakeholders and changed the way CASE did business. For example, to garner the support of the administration, CASE (1) sent out regular updates about how many CASE students had provided how many hours of service to how many community organizations—information that the university could include in its economic impact report to the state, (2) collaborated with University Relations to feed newspapers across the state stories about hometown CASE student's service activities, and (3) invited legislators to speak at required student trainings to show them what a fine job Rutgers is doing. Likewise, CASE wooed Rutgers's best professors by inviting them to find creative ways to add service learning placements to their courses, rather than telling them what they ought to teach and how. This ensured CASE courses across the curriculum from biology to visual arts, and broadened CASE's base of support among departments and the faculty. Critical for students, the addition of service learning to core departmental courses permitted students to make CASE part of their regular major, rather than a peripheral add-on. Finally, CASE organized a Community Partner Advisory Board (CPAB) to give the community access to Rutgers.

CPAB input resulted in two of the three major organizational changes CASE has made since 1994, all three of which enhanced CASE's capacity to teach the whole student. First, in 1996, CASE "inherited" the University's flagging Neighborhood Relations Program. NRP had been organized to provide student volunteers to help senior citizens living near Rutgers's main campus. CPAB, however, pointed out that senior citizens were already well served, and that if Rutgers wanted to help then NRP should support services not already being provided. Foremost among these were literacy programs and teen mentoring. CASE thus recruited student and faculty support for the creation of Rutgers Readers, a K–3 literacy program; and RU CHAMPS, a middle school mentoring program. Today NRP provides hundreds of students with structured but cocurricular service learning experiences. Second, in 1997–98, CPAB began to advocate for CASE to "get nonprofits on the Web." With CPAB support, CASE raised the money to develop njserves.org. Today, njserves.org offers student staff real-world work and service experience, serves the citizens of New Jersey, and draws funding from civic-minded corporate sponsors (Becton-Dickinson, Horizon-Mercy, Lucent, Microsoft, Novartis, Prudential, and PSE&G) that now support one-third of CASE's general operating budget.

The final mission and organizational changes CASE undertook in the late 1990s reflected CASE's own success and the accompanying need to find new funding sources. As word spread, CASE began to receive requests for technical assistance from universities across the United States and around the world. In these requests, CASE recognized both a logical extension of its mission—to help others to do for their universities, students, and communities what CASE does for Rutgers—and the means to broaden CASE's funding base. CASE created a new operating unit, Special Projects, to manage consulting projects. Special Projects now manages hundreds of thousands of dollars in grants from, for example, the U.S. State Department to develop CASE-like programs in the Baltics, Lebanon, and Poland; and advertises CASE's technical assistance offerings to generate revenues to support CASE operations and development. Of course, CASE students are involved in the development of all CASE training materials and all on-campus training visits, and some have traveled with CASE training teams to such distant destinations as Lebanon and Mongolia.

In sum, in the years since its founding in 1989 CASE has grown and thrived through a self-conscious effort to advance the CASE team's values and agenda, while attending carefully to the needs and concerns of its many and diverse constituencies. For the moment, CASE is well described by the most recent mission statement, drafted in January 2002 as part of a Baldrige-based organizational assessment, planning, and improvement exercise:

> The Rutgers Citizenship and Service Education program, composed of faculty, students and staff, exists to improve the practice of active citizenship and community service. We strive to deliver educational, training, and direct service programs that advance the knowledge, skills and attitudes essential to effective citizen participation.

> Through collaborative relationships, the Rutgers CASE program harnesses the resources of the broader community to promote civic engagement and invigorate civic life nationally and abroad.

Put differently, this far-reaching mission has permitted CASE to broaden the teaching and learning domain dramatically. CASE has introduced active learning pedagogies across the traditional curriculum and given students the opportunity to acquire knowledge, skills, and attitudes that cannot be learned in a traditional classroom; it has also made administrators, legislators, and nonprofit staffers into teachers and has converted soup kitchens, nursing homes, and church basements into classrooms. (To get a sense of the breadth of CASE's offerings and "campus" size, visit www.redbook.case.rutgers.edu.)

Organizational Tensions

Despite success, the CASE experience offers cautionary lessons, all related to the importance of an organization's place in a university's organizational chart. CASE lobbied hard to be located on the academic side of the house, and to report to the vice president for academic affairs. Without this, CASE could not have won faculty collaboration. However, CASE does not actually "do" any of the university's missions; rather it administers to them. But even though in this sense CASE is an administrative unit, it is headed by a tenured professor and reports to the vice president for academic affairs. It lacks the hardwired claim on resources that a dean or director of most administrative areas can make, and it has no routinized claim on university resources such as space or vehicles; it is also forced to raise funds externally for resources that are taken for granted by many units. Thus CASE's organizational limbo puts at risk a program that is routinely cited in public documents, testimony to the state legislature, and fundraising materials as a model of a university's commitment to serving the needs of its students, communities, and state.

Chapter Eight

Devoting More Attention and Resources to Leadership
Attracting, Developing, and Retaining Outstanding Leaders

Position Available

Seeking visionary, energetic, dedicated leader to guide the institution to new levels of excellence and innovation. Requires a substantial record of academic and administrative achievement, demonstrated commitment to the mission and goals of the institution, and an understanding of current national and global issues and trends in higher education, demonstrated success in resource development and marketing, a commitment to diversity, and an ability to communicate effectively with students, faculty, staff, alumni, members of the board, the community, and the general public. The individual should have an accessible and visible leadership approach, an open communication style, effective listening skills, superior interpersonal and organizational skills, a commitment to collaboration and shared governance, demonstrated ability to make decisive and responsive decisions, and should possess the skills necessary to be an effective advocate for the institution and for higher education. Experience in developing collaborative partnerships with community and business leaders, expertise and success in building a rich workforce, and familiarity with the use of technology are also essential.

Extraordinary challenges face higher education nationally, and leaders with exceptional capabilities are needed to help institutions meet these challenges. Individuals with the qualities described above are in demand everywhere within the academy. These are just some the capabilities sought in a candidate for a presidency, vice presidency, provost, or dean. With minor variations, they are also the desired attributes of associate deans, department chairs, directors, and other academic administrators, and also of leaders of administrative, student life, and auxiliary services areas.

Where do people with these capabilities come from? The ideal set of competencies is difficult, if not impossible, to find in any one person; thus the task goes beyond simply *locating* outstanding leaders. It includes encouraging, facilitating, and rewarding their development. What role have colleges and universities played— and what role should they play—in identifying and preparing individuals for the many vital leadership roles within the academy? This chapter focuses on these questions.

Higher Education Administration: Context and Contrasts

Colleges and universities today are exceedingly complex, providing an increasing range of educational services to a broad and ever-expanding array of constituencies. In earlier times, the essence of higher education institutions might have been adequately captured by the word *school,* but this imagery is increasingly less adequate and useful. Colleges and universities *are* schools, but they often are also libraries, contract research agencies, health services, hotels, restaurants, recreational facilities, purchasing services, career counseling services, police and fire departments, personnel services, athletic sponsors, patent offices, printing offices, computer services, facilities maintenance organizations, and on and on. Many of today's higher education institutions have all the complexity of (and provide as broad a range of services as) a municipality or a major corporation; the challenge of assuring excellence in each area of the contemporary college or university is daunting, to say the least.

Large and small institutions alike are confronted with critical issues related to external criticism, finances, quality, service, accountability, innovation, competition, and governance. Higher education's leaders are at center stage in efforts to meet the many challenges that must be successfully addressed to advance their institutions. In addition to their many institutional responsibilities, they have the exceedingly difficult task of interpreting the academy and its imperatives to the external world—and, conversely, interpreting the realities of the external world to the academy (R. Berdahl, personal conversation, Berkeley, Calif., Sept. 6, 2002). Whether one thinks of the academic, administrative, or service realm, leaders' responsibilities are numerous and varied. They include articulating and building consensus on the organization's mission and future directions, creating an appropriate climate, making necessary resources available, stimulating innovation and change, effectively managing day-to-day operations, as well as ensuring the development of plans and goals, the recruitment of high-quality faculty and staff, and the design and implementation of effective programs and services (Balderston, 1995; Birnbaum, 1992; Dalton and McClinton, 2002; Freeland, 2001; Gmelch and Miskin, 1995; Higgerson, 1996; Lucas, 1994; McLaughlin, 1996; Seagren, Creswell, and Wheeler, 1993; Rhodes, 2001). To be successful, one must have appropriate personal knowledge, experience, and skill, and also be able to impart the vision, motivation, and modeling necessary to engage and mobilize colleagues and external constituencies.

In all these respects, the responsibilities and expertise required of today's higher education leaders generally parallel those associated with leadership positions in business and other sectors about which so much has been written in recent years (for instance, Bratton, 1998; Knight and Trowler, 2001; Kotter, 2001; and Useem, 1998). However, many, if not most, of the similarities between leadership in higher education and organizations in other sectors end there. Leaders in other sectors do not generally find themselves in organizations that so highly prize individual autonomy, or have such limited discretionary resources and incentives at their disposal to reward or stimulate innovation and change. Leaders in other sectors also are not faced with the complexities of shared governance—a unique feature of the landscape of the academy.[1] At most colleges and universities, the governance structure includes appointed boards or regents, the president and senior administration, deans and directors, department chairs and unit managers, the faculty, faculty advisory groups, a senate, and in the case of some public institutions a system-level administrative group as well. Not surprisingly, this structure creates numerous organizational tensions among these groups, which are well known to those within the academy (Birnbaum, 1988, 1992; Rhodes, 2001; Weinstein, 1993). From the perspective of those occupying a leadership position at any of these levels within the institution, the challenges presented by the shared governance structure are formidable, to say the least. As Rhodes puts it: "Institutions once admired as modest models of prudent judgment and strong participatory government are now seen by some as archetypes of bureaucratic bumbling and learned inefficiency, where efficient management and decisive leaders are held hostage to a host of competing interests and divided loyalties, and where prompt, responsible actions and responsive decisions are delayed by prolonged debate or diluted by ideological wrangling. The development of responsible, effective, and balanced governance, leadership, and management is one of the most urgent priorities for the American university as it enters the new Millennium" (Rhodes, 2001, p. 235).

The Case of Academic Leaders

Nowhere are leadership challenges more pronounced than in academic units, and particularly academic departments, which present a microcosm of the opportunities and difficulties that exist for leaders throughout the institution. In decentralized organizations such as colleges and universities, the work of constituent divisions and departments is vital. Indeed, academic departments carry out many activities that are fundamental to the mission of higher education. Leadership positions within these units are pivotal within the academy (Seagren, Creswell, and Wheeler, 1993), and the most important link between administrators, faculty, programs, and students (Waltzer, 1975). Roach (1976) has estimated that 80 percent of all university decisions are made at the departmental level. According to Seagren and colleagues: "As administrators responsible for evaluating and rewarding staff, [academic leaders] promote or inhibit the advancement of individual careers. As advocates for faculty, they serve as important communication links between academic units and the administrative hierarchy of colleges and universities. As colleagues of faculty and staff in the department, they understand the daily frustrations and concerns of individuals employed in higher education institutions" (Seagren, Creswell, and Wheeler, 1993, p. 1).

Given the critical role played by academic department chairs, program directors, and deans, the contrast between these leadership roles and those in other sectors is particularly striking.

Compensation

One notable area of contrast is compensation. Individuals serving in important administrative positions in business and other sectors are generally highly rewarded for their contributions, but in many colleges and universities there are few tangible incentives for serving as a department chair or program director. The difference is particularly apparent in most research institutions, where serving in a departmental leadership role carries little added financial remuneration—often less than one would earn from teaching a summer session course or two, or from consulting for a few days. Moreover, in these institutions, departmental leadership typically does not contribute to one's professional advancement. To the contrary, it quite likely retards one's progress because it reduces the time one has to devote to scholarly work and publication.

The contrast in compensation is somewhat less extreme for deans and for departmental chairs and program directors at colleges and universities where administrators are recruited for permanent positions using different appointment and promotion criteria than those for faculty. In many universities, however, the limited rewards for serving in departmental leadership roles (which are widely acknowledged to be among the most important roles in the institution) represent an obvious contradiction that appears to be unique to higher education.

Leadership Development

Another significant difference between higher education and other sectors is the historic lack of attention to leadership development within the academy. Although leadership and professional development programs are commonplace within health care and government, and particularly in business, little attention and few resources have been devoted to these activities on most campuses, especially in academic affairs (Fogg, 2001, Munitz, 1995). Even in the case of institutions and disciplines that have initiated professional development programs, these efforts are generally quite limited in scope and reach. Similarly, formalized coaching/mentoring initiatives, multiperspective performance reviews, and programs for nominating and developing high-potential employees are familiar concepts in most large organizations in other sectors (Bennis, 2000),[2] but are uncommon in colleges and universities (Gmelch, 2000). Accountability and opportunities for developmental feedback are also often lacking for individuals serving in department chair and program positions, compared with faculty serving in teaching and research capacities for whom review criteria and procedures are generally in place.

Selection and Preparation

Approximately eighty thousand faculty members in the United States serve as department chairs in any year, and roughly one-fourth of these positions turn over annually (Gmelch and Miskin, 1993). Many, if not most, of these twenty thousand new chairs come to their position with little or no formalized preparation. The same can be said of program directors, and often deans. Gmelch and colleagues (Gmelch, 2000) note that deans usually come to the position without leadership training, without prior executive experience, and without a full understanding of the complexities or responsibilities the role entails (Wolverton and Gmelch, 2002).

One of the most fundamental shortcomings of the usual approach to leader selection and preparation is the failure to recognize the distinct set of competencies required for success as a leader compared with those required for success as a faculty member. Gmelch and colleagues (Gmelch, 2000; Gmelch and Seedorf, 1989; Gmelch and Miskin, 1993; and Gmelch and Parkay, 1999) note, for instance, that although faculty work is typically solitary and focused, leadership activities are generally social and fragmented. Faculty members have substantial autonomy in their work, while leadership tasks are structured and accountable; faculty members prepare manuscripts, administrators prepare memos, budgets, personnel requests, and accountability reports. Much of the work of faculty members is done in private, while leaders' work is largely public. As a faculty member, one is the recipient of resources, while administrators are resource custodians and providers. Having to spend time in the office daily, attend meetings, and perhaps wear clothes different from those of a graduate student can also be a shock to some new administrators. Because of these and other differences, the necessary competencies for success in the faculty role do not necessarily translate easily to leadership roles—indeed they often are at odds. Regrettably, in too many institutions, there is a perception that if an individual has a Ph.D. and is an effective faculty member, he or she is appropriately prepared to be an administrator—without recognizing that there are many unique capabilities and competencies involved.

Given the striking contrasts between roles, the socialization of new academic leaders can be quite painful for the individual *and* his or her colleagues, whose lives are directly affected by the turbulent trial-and-error learning process. As one faculty member noted, "Being chair means the end of your research for that period, and the possibility that you may do the job so badly that everybody—rightly—hates you" (Wilson, 2001b, p. A10). Often the process by which one evolves in an administrative capacity is so demoralizing that it leaves the incumbent with little desire to pursue further administrative opportunities in the future.

Role Attractiveness and Status

Another problem involving faculty members is that assuming an academic leadership role is not always seen as an attractive career choice for the classically trained Ph.D. To the contrary, at some institutions an individual who confesses enthusiasm about serving as an administrator may encounter suspicion or bewilderment on the part of colleagues. Once in the role, an individual may find himself or herself apologizing for the decision to move into leadership—a decision that is sometimes (jokingly?) referred to by colleagues as "crossing over to the dark side."

Regrettably, faculty members seem often unaware of the enormous difference leaders can make in their discipline and beyond when they lead and participate in departmental and institutional decisions. Too often, for example, there is difficulty finding someone willing—let alone eager—to serve as chair. Gmelch and Miskin (1995) report research findings indicating that nearly twice as many chairs serve because they are drafted by a dean or colleague or feel there is no alternative as those who serve for reasons of personal development and challenge. This problem is well illustrated by the title of an article in the *Chronicle of Higher Education* (Wilson, 2001b), discussing faculty perceptions of the roles and responsibilities of the department chair: "Beggar, Psychologist, Mediator, Maid: The Thankless Job of a Chairman."

A memo from a dean to the faculty of her college is another vivid example of the sometimes negative perceptions associated with academic leadership roles:

> While it doesn't seem possible, in January, Mark Johnson will have completed a three-year term as Chair of his department and has decided to take a well-deserved break from administration. Thank you, Mark, for serving your department and college in an excellent fashion.
>
> At the request of her department and dean, Mary Jones, against the wishes of her family, has agreed to assume the chair responsibilities for the spring semester. Starting on July 1, 2002, when her term as Graduate Director of the School ends, Jenny Smith, listening to the pleas of her department and dean, has agreed to accept a three-year term of office as Chair.
>
> Thank you, Mary and Jenny. Your colleagues and I appreciate your agreeing to take on the most important (and most difficult) role in the university.[3]

From the language and tone of the memo, one might think the faculty members in question were being recognized for their willingness to undertake hazardous waste cleanup work without the benefit of protective clothing, rather than for leading an academic department and program!

The cultural stigma associated with academic leadership roles is also illustrated in a tongue-in-cheek, David Letterman–style list of the "Top 10 Reasons Why Professors Become Chairs" (Gmelch and Miskin, 1975, p. 3). The list, Gmelch and Miskin noted, was written by one of the reviewers of their book manuscript prior to publication, as a humorous comment on the authors' research. Among the reasons: "Because you don't want someone else to do it even if you don't"; "Because your peers elected you, thinking you are useless at research and teaching and this way you can at least fill out administrative reports"; and "Because you temporarily became insane, forgetting why you came into academics . . . momentarily in a state of confusion, mistaking your little college or university for General Motors or Microsoft, thinking you will climb the ladder."

The stigma, jocularity, and sometimes blatant disrespect are no doubt both causes and effects of much of the difficulty associated with recruiting and developing outstanding academic leaders. Indeed, a national study by the U.S. Department of Education (1999) identified dissatisfaction with faculty leadership as one of the five leading faculty concerns.

Ultimate Consequences

Academic leaders have exceedingly important yet difficult roles. They are appointed to lead organizations made up of highly empowered colleagues who may well have played a role in their selection. Department chairs generally serve fixed terms and have limited incentives, sanctions, and discretionary resources at their disposal to stimulate or reward departmental advancement. To support their efforts, they receive modest compensation and little assistance preparing to be a leader in a culture that encourages shared governance and tolerates considerable flexibility in how individuals define and enact their institutional responsibilities. Program directors, and sometimes deans and even more senior academic administrators, face many of these same challenges.

Some individuals are successful in addressing the challenges they encounter and become strong and effective leaders. Many other talented potential leaders, however, are discouraged from seeking administrative roles. Moreover, others who are recruited become discouraged because they find they do not receive the level of recognition, respect, or esteem from colleagues that seems appropriate to the energy and expertise required of these roles.

The Natural Selection Paradigm

Academic leaders are certainly not unique in the problems they confront. Like academic administrators, individuals who occupy administrative positions in other college and university departments also face major challenges, and often with similarly limited resources, authority, and incentives available. Adding to the complexity of leadership roles are marketplace pressures throughout the academy imposing conditions that impinge upon and sometimes overwhelm the impact that leaders in a single department or unit can have (J. Morley, personal correspondence, Aug. 20, 2002).

How have colleges and universities identified and prepared individuals to provide the caliber of leadership required in higher education today? Ironically, this has not been a matter of great attention within the academy (ostensibly a learning organization). The approach most often used exemplifies what might be termed a natural selection paradigm. The general presumption has been that bright and talented individuals with appropriate expertise in their specialty areas will quite naturally come forth, rise to the occasion, and become effective leaders. A similar logic suggests that outstanding teachers or scholars—or the staff members who demonstrate superior technical skills—are natural candidates for administrators and should excel when placed in leadership positions; either they already have the necessary competencies, or they will quickly and easily develop them once in their new roles. Unfortunately, however, the record would seem to show that candidates for leadership positions don't come forth naturally, often don't arrive with appropriate leadership and administrative experience, and many times fail to excel in the new roles at the level they had in their previous positions.

In colleges and universities—as in other contexts where the natural selection paradigm is in play—the paradigm does have some advantages for the selection and development of leaders. The current system generally vests the individual with full responsibility for failure, requires the investment of few institutional resources, and ultimately is a rational basis for identifying potentially successful leaders. Eventually, the necessary learning may occur for those who persist. Even when this is the case, however, it occurs in a more inefficient, individualized, and isolated manner than might be necessary if preparation for this task were approached systematically and collectively. Moreover, the learning curve is steep and costly for all involved, and strong candidates who are unable to adapt quickly and independently to the environment experience unnecessary failures. Even for a candidate who is successful, the process of finding one's own way can result in extensive frustration (for the individual and for colleagues), disorientation, and even anger, as well as leading to costly mistakes and wasted time and energy.

The Need for an Education-Based Paradigm of Leadership Development

Leadership competencies—along with disciplinary and occupational competencies—have become increasingly essential in higher education today. Colleges and universities have become huge, fragmented, and very expansive enterprises. But our attitude toward their administration has changed at a far less dramatic rate than our institutions.

As Richard Freeland notes, "The challenge to . . . leaders is . . . to find ways to make academic communities reach their highest potentials while also flourishing in the intensely competitive area in which they must exist" (2001, p. 247).

There may have been a time when the natural selection paradigm was a reasonable approach—a simpler time when devoting more attention to attracting, selecting, developing, and retaining outstanding leaders could perhaps have been legitimately regarded as a luxury. This is no longer the case today, as the leadership challenges and requisite competencies for higher education administrators in all areas are among the most significant faced anywhere.

The need today is for presidents, chancellors, vice presidents, deans, chairs, directors, and other leaders who understand the challenges facing higher education, who possess the appropriate organizational and interpersonal competencies, and who are dedicated to working collaboratively with faculty and staff, and key constituencies to advance the purposes of colleges and universities.

To strengthen and broaden the available pool of qualified leadership, a new education-based paradigm is needed, one that embraces four tenets:

1. Strong leadership in higher education must become a higher priority. The academy needs a growing number of effective and committed leaders to ensure its appropriate role within contemporary society.
2. Exceptional scholars, teachers, or skilled practitioners do not automatically become effective leaders.
3. Effective leadership is not simply a matter of common sense.
4. The knowledge and competencies associated with effective leadership can be taught and learned with a substantial commitment of energy, time, and resources.

Leadership has been described simply as a practical and everyday process of supporting, coordinating, developing, and inspiring colleagues (Ramsden, 1998). *Defining* the nature of leadership may be quite simple, but *mastering* the concepts and competencies is certainly not. Notwithstanding high levels of self-confidence often in abundant supply within the academy, these core competencies do not necessarily come more easily to the many well-educated and talented people within the academic community than they do to others. Paradoxically, it may be that our own overconfidence on this topic is one of the most fundamental impediments to advancing our capabilities.

Whether one thinks of academic, student life, or administrative areas, it is clear that effective organizational leadership requires a different set of competencies than does providing effective leadership of one's own career. In an effort to achieve excellence in one's field of specialization, subject matter expertise is particularly vital. In leading one's colleagues, core competencies have to do with creating collective—rather than individual—excellence. Leadership of one's own career can often be accomplished working independently of one's colleagues *in* the system. Organizational leadership, however, requires building partnerships and working *with* and *through* the system and one's colleagues. In efforts to achieve individual excellence, disciplinary *content* is essential, and process skills in communication, interpersonal relations, and collaboration are a luxury. When the goal is organizational excellence, however, these skills become core competencies. This is the case for leaders in academic positions, and also for individuals in administrative and student affairs, and support service roles at all levels within colleges and universities.

Unquestionably, it *is* possible to enhance our individual and collective expertise in organizational leadership, and to apply our broadened insight and proficiency in a range of roles throughout the academy. Doing so, however, requires much greater attention to leadership development and practice than has been our tradition. It also requires us to place much greater emphasis on leadership research, incentives, education, and evaluation.

Advancing and Using Leadership Scholarship

Insight into effective leadership in higher education can be gleaned from the growing body of literature on the subject, much of which focuses on the leadership needs of particular roles such as president (for example, Balderston, 1995; Birnbaum, 1992; McLaughlin, 1996; Munitz, 1995), academic department chair or dean (Gmelch and Miskin, 1995; Gmelch, 2000; Higgerson, 1996; Knight and Trowler, 2001; Lucas, 1994; Roach, 1976; Waltzer, 1975), student affairs leader (Dalton and McClinton, 2002), and others. Many of the more general efforts to address issues of leadership are also relevant (Bennis, 1997; Bratton, 1998; Collins and Porras, 1994; Covey, 1991; Heifetz, 1994; Kotter, 2001; Tichy, 1997; Useem, 1998; and Witherspoon, 1997).

For those who study or reflect seriously on the topic of leadership, it becomes evident that intellectual ability, educational background, and disciplinary or technical accomplishment are not particularly good predictors of leadership effectiveness, unless they are accompanied by organizational knowledge and a variety of personal and interpersonal competencies—what Daniel Goleman and others (1997, 1998a, 1998b; Cherniss and Goleman, 2001; and Mayer and Salovey, 1997) have termed "emotional intelligence," or EQ. Emotional intelligence consists of personal competencies (self-awareness, self regulation, and motivation) and social competencies (empathy and social skills) all of which are critical to working effectively with colleagues and external constituencies and hence to success in leadership roles. Goleman offers a description of these EQ competencies and their importance in leadership roles:

- *Self-awareness:* the ability to recognize and understand one's own moods, emotions, and drives, and their effects on others; essential for effective leadership and realistic self-assessment
- *Self-regulation:* the capacity to control one's impulses and moods, and to think before taking action; contributes to leader integrity and trustworthiness, dealing with ambiguity, and openness to change
- *Motivation:* a passion for one's work and a propensity to energetically and persistently pursue goals; contributes to a leader's drive for achievement, commitment, and optimism
- *Empathy:* the capacity to understand others' emotions and reactions; essential for leader efforts to form effective relationships with staff, colleagues, and clients, relate effectively with individuals with diverse cultural backgrounds, and develop and retain talented colleagues

- *Social skills:* competency in building and maintaining inter-personal networks, establishing rapport, and creating common ground; important for persuasiveness, effectiveness in leading change, and creating and leading groups and teams (1998a, p. 7).

From the literature on emotional intelligence and studies of the role of communication competence in workplace success (Ruben, 1976; Ruben and Kealey, 1979), it appears that precisely the social and communication skills that are critical in collaboration, as discussed in Chapter Six, are even more vital when it comes to leadership. Documenting the role and contribution of these competencies to higher education leadership in particular is an important need, as is the translation of this knowledge into a framework for leadership education and assessment. Also needed are methods for assessing organizational leadership needs at a particular point in time, and tools for identifying and matching leaders' capabilities to these needs.

Improving Leadership Incentives

Having appropriate incentives for recruiting and recognizing leaders is another essential element for the development of a new paradigm for leadership development within the academy. The extent to which the lack of incentives is a problem may vary from position to position within a single institution, and from institution to institution and discipline to discipline. In general, however, higher education faces a broad challenge in offering sufficient incentives to encourage and recognize leadership excellence. This seems particularly critical in disciplines and technical areas in which individuals have loyalties to two communities: the college or university at which they work, and their technical or academic discipline with which they identify academically and professionally. From an institution's point of view, this is a double-edged sword. On the one hand, the stature of an institution is greatly influenced by the accomplishments and reputations of staff, and especially faculty, within their disciplines or areas of expertise. On the other hand, loyalties and attention to external professional communities may detract from the time, energy, and commitment faculty and staff members are willing and able to devote to their own institution. Given the traditional incentive systems and criteria for advancement—particularly for academics—the benefits for devoting effort to one's discipline are quite clear and tangible, while those associated with effort dedicated to one's college or university often are not.

New and creative incentive systems are needed to attract and retain exceptional leaders. Leaders must find it professionally and financially rewarding to invest time and effort in developing their expertise and commitment to institutional leadership. Colleges and universities must clearly articulate the importance of these contributions and recognize successes. Rhetoric alone, however, is insufficient, and even counterproductive since it breeds resentment and cynicism, unless buttressed by meaningful institutional incentives and rewards.

Enhancing Leadership Education

Education must be at the core of a new paradigm for the leadership development. Studies in the corporate arena indicate that it takes about ten years of preparation for an individual to attain an expert level of performance in a particular role (Ericsson, Krampe, and Tesch-Romer, 1993). Recognizing the importance of expediting the socialization and learning process, businesses spend an estimated $30 billion a year on training—roughly 1.4 percent of their payroll budgets—and a majority of those funds are directed toward training individuals who serve in administrative and professional positions (Meister, 1994).

Surveys of more than two thousand academic leaders indicate that fewer than 10 percent have leadership development programs in their institutions (Gmelch, 2000), and it seems likely that comparable surveys of leaders in other areas in colleges and universities would produce much the same findings: "In business . . . potential leaders are usually identified fairly early and are deliberately assigned positions that allow them to develop the all-around expertise necessary for top management. Their professional ambitions are understood and monitored. At most colleges and universities, however, a comparable grooming of possible future leaders would be frowned upon if not strongly criticized as inappropriate to the historical values of campus administration" (Munitz, 1995, p. 4).

As Gmelch (2000, p. 29) puts it, "We need a radical change in our approach to leadership development in higher education." Innovative educational programs addressing leadership issues and competencies are much needed throughout higher education. We need to replace programs that reflect the survival-of-the-fittest paradigm with an educational approach that benefits from the competencies for which others look to the academy as a standard of excellence: discovery, learning, and engagement.[4]

There are a growing number of degree programs; courses; and academic, cocurricular, professional, corporate, and community programs aimed at leadership development that are helpful models (Schwartz, Axtman, and Freeman, 1998). Various higher education organizations and associations, including the W. K. Kellogg Foundation, the American Council on Education, and the National Association of College and University Business Officers (NACUBO), have also begun to view leadership development as a priority, and programs are beginning to address this need.[5] As an outgrowth of the Kellogg Leadership for Institutional Change (LINC) initiative, about fifty colleges and universities—alone or in collaboration with others—have also begun to offer regional or state initiatives, and a growing number of institutions—including Penn State, Michigan, Harvard, Rutgers, Delaware, and Berkeley—are experimenting with leadership development programs.[6]

Leadership Development Program Goals

The development of campus-based programs begins with the articulation of a rationale, documentation of a need, clarification of goals, specification of program content and components, and identification of sources of support.

Although programs differ widely in structure and content, the fundamental purposes of leadership development initiatives generally pursue a number of goals:

- Creating a forum for reflecting on higher education, the institution, and the role of academic and administrative leadership positions
- Providing information on institutional policies, practices, procedures, and regulations that are essential for departmental administration

- Offering a forum for discussing issues and topics of concern and for answering questions
- Sharing contemporary research and personal experiences relative to leadership theory and effective practice
- Facilitating interdepartmental and interdisciplinary communication and problem solving
- Creating a collaborative and supportive network for campus leaders
- Providing information on university services and offices
- Accelerating the socialization process of new leaders
- Enhancing leaders' capabilities to support the mission, vision, and values of the unit and institution

Leadership Program Content and Method

To be effective and valuable, leadership programs must address salient needs and concerns. Ramsden (1998) found these general concerns among university leaders: maintaining quality with fewer resources; managing budgets; managing and leading academic people in times of rapid change, turbulence in the higher education environment, increasing student numbers, and changing student profiles; and balancing academic work with the demands of a leadership role because specific concerns and issues are quite likely to vary from institution to institution. Campus leadership needs assessments should be an important component of program planning and design. At Rutgers, for example, interviews and a survey of academic chairs indicated that academic policies and procedures, budgeting and funding, student-related concerns, faculty personnel issues, change and change management, faculty mentoring and motivation, staff personnel, and dispute resolution—while still maintaining a research program—were the priority issues.[7]

In addition to needs and concerns identified by potential program participants, leadership development programs also typically address a series of fairly standard topics. The agenda might include national, state, and local concerns relative to higher education; understanding and interfacing with external constituencies; regulatory and legal issues; budgeting; personnel and employee relations; campus opportunities and challenges; assessment and planning; work process analysis and improvement; and departmental performance measurement. Personal and interpersonal competency development should also be a focus

(Higgerson, 1996; Ramsden, 1998). This might include areas such as those associated with emotional intelligence and communication competence.[8]

Leadership can be taught and learned using the same methodologies that are applied in other subject matters and proficiencies addressed by higher education. Successful outcomes require effective instructional designs, appropriate instruction and mentoring, feedback on performance, and genuine desire by the learner. There is a general consensus that, ideally, leadership programs should be both theoretical and practical in approach, using methods that are both informational and experiential. Exemplary programs include action learning, feedback on leadership performance, exposure to senior leaders and strategic agendas, external coaching and mentoring, and cross-functional and job rotations (Giber, Carter, and Goldsmith, 2000). Case studies are also popular instructional methods,[9] and many successful organizations integrate what Noel Tichy (1997) describes as the "teachable point of view"—coherent and engaging leadership narratives that illustrate leadership concepts, values, and experiences.

Implementing Leadership Feedback and Review Systems

Systematic feedback and review of leaders and leadership practices is another core component of leadership development. Feedback and evaluation are appropriate for leaders for all the same reasons that student, faculty, and program review and assessment programs have become common practice.

A variety of strategies are available to make the feedback and review process a useful input for leadership development. The evaluation process could include the preparation and review of administrative portfolios (Seldin and Higgerson, 2002). Typically, review processes also include systematic gathering of information from those who see leaders in action. Probably the most beneficial model is the 360 degree approach, so named because it includes feedback from a variety of perspectives (the individual to whom a leader reports; peers; and those over whom the leader has responsibility) in an effort to yield a broad perspective on leadership effectiveness (Jones and Bearley, 1996; Lepsinger and Lucia, 1997; Milliman and McFadden, 1997, Peiperl, 2001). Through the use of various methods and multiple-points-of-view feedback, leaders have access to a range of information that should be useful in helping them assess and advance their effectiveness and development, and to establish meaningful improvement plans and goals.

Concluding Comments

Effective leadership is a pressing need in all organizations. For the higher education community, it has become a major priority. We need leaders who will help the academy understand, confront, and constructively address the many challenges we face, who can engage their colleagues and external constituencies in a more resolute commitment to self-assessment, dialogue, and ambitious institutional improvement goals. Newman and Couturier (2001) describe the need this way: "Capable leaders who not only create an institutional vision and strategy, but are also capable of drawing faculty, the administration, the board, alumni, and students into the process so that they understand, are energized by, and support the institutional direction" (p. 16).

Efforts to develop innovative approaches to identifying, recruiting, developing, and retaining outstanding leaders face a number of obstacles; economic considerations, cultural resistance, and structural impediments rank high among them. The record seems to suggest, however, that if these hurdles can be overcome, leadership programs are often well-received and can make important contributions.

The familiar survival-of-the-fittest approach to preparing and supporting leaders no longer serves our interests, if it ever did. A new paradigm is needed, one that reflects the academy's core values and competencies relative to discovery, learning, and engagement. Higher education needs a paradigm that reaffirms, for ourselves, the values and benefits of the kinds of educational experiences we have long advocated for others—and one that devotes the attention and resources necessary to effectively translate those values into practice.

Notes

1. Ramsden (1998) presents a most forceful statement about the leadership challenges posed by shared decision making within the academy: decision making "has come under pressure . . . because its weaknesses are more evident in a system where there are more

decisions to be made and where quick responses to external changes are at a premium. It is a slow form of decision making. It is intrinsically inward-looking. Its procedures are unwieldy. It exudes an air of protective self-interest. A higher education system whose institutions need to search for new funding sources, plan strategically, and compete with each other in a market with manifold clients no longer possesses the homogeneity and stability which can make collegiality an effective form of getting things done. . . . Academics tend towards criticism, skepticism, and sometimes destructive negativism. Collegiality allows these attitudes and behaviors [to] reign free" (p. 22). Clearly, this is not a perspective shared by many academics, who would assert that Ramsden overstates the negatives and fails, in this summary, to appropriately acknowledge the benefits. For instance, Noble (2001) speaks passionately of the need for "those who truly embody education, teachers and students, as well as the larger community that education is meant to serve in a democratic society [to] . . . reclaim this precious and unique social space as a realm of freedom, open access, debate, inquiry, and learning—a place, in short, where the habits and highest ideals of democracy are a way of life" (p. 32).

2. A recent study by Warren Bennis (2000) analyzed 350 companies with leadership development. Forty-four percent of them indicated they had a process for nominating and developing high-potential employees.

3. The text is verbatim. Names of the individuals involved were changed for obvious reasons.

4. These are the terms suggested by the Kellogg Commission. See Kellogg Commission (2001a).

5. See, for instance, "Chairing the Academic Department" (www.acenet.edu); *Institutional Effectiveness,* from the National Association of College and University Business Officers (www.nacubo.org/register_for_programs/); "Leading Your Department: A Workshop for Academic Chairs," Cornell University, www.sce.cornell.edu; and "Academic Chairpersons' Conference" sponsored by Kansas State University (www.dce.ksu.edu/academicchairpersons/).

6. See Kellogg Commission (2001b); "Breakthrough Leadership" (2003); "Leadership for Institutional Change Initiative" (2001); and Academic Leadership Program (www.academicleadership.rutgers.edu/).

7. These leadership needs of chairs and other academic administrators were identified through surveys, focus groups, and interviews undertaken at Rutgers University as a part of the W. K. Kellogg–Rutgers Academic Leadership Development Program in 1999. The author acknowledges the contributions of the members of the ALP initiative, particularly Gary Gigliotti, who coordinated the survey; and members of the planning committee: Paul Breitman, Dan Fishman, Barry

Qualls, Brent Ruben, Norman Schnayer, Karen Stubaus, and Sherrie Tromp; and Barbara Bender, who serves as current chair of ALP.

8. For a listing and discussion of topics associated with emotional intelligence, see Cherniss and Goleman (2001), Cooper and Sawaf, (1997), Goleman (1997, 1998a, 1998b), Mayer and Salovey (1997), and Weisinger (1998). For a review of those associated with communication competence, see Daly and Wiemann (1994); O'Hair, Friedrich, Wiemann, and Wiemann (1997); Spitzberg and Cupach (1984); Ruben (1976); and Ruben and Kealey (1979).

9. For interesting examples from a variety of contexts, see Bratton (1998); Kotter (2001); Knight and Trowler (2001); and Useem (1998).

Narratives

Devoting More Attention and Resources to Leadership: Attracting, Developing, and Retaining Outstanding Leaders

Attracting, developing, and retaining outstanding leaders is one of the most critical challenges facing the academy. A number of innovative programs are being developed to address these issues. In the first narrative in this section, Vice Provost Bobby Gempesaw describes the University of Delaware's integrative approach, which includes development, review, and incentives.

Next, Chet Warzynski and Brian Chabot, from Cornell, and Billie Willits and Leonard Pollack, from Penn State, describe evolving leadership development programs for faculty and staff at their institutions, and some of the challenges and benefits associated with implementation.

The significance of the leadership challenge is also being recognized and addressed at the regional level, as with the "Big Ten" CIC approach discussed in "The Committee on Institutional Cooperation's Academic Leadership Program" in Chapter Six, and at the national level by such national associations as the American Council on Education (ACE), the American Association for Higher Education (AAHE), and the National Association of College and University Business Officers. In the final narrative in this section, NACUBO President Jay Morley presents a view of the importance of leadership development and summarizes that organization's efforts to encourage and support these advances.

Recruiting and Supporting Academic Leaders at the University of Delaware

Conrado M. (Bobby) Gempesaw II
Vice Provost for Academic and International
Programs, University of Delaware

The successful management of a research university in the twenty-first century requires that the entrepreneurial spirit of the faculty be channeled toward common institutional goals. One crucial element in developing the pathways to achieve synergy in higher education is the selection and recruitment not only of excellent faculty but of outstanding administrators as well. The academic leadership sets the tone for campus governance and direction. To recruit and retain good academic leaders, the institution must provide the necessary governance structure and support. This narrative briefly describes the governance structure and support for academic administration at the University of Delaware.

As one of the oldest land-grant institutions in the nation (as well as a sea-grant, space-grant, and urban-grant institution), the University of Delaware started as a small private academy in 1743. Located in Newark, Delaware, the university enrolls more than twenty-one thousand students, including sixteen thousand undergraduates. With a total budget over $500 million, the university has more than one thousand faculty members and offers 124 undergraduate, 74 master's, and 37 doctoral degrees.

The university's thirty-two-member board of trustees includes four ex officio members: the governor of the state, the president of the university, the master of the State Grange, and the president of the State Board of Education. Of the remaining twenty-eight members, eight are appointed by the governor and twenty are elected by majority vote of the board. The senior administration officers include the president, provost, executive vice president and treasurer, four other vice presidents, and seven college deans. In addition, there are more than seventy department chairs and academic program directors. The university Faculty Senate has twenty standing committees, performs the functions assigned to faculty governance, and has responsibility for curriculum and related academic matters.

Academic Resource Management

During the last five years, the university has made substantial changes as part of an overall plan to decentralize academic resource management. The major changes include budget decentralization, benchmarking indirect cost returns, providing full tuition support for all funded graduate students, and carryover of unspent funds to facilitate long term planning. Each college dean is given an annual block budget to cover salaries plus operating funds. Salary savings from vacant positions and operating funds are available to the college and departments; vacant positions remain in the college but are subject to an annual position plan agreement with the Provost. In addition, each college has a benchmark for indirect cost returns. Any excess overhead beyond the benchmark goes to the college and department.

Deans and chairs can use budget decentralization and benchmarking indirect cost returns to enhance resources at the college and department levels. By setting a higher indirect cost return benchmark, the requested increase in the benchmark can be added to the block budget. The dollar increase in the benchmark is collected during the course of the year, while the block budget is increased at the start of the year. This allows additional recurring budget resources and permits flexibility in support of new initiatives.

Academic Leadership Development

The University of Delaware has been an active participant in the American Council of Education (ACE) Fellows program, hosting fellows and nominating UD faculty to the program. In the last seven years, UD has nominated at least four faculty leaders to participate in the program, with two of them selected in the nationwide competition. The university has also hosted three ACE Fellows from other institutions. The ACE Fellows were given specific assignments and worked with the president, the provost, and the executive vice president and participated in senior staff and deans council meetings.

The university also sponsors twice-yearly leadership workshops for department chairs and academic program directors. Initially, the workshops were focused on new chairs and program directors dealing with topics such as faculty evaluation, grievance procedures, and promotion and tenure issues. Over the last three years, as the program grew, the leadership workshops were expanded to include not only all department chairs but also directors of academic programs and centers. New topics added to the workshop include faculty workload policies; collective bargaining contract administration; and, more important, a detailed presentation of the university's academic and administrative budgets and projection for the coming years. The leadership workshop has grown from an average of fifteen to twenty participants to more than one hundred this year.

The department chairs and academic program directors have a formal organization, called the Chairs Caucus, that meets once a month during the academic year. Typically, the president meets with the caucus at the end of the academic year. The provost usually meets with the caucus at the beginning of the fall semester and at the end of the spring semester prior to the caucus meeting with the president. Other administrators are also invited throughout the year. Topics discussed include budgetary issues, undergraduate and graduate admissions, general education reform, undergraduate research, study abroad, honors program, and other related issues.

Evaluation of Academic Leaders

It is the policy of the University of Delaware that periodic evaluation of deans and chairs be conducted and that they serve at the pleasure of the provost and the president. Deans are subject to an annual review by the provost. Usually, a major in-depth review is conducted after the initial five years of appointment. Major in-depth reviews and evaluations of the dean can be initiated by the president, provost, or a petition of a simple majority of the college faculty.

Department chairs are appointed by the president of the university, upon the recommendation of the appropriate deans and the provost, for a term of five years subject to renewal. The president has the authority to replace a department chair at any time within a five-year term if, in the opinion of the president, the provost, and the appropriate dean, such action is warranted. The performance of each chair is reviewed annually by deans and evaluated in depth periodically. More intensive evaluations of chairs are scheduled at periods consistent with the five-year term of office; the time of evaluation is toward the end of the penultimate year of the term of office. An evaluation of the work of any department chair at other than the regular period may be initiated by the chair, dean, provost, president, or a simple majority of the members of the department.

Compensation and Benefits

As compensation for expected summer presence and activity, department chairs on a nine-month contract receive an amount equal to one-ninth of their base salary incremented during the period of service. Upon satisfactory completion of the first term of service as chair, the one-ninth portion becomes a permanent addition to their base salary. Under normal circumstances, a second term as chair does not result in the permanent addition of a second ninth to the base salary, but one-ninth of the base salary is continued during the period of service. Furthermore, departmental chairs on nine-month contracts receive an administrative supplement of $5,000 and those on eleven-month contracts an administrative supplement of $5,500 during the period of service as chair. In addition to merit percentage increases calculated on the base salary, the same percentage is applied annually to the chair's administrative supplement, which is then added to determine the new base salary.

There are also other benefits given by the university to all faculty that help in the recruitment and retention of academic leaders. The university has made available a sum of money for the financing of residential mortgages to assist in recruiting and relocating highly qualified faculty and professionals through obtaining appropriate housing within the vicinity of the university. One program makes a one-time $5,000 payment at settlement on the purchase of a primary residence. Another program targets a specific neighborhood in the community and extends a $5,000 cash loan at settlement, to be forgiven at the rate of $1,000 for each full year the eligible employee maintains the house as his or her primary residence, with the stipulation that the purchaser must remain an eligible employee for two years from the date of settlement.

The university offers excellent health, dental, and life insurance coverage along with a tuition remission program that allows up to two tuition remission requests per semester for each employee. The student must be either a spouse or a dependent child of the employee and must be a full-time matriculated undergraduate student. For retirement purposes, the university offers a match of 11 percent of annual base salary for every eligible employee who contributes a minimum of 4 percent of salary. Employees are also assisted in meeting the cost of annual expenses for services provided by physicians, technicians, opticians, and so on such as annual physical examinations, ob-gyn examinations, eye examinations, optical fittings, hearing examinations, and hearing aid fittings. Full-time employees can receive up to $175 per fiscal year.

Outcomes and Lessons Learned

In 1990, President David Roselle set four goals for the university: (1) to give students greater access to scholarship and financial aid; (2) to provide competitive compensation for faculty and staff; (3) to enhance the campus through state-of-the-art teaching, research, and learning facilities; and (4) to promote a student-centered campus. As part of the Middle States Higher Education self-study accreditation process in 2001, a faculty task force conducted a comprehensive survey designed to assess faculty opinion on issues such as the quality of academic community, facilities, faculty time allocation and employment, and university administration and governance.

The survey results show that faculty at the university set high standards of academic quality and rate the institution highly in meeting these standards. Ninety-seven percent approved of the attractiveness of the campus and facilities. Ninety percent of the respondents indicated they were satisfied with their professional life at the university. Seventy-nine percent of the faculty surveyed gave a high rating for the overall quality of the academic community, and 78 percent rated compensation as good to excellent. These results show a fairly high level of satisfaction among faculty at the University of Delaware.

The essence of academic administration support is not simply to allocate resources to academic programs but also to impart direction for efficient use of these resources. It is only through the proper use and shared governance of these resources that academic administrators and faculty will be effective in delivering outstanding academic programs. Finally, it is equally important that the institution develop an attractive compensation and benefit package not just to recruit but also to retain strong academic leaders.

Leadership Development at Cornell University

Chester C. Warzynski
Director, Organizational Development Services,
Office of Human Resources, Cornell University

Brian F. Chabot
Professor, Department of Ecology and Evolutionary
Biology, College of Agriculture and Life Sciences,
Cornell University

One of the biggest challenges facing institutions of higher education is how to get faculty to engage in some of the broader leadership roles addressing institutional, local, regional, and global issues while at the same time fulfilling their obligations to their teaching and research programs. Cornell is attempting to meet this challenge by developing future leaders through its academic and professional development programs. The case study in this narrative describes the evolution of leadership education for faculty and staff at Cornell and outlines a program that is making a difference in faculty and staff leadership.

As the land-grant university for the state of New York and a member of the Ivy League, Cornell University represents a unique combination of public and private institutions, including thirteen colleges and schools serving 13,650 undergraduate students, 5,600 graduate students, 2,990 faculty, and 9,400 support staff. Cornell includes two distinct and largely separate internal organizations: an administrative organization to handle the business requirements of the university and an academic organization to concentrate on the mission of the university. Within these two divisions is an array of highly decentralized and autonomous administrative and academic units serving multiple stakeholders (faculty, students, research sponsors, public agencies, citizens). The administrative division resembles a business organization in that it is hierarchical in structure and operates with a customer-driven culture. The academic division, on the other hand, is largely based on a disciplinary and departmental structure and includes the individualized teaching, research, and outreach programs of the faculty. The net effect is that the university closely resembles a complex adaptive system in which change occurs through environmental adaptation rather than through design or decision. Addressing leadership needs within this complex of cultures and structures has proven challenging.

Leadership education for faculty and staff began with initiatives largely within the College of Agriculture and Life Sciences (CALS) and were connected to national programs for land-grant universities. For example, the National Association of Agricultural Experiment Stations Directors ran a leadership program for department chairs sponsored by the National Association of Land-Grant Colleges, aimed at expanding the leadership capacity of faculty through general leadership knowledge and skill development.

In 1987, Cornell introduced a training program for total quality management (TQM). Although leadership was not the central focus for these activities, elements of leadership were implicit in the processes; it involved the whole university, and a large group of faculty and staff were engaged. Subsequently, a new program, Leadership for Institutional Change, was developed to replace TQM concepts with more contemporary organizational leadership skills. In a related but separate activity, the university contracted with the Zenger-Miller Corporation to make their proprietary materials available to support leadership skill development workshops. The overwhelming majority of participants in these two programs were involved with administration. Although progress was made with each of these endeavors, they did not attract sufficient numbers of faculty, they dealt with parts of leadership rather than taking a comprehensive approach, and they did not produce lasting change in leadership practices. To address these needs, the Discovering Leadership Program was created.

The Discovering Leadership Program

The Discovering Leadership Program (DLP), initiated in 1998,[1] has proven to have a lasting positive effect on its participants and on leadership behavior throughout the university. The goals of the DLP are to (1) increase self-awareness of participants about their personal leadership style, attitudes, skills, and behavioral impact on others; (2) improve communication and relationship-building skills for engaging and motivating others, building trust, establishing organizational culture, providing direction, giving and receiving feedback, and resolving conflict; (3) create new experiences around developing and leading project teams and complex organizations; (4) develop and practice a methodology and guidelines for leading, sponsoring, and supporting change; and (5) design and execute an individualized learning and action plan that makes a difference to the individual and organization. DLP is intended for senior executives, middle managers, and faculty members who are responsible for setting direction in their organization.

As the name indicates, the discovery process is the core of the program. Each participant works through a series of developmental exercises and activities to discover personal competencies and new ways of thinking about leadership and influencing others. This contingency approach to leadership is highly individualized, to match the highly individualized culture of the university. The developmental emphasis is on understanding and tapping into individual experience, information, knowledge, and energy to develop responses to organizational challenges. Personal development occurs through working with others to meet challenges, evaluating and reflecting on this experience, and distilling the lessons learned for future application—all within the supportive context of the group.

What makes DLP different from other leadership courses is that participants are engaged in a learning process that inspires trust and confidence in moving toward common goals and challenges. This stems not only from technical competencies that they acquire but also from establishing a strong inner understanding of each participant and his or her impact on others. Therefore the program goes beyond technique and focuses on fundamental issues of self-awareness, personal values, and interpersonal relationships.

Another theme of the program is that leadership qualities are not taught; rather, they are learned through experience. The program is based on an experiential process that takes time, requires persistence, and depends on the participant's interest and willingness to change. It is designed to arouse that inner desire for change, and to provide the experiences, intellectual framework, and practice necessary to produce the desired change.

Components of the Discovering Leadership Program

Each program is offered to twenty-four participants and consists of eleven days of developmental activities in three courses over a period of five months. Table 8.1 summarizes the major leadership challenges, strategies and skills, and methods and tools covered in the program. The first course, requiring five days and entitled Discovering the Leader Within, focuses on self-assessment, individual and group challenge, and peer support. Participants use an open space meeting technique, consisting of unstructured and informal discussions, to develop from their experience a model of leadership based on the qualities, skills, and actions of effective leaders. Using this framework as a baseline, participants work in teams through a series of physical activities on the Hoffman Challenge ("ropes") course. These experiential exercises help individuals get to know each other and facilitate group trust, relationship building, and group process.

Participants continue personal discovery with the Myers-Briggs Type Indicator and a 360 degree assessment completed before the course. This information yields insight into personal preferences, individual strengths, and opportunities for development. Armed with this information, participants work through an in-depth organizational simulation and experience what it feels like to play roles at various levels of the organization.

The simulation is followed by an in-depth analysis and application of the concept of dialogue and how it may be used to unhook leaders from their own—and their organization's—dysfunctional behavior and practices. Dialogue is a critical communication tool for influencing and relationship building. Finally, participants clarify their individual values and develop a personal mission and vision statement for giving direction to their leadership. The course concludes with each person designing and sharing a learning and action plan for dealing with his or her own leadership challenges.

Table 8.1. Leadership Challenges and Strategies.

Leadership Challenges	Strategies and Skills	Methods and Tools
Motivating commitment	Self-awareness, personal mastery, vision, mission, and values clarification	MBTI, 360 degree assessment, learning action plans
Communicating across roles and cultures	Giving and receiving feedback, dialogue (inquiry and advocacy), building relationships	Challenge Course (Ropes), open space technology, left-hand column exercise, role playing
Establishing shared values and goals	Strategic planning and visioning, culture development	Future search conference, values-clarification and alignment
Coordinating across disciplines and functions	Conducting effective meetings, facilitating group dynamics, team building	Organizational simulation, group problem solving, and decision making
Creating change for continuous improvement	Dealing with resistance to change and building sponsorship and support, project management	Action research and learning, organization development, project assignments
Developing accountability	Performance management, coaching, conflict resolution, mediation	Measurement, feedback and coaching, interest-based negotiation, organizational development

The second three-day course, on discovering teams, is held approximately eight weeks after the first course. This course focuses on the functional prerequisites of effective organizations and key strategies for building and leading teams. The group engages in a variety of organizational simulations and skill-building exercises to simulate leading in a complex and often competitive environment in which people have different agendas and approaches to getting their needs met. The participants learn the importance of assessing power in relationships and develop leadership skills in giving and receiving feedback, negotiation, and conflict resolution to supplement and reinforce the leadership process. Participants learn how to facilitate group dynamics and conduct effective meetings, design and build project teams, set organizational culture and develop a strategic plan, and resolve conflict.

In the final three-day course, Discovering and Leading Change, held eight weeks after the second one, participants learn how to engage others in designing a change process, dealing with resistance to change, and building sponsorship and support for change. The need to engage people in change processes is essential for successful leadership. Working in small groups, participants identify an organizational challenge or real-life project they would like to address. They next examine several methodologies for leading change and develop a set of questions for engaging others in the change process. Working on their project, the members of each group collaboratively design a change plan. The last step is for participants to present and defend their plan for change before the entire group and to evaluate its effectiveness in terms of whether it increased their understanding, added new information or knowledge to the group, increased motivation, improved relationships and teamwork, and enhanced support for the change. This exercise brings together the lessons, tools, skills, and strategies from the entire course and applies them to a real situation.

In the final exercise, participants revisit the results of their 360 degree report and revise their personal goals, action plans, and visions. They also determine and report on how they intend to use their newly developed leadership knowledge and skills.

Between the three courses, participants receive coaching on their learning and action plans. The results of their efforts are summarized and shared in stories, many of which are communicated to the Cornell University Leadership Development listserv. In addition, the entire group of graduates meets annually for a one-day reinforcement program to share stories, evaluate and benchmark leadership practices, and create tools and visions for leadership. What is emerging from these sessions is a community of leadership practice in which the qualities and methods of successful leaders are being benchmarked and distributed throughout the university, and a vision of leadership is taking form.

Involving Faculty

Although Discovering Leadership is considered successful, one of the continuing challenges is to get faculty to participate in the program. Generally, faculty members are not fully aware of their leadership roles in the university. There is a culture of cynicism among faculty regarding committees, assuming formal leadership roles, and any skill development related to these activities. Leadership outside one's teaching and research program is not considered a key factor in promotion and tenure—that is, it is not rewarded. Consequently, faced with many competing demands and limited time, leadership development does not assume a high priority. Fortunately this is not true of everyone; there is a significant group of faculty who understand the value of good citizenship. It is these faculty members that participate in Discovering Leadership.

Three factors have facilitated the recruitment of faculty to this program. The first is the positive reputation of the program. Alumni of the program have been enthusiastic advocates and recruiters of colleagues. The second is that some faculty members currently serve in—or anticipate serving in—leadership roles in their units. Serving in a leadership capacity produces any number of teachable moments, which often heighten awareness of the value of more formalized leadership development programming. Also, a number of departments have rotating chairs, with the next chair being identified well before taking office. This allows ample preparation time for the incoming chair. A third factor is the support by particular colleges of leadership development efforts. New faculty entering the College of Agriculture and Life Sciences, and several other colleges, are exposed to skill development workshops in their first few years, and these experiences significantly reduce resistance to further development programs.

Outcomes

Two particularly gratifying outcomes are the continuing interest of past participants in leadership development and growing recognition of the value of this experience among university leaders. We hold annual refresher conferences that are well attended and allow us over time to gauge the value of aspects of the DLP. The value of the program to participants is sustained. Also, increasingly participation in new workshops is being encouraged both by recommendations of past participants and by department chairs and deans who are recognizing the value of this experience for people in their organizations.

Over the past four years, 169 leaders, representing every college and school, have completed the Discovering Leadership Program, including 16 faculty members, 3 associate deans, 2 assistant deans, 5 academic chairs, and 18 academic staff. According to evaluations of participants, the program has been highly beneficial to the individual leaders and their departments. Individuals commonly report in their evaluations that they achieved a greater self-awareness of their values and purpose; greater understanding of personal style, attitudes, and behaviors; and a clearer understanding of the impact they have on other people. Also frequently reported in the evaluations are increased self-confidence, optimism, renewed energy, and greater sense of community. A summary of participant evaluations is in Table 8.2.

The outcome participants report most frequently is an increased sense of renewal and commitment, together with a set of practical tools for addressing real organizational problems. In the words of one faculty member: "Going through the course on experiencing leadership has been an eye-opener for me. It not only redefined leadership for me (from front-runner to motivator and team-member), but the course supplies important tools to deal with real-life people issues. It has become clear to me that in our line of business people are our biggest asset, probably more so than any other industry. Investing time and effort into shaping the leaders in such an organization evidences great wisdom and insight in the very core of our existence."

Another indicator of the program's effectiveness is the demand from faculty and staff to participate in the program. There is a list of seventy-nine nominees, including twenty-one faculty, on the waiting list. In addition, two internal divisions—Cornell Information Technologies, and Administration, Facilities, and Finance—are engaged in making the program available to all their managers and leaders, and two other internal units are interested in offering the program to their managers in the near future.

Table 8.2. Participant Reaction.

Group	Information	Skills	Effect	Overall
Pilot	4.6	4.5	4.2	4.5
Control group	4.0	4.3	4.8	4.4
Group average	4.2	4.4	4.5	4.6

N=169; Rating: 5 = high; 1= low

Conclusion

The Discovering Leadership Program evolved from several previous efforts at Cornell to develop improved leadership capacity around evolving institutional needs. Discovering Leadership was designed to address a set of critical challenges at Cornell University by fostering (1) self-awareness around personal values, mission, and vision, and impact on others; (2) a set of competencies and capabilities for communicating, building relationships and teams, and managing performance; (3) a set of roles and activities to effectively lead change and counteract organizational mind-sets, structure, and politics; and (4) a performance management accountability system. The program encourages participants to develop their own leadership approach through a process of discovering their own strengths and weaknesses. It also emphasizes the importance and value of analyzing their own experiences and needs—as well as the experience and needs of their particular work group—to better meet the challenges of academic and administrative leadership within Cornell and higher education today.

Note

1. Roxi Bahar Hewertson, director of administration, finance, and facilities; Clint Sidle, director of the Park Leadership Fellows Program in the Johnson Graduate School of Management; and Chet Warzynski, director of the organizational development series, originated the Discovering Leadership Program and were involved in developing it into a universitywide program.

Penn State's Excellence in Leadership and Management Program

Billie S. Willits
Associate Vice President for Human Resources,
Pennsylvania State University

Leonard E. Pollack
Manager, Human Resource Development Center,
Pennsylvania State University

Founded in 1855, Pennsylvania State University is a state-related, land-grant institution with more than eighty-one thousand undergraduate and graduate students; approximately sixteen thousand full-time faculty, staff, and technical service employees; and twenty-four campus/college locations throughout the Commonwealth of Pennsylvania. Given Penn State's commitment to the integration of teaching, research, and public service, it is important that all aspects of this single university function together for the good of the institution.

In 1995, after a number of years of focus on quality improvement, and with a new president, the Penn State community conducted a survey of faculty, staff, and technical service employees to assess the culture of the university to garner input for setting strategic goals. The Office of Human Resources led the initiative in conjunction with the Provost's Office and the Office of Quality and Planning.

Significant to the survey was a thorough study of what the university said it valued. These values were gleaned from a content analysis of strategic plans, reward and recognition practices, documents of the board of trustees, and the president's "State of the University" addresses. Faculty and staff expertise was tapped for the design of the content and questions. A third-party consulting group was used to finalize, distribute, receive, and analyze the responses. The survey was distributed and analyzed in spring 1996.

Results of the survey indicated that the university would better meet its mission and vision if it emphasized professional development of leadership skills and tools throughout the community. Specifically, the survey indicated a need to enhance coaching skills, improve access to professional development, strengthen vertical communications, increase mutual respect and teamwork, and foster support for university values.

In addition to the survey results, a number of other forces were driving the need for leadership and management development at Penn State. Among them were the university's quest for empowering and humanizing management, furthering continuous quality improvement, enhancing the strategic planning process, advancing the framework for fostering diversity, heightening attention to professional development in annual staff reviews, and finding news ways to encourage increased productivity.

These driving forces collectively pointed to the benefits of accelerating the transition of Penn State's leadership and management practices from a traditional, hierarchical approach to a more participative, empowering model. In general, the evolution of the landscape within which Penn State operates warranted a management and leadership paradigm with increased emphasis on coaching, guiding, enabling, and facilitating. As an integrated response to these influences, the Office of Human Resources began planning for a series of leadership and management development opportunities for faculty, staff, and technical service employees.

In early 1997, a universitywide design team representing all stakeholders was established to craft an overall vision for leadership development at Penn State. The design team solicited input from faculty, academic administrators, staff, and administrators to obtain perspective, decided to use seminars as the main format for leadership development, and identified the general issues to be addressed in the seminars. The design team submitted a proposal to the central administration for the Excellence in Leadership and Management curriculum. The proposal included guidelines for both program content and learning activities. For example, seminars were to enhance participants' coaching, enabling, empowering, and facilitating skills; management concern for people; commitment to diversity and respect for others; teamwork, collaboration, and partnerships; personal and professional development; ethics and integrity; and excellence in individual and group performance.

In terms of learning activities, the proposal called for seminars that were to be participative, developmental, skill-based, and performance-oriented. Toward this end, there was a focus on the development of practical skills and the use of realistic case studies to achieve behavioral and organizational impact. Active and collaborative learning activities were created to advance quality and the quest for excellence; initiative and self-management; creativity and innovation; and critical thinking, judgment, and problem solving.

Penn State's central administration accepted the proposal and offered to support about 75 percent of all costs, with the balance supported by participants' departments. With central support, the Human Resource Development Center engaged faculty and staff with the requisite expertise to develop and deliver the programming. Review teams were established to critique the seminar material and to ensure consistency with preestablished design guidelines. In addition, each program was piloted and refined as appropriate.

In addition to taking on curriculum oversight, the design team also tapped marketing professionals in the university to submit articles, letters, memos, and even "sound bites" for use by deans and administrators. Marketing communications were intended to inform the community continuously of the existence of the Excellence in Leadership and Management programs, highlight program benefits, encourage participation, and stand as a reminder that the skills emphasized in the programs need to be used in the departments on an ongoing basis.

How the Program Works

The proposal was implemented in two phases. The first, initiated in 1998, included two programs: the Penn State Leader, and Mastering SuperVision. The second phase, launched in 2000, also included two programs:—Management Institute, and the Leadership Academy.

Each program in the curriculum shares a common foundation of eight core values for leadership and management at Penn State. All four programs are structured to facilitate networking to strengthen relationships among participants from different units and foster broader understanding of the university. Table 8.3 is an overview of the distinctive features of each program.

Table 8.3. Overview of Excellence in Leadership and Management Program.

Program	Highlights
The Penn State Leader	Major theme: Each person can be a leader in his or her role at the University
Audience: All faculty, staff, and technical service employees	Key topics: Current concepts and principles in leadership, leading in the context of Penn State values and culture, leadership in a rapidly changing world
Classroom time: 8 hours	Salient learning activities: Self-assessment of leadership behaviors, simulations of key leadership challenges in higher education, discussion of assigned readings, use of deans and executives as guest speakers
Mastering SuperVision	Major theme: Supervisors are encouraged to be visionary in leading their work groups
Audience: Faculty and staff in "supervisory roles"	Key topics: Penn State priorities for leadership and management, interpersonal skills, performance management, creating an environment of mutual trust, meeting special supervisory challenges
Classroom time: 56 hours	Salient learning activities: Systematic skill development with modeling and practice, realistic case studies, application-oriented group project
Management Institute	Major theme: Strategic leadership and management of a department or work unit
Audience: Managers and directors	Key topics: Leadership in the context of Penn State values and priorities; enhancing organizational effectiveness through planning, assessment and improvement; managing budgets; optimizing time and managing stress

continued

Table 8.3. *(continued)*

Program	Highlights
Classroom time: 37 hours	Salient learning activities: 360 degree development process that results in an individualized leadership development plan, access to a Web-based Leadership and Management Resource Center, realistic case studies, speakers with nationally recognized expertise, multidimensional case studies requiring integration and application of skills
Leadership Academy	Major theme: Strategic leadership and management of an academic department or division
Audience: New academic department heads and division directors	Key topics: Leadership in the context of Penn State values and priorities; enhancing organizational effectiveness through planning, assessment and improvement; managing budgets; optimizing time and managing stress
Classroom time: 32 hours	Salient learning activities: 360 degree development process that results in an individualized leadership development plan, access to a Web-based Leadership and Management Resource Center, realistic case studies, speakers with nationally recognized expertise, multidimensional case studies requiring integration and application of skills

Participants in the Excellence in Leadership and Management programs are typically nominated by deans and executives, although self-nominations are also accepted. Nominees are generally assigned to heterogeneous sections that differ in terms of organizational area, years of experience, gender, ethnicity, and position. Feedback from participants indicates that the heterogeneous groups strengthen working relationships across departments and promote broad understanding of the institution. To reach faculty and staff at all Penn State locations, numerous sections of each program in the curriculum are offered each year at the University Park campus, and regionally across the Commonwealth.

Summary of Outcomes and Recommendations

Ultimately, the value of the four programs is best summarized in a quote from President Graham Spanier: "Penn State aspires to be a humane institution that delivers programs and services of the highest quality. This vision calls for strong leadership and effective management at all levels. Toward this end, the University has launched a more systematic approach to professional development that is focused on excellence in leadership and management."

We are pleased with our progress and the results to date. As of fall 2002, more than twenty-two hundred individuals have enrolled, with the largest number having completed the Penn State Leader Program (1,371) and Mastering SuperVision (726). Participants representing virtually every area of the university have attended Excellence in Leadership and Management programs. Participation across areas of the university reflects the combined effects of the success of the programs, the practice of annually soliciting nominations for participants from all deans and executives, and public statements of support from Penn State's central administration.

Feedback is systematically gathered from participants and other stakeholders through immediate and follow-up evaluations, to determine the effectiveness of the four programs and to identify ways the programs can be improved. Specifically, feedback forms with open-ended questions and Likert-type scales are completed by participants immediately after each session of each program. The open-ended questions ask participants to describe how they will apply expertise gained in the session, to suggest improvements, and to describe specific ways in which the program exceeded their expectations. As shown in Table 8.4, mean overall ratings for these evaluations consistently range from 3.00 to 4.00 on a five-step scale, indicating that all four programs are exceeding participant expectations.

**Table 8.4. Mean Overall Program Ratings: 2000–01
Through Fall 2002 (Five-Step Scale).**

Program	2000–2001	2001–2002	Fall 2002
The Penn State Leader	4.04	3.78	3.48
Mastering SuperVision	3.67	3.69	3.87
Management Institute	3.48	3.70	3.84
Leadership Academy	3.26	Program not offered	3.93

Mastering SuperVision, the Management Institute, and the Leadership Academy are also assessed by six-month follow-up evaluations completed by participants, individuals who report to participants, and individuals to whom participants report. These follow-up evaluations focus on the participants' application of skills acquired in the programs and on the organizational impact of their application efforts. As with the immediate evaluations of each session, the six-month overall program evaluations indicate that each program is consistently exceeding stakeholder expectations in terms of impact, usefulness, and perceived benefits. For example, six-month follow-up assessments involving 364 participants in Mastering SuperVision showed that:

- All three groups surveyed—participants (88.1 percent), persons to whom participants report (79.8 percent), and people who report to participants (58.8 percent)—indicated they are satisfied or very satisfied with the impact of Mastering SuperVision on job performance.
- All groups felt the participants' effectiveness as supervisors increased as a result of the program; participants perceived a 36 percent increase in effectiveness, persons to whom participants report perceived a 35 percent increase, and persons who report to participants perceived a 17 percent increase.
- Just over 42 percent of the participants indicated that a moderate level of support was received in refining and applying

the skills learned in the program. Obstacles included time, lack of upper level management support, and workload.
- More than 80 percent of the participants considered Mastering SuperVision to be a high-quality, worthwhile professional development activity.

On the basis of these experiences and assessment results, a number of conclusions and recommendations for future refinement have been reached:

- Use data to verify the need for management development
- Show how leadership development supports the institution's strategic priorities
- Create a proposal outlining each program, with input from all stakeholder groups
- Establish a cost-effective implementation strategy
- Project future benefits, especially cost savings
- Develop stakeholder consensus on a shared vision of the optimal management paradigm for the institution
- Reinforce institutional values and priorities throughout each program
- Tailor program content to the needs and interests of the target audience
- Help participants' "bosses" to actively support application efforts
- Maintain frequent, two-way communications with all stakeholder groups
- Capitalize on expertise within the institution to develop, review, or deliver the program
- Use a variety of stimulating, interactive learning activities
- Evaluate often, and use the data continuously to improve each program

These and other suggestions guide us as we continue to look for ways to improve our programs to enhance leadership development throughout the university.

The Business of Higher Education

James E. Morley, Jr.
President, National Association of College
and University Business Officers

The National Association of College and University Business Officers (NACUBO) was formed in 1962 to promote sound management and financial practices within colleges and universities. The association is structured as an institutional membership organization and has a voting membership of more than twenty-one hundred public and private colleges and universities. The member institutions represent the full spectrum of missions, from research-intensive to community college. Typically, each institution designates its chief financial officer, chief business officer, or chief administrative officer as its primary representative and lead contact to NACUBO. Although the most senior financial, business, and administrative officers are the association's primary audience, we recognize that individuals in various other roles on campus have financial and administrative needs and responsibilities, so all employees of a member institution are eligible to benefit from our programs and services, and to participate in many ways as volunteers.

Historical Perspective

The 1950s and the 1960s were simpler times in higher education. Faculty exercised considerably more influence than today, there were fewer government regulations, tuitions were low, students were sent home if they did not meet either academic or code of conduct standards, and litigation was not a "line of business."

There was no competition from a for-profit sector. The traditional not-for-profit sector monopolized the issuance of college degrees, aided by the barriers of accreditation and the high cost of entry for both physical facilities and faculty talent.

Institutions were smaller and far less complex fifty years ago. This was true of even the flagship public institutions. For example, in 1950, Penn State's enrollment was 11,132 students (compared with 40,571 students in 2000). Penn State's expenditures were approximately $22 million, while in 2000 the figure was more than $2.2 billion. Over the last fifty years, we have seen the number of postsecondary degree-granting institutions increase from about 1,850 in 1950 (NCES, 2001) to 4,180 in 2000 (*Chronicle of Higher Education Almanac,* 2002). Enrollments have risen from 2.3 million to 14.8 million students (NCES, 2001). The aggregate expenditures of these institutions have grown from approximately $2.2 billion (NCES, 2001) to $280 billion (NCES, 2001). The number of faculty has increased from 250,000 to one million over the last five decades (NCES, 2001). Research activity and dollars have increased from approximately $250 million in the early 1950s to $31 billion in 2000 (National Science Foundation, 2000). In short, postsecondary education has become a significant industry.

Major changes have also occurred in the pattern of support for higher education from federal, state, and local governments. In 1950, this support was approximately $500 million from the federal government, just under $500 million from state governments, and about $61 million from local governments (NCES and IPEDS, 2000). By contrast, in 2000 federal support (excluding student financial aid) was nearly $24 billion, state support was close to $44 billion, and local government support was approximately $1.4 billion (NCES and IPEDS, 2000).

Implications for Campus Leadership

Today's colleges and universities are complex organizations, seeking to carry out their traditional academic missions yet forced to do so in a complex and highly competitive environment. State budget reductions and endowment shrinkage in the last few years are major sources of concern, for public as well as private institutions. Competition for resources has intensified not only with for-profit and other institutions of higher education but also with law enforcement, K–12 education, and health care.

Moreover, the breadth of programs and services provided by many colleges and universities has broadened substantially. This tremendous growth has mirrored the importance of a college education and the increase of academic research and public service in the fabric of the U.S. economy and social structure. From a federal and state policy perspective, the missions of our nation's colleges and universities have expanded to become engines to promote social change, encourage economic growth, and address pressing needs, including improving health care systems and services and contributing to scientific and technological advances (such as leading the development of the World Wide Web).

These profound changes have transformed the requirements for effective leadership in colleges and universities, particularly for those people concerned with business and financial aspects of the institution. In the 1950s, the primary institutional responsibilities of the senior financial officer included the controller and accounting functions, and the position usually carried a title such as business manager, controller, or chief accountant. The demands placed on administrative leaders just a few decades ago pale in comparison to the challenges of the current period. Senior campus executives in this new decade must manage complex health systems, economic development projects, and technology transfer programs, to name a few responsibilities that have been added to the portfolio.

Our colleges and universities can no longer just be "administered"; those in positions of authority and responsibility must lead. Individuals with business or financial responsibility and authority, at every level and in every department, must possess an array of leadership, organizational, and interpersonal competencies, in addition to technical financial knowledge and skills. Among the capabilities that need to be honed are:

- Strategic and systemwide thinking
- Understanding technology as a tool and strategy
- Planning and resource allocation
- Collaboration
- Change management
- Communication

The Mission Focus and Organizational Transition at NACUBO

The fundamental mission of NACUBO—advocacy, knowledge and professionalism, and community building—has not changed as the role of the chief business officer has evolved. What has changed is the scope and extent of member needs in these three areas and the sophistication required by NACUBO to respond. Clearly, the role of NACUBO's primary audience has changed from *transactional*—the administering of financial and business transactions—to *strategic,* and the challenge for the association is to transform itself to meet this new set of needs. Toward this end, NACUBO has undertaken a number of new initiatives. The first is an expansion of membership on the board of directors to bring a campuswide perspective to our planning and deliberations. Accordingly, the board now includes a president, provost, attorney, chief information officer, and government relations executive.

Secondly, NACUBO has established a number of new partnerships. We recognize that our structure, programs, and services must increasingly address the needs of cabinet-level executives who also manage numerous line organizations, and who must interface with administrators in all other areas of their institutions. We know also that effective campus leadership requires the effective collaboration of many campus departments, among them information technology, human resources, facilities, and student affairs. Thus NACUBO is developing new partnerships and collaborative programming with associations that serve administrators in these other university departments. For example, we have undertaken joint programming with EDUCAUSE: Transforming Education through Information Technologies (the higher education technology association); the College and University Professional Association for Human Resources (CUPA-HR); the Association of Higher Education Facilities Officers (APPA); and the National Association of Student Personnel Administrators (NASPA). NACUBO has also supported the development and expansion of the National Consortium for Continuous Improvement in Higher Education (NCCI). On a broad scale, we have championed the work of the Council of Higher Education Management Associations (CHEMA), a group of thirty associations, including those just listed, who share best practices to improve campus operations and member services.

We have also developed our own professional development programs to address the need for greater collaboration among campus constituents that reflect the changing relationships on campus. For example, our technology program, the Business of Information Technology (BIT '03), focuses on issues surrounding technology on campus that our membership needs to attend to, while ensuring a partnership with the chief information officer on campus. We also collaborate with EDUCAUSE on a joint forum, bringing chief information officers and chief financial officers together to address issues of common concern.

Third, we are building the capacity of our volunteers to contribute their expertise through presidential advisory councils, particularly our accounting and tax councils and constituent councils for community colleges, small colleges, comprehensive and large institutions, and research universities. A technology council is being added in 2003 to the list of current councils.

Leadership development programming represents a fourth, and particularly important, area. Currently, NACUBO has several programs targeting senior business officers. The Executive Symposium brings senior business and administration leaders together to consider major issues and develop critical leadership skills, as well as share insights and knowledge related more to leadership theory and practice. The New Business Officer program has a short primer on higher education leadership for those who have been a chief business officer for three years or less. The Organizational Effectiveness series provides education for business and financial leaders in the areas of organizational assessment and planning, and change management. We are also developing a new workshop, Foundations for Professional Advancement, for those preparing to serve as members of a president's cabinet. Other planned programs include a national forum that will bring presidents and chancellors and their cabinet-level officers and other higher education leaders together to identify and share perspectives on the most significant strategies and practices for responding to today's demands for campuswide operational excellence. Finally, our ongoing program of publications is intended to further meet the evolving leadership needs of today's business and financial officers.

Conclusion

This narrative describes the fifty-year evolution of the increasing complexity and importance of business and administrative affairs on campuses. Five decades ago, the business and academic functions of the academy were easily separated, as were the roles of those responsible for each position. Increasingly, financial and business considerations permeate all aspects of higher education administration. Today's business officers must not only have technical and financial skills; they must also possess the competencies necessary to administer a large, complex organization. Moreover, they must be teachers and facilitators, willing and able to share their expertise with all those in the institution whose responsibilities involve business, financial, and marketplace considerations— a roster that includes nearly all administrators, and many other staff as well as a growing number of faculty.

Campus leaders face internal and external challenges that were unfathomable just a decade ago. These realities have generated the imperative for those in positions of responsibility and authority to adopt a new perspective on the importance of leadership in all areas of higher education. New organizational structures, staffing, and support infrastructure must be considered and implemented if our colleges and universities are to maintain their position of value in society, as well as meet the challenges of today and tomorrow. Business and administrative officers must act on these challenges because in today's higher education environment, where higher education is a business more than in any previous era, business and administrative aspects have a profound impact on both nonacademic and academic arenas across an institution. Higher education associations such as NACUBO must accept the challenge of modifying and strengthening programs and services to meet the emerging leadership needs of the higher education community.

Chapter Nine

More Broadly Framing Our Vision of Excellence

Pursuing Excellence in All That We Do

Through teaching, scholarship, and outreach, higher education extends to its constituencies a range of benefits that come in many forms. For all our contributions and achievements in these areas, it is quite remarkable that the academy is a target of criticism and wavering support on many fronts.

Much of this book has been an exploration of the reasons for this circumstance and a discussion of the challenges that confront us in our efforts to be more fully understood and appreciated. In the final analysis, it seems quite likely that much of the problem comes down to this: as celebrated as we are for academics, our colleges and universities are far less praiseworthy when it comes to how we engage and form relationships with our constituencies, and how we function as organizations.

Of the various challenges enumerated and discussed in the book, none is more fundamental than the need for a more inclusive vision of excellence to which we can aspire, one that challenges us to become models of excellence not just in academics but in all that we do.

Academic Excellence: A Necessary But Not Sufficient Condition

U.S. higher education is the international standard of excellence in academics. Our faculties are widely recognized for their leadership in the advancement of all spheres of human knowledge. We attract bright and motivated students to our campuses from around the world; we graduate alumni who benefit personally, socially, and occupationally from their time with us, and they go on to contribute in myriad ways to society. Yet the academy is also the target of criticism for alleged resistance to change, self-absorption, detachment, inefficiency, and unresponsiveness, even from those who have benefited most from our efforts. Our work is admired and treasured on the one hand, but criticized and often underfunded on the other.

One explanation for this apparent contradiction can be found in the realization that there are any number of ways to define and assess excellence. The criteria that are most familiar within the academy generally emphasize academic dimensions and are based on assessments of faculty credentials, program ratings by peers, student qualifications, research accomplishments, and other measures of academic standing.

For the academy's beneficiaries, however, there are also other ways of thinking about excellence that have become increasingly salient. One alternative conceptualization of excellence focuses on the extent to which colleges and universities meet—or fail to meet—their needs and expectations. Criteria associated with this view of excellence typically include considerations as to the value, user-friendliness of systems, availability and ease of access to facilities, responsiveness, attractiveness of facilities, campus social life, safety, and the quality of encounters with representatives of the institution.

To many within the academy, such considerations may seem rather trivial. These are, after all, standards of the sort one would use to judge any organization that provides services—an airline, a hotel, or a hospital. Criteria such as these are largely unrelated to the unique mission of higher education and seem of far less importance than considerations that typically occupy the attention of the academic community. Be that as it may, these factors can be powerful forces that shape the image of the academy in the minds of our constituencies as they encounter our institutions every day. Unfortunately, assessments based on standards such as these can interact with, cloud, and sometimes overshadow assessments based on academic criteria. Is it really all that surprising, for instance, that traveling to several buildings to get registration materials processed, spending an hour driving around looking in vain for a place to park to attend class, or encountering an inconsiderate faculty or staff member can easily overpower and outlast a potentially more positive impression created by a stimulating class lecture also attended that day? This outcome is not all that different from having the rudeness of a flight attendant and the late departure of a flight leave us with an impression that overshadows the fact that we arrived on time, safe and sound at our destination. The things we do best in colleges and universities—which generally have to do with academics—often have benefits that are abstract, deferred, and intangible in the short run. The things we do less well are highly visible, immediate, and usually more tangible.

Recognizing the impact of nonacademic criteria helps to explain the sometimes puzzling instances in which the public reputation and support for a particular institution seems to greatly exceed the level of respect one would attribute on the basis of academic criteria alone. A warm and welcoming campus culture, safe and attractive facilities, friendly faculty and staff, spirited cultural and athletic events, positive attitudes on the part of alumni, and fond memories of visits to campus in previous years can be very important. For better or for worse, they can mediate and shape judgments of institutional excellence and influence reputations, enrollment decisions, referrals, recommendations, and financial support—and ultimately the flow of resources available to support instruction, research and outreach, and all other activities.

Service Excellence

As important as it is—and always will be—to conceptualize and assess the quality of higher education in terms of measures of *academic excellence*, it is also important to be mindful of other influential ways of defining excellence. Dimensions of *service excellence* are the basis for one such evaluative perspective; those of *operational excellence* are another.

The term *service* is used here as a way of talking about the communication processes through which colleges and universities create and maintain relationships with individuals through instructional, research, public service and outreach, cocurricular, administrative, and service activities. It includes all forms of interaction between colleges and universities and their many constituencies. Essentially, the concept of *service excellence*[1] corresponds quite closely to what the Kellogg Commission has called *engagement*.[2]

Communication is fundamental to service excellence. All communication events have both a *content*—or informational—dimension, and a *relational* component (Watzlawick, Beavin, and Jackson, 1967). The content dimension is the information conveyed through class lectures, journal articles, class discussions, Websites, cocurricular programs, or brochures. The relational dimension is the tone and climate, and the kind of relationship that is created in the process. As information is conveyed, relationships of one kind or another are shaped.

Service excellence is a way of referring to the kind of relationships that are formed through interaction—how our information and expertise is delivered—and the way we think about, create, and maintain connections with those with whom we are engaged. Service excellence, then, points to the importance of communication that is effective in two distinct respects: (1) successful information flow, as a traditional goal of instruction, scholarship, or outreach; and (2) successful interaction in terms of establishing and maintaining strong and meaningful relationships and an affinity between the institution and its beneficiaries, through which a commonness of understanding is a by-product. As educators, sharing information is the cornerstone of what we do. Yet if we are to be successful, matters of relationship are as important as matters of content in our communication with the beneficiaries of our work. In fact, the two are inseparable.

The Neglected Dimension of Communication

Historically, the academy has paid much less attention to the relationship dimension of communication than it has to the content dimension in setting goals, planning, and evaluating outcomes. Other sectors—particularly those dependent on consumer loyalty and good will—have seen the wisdom of devoting resources to the concepts of service and relationships. In some cases, the motives may have been altruistic; certainly more often they are pragmatic. One consequence is that our beneficiaries often compare colleges and universities to leading organizations in other sectors, and we sometimes come up short in comparison.

The very idea of making such comparisons is annoying to many of us. Much of the resistance comes in response to the implication that students, parents, employers, or other beneficiaries should be labeled or regarded as consumers or customers. Such terms are often seen as implying that external groups should be deciding what they should be taught, and perhaps ultimately by whom.[3] The further implication is that if this were to happen, the result would be an erosion of the quality-control role of faculty and staff, which in turn would lead to a deterioration of quality and a dumbing down of what is taught (and of the qualifications required of the teachers). It is often noted in such discussions, and correctly so, that students, parents, and employers are limited in their ability to assess what they really need from higher education; the educational goals of the academy involve preparing individuals not only for life and work today, but for leadership and coping in relationships, a working environment, and a society the needs of which none of us can be certain about today—least of all eighteen- or nineteen-year-old undergraduate students or employers hiring entry-level workers. As compelling as all such discussions are, they often seem to generate more heat than light and obscure a more fundamental issue: as professionals, we have an obligation to be knowledgeable and concerned about both the content and relationship dimensions of our communication, recognizing that both are necessary to the fulfillment of our goals.

A Shared Responsibility

Clearly, students and other constituencies also have responsibility for creating and maintaining effective communication relationships. Students are collaborators in the learning process, as the Wingspread Report (Wingspread Group on Higher Education, 1993, p. 16) so clearly articulated: "Students, at any level of education . . . have a major obligation for their own success. Too many students do not behave as though that were the case." The report goes on to note that many students and parents fail to appreciate that success in life requires hard work on campus, and dedication to a lifetime of learning.

We know that sometimes students and others fail to recognize their responsibilities as collaborators. This does not, however, excuse our responsibility for this outcome. Rather, their failure to understand their role is additional evidence of a deficiency in the academy's communication efforts. We certainly are in a better position than our beneficiaries to understand the learning process and the demands it makes on all parties. Shaping—or reshaping—their understanding of these dynamics is yet another challenge that we must accept. Because of our professional expertise, knowledge, and institutional power base, the responsibility rightly falls to us to educate students and others as to how to be effective partners in the learning process, and how to most fully benefit from the learning opportunities the academy offers.

Concerns about students-as-customers have their parallels in other areas of academic endeavor. Funding agencies and other research sponsors can be characterized as customers (Lawrence, 1995). Likewise, their influence could be seen as contributing to a loss of quality control of faculty research agendas or the dumbing-down of scholarship (Carey, 2000; Noble, 2001; Scott, 2002; Slaughter, 2001). It can also be argued that community or professional outreach activity, designed to serve and satisfy the community, state, region, or professional or academic community, carries attendant risks of compromising quality. Nevertheless, educational impact, critical review, and funding support are all possible only when one's instructional, scholarly, or outreach endeavors connect in some meaningful way with those who find that work to be of interest and value. Whenever there is the necessity or desirability of engaging with others, there is the attendant risk of influence in either, or both, directions. At times, undesirable influence occurs in collaborative relationships. Yet without such risks, there can be no interaction, and the many potential benefits that can be derived from collaborative relationships—from the perspective of both communication content and relationships—are impossible.

Organizational Relationships: A Broader Perspective

In seeking an understanding of the importance of engagement between the academy and its many constituencies, it can be helpful to broaden the context of thought to include diverse organizational settings, where issues of communication, relationship, service, and collaboration are also of concern. Three such settings are industrial workplaces, community colleges, and health care facilities.

Productivity in the Industrial Workplace

Readers may recall what has come to be called the "Hawthorne Effect"—an idea that has considerable relevance to matters of communication and relationship development. It was first advanced by F. J. Roethlisberger and William J. Dickson in the classic two-year study of workers at the Western Electric Company Hawthorne Works in Chicago. Their study was described in detail in the book *Management and the Worker* (1941). The research focused on working conditions, morale, and productivity. Roethlisberger and Dickson set up experimental work rooms and groups to study the impact of such factors as the length of the work day, length of the work week, and the introduction of breaks during the day. Who would have guessed that what began as a rather routine study of factors associated with increased productivity would produce results the authors referred to as "astonishing" (Roethlisberger and Dickson, 1941, p. 87)?

When they analyzed their data, they found, much to their amazement, that regardless of what specific changes they introduced into the experimental environment—for instance, whether they shortened working hours, days, and weeks or not—worker productivity increased. Every change they made in the subject's working conditions seemed to increase productivity. They assumed the finding must somehow be the result of some unrecognized factors in the experimental environment, so they systematically examined the relationship between environmental factors and variations in productivity. Still they found no explanation. By the end of the two-year study, efforts to explain the increased productivity had resulted in an examination of every imaginable explanation, including environmental factors, worker fatigue and monotony, wage incentives, and method of supervision. They went to such levels of detail as to test for the possible impact of temperature, humidity, even seasonal variation.

After all was said and done, their conclusion was this: differences in productivity were not due to specific changes in the experimental design nor to the environmental conditions. Rather, greater productivity resulted from the positive interpersonal relationships and unusual level of supervisor attention that was present in the experimental group at every phase of the research. The experiment had fostered closer working relations and established greater worker confidence and trust in their supervisors than was present in the normal working group situation. Supervisor-worker relations in the experimental room were discovered to have more the flavor of an office than a shop, creating an atmosphere in which workers had become the focus of a considerable amount of attention from top management. Indeed, it was the increased attention and more collaborative relationships between supervisors and workers that heightened productivity.

Retention in Community Colleges

In another classic work, *Pygmalion in the Classroom,* Robert Rosenthal and Lenore Jacobson (1968) reported on their research on the impact of teacher expectations on students' intellectual development. They argued persuasively that when teachers expect high or low performance from particular students, their own behavior toward these students is sufficiently different to produce these outcomes through a "self-fulfilling prophecy." That is, if I as a teacher believe John to be a talented child, I'll treat him as if he were talented, and he will be become more talented because of my expectations and behavior toward him and his responses to them.

Further studies examined this contention in some depth. Not all studies produced the so-called Pygmalion effect, and controversies swirled as to whether these inconsistencies were the result of inappropriate research methods, or whether there were underlying problems with the theory. Despite occasionally inconsistent findings, the weight of evidence supports the original theory: teachers' beliefs that particular students are of superior or inferior ability tend to lead to student achievement levels consistent with the expectations. When teachers' expectations are high and they relate to their students accordingly, student performance matches these expectations; conversely, when teachers have low expectations and relate to students in a consistent manner, lower levels of performance result (Seaver, 1973).

In 1986, John Herrling, a doctoral candidate in the Rutgers Graduate School of Education, undertook a thesis study designed to gain a better understanding of the dynamics of student adaptation to junior college life. It is well documented in the literature that attrition rates are high during the first semester of enrollment, and a chief goal of this study was to try to identify the factors leading to this outcome. Herrling designed an ethnographic study in which he met with students at several points during the semester for open-ended, taped conversations about the process of adapting to college, with the goal of gaining in-depth understanding of the dynamics of adaptation and attrition processes from the student's point of view.

In designing the study, an important consideration was selecting a large enough initial sample of students. Otherwise, if too many students dropped out during the semester it would not be possible to make comparisons between "dropout" and "successful adapter" groups at the conclusion of the study. Herrling determined that the average first-semester attrition rate for the institution where the study was taking place was 30 percent to 40 percent. He wanted the final sample size to be in the range of twenty students, so he began with a random sample of thirty-two students, reasoning that even with a 40 percent dropout rate he would be left with a study population of nineteen or twenty students who would complete the first semester. But Herrling was to be very surprised by his results. At the end of the first semester, only three of the thirty-two students had left the college—an attrition rate of 9 percent, rather than the usual 30–40 percent.

How can such a finding be explained? Initially, Herrling suspected that somehow the initial sample had been a biased one. However, a reexamination of the sample demographics confirmed that the group was entirely representative in terms of high school grades, SAT scores, curriculum being studied, and other relevant considerations. After much deliberation and careful analysis of the tapes and transcripts from the interviews, he concluded that rather than being an unfortunate outcome of an unrepresentative sample, the low attrition rate in the study group was instead a truly significant finding in its own right. Unlike the typical group of college students, this group of thirty-two in effect had their own personal counselor and were meeting and communicating with him regularly throughout the semester. Through the relationships that resulted, a genuine interest was expressed by the college in the concerns and experiences of this group of students, which in turn had a dramatic impact on attrition.

Patient Care in Health Settings

A number of researchers have emphasized the patient perspective in their efforts to better understand the dynamics of health care and health care relationships, among them Ellmer and Olbrisch (1983); Greenfield, Kaplan, and Ware (1985, 1986); Kaplan, Greenfield, and Ware, (1989); Leebov (1988); Pascoe (1983); Ruben (1985, 1989, 1992); Waitzkin (1984, 1986); and Ware and Davies (1983). One focus of my own research (Ruben, 1993c) has been to study what patients most remember from hospital stays and visits to health centers, paralleling the research done with undergraduate students discussed in Chapter Seven. The research involved nearly four thousand patients at six hospitals and health services.[4] In the study, patients were asked to: "Think back to your stay at the hospital (or visit to the health center) and describe, in a sentence or two, your most memorable positive or negative experience. (This can be any experience related to the hospital [or center], its staff, or services)."

The open-ended responses were then content-analyzed and categorized, and frequencies were calculated. Six categories of most memorable experiences emerged:

1. Clinical or technical facets of the treatment (abbreviated as *clinical*)
2. The institution's policies and procedures (abbreviated as *policies*)
3. The institution's facilities and accommodations (abbreviated as *facilities*)
4. Aspects of their treatment relating to personal treatment or interpersonal communication (abbreviated as *interpersonal*)
5. The quality or quantity of information provided (abbreviated as *information*)
6. Other (abbreviated as *other*)

Contrary to what health care providers might predict, the study revealed that patients do *not* most remember the clinical or technical care they receive. In five of the six populations studied, the clinical category ranked second; in the case of the ambulatory health care center, the rank was third. Overall, "clinical" aspects of care accounted for only 27 percent (304 out of 1,125) of remembered experiences. Health care facilities—which included food, in the case of the hospitals—were even less significant to the more lasting memories of health care. Facilities ranked fourth overall, accounting for only 7.3 percent (82 of 1,125) of the experiences reported. A rather remarkable finding was that more patients' most memorable experiences (525 of 1,125) were related to the quality of their relationships with caregivers, and the way they were treated personally, than to any other factor (Ruben, 1993c).

The results of this study tell us nothing definitive about how patients were *actually* cared for. They do, however, say a great deal about the criteria they themselves use in reflecting upon the quality of care they receive. By implication, the study also offers insights about probable sources of satisfaction and dissatisfaction among patients and helps us understand the basis upon which images of health services are formed. The findings from these projects argue convincingly that patients in a variety of health care settings place a high premium on personal treatment, interpersonal communication, and relationships in forming their impressions of a health care institution and its staff.

Implications for Higher Education: Relationship Challenges in the Academy

Although all of the settings examined are quite different in a number of respects, each involves many of the same issues that are of concern in higher education. The Western Electric study focused on productivity in the workplace, the Herrling study on adaptation to community college life, and the Ruben study on patient perceptions of the quality of health care. Common to each is the centrality of relationships and the role of communication. All three cases are a persuasive lesson about the power of being noticed, paid attention to, listened to, and cared about. Whether we take our lessons from employees, students, patients, our own experience, or the theoretical and research literature, the relevance of these insights for enhancing the quality of the educational experiences of our beneficiaries is striking in a number of respects. The core principles are eloquently and simply articulated in these comments by Paul O'Neill, former secretary of the U.S. Department of the Treasury:

- Every human being wants to be treated with dignity and respect, every single day.
- People want to make a contribution with what they do; they want their lives to have meaning.
- All people want someone to notice what they do (Phillips-Donaldson, 2002, p. 25).

Technical Competence and Communication Competence

In each of the settings discussed, and in many others, the initial impulse is to assume that the perception and reality of excellence is fundamentally related to the technical work of the enterprise and the expertise of its personnel. Thus, when thinking about factors associated with excellence in industrial production, the tendency is to focus on assembly line and environmental factors.

In the case of health care, which most closely parallels higher education, the tendency is to think first of clinical factors when conceptualizing health care excellence. Health care institutions and professionals traditionally focus on clinical goals, competencies, and outcomes in much the same way that higher education has historically emphasized academic quality. As important to effective health care as factors related to clinical quality are, caregiver communication competence, the availability of appropriate information, effective collaboration among members of the health care team, and the structure and responsiveness of the health care environment are also important. Effective and satisfying medical care requires attention not only to clinical excellence but also to excellence in interpersonal communication and organizational matters (Ruben, 1989).

It is difficult, perhaps impossible, for most patients to assess the clinical and technical level of the care they receive, or the competence of their caregivers. Similarly, students, parents, and the public at large are limited in their ability to judge the quality of college or university faculty. In both settings, impressions are often based on what beneficiaries can easily see and comprehend: the apparent level of preparation, the extent of professionalism and courtesy, the manner in which questions are responded to, and the way they are treated as people. There are many positive encounters between stakeholders and members of higher education institutions. Unfortunately, however, research shows that the impact of negative interactions is often considerably greater (Day, 1977). People recall and repeat stories about negative events at least seven to ten times more often than they retell stories about positive ones.[5] What this means is that not-so-wonderful encounters—whether in the workplace, health care, higher education, or another setting—have a disproportionately large impact.

Service excellence and quality relationships are not simply matters of appearance—of strategic management, public relations, bedside manner, or social nicety. Nor is their impact merely a matter of impressions and image management. Considerably more is at stake. In health care, excellence in service—communication and relationships—often influences patient understanding, patient compliance with provider recommendations, health care status, the likelihood of patients taking responsibility for managing their own health care, and even health outcomes (Greenfield, Kaplan, and Ware, 1985, 1986; Inui, Yourtee, and Williamson, 1976; and Kaplan, Greenfield and Ware, 1989).

Much the same can be said of higher education. As with patients, how our students and other stakeholders are treated has the potential to affect not only how they think about and value our institutions but also our ability to help them learn, make productive use of their knowledge, and become self-directed and self-motivated lifelong learners. Whether one thinks of the workplace, the health care facility, or the college or university, the goal should be to ensure technical and disciplinary excellence, as well as service excellence, because it is clear that they are inseparably linked to the outcomes for which we strive.

Asymmetrical Relationships

One of the particular challenges in workplace and health care settings, as in higher education, relates to the dynamics of asymmetrical encounters. As with the manager and production worker, the caregiver and patient, the attorney and client, or the librarian and the information seeker, the relationship between a teacher and student is asymmetrical. In each relationship, the experience, expertise, and power are unevenly distributed. Both parties to such relationships can be said to share a purpose for coming together, but they seldom share perspectives on the situation or the communication processes involved. Asymmetrical interactions of this kind pose a particular communication challenge in terms of the content, and especially in the relationship dimension of communication.

For their part, the professional—or, in some cases, simply the more experienced and powerful party—comes to the encounter with considerable background knowledge and expertise, being at home in the physical and symbolic context in which the interaction is occurring, familiar with terminology and policies, comfortable with the tasks at hand, and generally equipped with substantial experience regarding the range of problems and circumstances that present themselves. Ideally, the expert in such a circumstance seeks to provide the necessary information, guidance, or direction in a manner that helps to ensure that the other party will be attentive and receptive to the information; satisfied with the encounter; and left with a positive impression of the expert, the process, and the institution involved.

The worker, patient, or student is coming to the interaction for supervision, information, or guidance and oftentimes is also seeking attention and reassurance from someone with more influence, knowledge, or experience. The recipient does not have the benefit of the expert's experience, comfort, or power, and in such circumstances even "routine" information-seeking or problem-solving tasks can be intimidating. This may be the case when an employee approaches a manager to discuss the possibility of a raise or promotion, or in critical health care circumstances when a patient comes to a physician for a diagnosis or treatment recommendations. In asymmetrical encounters, the impact of "small" things— tone of voice, eye contact, interest or respect shown—can be greatly magnified. Unfortunately but predictably, in such interactions a preoccupied supervisor, physician, or teacher who is regularly or excessively late for scheduled appointments or who responds to a question in a way that is perceived to be condescending unintentionally and unknowingly erects substantial barriers to effective communication and service excellence, detracting from his or her ability to render the expertise and guidance for which he or she is trained. Although barriers of this kind can emerge in any interpersonal interaction, they are a particular concern in asymmetrical relationships.

When they arrive at college, students enter a university environment that is unfamiliar. Over the course of an average week, they may well have dozens of encounters with representatives of the institution who have considerably more expertise and experience, and substantial influence over their future—whether in terms of class assignments, grades, making up a missed exam, course schedules, housing arrangements, or the possibility of having a parking fine rescinded. In such encounters, relationship dimensions of communication take on particular importance in defining the event from a student's point of view. If a student encounters the right person in the right office in the right mood on the right day, things go very well. If not, they don't.

Achieving better predictability in how we relate to our beneficiaries and one another must become a higher priority. In large measure, these inconsistencies may be understandable because higher education has never really dedicated itself to excellence in this domain, certainly not in any of the ways that it has been dedicated to excellence in academics. We don't think much about service excellence, we don't talk much about it, we don't do much to assess how well we do it, and we do little to recognize or reward the competencies and outcomes that could help institutionalize it as a part of our culture—certainly not nearly to the extent that is true for organizations such as Disney or Nordstrom, which are widely viewed as exemplifying very high standards of service excellence. This circumstance needs to change for higher education, as it has in other sectors.

The problem of effective relationships in higher education must become everyone's responsibility. Administrators, faculty, staff, teaching assistants, part-time faculty—all university employees—are ambassadors of the institution in communication encounters with present and potential students, visitors, family members, alumni, donors, colleagues at other institutions, and the public. Through these interactions, ongoing and lasting impressions are formed—impressions that are the basis for stories that are told and retold, sometimes for years, to the benefit or detriment of service and also academic goals. Collectively, these images shape institutional reputation, applicant preferences, patterns of financial and moral support, attitudes toward higher education, and perhaps even thoughts and attitudes regarding the learning process.

Operational Excellence

How colleges and universities function as organizations is another immediate, tangible, and highly visible contributor to impressions of higher education. Leaders from business and health care around the world look to the academy as the benchmark of superior scholarship, but there is certainly no groundswell of interest in emulating how higher education institutions organize and carry out operational aspects of their work.

For most who have had extended contact with a college or university, it is not difficult to think of any number of situations where work processes and operational procedures were less than ideal. Not surprisingly, when asked "What is the one thing you would do to improve colleges and universities?" the most frequent response among a sample of one thousand respondents who rated themselves as knowledgeable about higher education was "make them more efficient" (36 percent), followed by "lower prices" (26 percent). Both of these complaints surpassed "eliminate tenure" and other familiar topics of criticism (National Center for Postsecondary Improvement, 2001).

Some operational deficiencies affect students and other external constituencies; many also affect faculty and staff. The situation may involve a transfer student and her parents, who find themselves forced to travel around campus searching for one administrative office after another to take care of various tasks. Or it may be a faculty member who discovers that it will take months for the reviews and approvals necessary to offer a new course. It could also be the recognition by a staff member that reimbursement for travel takes six weeks from submission of paperwork at her institution, while she has neighbors who work in private sector organizations where payments are made at one's home, bank, or designated charge account within forty-eight hours of submission.

There are many examples of how operational and infrastructure issues contribute to the success of the institution: Boyer (1997) makes this point quite effectively in a discussion of a study of campus life on twenty-nine college campuses: ". . .When [the researchers] asked students what influenced them most during their visit to a campus, about half mentioned 'the friendliness of students we met.' But it was the buildings, the trees, the walkways, and the well-kept lawns that overwhelmingly won out. The appearance of the campus is, by far, the most influential characteristic during campus visits, and we gained the distinct impression that when it comes to recruiting students, the director of buildings and grounds may be more important than the academic dean" (p. 17).

One significant factor contributing to operational deficiencies at many institutions is limited resources. Among the consequences are long-deferred maintenance of buildings and grounds, less than state-of-the-art information systems at most institutions, and sometimes staff shortages. Addressing these operational problems is generally possible only with additional funding. Many other frequently mentioned operational problems, however, are not directly dependent on increased resources. These include inadequacies in internal communication, difficulties coordinating processes that involve more than one department, inattention to streamlining decision making and work process cycle time, complacency, inadequate standards of comparison with other institutions and sectors, and the absence of a commitment to continuous improvement efforts. Observers note that attention to improvements in these areas would result not only in greater efficiency and satisfaction but also in dollar and time savings, both of which would be helpful for addressing areas where increased funding is required.

A topic that merits special attention in this discussion is organizational culture. An interesting universitywide study examining campus operations concluded that a core problem was a cultural tradition emphasizing control and regulation, rather than service and support (*Report of the Committee on Administrative Systems Efficiency,* 1992). Clearly, this finding is not unique to any one institution. On many campuses, processes that reflect the values of control and regulation work quite well. Examples might be issuing parking tickets, billing for accounts receivable, or monitoring completion of degree requirements—these processes operate with exceptional effectiveness and efficiency in most colleges and universities. In many of those same institutions, it is likely that the supportive and facilitative "counterparts" of these same operational processes—for example, processes for acquiring parking permits and parking spaces, obtaining a return on funds from overpaid bills, or securing help with on-time graduation—are not nearly as exemplary. That this is the case has not gone undetected by our stakeholders.

Across higher education, the challenge is to increase ease of effectiveness, efficiency, access, coordination, and responsiveness in all aspects of our work—academic, cocurricular, ancillary, and support. Achieving these goals requires more attention to the methodical analysis, documentation, and improvement of mission-critical and support work processes to ensure that systems and procedures function better, more easily, more quickly, with reduced waste and rework, less duplication of effort, and more satisfaction for all involved. Improvements of this kind require the academy to be aggressively self-critical, to employ our research expertise and tools to analyze our own work processes, and most especially to look to other organizations and other sectors for ideas that we can emulate.

Whether the goal is to improve systems for supporting instruction, research, or public service; tracking systems for student applications; effective handling of large numbers of individuals; or rapid processing of travel expenses, there is much to gain by comparisons not only with other colleges and universities but also with health care, government, and business. Though we are unique in some respects, we also have much in common with other sectors. In areas such as the determination of instructional content and research directions, factors such as creativity, individuality, and academic freedom are absolutely vital and must be preserved. In many other areas—handling requests for building repairs, ordering supplies, recouping travel monies promptly, securing parking permits, gaining approvals on grants submissions, maintaining attractive facilities, copying course materials—creativity and individual uniqueness are not assets. In these areas, the need is not for creativity and freedom of personal choice but for well-developed, standardized, predictable, reliable, and cost-effective processes and procedures, and we should be willing and able to learn from others who have superior approaches in these areas.

Concluding Comments

There can be little doubt as to the importance of service excellence and operational excellence. Deficiencies in either area undermine faculty and staff morale, interfere with and overshadow excellence in academics, and limit the ability of colleges and universities to achieve their missions or aspirations for the future.

Higher education needs a broader, more inclusive view of excellence—one that emphasizes the importance of higher standards of performance in academics, as well as in service and operational dimensions of our work. Excellence in practice demands superiority in all three.

Notes

1. There is no fully satisfactory term or phrase to convey this idea. Whether one selects "engagement," "interaction," "relationship," or "service," there is a potential for misinterpretation. The reference to "service" and "service excellence" was used by the author in Ruben (2001d) and earlier in "The Ivory Tower—2000: Images, Ironies and Opportunities," Rutgers University Daniel Gorenstein Memorial Lecture, Apr. 17, 2000; it is being continued here for purposes of consistency. The intended meaning of *service* in this context is generic, referring to all interaction, and not more limited usages as in "public service" or "support services."

2. The Kellogg Commission (1999b, p. vii) describes "engagement" this way: "Engagement goes well beyond extension, conventional outreach, and even most concepts of public service. Inherited concepts emphasize a one-way process in which the university transfers its expertise to key constituents. Embedded in the engagement ideal is a commitment to sharing and reciprocity." National Association of State Universities and Land-Grant Colleges, Office of Public Affairs, 1 Dupont Circle NW, Suite 710, Washington, DC 20036–1191 (www.nasulgc.org/Kellogg/kellogg.htm).

3. For instance, see McMillan and Cheney (1996); Noble (2001); Schwartzman (1995); Scott (2002); Slaughter (2001); and Trout (1997a).

4. The research consisted of surveys of a total of 3,868 patients at six institutions in the Northeast.

5. According to studies conducted by the Technical Assistance Research Program (TARP) for the White House Office of Consumer Affairs, the average consumer who has a problem with an organization tells nine to ten people. The research also indicates that organizations don't hear from 96 percent of those who are dissatisfied. See discussion in Albrecht and Zemke (1985).

Narratives

More Broadly Framing Our Vision: Pursuing Excellence in All That We Do

The most fundamental challenge facing higher education—of which the other challenges discussed in the previous chapters are in many ways derivative—is that of advancing a more inclusive view of excellence for the academy. An institution's vision shapes priorities and resource allocations, influences the kind of activities and actions rewarded and encouraged, and sets the motivating context for the many daily decisions and choices made by faculty and staff throughout the institution. In one way or another, all of the chapters and narratives presented in *Pursuing Excellence in Higher Education* address these critical issues. In the preceding chapter, issues of purpose and aspiration were the central focus.

It is clear that in the experiences of students and other groups for whom we provide programs and services, there are often no clear lines of demarcation among the academic, service, and operational dimensions of our work. Typically, the perception and effectiveness of our instructional, research, and outreach activities depend on a smooth and seamless integration of any number of university processes.

The narratives in this section describe efforts to broaden our vision of excellence. The first is a summary of the work of the Kellogg Commission on the Future of State and Land-Grant Universities. As described by its executive director, John Byrne, the commission brought together presidents from twenty-five colleges and universities to reaffirm the foundational goals of the state and land-grant institutions, and to articulate a broadened and refined vision for the future. The process and the reports produced by the commission call upon the academy to reexamine how we characterize our core mission; focus additional attention on the student experience and campus culture; devote new energies to exploring the role colleges and universities should play in lifelong teaching and learning; and enrich our engagement with students, the community, the state, and the nation.

Within colleges and universities, efforts to pursue a broader perspective on excellence take a variety of forms. One excellent example is the Penn State Expo, described by Louise Sandmeyer and Carol Lindborg Everett. The Expo brings together faculty, administrators, and staff involved in campus innovations in academics, service, and operational departments to share information and experiences, and to reinforce a shared sense of purpose.

In the final narrative, University of California–Berkeley Chancellor Robert Berdahl and Center for Organizational Effectiveness Director Phyllis Hoffman present an articulate and persuasive case for a vision of excellence that extends beyond academics; they give an overview of efforts under way there to implement this new perspective.

Taking Charge of Change: The Kellogg Commission on the Future of State and Land-Grant Universities

John V. Byrne
Former Executive Director, Kellogg Commission on the Future of State and Land-Grant Universities, and President Emeritus, Oregon State University

"Unprecedented problems confront our campuses. We face seismic shifts in public attitudes. We are challenged by new demographics and exploding technologies. We are beset by demands to act accountably toward students, parents, communities, and taxpayers. An increasingly skeptical press questions our priorities.

"Institutions ignore a changing environment at their peril. Like dinosaurs, they risk becoming exhibits in a kind of cultural Jurassic Park: places of great interest and curiosity, increasingly irrelevant in a world that has passed them by. Higher education cannot afford to let this happen. We must take charge of change" (Kellogg Commission, 1996).

With these words in June 1996 the Kellogg Commission announced itself to the academic community. The Commission's role: to stimulate, and serve as a catalyst for reform on the campuses of America's public universities. The Commission wouldn't have the authority to mandate change on any campus, but it would express the need for change, would press for change, and would work with campus leaders to find ways to make change a way of life on American's public university campuses.[1]

In the early 1990s, recognizing the need to reform how students were being prepared for twenty-first-century careers in food systems, the W. K. Kellogg Foundation funded a new program, the Food Systems Profession Education Initiative. The success of this program inspired Peter Magrath, president of the National Association of State Universities and Land-Grant Colleges (NASULGC), to consider that a similar program involving the leaders of public universities, acting collectively, might stimulate reforms in all of public higher education. As a result, NASULGC submitted a proposal to the Kellogg Foundation requesting funding for a "commission" of public university CEOs that would stimulate higher education reform. In May 1995, the foundation appropriated $1.1 million to be expended over four years to establish the Kellogg Commission on the Future of State and Land-Grant Universities.

The Kellogg Commission originally included the presidents and chancellors of twenty-four land-grant, urban, and other universities, the president of NASULGC, and the former president of Oregon State University, who served as the commission's executive director. The commission later expanded to twenty-five universities; as presidents and chancellors retired or took on other higher education positions, they remained on the commission as emeritus members.

A board of seven nonacademic advisors[2] participated in the commission meetings to provide the "nonuniversity" citizen's perspective. From its first meeting in January 1996 through the final meeting in March 2000, the commission met three or four times each year to address issues of significance to national higher education. The president of the Kellogg Foundation, William Richardson, opened both the first meeting and the final one, thereby signaling the importance the foundation attributed to the work of the commission. A steering committee consisting of commission leaders and key NASULGC staff met between commission meetings to guide the operational and logistical aspects of commission activities.[3]

The Agenda

At the first meeting, in January 1996, five topical issues were identified as an agenda. As the commission approached the end of that four-year term, it added the sixth topic:

1. The student experience
2. Student access
3. The engaged institution
4. A learning society
5. Campus culture
6. The covenant or partnership between the public and the public's universities

Early in their deliberations, the commissioners recognized that published reports were an important tool in achieving their goal to stimulate reform on America's public campuses. James Harvey, a professional writer, attended all the commission's meetings, engaged in the discussions, and subsequently prepared draft reports, which were then reviewed thoroughly by the commission. Ultimately, six final reports were prepared and published and distributed by NASULGC. Each report focused on one of the issue areas.

The commission chose to address "the student experience" first. As the discussions proceeded, the members came together as an effective and cohesive group, capable of frank discussion marked by a high level of mutual respect. While the first report on the student experience was taking form, it became obvious that the work of the commission needed to be streamlined, or its agenda might never be completed. Therefore, the commission formed four focus groups, one for each of the remaining issue areas; in a sense, the remaining four issues were developed on four parallel tracks. Later, a fifth focus group was created to address the covenant between the public and its universities. On the day of each meeting, each focus group met separately at breakfast to discuss their issue. At the following meeting of the full commission, the next two issues due to have reports published were discussed. This system worked well. It gave every commissioner the opportunity to be involved substantively and the commission was able to complete its agenda, and its published reports, in a timely manner.

The published reports stressed educational ideals, principles, and tenets fundamental to effective public higher education in a world undergoing increasingly rapid change. Sidebars in each report gave specific examples of best practices already in place at various public universities throughout the country. Each report included recommendations and suggested actions for reform; in all, there were some forty recommendations and more than seventy suggested actions included in the reports. The commission, through NASULGC, also published data summaries to accompany the reports on the student experience, student access, the engaged institution, and a learning society. The reports were well received by the academic community and were applauded by the W. K. Kellogg Foundation board of trustees (Kellogg Commission, 1996, 1997, 1998, 1999a, 1999b, 2000a, 2000b, 2001b).

The most recently published Kellogg Commission report often became part of the agenda for NASULGC's council and commission meetings. The responses of these groups were important to the commission. In addition, at each NASULGC annual meeting a special session was convened to address a specific Kellogg Commission issue area. These sessions were often attended by three hundred to five hundred participants, attesting to the high level of interest in the work of the commission. The commissioners, the president of NASULGC, and the executive director were frequently invited to speak about the commission's work to universities and other educational organizations throughout the United States and the rest of the world, notably to the Association of Governing Boards (Washington, D.C.), the Salzburg Seminar in Austria, the Alliance of Universities for Democracy (Sofia, Bulgaria), and the Organization for Economic Cooperation and Development (Paris).

To further stimulate reform on individual campuses, the commission initiated a number of regional meetings on the campuses of participating institutions. The first of these meetings was held at Iowa State in September 1997. Subsequent meetings were held at Washington State University, University of Nebraska, Arizona State University, Texas A&M University, University of Vermont, Clemson University, University of New Orleans, and University of Illinois. The meetings were effective in highlighting the work of the commission and in assisting the host institution to move forward on its own agenda for reform.

For the final meeting of the Kellogg Commission, in March 2000, each commission institution invited and sponsored five stakeholders, civic leaders, legislators, faculty, or administrators. The focus of that meeting, held in Washington, D.C., was the nature and process of engagement with the societies our public universities serve. The exchange of ideas among those present, both academic and nonacademic, was important to the reform that continues to be achieved after the Kellogg Commission completed its formal work. The sixth, and final, report of the Kellogg Commission, "Renewing the Covenant: Learning, Discovery, and Engagement in a New Age and Different World," was released at the time of the final meeting.

To maintain the momentum of the reform generated by its work, the commission formed an "implementation group,"[4] supported with remaining funds from the commission's grant, plus additional funds from another Kellogg grant to NASULGC. These funds enabled the group to conduct a survey of perceptions of reform at thirty-six public universities (including the Kellogg Commission institutions), host a workshop in June 2001, and publish in a single volume the executive summaries of all six of the Kellogg Commission reports.

Institutional Change: 2000—A Survey of Reform at Thirty-Six Public Universities

During the summer and fall of 2000, the Implementation Group surveyed forty public universities, including the commission institutions, about education reform on their campuses. The purpose of the survey was to assess perceptions of reform and to stimulate continued thought and action concerning the need for and the nature of higher education reform.

The survey questionnaire was organized according to the five areas addressed by the Kellogg Commission: student experience, student access, the engaged institution, a learning society, and campus culture. Responses were requested from four levels at each institution: president; dean of agriculture; other dean, vice president, or director; and faculty leader. Those receiving the questionnaire were asked to respond to forty-three questions directly related to the commission's recommendations. More than ninety questionnaires were returned from thirty-six universities. Although differences between perception and reality do occur, collectively the responses reflected the progress of reform occurring in today's public university. Respondents also described examples of progress on their campus, identified impediments to change, and suggested reform that should be happening.

June 2001 Workshop: A Vision for Change

At the post–Kellogg Commission Workshop on Higher Education Reform, "A Vision for Change," held June 11 and 12, 2001, in Atlanta, more than one hundred participants representing fifty universities shared information about reform on their campuses. The workshop addressed the requirements for changing an organization, established a forum for presentation by a number of universities of examples of successful and unsuccessful efforts to institute change, and offered participants the opportunity to share lessons learned while attempting reform.

The impact of the Kellogg Commission has been felt throughout American public higher education. The commission reports have enhanced the awareness of the need for education reform. More than thirty-six thousand copies of the reports have been distributed. They have stimulated campus discussions leading to revision of promotion and tenure guidelines and the very missions of American universities. The integration of learning, discovery, and engagement, as recommended by the commission, is being adopted as the core mission at an increasing number of public universities.

The University of Georgia has initiated a new publication devoted to engagement, the *Journal of Higher Education Outreach and Engagement,* and engagement is being introduced as a legitimate activity recognized in promotion and tenure guidelines at many universities. Several of the higher education associations are promoting passage by the U.S. Congress of a Millennial Partnership Act, the information-age equivalent of the original land-grant acts, with sufficient funding to create a genuine national learning society. Another major effort is being made to address questions related to food and society. The Kellogg Commission on the Future of State and Land-Grant Universities stimulated all these activities. The work of the commission has laid a foundation for the continuing reform of public higher education in America. By any measure, the Kellogg Commission was a success.

Notes

1. The commissioners and their staffs, the advisory board, the NASULGC staff (especially Michael Vahle), Carol Mason of Oregon State University, James Harvey, the implementation group, and the leadership of the W. K. Kellogg Foundation (including William

Richardson, president; Richard Foster, vice president for programs; and Gail Imig, program officer) all contributed substantially to the success of the work of the commission.

2. Advisory board members: Roger R. Blunt, Sr. (chair), chairman and CEO, Essex Construction Corp. and Blunt Enterprises, Maryland; Paula Butterfield, superintendent, Bozeman, Montana, Public Schools and Mercer Island, Washington, Public Schools; Wenda Weekes Moore, trustee, W. K. Kellogg Foundation, Michigan; Donald E. Petersen, former chairman and CEO, Ford Motor Co., Michigan; Walter Scott, Jr., president, Peter Kiewit Sons, Inc., and Level 3 Communications, Inc., Nebraska; Mike Thorne, executive director, Port of Portland, Oregon; Edwin S. Turner, president, EST Enterprises, Missouri.

3. Steering committee members: C. Peter Magrath, president, NASULGC; John Byrne, executive director, Kellogg Commission; Richard Foster, W. K. Kellogg Foundation; James Harvey, Harvey and Associates; Richard Stoddard, director of federal relations, Ohio State University; Teresa Streeter, executive associate to the president, NASULGC; Michael Vahle, staff assistant to the Kellogg Commission. Others who participated: Roselyn Hiebert, director, public affairs, NASULGC; Cheryl Fields, Hiebert's successor as director of public affairs; Joseph Kunsman, director, academic programs in agriculture and natural resources, NASULGC; and Stephen MacCarthy, executive director, university relations, Pennsylvania State University.

4. Implementation group members: Ted Alter, Pennsylvania State University; John Byrne, Oregon State University, retired; Maury Cotter, University of Wisconsin-Madison; Brent Ruben, Rutgers University; Louise Sandemeyer, Pennsylvania State University; Dick Stoddard, Ohio State University; and Michael Vahle, NASULCG.

Building Community and Shared Vision Through "The Quality Expo"

Louise Sandmeyer
Director, Office of Planning and Institutional Assessment, Pennsylvania State University

Carol Lindborg Everett
Associate Director, Office of Planning and Institutional Assessment, Pennsylvania State University

On most campuses, it is rare to see a member of the Office of Physical Plant engaging in a discussion about how he has implemented a new online inventory system, with a faculty member who teaches large freshmen chemistry classes and has put her syllabus and notes online to free additional classroom time for problem-based learning. Such interchanges do not happen naturally in most institutions of higher learning. Sometimes it is difficult for faculty to interact with other faculty outside of their discipline or college. Staff may find their interactions with others restricted to those who work in their immediate office. Individuals find themselves separated not just by physical location but also by discipline, hierarchy, and educational status. In such an environment, how does cross-unit learning occur? How are organizational silos broken down? How is interdependency understood and fostered? How does collaboration occur? How does the university share a broadly defined vision of excellence?

One answer might be to build a culture for improvement-driven planning. Daniel Seymour, in his book *On Q: Causing Quality in Higher Education,* states that "a college or university operates as a collection of isolated individual parts; strategic quality management is a unifying force that advances an integrated, purposeful whole" (1989, p. 31). To advance institutional quality and institutional effectiveness, it is essential to have collaboration, teamwork, and a shared vision. A culture for quality cannot result without building an interdependent culture for collaboration.

Celebrating Quality and Building a Shared Vision of Excellence

Penn State builds community and promotes a collaborative approach to institutional excellence through what we call a "Quality Expo," an event that has been held each spring for the past ten years. The expo is sponsored by the Office of Planning and Institutional Assessment, an organization formed to provide leadership and support for improvement, planning, and assessment initiatives at the unit and institutional levels. The university originally embarked on its continuous quality improvement effort in 1991 under the leadership of then-provost John Brighton. From the beginning, improvement, collaboration, and teamwork were recognized, acknowledged, and celebrated through what was originally called the Continuous Quality Improvement (CQI) Team Fair, and later the Quality Expo. The unifying theme of each expo has been "Share, Learn, and Celebrate."

At the 2002 expo, thirty-eight exhibits representing forty-three teams and 305 individuals demonstrated how services have been enhanced through user-centered information technologies in academics, services, and operations (Table 9.1). In the President's Hall at the Penn Stater conference center on the University Park campus, booths were set up and students, faculty, staff, and administrators shared their stories of organizational change and technological innovations. A visitor would have heard a faculty member and a student affairs administrator discuss the use of student e-portfolios to enhance learning; a staff assistant and the assistant registrar talk about their work together on a team that reengineered course scheduling through the use of technology; and two career counselors located at different campuses explain how their virtual team has created greater opportunities for cross-campus collaboration.

**Table 9.1. Quality Expo Teams Focused on
"Academics," "Operations," and "Services."**

	1993	1994	1995	1996	1997	1998	1999	2000	2001	2002	TOTAL
Academic	12	12	11	25	21	24	23	15	12	10	165 (34%)
Operations	5	7	6	8	20	24	15	20	17	11	133 (27%)
Service	11	8	22	13	36	30	13	19	13	22	187 (39%)
TOTAL	28	27	39	46	77	78	51	54	42	43	485 (100%)

The expo is about rewarding collaboration and teamwork. Recognition, gratitude, and celebration are critical to the success of any quality initiative. Although the values of individualism and competition are important to the advancement of scholarship and are rewarded in the academy, the teams in the expo don't compete for recognition. There is no "best in show." All team efforts are celebrated, whether the outcome has resulted in considerable cost savings to the university (for example, through the use of a purchasing card) or has involved reducing the time it takes to streamline a process (such as registering for a course or cleaning a classroom).

In 1993, Penn State's first CQI Team Fair highlighted the efforts of twenty-eight teams made up mostly of staff members. Each year since then it has grown; it now showcases the quality improvement efforts of students, faculty, and staff and highlights the successes of interdisciplinary and multiunit teams.

Collaboration and Community That Extends Beyond Our Own Campus

In recent years the expo has been expanded to include other events, such as conferences and workshops designed to attract a national audience of people interested in issues of organizational effectiveness and improvement. In 1998, the expo was preceded by a quality conference, which was attended by 150 conferees, one-third of whom were from institutions other than Penn State. In 2001, Associate Vice Chancellor Ron Coley, UC Berkeley, and Chet Warzynski, director of organizational development and employment services at Cornell University, offered a workshop on the balanced scorecard approach to performance assessment (Kaplan and Norton, 1996a). The workshop was cosponsored by the National Consortium for Continuous Improvement (NCCI). In the past several years, in addition to Penn State team exhibits there have been exhibits from the University of Wisconsin–Madison, Slippery Rock University, Bloomsburg University, Rutgers University, the University of Missouri–Rolla, Ohio State University, and the California State University System. Just as the expo offers opportunities for cross-unit learning within Penn State, in recent years it has facilitated networking among diverse institutions whose size and mission may vary but that have a common interest in enhancing quality through collaboration.

"The expo provides an opportunity to celebrate the diversity of the university community by bringing together teams from different units and campus locations. The teams have worked on processes that vary widely but share the common theme of improving the quality of education and better serving the citizens of Pennsylvania," says Rodney Erickson, Penn State's executive vice president and provost.

"CQI has made Penn State more aware of whom we serve and how we can meet and exceed their expectations through improved processes. It has supported a culture where teamwork and collaboration are valued, and innovation and change are encouraged," says Erickson.

Planning the Expo

Just as the expo exhibitors represent both the academic and administrative areas of the university, so too the team of volunteers who plan and execute the event with the support of the Office of Planning and Institutional Assessment reflect this diversity. The expo planning team is made up of a grassroots group of volunteers who have a vested interest in organizational effectiveness and improvement. Members' familiarity with quality concepts and tools in their day-to-day work and on CQI teams contributes to the work of the planning team, where brainstorming, flowcharting, benchmarking, and assessment all take place. Team membership changes slightly each year and members have included, for example, the assistant development director in the college of business, the director of a technology center, a staff assistant in the department of materials science and engineering, a network analyst in the office of undergraduate admissions, a director in auxiliary and business services, a human resources manager, and the director of telecommunications.

The planning team's goals are (1) to create a vehicle to successfully recognize teams and individuals who participate in quality improvement initiatives; and (2) increase the dissemination of information about improvement initiatives to the university community, which in turn increases the number of teams and quality activities.

The Quality Expo has shown measurable success for ten straight years, under the administration of three presidents and two provosts, with the participation of exhibitors and guests from dozens of universities. The fact that several universities have initiated similar events after observing the success of Penn State's event offers additional evidence of its value and impact.

Several lessons have been learned over the past decade. The expo is successful because it is easy for people to participate. There is no cost to the exhibitors. The Office of Planning and Institutional Assessment coordinates venue setup, technical support, marketing and publicity, printing programs, banners and posters, and development of evaluation instruments.

Although continuous improvement is about pushing decision making downward in the organization, it is important that there be both grassroots involvement and top leadership commitment for the expo to be successful. The event is inclusive and welcoming to faculty, staff, and students from across the university; it encourages conversation across disciplines, units, and campuses. This occurs because supervisors and managers encourage teams to exhibit, exhibitors' coworkers attend the event to show their support, and administrators visit booths and engage in discussion with exhibitors and visitors about improvement and innovation. It may be jargon to put it in these terms, but the expo gives university leaders the opportunity to "walk the talk."

One of the early lessons Penn State learned through its partnerships with Du Pont and IBM is that if exceeding customer expectations is a goal, then the organization must first meet the expectations of its employees. Systems for recognition and reward must align with institutional values. If the institution states that it values continuous learning and improvement, teamwork, collaboration, and community, then it must recognize and reward those behaviors. The Quality Expo is one such venue for learning, rewarding, and celebrating these core values.

The nature of the exhibits featured in the expo evolves and changes depending upon where the university is in its quality improvement efforts. The desire for improvement and excellence occurs in academics, services, and operations. However, the adoption of continuous improvement and the process focus initially appear more applicable to the areas of services and operations. Thus, in the first years of the expo, most of the exhibits dealt with improving administrative processes such as shortening wait times, streamlining office procedures, and reducing inventories. Exhibits in recent years have celebrated the progress made in the university's core activities, such as the teaching and learning process that occurs in the classroom and methods for improving the quality of academic programs. Discussions with exhibitors indicate that not only are the core processes being addressed but competencies in collaboration have also been strengthened. The expo is a forum that brings together faculty and staff who share the goal of improvement. A tenet of the continuous improvement model is that organizations are systems, and what occurs in one area will have an impact upon other areas. For example, academics, services, and operations are interdependent, especially from the perspective of those for whom we provide services. Teamwork, collaboration, and communication are the tools that help the university achieve change and leverage this interdependency. The expo furnishes a definition of community that goes beyond role and discipline-based cultural divisions. At Penn State, our goal is to ensure that quality improvement connects individuals from throughout the university with broader institutional goals and values and, in the process, engages their interest and commitment to a shared vision of excellence.

Organizational Change at Berkeley: A Work in Progress

Robert M. Berdahl
Chancellor, University of California, Berkeley

Phyllis Hoffman
Director, Center for Organizational
Effectiveness, University of California, Berkeley

The University of California, Berkeley, is the flagship of California's public university system. Its undergraduate enrollment exceeds 23,000 and graduate enrollment more than 8,800. Berkeley's faculty of 1,400-plus consists of seven Nobel laureates, 17 MacArthur Fellows, 119 members of the National Academy of Sciences, 70 Fulbright Scholars, and three Pulitzer Prize winners. UC Berkeley ranks third nationally among all institutions in the number of freshmen who are National Merit Scholars. Berkeley also produces more graduates who go on to earn Ph.D.s than any other university in the country.

Making Organizational Effectiveness a Top Priority for Berkeley

When I arrived as chancellor of UC Berkeley in July 1997, I expected to find that all aspects of Berkeley would reflect the excellence of its

The authors wish to express their gratitude to Katherine Mitchell, internal organizational development consultant, Center for Organizational Effectiveness, for her helpful assistance in the preparation of this narrative.

academic reputation. Excellence in academics must surely be, at least in part, a consequence of high-quality business and administrative functions. What I found surprised me. Business practices and administrative operations were simply not on par with the quality one would expect to be associated with Berkeley. Capital projects routinely were seriously over budget and late in completion; bills submitted to the university by service providers, including reimbursements to faculty, were not paid in a reasonable time period; some administrative offices were not operating in an efficient, or even a modern, manner; bureaucratic policies, built up over time, clogged the efficiency of many operations; and some units seemed not to remember that their primary function was to serve their various constituencies.

Berkeley's faculty, staff, and students take great pride in being associated with one of the world's leading public research universities. The campus's organizational effectiveness, however, had not kept pace with its academic reputation. In most cases, these failings were not a consequence of incompetent staff or administrators; nor were they a result of indifference or ill will. Rather, a level of tolerance for such inefficiencies had developed so that when asked why things were done as they were, people would shrug and say, "That's just 'the Berkeley way.'" It was thus a part of the Berkeley culture.

As chancellor, I challenged the campus community to join me in addressing this issue and designated "operational excellence"—now called "organizational effectiveness"—as one of my top priorities: "It's time for a change at Berkeley. We need to examine all aspects of how we conduct our business with the aim of streamlining decision making and infusing our campus community with a service orientation. We must make certain that the same ethos of excellence that marks our teaching and research permeates our entire organization. Organizational effectiveness is everyone's responsibility."

As is almost always the case in universities, the exploration of a new idea begins with the appointment of a committee. In this case, the Chancellor's Exploratory Committee on Continuous Improvement (CECCI) was created and charged with examining how to "improve organizational effectiveness across the campus by streamlining processes, and providing professional development and continuous improvements."

CECCI spent several months researching continuous improvement practices in business and higher education, and studying prior change initiatives at Berkeley. The committee was especially interested in identifying lessons learned from previous change efforts and concluded that Berkeley could benefit from the philosophy and tools of continuous improvement, so long as the approaches were appropriately adapted to our organizational culture. The committee, chaired by Ron Coley, associate vice chancellor for business and administrative services, recommended the establishment of a central office for continuous improvement that reported to the Office of the Chancellor.

To aid the new office in its initial phase, the committee issued five recommendations, excerpted here:

1. Institutionalize continuous improvement throughout the campus by establishing a small office that reports to the chancellor, with central funding and a dedicated staff; the office would:

   Offer a range of useful models and tools for planning and improvement

   Provide consultative services to help guide planning and improvement efforts upon request

   Create learning opportunities to help people develop skills that will support their efforts

   Furnish an assessment model that units can use to self-study their operations and focus their improvement efforts, and consultative help in using the model

   Work to lessen the rigidity of organizational boundaries through collaboration and consultation

   Support efforts to improve internal communication and the sharing of information

   Support inclusive strategic planning at all levels of the university

2. The Office of the Chancellor and the committee should model continuous improvement.

3. The office of continuous improvement should be responsible for developing and making available planning and process improvement tools and become an integral component of continuous improvement at UC Berkeley.

4. Emphasize the meaningful assessment and development of employees at all levels.
5. Formalize professional affiliations with recognized leaders in organizational excellence:
   Establish a partnership with Hewlett-Packard
   Maintain affiliations with established leaders in continuous improvement in higher education

Establishing the Center for Organizational Effectiveness (COrE)

As the first step toward implementing CECCI's recommendations, the Center for Organizational Effectiveness (COrE) was established in February 1999; Phyllis Hoffman was named director. COrE was constituted as a small, centrally funded unit reporting to the associate chancellor–chief of staff to the chancellor. As director of the center, I realized that COrE faced a significant early challenge: How could this new center assist university departments in improving their work processes without itself becoming a part of the same bureaucracy?

Reviewing CECCI's recommendations in consultation with on- and off-campus advisors, COrE's staff outlined organizing principles for the center. Although the particular services that we provide to campus have changed as the center has evolved over time, these principles continue to guide our decision making.

Create a Critical Mass of Campus Champions

Needing to build a critical mass of campus champions who would support the organizational effectiveness priority, COrE decided to respond to as many requests for help as possible. This initial "breadth" approach reinforced that organizational effectiveness was a top priority for Berkeley and demonstrated how the center could provide assistance.

Pull Rather Than Push

As recommended by CECCI, we worked with campus clients who voluntarily sought consultation. This strategy confirmed a fundamental principle of community organizing: attracting voluntary early adopters interested in making improvements results in greater commitment to implementing positive changes and builds solid allies.

Invest in Projects Where the Person-in-Charge Is Actively Involved

Improvement requires the active involvement of leaders and managers who are accountable for operations. We chose to invest in projects where the senior administrator of the unit took direct responsibility for the effort, resisting appeals from employees and managers to "come in and fix things."

Work Both "Top Down" and "Bottom Up"

Previous campus efforts to improve effectiveness had more success when both leaders and grassroots staff demonstrated commitment to a shared goal. Working from the top down, COrE involved itself in projects with members of the chancellor's office and cabinet. At the same time, the center sponsored several seminars and made multiple presentations about organizational effectiveness to groups of interested staff and faculty members. Strategically placed within the Office of the Chancellor, COrE bridged the gap between active top-down initiatives and positive bottom-up improvement efforts by facilitating communication across organizational boundaries.

Collaborate with Other Change Agents on Campus

When COrE was established, many individuals—managers, human resource professionals, and informal leaders—had created positive change within their own spheres of influence but faced limits on their ability to affect systemic issues campuswide. As a hub for organizational effectiveness on campus, COrE convened members of these groups to leverage individual efforts for maximum impact.

Assessment, Planning, and Improvement

COrE's initial breadth approach achieved its purpose of creating a critical mass of supporters for organizational effectiveness. By the end of the center's second year, however, it became evident that this strategy would not produce sustainable change at Berkeley. Although successful department-specific projects achieved local change, these efforts could not address root causes of campuswide systemic issues. We began redirecting our resources to work on projects that addressed systemic issues having campuswide impact, led by individuals who were ready and positioned to make positive change. Two of these systemic issues were pivotal:

1. *Setting priorities:* Berkeley's decentralized and fiercely independent culture makes it challenging to articulate a set of outcome-oriented priorities for the campus as a whole. Administrators face difficult decisions about what *not* to do because not doing something can negatively affect an individual student, faculty, or staff member; increase risk or liability; or offend an important constituent group.

2. *Performance management:* Many of Berkeley's managers and academic administrators struggle to translate organizational priorities into effective staff performance.

Our experience in addressing these systemic issues has shown us the importance of identifying and working with campus leaders who are ready to be levers for change. Although many campus leaders already know how to solve their problems, they find that their effectiveness increases with focused time and confidential, professional support from a COrE consultant to fully examine the ramifications of potential strategies and actions. By working in partnership with COrE, leaders are better equipped to identify and achieve desired outcomes, clarify their vision and direction, establish priorities, set realistic expectations, and implement an action plan.

To address the challenges of assessment and priority setting, performance management and leadership, we have used a variety of approaches, among them the balanced scorecard (Kaplan and Norton, 1996a), which has been used extensively in our Business and Administrative Services division; a work process improvement methodology, called Ford RAPID, developed by Ford Motor; and the *Excellence in Higher Education* framework for organizational assessment and improvement (Ruben, 2001a, 2003a), an adaptation of the Malcolm Baldrige model (Baldrige National Quality

Program, 2002e, 2003a). The application of the balanced score-card within business and administrative services at Berkeley is explained in a narrative by Ron Coley and Paul Dimond elsewhere in this book (see Chapter Four). In the next section, we briefly describe our application of the Excellence in Higher Education program.

Early on, the CECCI identified the Baldrige National Quality Program (2003a) criteria as the clear gold standard for organizational assessment and improvement in the private sector. They also became acquainted with *Excellence in Higher Education* (Ruben, 2001b, 2001c, 2003a, 2003b), a Baldrige-based program tailored specifically to the needs and culture of higher education. We piloted the *EHE* program with four units in the Business and Administrative Services division (mail services, parking and transportation, physical plant, and printing services) and subsequently introduced it in a number of other departments, including the Academic Personnel Office, Business and Administrative Services Senior Managers, Chancellor's Immediate Office, Graduate Division and Research, Office of Laboratory Animal Care, and University Police. The *EHE* workshop program has been customized—"Berkeleyized"—in various ways. Campus examples have been used to demonstrate the relevance of the seven *EHE* criteria to the UC Berkeley community. A short questionnaire—the Organizational Effectiveness Inventory—was developed and used to introduce people to the *EHE* framework. Modules were also created for each of the *EHE* categories, so that each can be used either as the basis for stand-alone workshops or integrated as a module into a larger organizational effectiveness effort.

A Work in Progress

In the years since the establishment of COrE, we have learned a good deal about the difficulty of fostering meaningful and lasting change; we have also gained insight into what we believe are essential ingredients for success in such efforts:

- *A catalyst:* an urgency for change, in our case created by a vision articulated by the chancellor and reinforced by CECCI, acknowledging the negative impacts of organizational ineffectiveness on our academic programs.

- *Committed sponsorship:* leadership and support from the very top, as well as several midlevel managers championing organizational improvement in their own areas, motivating faculty and staff to personally engage in change efforts. In our case, committed sponsorship was demonstrated in part by the placement of COrE in the chancellor's immediate office, which has also facilitated COrE staff members' access to all levels of the organization.

- *Emerging clarity of purpose and scope:* a clear sense of direction and priority. As we enter our fourth year, we have greater clarity and focus as a center, with three primary areas in which we offer services to the campus: organizational assessment, strategic and action planning, and work process improvement. We also now have more clarity on what projects we will refer to other on-campus resources and off-campus consultants. Additionally, we have realized that creating campus momentum toward organizational effectiveness requires moving beyond work process improvement to helping leaders at all levels develop self-awareness and courage to lead change themselves.

- *Building a foundation for organizational planning across the campus:* connecting with other campus change agents—campus leadership teams, special task forces, campuswide planners, and other organizational development specialists—to move organizational planning forward.

- *Sufficient financial and human resource base:* ongoing financial support and staff members who have the appropriate set of skills, experiences, and perspectives. This has also meant that we must have the spirit and energy to accomplish a great deal with a small staff.

Through our work, we have been reminded that Berkeley is a fascinating place, full of bright, well-intentioned people who are intensely committed to the university's educational mission. One of our ongoing challenges in facilitating organizational effectiveness has been overcoming widespread cynicism about the possibility for organizational change while supporting a growing network of change champions at all levels. By strategically deploying COrE's limited resources and forming partnerships with other change agents, we infuse hope and energy into the system, and we help set realistic expectations about what this large, public, political system can achieve. At the same time, we challenge elements of the status quo while preserving our freethinking, collegial culture.

Berkeley's long-term change effort is gaining momentum. UC Berkeley faces a period of economic constraint and particularly tough choices. As we face this and other institutional challenges, we are committed to building upon our tradition of excellence to make UC Berkeley an even more effective and distinguished institution in the years ahead.

Chapter Ten

Excellence in Practice
Asking More of Ourselves and Our Institutions

This book examines eight challenges facing colleges and universities, each of which is a core issue with broad significance within the higher education community from philosophical and practical perspectives. Even though each challenge represents a problem, each is also an opportunity to reexamine and clarify our sense of purpose, reaffirm our guiding principles, and reconcile differences between traditional academic values and the demands of an increasingly competitive marketplace for educational services. This final chapter is a brief review of these challenges, with closing observations on their implications.

Broadening Public Appreciation for the Work of the Academy: Committing Ourselves to Dialogue

Higher education needs broadened understanding, appreciation, and support for its work among many constituencies and publics. Achieving this purpose requires more genuine commitment to dialogue—more dedicated listening and more clearly articulated and persuasive explanations of our purposes and aspirations, presented in ways that are more sensitive to the perspective, experience, and education of those with whom we are speaking.

The reasons for lack of knowledge and misunderstanding of the academy are many and can often be traced to the sheer complexity of our institutions, their missions, and the number of constituencies we serve. The range of services and potential points of intersection between the academy and its constituencies presents a challenge, but it can also be an opportunity if we approach it as such. Doing so requires the concerted effort of all of us—administrators, faculty, and staff (and students)—not simply of those professionals within the institution whose job description calls for attention to these matters.

Creating shared perspectives should be an implicit goal of every encounter with constituents—beginning with the first exposure that potential students, family members, and visitors have to an institution, and permeating each subsequent interaction between the individual and institution over the course of his or her lifetime—as a student, alumni, employer, visitor, participant in university events, potential donor, and lifelong member of the college or university community.

Better Understanding and Addressing the Needs of Workplaces: Bridging the Gap Between the World of the Academy and the World of Work

The academic community can benefit greatly from increasing dialogue about the workplace, and the knowledge and competencies needed for entry, advancement, and leadership within all sectors. Some perceive a substantial difference between the education provided by most institutions and the needs of the workplace, but this perception may be exaggerated. A closer look at the clusters of competencies that are viewed as necessary to workplace success reveals many similarities to those traditionally valued within the academy. That many perceive otherwise speaks to the need for increased interaction and engagement between the world of higher education and the world of work.

The increased dialogue should be targeted to broadening shared understanding of the knowledge and competencies that are important to success in the workplace; the most effective approaches for teaching and learning these competencies; the respective roles best played by the academy and the workplaces in providing this education; and possibilities for working more collaboratively in research, instruction, and outreach efforts relative to this issue.

Becoming More Effective Learning Organizations: Clarifying Goals and Evaluating Outcomes

Given the mission of the academy, few challenges seem more basic than becoming model learning organizations. Clarifying goals, developing methods for evaluating and monitoring our achievements relative to these goals, and creating a climate that is open to learning from any and all pertinent sources are among the activities that are characteristic of such organizations. An important element of this process is the translation of institutional missions, aspirations, and goals into indicators of organizational achievement so that successes—as well as failures—can be highlighted and used as sources of learning and improvement. Identifying and using a cluster of organizational indices, an organizational dashboard, can help to sharpen focus, foster a shared sense of possibilities and priorities, and allow each faculty and staff member in the institution to see the connection between his or her work and the purposes and future directions of the institution.

Given the benefits, the importance of being proactive in defining and using excellence measures cannot be overemphasized. The alternative is to wait until accountability or performance measures are defined and imposed by others, more often than not by groups that have a considerably more restricted view of what constitutes excellence than do administrators, faculty, and staff within the program, department, or institution. The selected indicators must emphasize academic dimensions of excellence, but it must also take account of factors that are judged to be important to those for whom our programs and services are created—and to faculty and staff—as well those that are critical to operational and financial effectiveness.

Integrating Organizational Assessment, Planning, and Improvement: Making Organizational Self-Study and Change Everyday Activities

There is a pressing need to implement integrated approaches to assessment, planning, and improvement in academic *and* administrative departments, and indeed entire institutions. Such approaches should acknowledge the uniqueness of each department, but they can also encourage the identification and sharing of effective practices across departments and institutions.

Baldrige-based frameworks adapted to the special languages and culture of higher education offer programs, departments, and institutions a model for addressing these formidable challenges. Excellence in Higher Education is one such program, and the North Central Accrediting Association's Academic Quality Improvement Program is another. Programs based on the Baldrige model help to identify strengths and areas for improvement that translate into strategic and action plans, clarify mission and aspirations, create common language for organizational analysis and improvement, and encourage a focus on the perspectives of stakeholders. Moreover, they pose a standard of comparison using an accepted assessment framework, and they guide the establishment of benchmark comparisons and learning across departments and institutions. These programs also help departments and institutions prepare for external review and accreditation, increase the shared commitment to institutional change and advancement, and foster a culture of ongoing self-assessment and continuous improvement.

Enhancing Collaboration and Community: Aligning the Rhetoric and Reality of Campus Culture

Respect for individual differences and collegiality are core values within the academy, and nearly every institution visibly endorses the principles of mutual respect, cooperation, collaboration, and community. Despite our ongoing articulation of these values, significant gaps between the rhetoric and reality continue to challenge our good intentions. Some of the problem areas are already a focus of attention; others, as in cultural gaps based on differences in occupational roles, disciplines, or technical specialties, have received less attention but are of no less concern.

Occupational and role-based cultures—such as those that may develop among faculty, administrative, and staff groups within particular academic or administrative departments—serve necessary and important functions within colleges and universities, as they do in organizations in other sectors. However, they may also interfere with organizational excellence, undermine our shared sense of institutional purpose and vision, detract from campus cohesion and institutional pride, and most important undermine our ability to create the kind of exemplary teaching and learning environment to which the academy is dedicated. There is a need to promote and cultivate collaborative values and competencies among faculty, administrators, and staff. We also need to identify and experiment with boundary-spanning organizational models, and to introduce incentive and recognition systems to reward collaborative efforts, along with individual accomplishment.

Recognizing That Everyone in the Institution Is a Teacher: Focusing on the Student Experience

Members of the faculty *and* all members of the administrative, professional, and support groups teach through each and every one of the tens of thousands of interpersonal encounters with students, guests, and one another that transpire daily on every campus. *Together,* we are the face of the institution. Important lessons are being taught in classrooms and laboratories through lectures and other planned activities, but also through any number of unplanned events—through the kind of organizations we design, through how we do our work, and through the way we relate to students, other stakeholders, and one another. Together, we are presenting a complex and diverse array of lessons—for the next generation of doctors, teachers, engineers, artists, corporate managers, health care providers, lawyers, and civic leaders.

It is essential that the lessons we are teaching be created by design, rather than by default. To achieve this goal, we must be clear as to what kinds of organizations, relationships, and environments we offer as models. Excellence in education is not, then, solely a faculty matter. We are all instructors and stewards of the student learning experience. We share responsibility for shaping the learning environment and for shaping the perception—and the reality—of teaching excellence.

Devoting More Attention and Resources to Leadership: Attracting, Developing, and Retaining Outstanding Leaders

Extraordinary times require extraordinary leaders—leaders who are broadly knowledgeable about the work of the academy, able to relate effectively with the many internal and external constituencies,

capable of engaging and mobilizing colleagues toward a shared
vision of excellence, and appropriately recognized and rewarded for
their contributions. Exceptional leaders are needed in all areas and
at all levels within colleges and universities.

The time-honored approaches used by the academy to identify, recruit, prepare, and retain leaders are increasingly inadequate
today. A new leadership development paradigm is needed, one that
uses the academy's core educational values and competencies and
allows those of us within the academy to benefit from the kinds of
developmental experiences we have long advocated and provided
for others. In support of this approach, we need to encourage
further study of leadership in higher education, offer meaningful
incentives and rewards, create more meaningful leadership
development opportunities, and implement systematic leadership-
effectiveness review processes.

More Broadly Framing Our Vision: Pursuing Excellence in All That We Do

Undoubtedly, the most fundamental need is for a new, more inclusive vision of excellence to which we can aspire. Our mission statements and much of the work of the academy are dedicated to the
pursuit of academic excellence. Yet excellence in academics is very
much dependent upon establishing and sustaining excellent relationships with our beneficiaries, and upon developing effective and
efficient organizations. In the day-to-day experiences of students,
faculty, and staff, the lines between academic, service, and operational aspects of a university often become blurred. The result is
impressions and images of an institution that are influenced not
only by efforts at academic and scholarly excellence but also by the
way individuals are treated by faculty and staff, the responsiveness
and user-friendliness of systems and procedures, and the effectiveness and efficiency of the infrastructure. These combined perceptions, recollections, and accounts from others translate into
important decisions that affect institutional reputation; student
recruitment; alumni support; faculty and staff morale; and the flow
of resources to support learning, discovery, and engagement.

The interdependency of academic, service, and operational
excellence is fundamental; unfortunately, the consequences of deficiencies in service and operational areas are often more obvious

than the contributions made by academics. Today, more dramatically than in previous times, excellence in higher education requires a commitment to high standards in all three domains.

Concluding Comments

As I wrote in the opening chapter of this book, the term *ivory tower* was first used to refer to a kind of sanctuary, a retreat from the realities of the day (Sainte-Beuve, 1869). The ivory tower image of the academy, however—a place that is different and disconnected from the "real" world—is a myth. There are those who would argue that this was never an appropriate characterization of higher education, but few would suggest that this portrayal is appropriate today. For better or worse, higher education is confronted by all the operational, financial, and cultural challenges that face other organizations.

Those who care deeply about higher education abhor the thought of operating colleges and universities as "consumer-driven" organizations guided solely by economic and marketplace considerations. Yet the image of the ivory tower—where purpose and direction are set without regard to the perspectives of the many groups and organizations upon whose support our institutions depend—is equally untenable.

The Kellogg Commission (2001b) described it this way: "Our key challenge is two-fold. We must maintain our legacy of world-class teaching, research, and public service. At the same time, in a rapidly changing world, we must build on our legacy of responsiveness and relevance" (p. 1).

An institution's vision and its core ideology set the context that motivates and guides the practices through which the organization is defined and redefined. What is called for now is a new, broader, and more inclusive view of organizational excellence. This new vision should underscore the importance, interdependence, and creative tensions of the goals of academic, service, and operational excellence. It should identify the academy as a place that *advances* knowledge, and one that *applies, tests,* and *uses* that knowledge to improve its own functioning—one that clarifies and *studies* best practices in health care, education, business, humanities, and the arts, *and employs* those best practices that are relevant to our work.

Translating this vision into reality requires that we ask more of ourselves and our institutions as we work together to create contemporary centers of learning that are the embodiment of the best organizational principles and practices possible. In addition to giving consideration to the kinds of institutional improvements suggested in the preceding chapters and narratives, there are also more personal challenges confronting those of us who are fortunate enough to work in a university environment.

Perhaps the most important task facing all of us—faculty, administrators, and staff—is to continually remind ourselves of the vital role we play as full-time ambassadors for our institutions in each and every interaction with students, parents, alumni, and the public. Every conversation we have presents an opportunity for us to play a significant personal role in helping to enrich the understanding and support for the purposes and aspirations of our college or university, and higher education in general.

The primary additional challenge for those of us who serve in administrative or other staff roles is to recognize that as we carry out the duties of our respective positions, we are also teachers. In every decision or action that we take, whether at our desks or elsewhere on campus, we are teaching others about organizational life, interpersonal relations, conflict resolution, the importance of pride in one's work, and myriad other critically important lessons. In each instance we are conveying not only our personal values but the values of our institution—regardless of our job descriptions. We are all personally and directly involved in creating learning experiences that help to shape the thoughts, attitudes, and behaviors of tomorrow's citizens, parents, and leaders.

For those of us who are faculty members, pursuing this more inclusive vision of excellence calls upon us to become as dedicated to the advancement of our departments and institutions as we are to our own scholarship and disciplines, as concerned with the quality of the lived experience of our students within our institutions as we are with the quality of the content and delivery of our courses over which we have more direct control, and as committed to dialogue and collaboration with administrators and staff as we are with our academic colleagues. Put simply, for us, excellence in practice means reinventing the significance of the phrase "the faculty are the university."

References

"Academic Chairpersons' Conference." Kansas State University, 2001. (www.dce.ksu.edu/dce/cl/academicchairpersons/)

Albrecht, K., and Zemke, R. *Service America.* Homewood, Ill.: Dow-Jones/Irwin, 1985.

Albrighton, F., and Thomas, J. *Managing External Relations.* Buckingham, England: Open University Press, 2001.

Allen, R., and Chaffee, E. "Management Fads in Higher Education." Paper presented at the Annual Forum of the Association for Institutional Research, Minneapolis, May 1981.

American Association of Higher Education. *Service-Learning in the Disciplines* (18 vols.). Washington D.C.: American Association for Higher Education, 1997–2000.

American Association for Higher Education. *Assessment Forum.* Washington, D.C.: American Association of Higher Education, 2002. (www.aahe.org/assessment/)

American Association for Higher Education, American College Personnel Association, and National Association of Student Personnel Administrators. *Powerful Partnerships: A Shared Responsibility for Learning. A Joint Report.* June 1998. (www.aahe.org/teaching/tsk_frce.htm)

American Association for Higher Education, American College Personnel Association, and National Association of Student Personnel Administrators, 1998. (www.naspa.org/resources/partnership.cfm)

American College Personnel Association. *The Student Learning Imperative: Implications for Student Affairs.* Washington, D.C.: American College Personnel Association, 1994.

American Council of Education. "Chairing the Academic Department." 2002. (www.acenet.edu)

Antonio, A. L. "Diversity and the Influence of Friendship Groups in College." *Review of Higher Education,* 2001, *25*(1), 63–89.

Applegate, J. L. "Engaged Graduate Education: Skating to Where the Puck Will Be." *National Communication Association Spectra,* Sept. 2001, pp. 2–5.

Ashkenas, R., Ulrich, D., Jick, T., and Kerr, S. *The Boundaryless Organization.* San Francisco: Jossey-Bass, 2002.

389

Astin, A. W. *What Matters in College?* San Francisco: Jossey-Bass, 1993.

Balderston, F. *Managing Today's University: Strategies for Viability, Change and Excellence* (2nd ed.). San Francisco: Jossey-Bass, 1995.

Baldrige National Quality Program. *The 2000 Criteria for Performance Excellence in Education.* Gaithersburg, Md.: National Institute of Standards and Technology, National Quality Program, 2000.

Baldrige National Quality Program. "Malcolm Baldrige National Quality Award." (Factsheet from NIST.) 2002a. (www.nist.gov/public_affairs/factsheet/mbnqa.htm)

Baldrige National Quality Program. "Malcolm Baldrige National Quality Award Application Data, 1988–2001." (Factsheet from NIST.) 2002b.(www.nist.gov/public_affairs/factsheet/nqa_appdata.htm)

Baldrige National Quality Program. National Institute for Standards and Technology (NIST) Website. (www.quality.nist.gov/. Aug. 2002c)

Baldrige National Quality Program. "State, Local and Regional Awards." Gaithersburg, Md.: Baldrige National Quality Program, 2002d.

Baldrige National Quality Program. *The 2002 Criteria for Performance Excellence.* Gaithersburg, Md.: National Institute of Standards and Technology, National Quality Program, 2002e. (www.quality.nist.gov/)

Baldrige National Quality Program. *The 2002 Criteria for Performance Excellence in Business.* Washington, D.C.: National Institute of Standards and Technology, 2002f. (www.quality.nist.gov/Business_Criteria.htm 2002f)

Baldrige National Quality Program. *The 2002 Criteria for Performance Excellence in Education.* Washington, D.C.: National Institute of Standards and Technology, 2002g. (www.quality.nist.gov/Education_Criteria.htm)

Baldrige National Quality Program. "2001 Malcolm Baldrige National Quality Award Education Category." (Factsheet from NIST.) 2002h. (www.nist.gov/public_affairs/factsheet/education.htm)

Baldrige National Quality Program. *The 2003 Criteria for Performance Excellence in Business.* Washington, D.C.: National Institute of Standards and Technology, 2003a. (www.quality.nist.gov/Business_Criteria.htm)

Baldrige National Quality Program. *The 2003 Criteria for Performance Excellence in Education.* Washington, D.C.: National Institute of Standards and Technology, 2003b. (www.quality.nist.gov/Education_Criteria.htm)

Becher, T., and Trowler, P. R. *Academic Tribes and Territories* (2nd ed.). Buckingham, England: Open University Press, 2001.

"Belmont University Alternate Self-Study: A Self-Assessment in Response to the Malcolm Baldrige National Quality Award Criteria for Education." (University internal document.) Nashville, Tenn.: Belmont University, 2000.

Bennett, J. B. *Collegial Professionalism.* Phoenix, Ariz.: American Council on Education/Oryx Press, 1998.

Bennis, W. *Managing People Is Like Herding Cats.* Provo, Utah: Executive Excellence, 1997.

Bennis, W. In D. Giber, L. Carter, and M. Goldsmith (eds.), *Linkage Inc.'s Best Practices in Leadership Development Handbook.* San Francisco: Jossey-Bass, 2000.

Berquist, W. H. *The Four Cultures of the Academy.* San Francisco: Jossey-Bass, 1992.

Biemiller, L. "North Central Association Unveils an Alternative Accreditation Plan." *Chronicle of Higher Education,* Apr. 3, 2000. (http://chronicle.com/daily/2000/04/20000040304n.htm)

Birnbaum, R. *How Colleges Work.* San Francisco: Jossey-Bass, 1988.

Birnbaum, R. *How Academic Leadership Works: Understanding Success and Failure in the College Presidency.* San Francisco: Jossey-Bass, 1992.

Birnbaum, R. *Management Fads in Higher Education.* San Francisco: Jossey-Bass, 2001.

Bowman, J. C., and Ruben, B. D. "Patient Satisfaction: Critical Issues in the Implementation and Evaluation of Patient Relations Training." *Journal of Healthcare Education and Training,* 1986, *1*(2), 24–27.

Boyer Commission. *Reinventing Undergraduate Education: A Blueprint for America's Research Universities.* Stony Brook, N.Y.: State University of New York at Stony Brook, for the Carnegie Foundation, 1998.

Boyer, E. L. *Scholarship Reconsidered: Priorities of the Professoriate.* San Francisco: Jossey-Bass, 1997.

Brancato, C. K. *New Corporate Performance Measures.* New York: Conference Board, 1995.

Braskamp, L. A., and Ory, J. C. *Assessing Faculty Work.* San Francisco: Jossey-Bass, 1994.

Bratton, W. *Turnaround.* New York: Random House, 1998.

"Breakthrough Leadership." Special Issue: Harvard Leadership Development Program. *Harvard Business Review,* Dec. 2001, *79*(11).

Broadhead, J. L. *The 1999 Annual Report.* Foundation for the Malcolm Baldrige National Quality Award, 2000. (www.quality.nist.gov/law.htm)

Burke, J. C. *Performance-Funding Indicators: Concerns, Values, and Models for Two- and Four-Year Colleges and Universities,* Albany. N.Y.: Nelson A. Rockefeller Institute of Government, 1997.

Burke, J. C., and Minassians, H. "Linking State Resources to Campus Results: From Fad to Trend—The Fifth Annual Report." 2001. (www.rockinst.org/publications/higher_ed/5thSurvey.pdf)

Burke, J. C., and Serban, A. M. *Performance Funding and Budgeting for Public Higher Education: Current Status and Future Prospects.* Albany, N.Y.: Nelson A. Rockefeller Institute of Government, 1997.

Burtha, M. "Knowledge Networking at Johnson and Johnson." Presentation at the Doctoral Colloquium, Graduate School of Applied and Professional Psychology, New Brunswick, N.J.: Rutgers University, Mar. 2002.

Camp, R. C. *Business Process Benchmarking: Finding and Implementing Best Practices.* Milwaukee, Wis.: American Society for Quality Press, 1995.

Caplow, T., and McGee, R. J. *The Academic Marketplace.* New Brunswick, N.J.: Transaction, 2001.

Carey, J. W. *The Engaged Discipline.* (Carroll C. Arnold Distinguished Lecture Series.) Boston: Allyn and Bacon, 2000.

Carnegie Foundation for the Advancement of Teaching. *National Survey on the Reexamination of Faculty Roles and Rewards.* Menlo Park, Calif.: Carnegie Foundation for the Advancement of Teaching, 1994.

Carnegie Foundation for the Advancement of Teaching. July 2002. (www.carnegiefoundation.org/Classification/index.htm)

Carson, B. H. *Change.* Nov.–Dec. 1996, pp. 11–17.

Chang, M. J. "Improving Racial Dynamics on Campus." *About Campus,* 2002, 7(1), 2–8.

Cherniss, C., and Goleman, D. *The Emotionally Intelligent Workplace.* San Francisco: Jossey-Bass, 2001.

Chronicle of Higher Education Almanac, Vol. 49, Aug. 30, 2002. (Table on p. 15. Source for table: U.S. Department of Education 2000–01.)

Clifton, R. A., and Rubenstein, H. "Collegial Models for Enhancing the Performance of University Professors." Fraser Institute Digital Publications, July 2000. (www.fraserinstitute.ca/admin/books/files/CollegialModels.pdf)

Collins, J. C., and Porras, J. I. *Built to Last.* New York: HarperCollins, 1994.

Collis, D. "'When Industries Change' Revised: New Scenarios for Higher Education." In M. E. Devlin and J. W. Meyerson (eds.), *Forum Futures: Exploring the Future of Higher Education-2000 Papers.* San Francisco: Jossey-Bass, 2001.

Cooper, R. K., and Sawaf, A. *Executive EQ: Emotional Intelligence in Leadership and Organizations.* New York: Penguin Putnam, 1997.

Covey, S. R. *Principle-Centered Leadership.* New York: Fireside, 1991.

Dalton, J. C., and McClinton, M. (eds.). *The Art and Practical Wisdom of Student Affairs Leadership.* New Directions for Student Services, no. 98. San Francisco: Jossey-Bass, 2002.

Daly, J. A., and Wiemann, J. M. (eds.). *Strategic Interpersonal Communication.* Hillsdale, N.J.: Erlbaum, 1994.

Day, R. L. *Advances in Consumer Satisfaction, Dissatisfaction, and Complaining Behavior.* Bloomington: Indiana University, 1977.

Doerfel, M. L., and Ruben, B. D. "Developing More Adaptive, Innovative and Interactive Organizations." In B. E. Bender and J. H. Schuh (eds.), *Using Benchmarking to Inform Practice in Higher Education.* New Directions in Higher Education, no. 118. San Francisco: Jossey-Bass, 2002.

Ellmer, R., and Olbrisch, M. E. "The Contribution of a Cultural Perspective in Understanding and Evaluating Client Satisfaction." *Evaluation and Program Planning,* 1983, *6,* 275–281.

"Enhancing Faculty Performance Through Collegially Grounded Reward Systems." *Academic Leader,* June 2002, *19*(6), 5.

Ericsson, K. A., Krampe, R. T., and Tesch-Romer, C. "The Role of Deliberate Practices in the Acquisition of Expert Performance." *Psychological Review,* 1993, *100*(3), 363–406.

Ewell, P. "Developing Statewide Performance Indicators for Higher Education." In S. S. Ruppert (ed.), *Charting Higher Education Accountability: A Sourcebook on State-Level Performance Indicators.* Denver: Education Commission of the States, 1994.

Federal Quality Institute. "Lessons Learned from High-Performing Organizations in the Federal Government." In *Federal Quality Management Handbook.* Washington, D.C.: Federal Quality Institute, 1994.

Flanagan, J. C. "The Critical Incident Technique." *Psychological Bulletin,* July 1954, *51,* 327–357.

Fogg, P. "Can Department Heads Be Trained to Succeed?" *Chronicle of Higher Education,* Oct. 19, 2001, *48*(8), A10-A11.

Frank, R. H. "Higher Education: The Ultimate Winner-Take-All Market?" In M. E. Devlin and J. W. Meyerson (eds.), *Forum Futures: Exploring the Future of Higher Education-2000 Papers.* San Francisco: Jossey-Bass, 2001.

Freeland, R. M. "Academic Change and Presidential Leadership." In P. Altback, P. J. Gumport, and D. B. Johnstone (eds.), *Defense of American Higher Education.* Baltimore: Johns Hopkins University Press, 2001.

Friedman, D., and Hoffman, P. H. "The Politics of Information: Building a Relational Database to Support Decision-Making at a Public University." *Change,* May/June 2001, *33*(3), 51–57.

Gardiner, L. F. *Redesigning Higher Education* (ASHE-ERIC Higher Education Report no. 7). Washington, D.C.: George Washington University, 1994.

Garvin, D. A. "Building a Learning Organization." In *Knowledge Management.* Cambridge, Mass.: Harvard Business School Press, 1998.

Giber, D., Carter, L., and Goldsmith, M. *Best Practices in Leadership Development Handbook.* San Francisco: Jossey-Bass, 2000.

Gmelch, W. H. "Leadership Succession: How New Deans Take Charge and Learn the Job." *Journal of Leadership Studies,* 2000, *7*(30), 68–87.

Gmelch, W. H., and Miskin, V. D. *Strategic Leadership Skills for Department Chairs.* Boston: Anker, 1993.

Gmelch, W. H., and Miskin, V. D. *Chairing an Academic Department.* Thousand Oaks, Calif.: Sage, 1995.

Gmelch, W. H., and Parkay, F. P. "Becoming a Department Chair: Negotiating the Transition from Scholar to Administrator." Paper presented at American Educational Research Association Conference, Montreal, Canada, Apr. 1999.

Gmelch, W. H., and Seedorf, F. "Academic Leadership Under Siege: The Ambiguity and Imbalance of Department Chairs." *Journal for Higher Education Management,* 1989, *5,* 37–44.

Goleman, D. *Emotional Intelligence.* New York: Bantam Books, 1997.

Goleman, D. "What Makes a Leader?" *Harvard Business Review,* Nov.-Dec., 1998a.

Goleman, D. *Working with Emotional Intelligence.* New York: Bantam Books, 1998b.

Greene, H., and Greene, M. *The Public Ivies: America's Flagship Universities.* New York: HarperCollins, 2001.

Greenfield, S., Kaplan, S., and Ware, J. E. "Expanding Patient Involvement in Care: Effects on Patient Outcomes." *Annals of Internal Medicine,* 1985, *102,* 520–528.

Greenfield, S., Kaplan, S., and Ware, J. E. "Expanding Patient Involvement in Care: Effects on Blood Sugar." *Annals of Internal Medicine,* 1986, *34*(2), 819A.

Gudykunst, W. D. *Bridging Differences.* Thousand Oaks, Calif.: Sage, 1991.

Hammer, M., and Champy, J. *Reengineering the Corporation.* New York: HarperCollins, 1993.

Harari, O. *The Leadership Secrets of Colin Powell.* New York: McGraw-Hill, 2002.

Harrison, B. T., and Brodeth, E. "Real Work Through Real Collegiality: Faculty Seniors Views on the Drive to Improve Learning and Research." *Journal of Higher Education Policy and Management,* 1999, *21*(2), 203–214.

Harvard Leadership Development Program, Jan. 2003. (http://atwork. harvard.edu/pdf/LeadFoundations.pdf)

Hebel, S. "Public Colleges Emphasize Research, But the Public Wants a Focus on Students." *Chronicle of Higher Education,* May 2, 2003, *49*(34), A14-A15.

Heifetz, R. A. *Leadership Without Easy Answers.* Cambridge, Mass.: Harvard University Press, 1994.

Herrling, J. L. "Student Adaptation to a Community College." Doctoral dissertation, Rutgers University, New Brunswick, N.J., 1986.

Herzberg, F., Mauzner, B., and Snyderman, B. *The Motivation to Work.* New York: Wiley, 1959.

Hexter, E. S. *Case Studies in Strategic Performance Measurement.* New York: Conference Board, 1997.

Higgerson, M. L. *Communication Skills for Department Chairs.* Bolton, Mass.: Anker, 1996.

Hurtado, S., Milem, J. F., Clayton-Pedersen, A. R., and Allen, W. R. *Enacting Diverse Learning Environments: Improving the Climate for Racial/Ethnic Diversity in Higher Education Institutions.* (ASHE-ERIC Higher Education Report no. 26:8.) Washington, D.C.: George Washington University, 1998.

"Improve Learning Through Academic/Student Affairs Collaboration." *Academic Leader,* Aug. 2002, *18*(8), 3–4.

IPEDS [Integrated Postsecondary Education Data System] Peer Analysis System (http://nces.ed.gov/ipedspas/). National Center for Education Statistics, 1995.

IPEDS [Integrated Postsecondary Education Data System] Peer Analysis System (http://nces.ed.gov/ipedspas/). National Center for Education Statistics, 1997.

IPEDS [Integrated Postsecondary Education Data System] Peer Analysis System (http://nces.ed.gov/ipedspas/). National Center for Education Statistics, 1999.

IPEDS [Integrated Postsecondary Education Data System] Peer Analysis System (http://nces.ed.gov/ipedspas/). National Center for Education Statistics, 2001.

Inui, T. S., Yourtee, E. L., and Williamson, J. W. "Improved Outcomes in Hypertension After Physician Tutorials." *Annals of Internal Medicine,* 1976, *84,* 646–651.

Irgang, P. "When a Wet Vac Counts More Than a Ph.D." *Chronicle of Higher Education,* Jan. 21, 2000, p. B8.

Jackson, N., and Lund, H. *Benchmarking for Higher Education.* London: Society for Research into Higher Education and Open University Press, 2000.

Johnson, C. N. "Annual Quality Awards Listing." *Quality Progress,* Aug. 2002, *35*(8), 48–57.

Johnson, R., and Seymour, D. "The Baldrige as an Award and Assessment Instrument for Higher Education." In D. Seymour (ed.), *High Performing Colleges I: Theory and Concepts.* Maryville, Mo.: Prescott, 1996.

Jones, J. E., and Bearley, W. L. *360° Feedback: Strategies, Tactics, and Techniques for Developing Leaders.* Amherst, Mass.: HRD Press, 1996.

Juran, J. M. "World War II and the Quality Movement." In B. D. Ruben (ed.), *Quality in Higher Education.* New Brunswick, N.J.: Transaction, 1995.

Kaplan, R. S., and Norton, D. P. "The Balanced Scorecard—Measures That Drive Performance." *Harvard Business Review,* Jan-Feb. 1992, *70*(1), 71–79.

Kaplan, R. S., and Norton, D. P. "Putting the Balanced Scorecard to Work." *Harvard Business Review,* Sept-Oct. 1993, *71*(5), 134–147.

Kaplan, R. S., and Norton, D. P. *The Balanced Scorecard.* Cambridge, Mass.: Harvard Business School, 1996a.

Kaplan, R. S., and Norton, D. P. "Using the Balanced Scorecard as a Strategic Management System." *Harvard Business Review,* Jan-Feb., 1996b, *74*(1), 75–85.

Kaplan, R. S., and Norton, D. P. *The Strategy-Focused Organization.* Cambridge, Mass.: Harvard Business School, 2001.

Kaplan, S. H., Greenfield, S., and Ware, J. E. "Assessing the Effects of Physician-Patient Interactions on the Outcomes of Chronic Disease." *Medical Care,* 1989, *27*(3, Supplement), S110-S127.

Kealey, D. J., and Ruben, B. D. "Cross-Cultural Personnel Selection: Issues, Criteria, Methods." In R. W. Brislin and D. Landis (eds.), *Handbook of Intercultural Training: Vol. 1.* New York: Pergamon Press, 1983.

Kellogg Commission. "Taking Charge of Change: Renewing the Promise of State and Land-Grant Universities." Washington, D.C.: National Association of State Universities and Land-Grant Colleges, 1996. (www.nasulgc.org/Kellogg/kellogg.htm)

Kellogg Commission. *Returning to Our Roots: The Student Experience.* Washington, D.C.: National Association of State Universities and Land-Grant Colleges, 1997. (www.nasulgc.org/Kellogg/kellogg.htm)

Kellogg Commission. *Returning to Our Roots: Student Access.* Washington, D.C.: National Association of State Universities and Land-Grant Colleges, 1998. (www.nasulgc.org/Kellogg/kellogg.htm)

Kellogg Commission. *Returning to Our Roots: A Learning Society.* Washington, D.C.: National Association of State Universities and Land-Grant Colleges, 1999a. (www.nasulgc.org/Kellogg/kellogg.htm)

Kellogg Commission. *Returning to Our Roots: The Engaged Institution.* Washington, D.C.: National Association of State Universities and Land-Grant Colleges, 1999b. (www.nasulgc.org/Kellogg/kellogg.htm)

Kellogg Commission. *Renewing the Covenant: Learning, Discovery, and Engagement in a New Age and Different World.* Washington, D.C.: National Association of State Universities and Land-Grant Colleges, 2000a. (www.nasulgc.org/Kellogg/kellogg.htm)

Kellogg Commission. *Returning to Our Roots: Toward a Coherent Campus Culture.* Washington, D.C.: National Association of State Universities and Land-Grant Colleges, 2000b. (www.nasulgc.org/Kellogg/kellogg.htm)

Kellogg Commission. "Leadership for Institutional Change Initiative." 2001a. (www.leadershiponlinewkkf.org; http://cuinfo.cornell.edu/LINC; http://www.fspe.org/linc)

Kellogg Commission. *Returning to Our Roots: Executive Summaries of the Reports of the Kellogg Commission on the Future of State and Land-Grant Universities.* Washington, D.C.: National Association of State Universities and Land-Grant Colleges, 2001b. (www.nasulgc.org/Kellogg/kellogg.htm)

Kennedy, D. *Academic Duty.* Cambridge, Mass.: Harvard University Press, 1997.

Kezar, A., Hirsch, D J., and Burack, C. (eds.). *Understanding the Role of Academic and Student Affairs Collaboration in Creating a Successful Learning Environment.* New Directions for Higher Education, no. 116. San Francisco: Jossey-Bass, 2001.

King, P. "Improving Access and Educational Success for Diverse Students: Steady Progress But Enduring Problems." In C. S. Johnson and H. E. Cheatham (eds.), *Higher Education Trends for the Next Century: A Research Agenda for Student Success.* Washington: D.C.: American College Personnel Association, 1999.

Knight, P. T., and Trowler, P. R. *Departmental Leadership in Higher Education.* Buckingham, England: Open University Press, 2001.

Koepplin, L. W., and Wilson, D. A. *The Future of State Universities.* New Brunswick, N.J.: Rutgers University Press, 1985.

Komives, S. R., Lucas, N., and McMahon, T. R.. *Exploring Leadership: For College Students Who Want to Make a Difference.* San Francisco: Jossey-Bass, 1998.

Kotter, J. P. "What Do Leaders Really Do?" *Harvard Business Review,* 2001, *79*(11), 85–97.

Kuh, G. D. "Assessing What Really Matters to Student Learning," *Change,* May–June 2001a, *33*(3), 10–17, 66.

Kuh, G. D. "College Students Today: Why Can't We Leave Serendipity to Chance?" In P. G. Altbach, P. J. Gumport, and D. B. Johnstone (eds.), *In Defense of Higher Education.* Baltimore, Md.: Johns Hopkins University Press, 2001b.

Kuh, G. D., Douglas, K. B., Lund, J. P., and Ramin-Gyurmek, J. *Student Learning Outside the Classroom.* (ASHE-ERIC Higher Education Report No. 8.) Washington, D.C.: George Washington University, 1994.

Kuhn, T. S. *The Structure of Scientific Revolutions* (2nd ed.). Chicago: University of Chicago Press, 1970.

Lathrop, J. P. *Restructuring Health Care.* San Francisco: Jossey-Bass, 1993.

Lawrence, F. L. "Preface." In B. D. Ruben (ed.), *Quality in Higher Education.* New Brunswick, N.J.: Transaction, 1995.

"Leadership for Institutional Change Initiative," 2001. (www.leadership onlinewkkf.org; http://cuinfo.cornell.edu/LINC)

"Leading Your Department: A Workshop for Academic Chairs." Cornell University, 2002. (www.sce.cornell.edu)

Leebov, W. *Service Excellence: The Customer Relations Strategy for Health Care.* Chicago: American Hospital Association, 1988.

Lepsinger, R., and Lucia, A. D. *The Art and Science of 360° Feedback.* San Francisco: Jossey-Bass, 1997.

Levine, A., and Cureton, J. S. "College Life: An Obituary." *Change,* May–June 1998, *30*(3), 12–17.

Light, R. J. *Making the Most of College: Students Speak Their Minds.* Cambridge, Mass.: Harvard University Press, 2001.

Lucas, A. E. *Strengthening Departmental Leadership.* San Francisco: Jossey-Bass, 1994.

Magolda, M. B. "Engaging Students in Active Learning." In G. S. Blimling, E. J. Whitt, and associates (eds.), *Good Practice in Student Affairs.* San Francisco: Jossey-Bass, 1999.

Marchese, T. "Not-So-Distant Competitors." *American Association for Higher Education Bulletin,* May 1998, pp. 3–7.

Marszalek-Gaucher, E., and Coffey, R. J. *Transforming Healthcare Organizations.* San Francisco: Jossey-Bass, 1990.

Mayer, J. D., and Salovey, P. "What Is Emotional Intelligence?" In P. Salovey and D. J. Sluyter (eds.), *Emotional Development and Emotional Intelligence.* New York: Basic Books, 1997.

McClelland, D. C. *The Achieving Society.* New York: Irvington, 1976.

McDonald, W. M. (ed.). *Creating Campus Community.* San Francisco: Jossey-Bass, 2002.

McLaughlin, J. B. (ed.). *Leadership Transitions: The New College President.* New Directions for Higher Education, no. 93. San Francisco: Jossey-Bass, 1996.

McMillan, J. J., and Cheney, G. "The Student as Consumer: The Implications and Limitations of the Metaphor." *Communication Education,* 1996, *45*(1), 1–14.

Meister, J. C. *Corporate Quality Universities.* Burr Ridge, Ill.: Irwin, 1994.

Merwick, D. M., Godfrey, A. B., and Roessner, J. *Curing Healthcare.* San Francisco: Jossey-Bass, 1990.

Middle States Commission on Higher Education. *Characteristics of Excellence in Higher Education: Eligibility Requirements and Standards for Accreditation.* Philadelphia: Middle States Commission on Higher Education, 2002.

Miller, J. G. "Living Systems." *Behavioral Science,* 1965, *10,* p. 10.

Milliman, J. F., and McFadden, F. R. "Toward Changing Performance Appraisal to Address TQM Concerns: The 360-Degree Feedback Process." *Quarterly Management Journal*, 1997, *4*(3), 44–64.

Moll, R. *The Public Ivys.* New York: Viking Penguin, 1985.

Munitz, B. "Wanted: New Leadership for Higher Education." (California State) *University Information Bulletin*, Nov. 28, 1995, *52*(15). Adapted from B. Munitz, *Planning for Higher Education,* Society for College and University Planning, Ann Arbor, Mich., Fall 1995.

National Association of College and University Business Officers. *Institutional Effectiveness.* 2002. (www.nacubo.org/register_for_programs)

National Association of State Universities and Land-Grant Colleges (NASULGC). *Shaping the Future: The Economic Impact of Public Universities.* Washington, D.C.: National Association of State Universities and Land-Grant Colleges, 2001.

National Center for Education Statistics (NCES). *Digest of Education Statistics 2001.* Washington, D.C.: U.S. Department of Education, Office of Educational Research and Improvement, 2001.

National Center for Education Statistics (NCES). *The Condition of Education 2002.* (NCES Report no. 2002–025.) Washington, D.C.: U.S. Department of Education, Office of Educational Research and Improvement, 2002a.

National Center for Education Statistics (NCES). *Digest of Education Statistics 2001.* (Publication 2002–130.) Washington, D.C.: U.S. Department of Education, Office of Educational Research and Improvement, 2002b.

National Center for Education Statistics (NCES) and Integrated Postsecondary Education Data System (IPEDS). *Enrollment in Postsecondary Institutions, Fall 2000 and Financial Statistics, Fiscal Year 2000* (report). Washington, D.C.: U.S. Department of Education, 2000.

National Center for Postsecondary Improvement. "Revolution or Evolution? Gauging the Impact of Institutional Student-Assessment Strategies." *Change,* Sept.–Oct. 1999, *31*(5), 53–55.

National Center for Postsecondary Improvement. "A Report to Stakeholders on the Condition and Effectiveness of Postsecondary Education." *Change,* Sept.–Oct. 2001, *33*(5), 23–38.

National Science Foundation, Division of Science Resources Statistics. *Survey of Research and Development Expenditures at Universities and Colleges, Fiscal Year 2000.* (Publication no. NSF 02–308; report Academic Research and Development Expenditures: Fiscal Year 2000, Section B, Table B-1, p. 9.) Washington, D.C.: National Science Foundation, 2000.

National Survey of Student Engagement. (Indiana University Center for Post-secondary Research and Planning.) 2002. (www.iub.edu/~nsse/)

Newman, F., and Couturier, L. K. "The New Competitive Area: Market Forces Invade the Academy." *Change,* Sept.–Oct. 2001, *33*(5), 10–17.

Noble, D. "The Future of the Faculty in the Digital Diploma Mill." *Academe,* Sept.-Oct. 2001, *87*(5), 27–42.

North Central Accrediting Association. Higher Learning Commission's *Academic Quality Improvement Project.* July 2002. (http://AQIP.org)

Norton, J. "Transforming Teacher Education: The Samford University Example." Oct. 1999. (www.middleweb.com/samford.html)

Nyquist, J. "Re-envisioning the Ph.D." May 9, 2001. (www.grad.washington. edu/envision)

O'Brien, G. D. *All the Essential Half-Truths About Higher Education.* Chicago: University of Chicago Press, 1998.

O'Hair, D., Friedrich, G., Wiemann, J. M., and Wiemann, M. O. *Competent Communication* (2nd ed.). New York: St. Martin's Press, 1997.

Pascarella, E. T. "Identifying Excellence in Undergraduate Education: Are We Even Close?" *Change,* May/June 2001, *33*(3), 19–23.

Pascoe, G. C. "Patient Satisfaction in Primary Health Care: A Literature Review and Analysis." *Evaluation and Program Planning,* 1983, *6,* 185–210.

Peiperl, M. A. "Getting 360° Feedback Right." *Harvard Business Review,* Jan. 2001, *79*(1), 142–147.

Pfeffer, J., and Fong, C. T. "The End of Business Schools? Less Success Than Meets the Eye." *Learning and Education,* Sept. 2002, *1*(1), 78–95.

Phillips-Donaldson, D. "On Leadership." *Quality Progress,* Aug. 2002, *35*(8), 24–25.

Porter, M. E. "Capital Disadvantage: America's Failing Capital Investment System." *Harvard Business Review,* Sept.-Oct. 1992, *70*(5), 65–82.

"Preparing Future Faculty Program" (www.preparing-faculty.org/PFFWeb. Contents.htm). July 2002.

Qayoumi, M. *Benchmarking and Organizational Change.* Alexandria, Va.: Association of Higher Education Facilities Officers, 2000.

Ramsden, P. *Learning to Lead in Higher Education.* London: Routledge, 1998.

Report of the Committee on Administrative Systems Efficiency. New Brunswick, N.J.: Rutgers University, 1992.

Rhodes, F. H. *The Creation of the Future: The Role of the American University.* Ithaca, N.Y.: Cornell University Press, 2001.

Roach, J.H.L. "The Academic Department Chairperson: Roles and Responsibilities." *Educational Record,* 1976, *57*(1), 13–23.

Rockefeller Institute of Government. "What's New." June 2002. (www. rockinst.org/higheduc.htm)

Roethlisberger, F. J., and Dickson, W. J. *Management and the Worker.* Cambridge, Mass.: Harvard University Press, 1941.

Rosenthal, R., and Jacobson, L. *Pygmalion in the Classroom.* Austin, Tex.: Holt, Rinehart and Winston, 1968.

Ruben, B. D. "Assessing Communication Competence for Intercultural Communication Adaptation." *Group and Organization Studies,* 1976, *1*(3), 334–354.

Ruben, B. D. "Toward a Theory of Experience-Based Instruction." *Simulations and Games,* 1977, *8*(2), 211–231.

Ruben, B. D. "Human Communication and Cross-Cultural Effectiveness." *International and Intercultural Communication Annual,* 1978, *4,* 95–105.

Ruben, B. D. "Intrapersonal, Interpersonal and Mass Communication Processes in Individual and Multi-Individual Systems." In G. Gumpert and R. Cathcart (eds.), *Intermedia: Interpersonal Communication in a Media World* (2nd ed.). New York: Oxford University Press, 1983.

Ruben, B. D. *The Bottomline: A Patient Relations Training Program.* Morristown, N.J.: Morristown Memorial Hospital, 1985.

Ruben, B. D. *Patient Perceptions of Quality of Care: Survey Results.* No. 2, 1986. Unpublished Report.

Ruben, B. D. *Patient Perceptions of Quality of Care: Survey Results.* No. 3, 1987. Unpublished Report.

Ruben, B. D. "The Health Caregiver-Patient Relationship: Pathology, Etiology, Treatment." In E. B. Ray and L. Donohew (eds.), *Communication and Health: Systems and Applications.* Hillsdale, N.J.: Erlbaum, 1989.

Ruben, B. D. *Communicating with Patients.* Dubuque, Iowa: Kendall/Hunt, 1992.

Ruben, B. D. "Building Effective Client and Colleague Relationships: Insights from Patients, the Factory, the Classroom, and the Pet Shop." In B. D. Ruben with N. Guttman (eds.), *Caregiver-Patient Communication: Readings.* Dubuque, Iowa: Kendall/Hunt, 1993a.

Ruben, B. D. "Integrating Concepts for the Information Age: Communication, Information, Mediation, and Institutions." In J. R. Schement and B. D. Ruben (eds.), *Information and Behavior.* Vol. 4: *Between Communication and Information.* New Brunswick, N.J.: Transaction, 1993b.

Ruben, B. D. "What Patients Remember: A Content Analysis of Critical Incidents in Health Care." *Health Communication,* 1993c, *5*(2), 99–112.

Ruben, B. D. "The Quality Approach in Higher Education: Context and Concepts for Change." In B. D. Ruben (ed.), *Quality in Higher Education.* New Brunswick, N.J.: Transaction, 1995a.

Ruben, B. D. *Quality in Higher Education.* New Brunswick, N.J.: Transaction, 1995b.

Ruben, B. D. *Tradition of Excellence: Higher Education Quality Self-Assessment Program.* Dubuque, Iowa: Kendall/Hunt, 1995c.

Ruben, B. D. "What Students Remember: Teaching, Learning and Human Communication." In B. D. Ruben (ed.), *Quality in Higher Education.* New Brunswick, N.J.: Transaction; 1995d.

Ruben, B. D. "Simulations, Games and Experience-Based Learning: The Quest for a New Paradigm for Teaching-and-Learning." *Simulations and Games,* 1999, *30*(4), 498–505.

Ruben, B. D. "Communication and the Quality of Care: Insights from the Hospital, the Factory, the Classroom and the Pet Shop." In L. Lederman and W. D. Gibson (eds.), *Communication Theory: A Casebook Approach.* Dubuque, Iowa: Kendall/Hunt, 2000a.

Ruben, B. D. *Excellence in Higher Education 2000: A Baldrige-Based Guide to Organizational Assessment, Planning, and Improvement.* Washington, D.C.: National Association of College and University Business Officers, 2000b.

Ruben, B. D. *Excellence in Higher Education 2000: Facilitators Guide.* Washington, D.C.: National Association of College and University Business Officers, 2000c.

Ruben, B. D. *Excellence in Higher Education 2000: Workbook.* Washington, D.C.: National Association of College and University Business Officers, 2000d.

Ruben, B. D. *Excellence in Higher Education 2001–2002: A Baldrige-Based Guide to Organizational Assessment, Planning, and Improvement.* Washington, D.C.: National Association of College and University Business Officers, 2001a.

Ruben, B. D. *Excellence in Higher Education 2001–2002: Facilitator's Guide.* Washington, D.C.: National Association of College and University Business Officers, 2001b.

Ruben, B. D. *Excellence in Higher Education 2001–2002: Workbook.* Washington, D.C.: National Association of College and University Business Officers, 2001c.

Ruben, B. D. "We Need Excellence Beyond the Classroom." *Chronicle of Higher Education,* July 13, 2001d, *47*(44), B15–B16.

Ruben, B. D. *Excellence in Higher Education 2003–2004: A Baldrige-Based Guide to Organizational Assessment, Improvement, and Leadership.* Washington, D.C.: National Association of College and University Business Officers, 2003a.

Ruben, B. D. *Excellence in Higher Education 2003–2004: Facilitator's Guide.* Washington, D.C.: National Association of College and University Business Officers, 2003b.

Ruben, B. D. *Excellence in Higher Education 2003–2004: Workbook and Scoring Guide.* Washington, D.C.: National Association of College and University Business Officers, 2003c.

Ruben, B. D, and Bowman, J. C. "Patient Satisfaction: Critical Issues in the Theory and Design of Patient Relations Training." *Journal of Healthcare Education and Training,* 1986, 1(1), 1–5.

Ruben, B. D., and DeAngelis, J. A. "Succeeding at Work: Skills and Competencies Needed by College and University Graduates in the Workplace: A Secondary Analysis of Quantitative and Qualitative Literature." Report presented to Conference Board, New York, 1998.

Ruben, B. D., and Kealey, D. J. "Behavioral Assessment of Communication Competency and the Prediction of Cross-Cultural Adaptation." *International Journal of Intercultural Relations,* 1979, *3*(1), 15–47.

Ruben, B. D., and Kim, J. Y. (eds.). *General Systems and Human Communication Theory.* Rochelle Park, N.J.: Hayden, 1975.

Ruben, B. D., and Lehr, J. *Excellence in Higher Education: A Guide for Organizational Self-Assessment, Strategic Planning and Improvement.* Dubuque, Iowa: Kendall/Hunt, 1997.

Ruben, B. D., and Ruben, J. M. *Patient Perceptions of Quality of Care: Survey Results.* No. 4, 1987. Unpublished Report.

Ruben, B. D., and Ruben, J. M. *Patient Perceptions of Quality of Care: Survey Results.* No. 5, 1988. Unpublished Report.

Ruben, B. D., and Stewart, L. P. *Communication and Human Behavior* (4th ed.). Boston: Allyn and Bacon, 1998.

Rummler, G. A., and Brache, A. P. *Improving Performance.* San Francisco: Jossey-Bass, 1995.

Rutgers University Teaching Assistant Project. July 2002. (http://taproject.rutgers.edu)

Ruud, G. "The Symbolic Construction of Organizational Identities and Communities in a Regional Symphony." *Communication Studies,* 1995, *46,* 201–221.

Ruud, G. "The Symphony: Organizational Discourse and the Symbolic Tensions Between the Artistic and Business Ideologies." *Journal of Applied Communication Research,* 2000, *28*(2), 117–143.

Sainte-Beuve, C. A. *Pensées d'Août.* In M. Villemain (ed.), *Poesies completes de Sainte-Beuve.* Paris: Charpentier, 1869.

Sax, L. J., Astin, A. W., Arredondo, M., and Korn, W. S. *The American College Teacher: National Norms for 1995–96 HERI Faculty Survey.* Los Angeles: Higher Education Research Institute, 1996.

Schroeder, C. C. "Partnerships: An Imperative for Enhancing Student Learning and Institutional Effectiveness." In J. H. Schuh and E. J. Whitt (eds.), *Creating Successful Partnerships Between Academic and Student Affairs.* No. 87. San Francisco: Jossey-Bass, 1999.

Schuh, J., and Bender, B. (eds.). *Benchmarking in Higher Education.* San Francisco: Jossey-Bass, 2002.

Schwartz, M. K., Axtman, K. M., and Freeman, F. H. (eds.). *Leadership Education: A Source Book of Courses and Programs* (7th ed.). Greensboro, N.C.: Center for Creative Leadership, 1998.

Schwartzman, R. "Are Students Customers? The Metaphoric Mismatch Between Management and Education." *Education,* 1995, *116*(2), 215–222.

Scott, J. W. "The Critical State of Shared Governance." *Academe,* July-Aug. 2002, *88*(4), 41–48.

Seagren, A. T., Creswell, J. W., and Wheeler, D. W. *The Department Chair.* ASHE-ERIC Higher Education Reports, 1993, *22*(1).

Seaver, W. B. "Effects of Naturally Induced Teacher Expectancies." *Journal of Personality and Social Psychology,* 1973, *28*(3), 333–342.

Seldin, P., and Higgerson, M. L. "The Administrative Portfolio." *AAHE Bulletin,* Jan. 2002, *54*(5), 3–6.

Selingo, J. "Businesses Say They Turn to For-Profit Schools Because of Public Colleges' Inertia." *Chronicle of Higher Education,* July 14, 1999. (http://chronicle.com/daily/99/07/99071401n.htm)

Selingo, J. "What Americans Think About Higher Education." *Chronicle of Higher Education,* May 2, 2003, *49*(34), A10-A15.

Seymour, D. T. *On Q: Causing Quality in Higher Education.* New York: American Council on Education, and Macmillan, 1989.

Showalter, E. "The Risks of Good Teaching: How 1 Professor and 9 T.A.'s Plunged into Pedagogy." *Chronicle of Higher Education,* July 9, 1999, p. B4.

Shulman, J. L., and Bowen, W. G. *The Game of Life.* Princeton, N.J.: Princeton University Press, 2001.

Slaughter, S. "Professional Values and the Allure of the Market." *Academe,* Sept.-Oct. 2001, *87*(5), 22–26.

Snow, C. P. *The Two Cultures.* Cambridge, England: Cambridge University Press, 1993.

"South Carolina's 'Performance Indicators.'" *Chronicle of Higher Education,* Apr. 4, 1997, *43*(30), A27.

Spangehl, S. D. "Aligning Assessment, Academic Quality, and Accreditation." *Assessment and Accountability Forum,* 2000, *10*(2), 10–11, 19.

Spangehl, S. D. "Talking with Academia About Quality: The North Central Association of Colleges and Schools Academic Quality Improvement Project." In B. D. Ruben (ed.), *The Ivory Tower and the Marketplace:*

Reconciling Irreconcilable Differences in Higher Education. San Francisco: Jossey-Bass, 2003.

Spence, L. D. "The Case Against Teaching." *Change,* Nov.-Dec. 2001, *33*(6), 11–17.

Sperling, J. G., and Tucker, R. W. *For-Profit Higher Education: Developing a World-Class Workforce.* New Brunswick, N.J.: Transaction, 1997.

Spitzberg, B. H., and Cupach, W. R. *Interpersonal Communication Competence.* Thousand Oaks, Calif.: Sage, 1984.

Terenzini, P. T., and Pascarella, E. T. "Living with Myths: Undergraduate Education in America." *Change,* 1994, *26*(1), 28–32.

Thayer, L. *Communication and Communication Systems.* Homewood, Ill.: Irwin, 1968.

Tichy, N. M. *The Leadership Engine.* New York: HarperCollins, 1997.

Tierney, W. G. (ed.). *Assessing Academic Climates and Cultures.* New Directions for Institutional Research, no. 68. San Francisco: Jossey-Bass, 1990.

Tierney, W. G. *Building Communities of Difference: Higher Education in the Twenty-First Century.* Westport, Conn.: Bergin and Garvey, 1993.

Trout, P. A. "Disengaged Students and the Decline of Academic Standards." *Academic Questions,* Spring 1997a, 10(2) 46–55.

Trout, P. A. "What the Numbers Mean." *Change,* Sept.-Oct., 1997b, *29*(5), 25–30.

Tucker, R. W. *For-Profit Higher Education.* New Brunswick, N.J.: Transaction, 1997.

Ulschak, F. L. *The Common Bond.* San Francisco: Jossey-Bass, 1994.

University of Wisconsin System. "Introduction." (n.d.) (uwhelp.wisconsin. edu)

Useem, M. *The Leadership Moment.* New York: Random House, 1998.

U.S. Census Bureau. "2001 Supplementary Survey." (www.census.gov/acs/ www/Products/Ranking/SS01/R07T040.htm)

U.S. Department of Education. "The National Survey of Postsecondary Faculty." 1999. (www.nea.org/he/heupdate/vol8no2pdf)

U.S. Department of Education. *Projections of Education Statistics to 2011* (30th ed.). (National Center for Education Statistics: NCES 2001–083.) Washington, D.C.: U.S. Department of Education, Oct. 2001.

Veblen, T. *The Higher Learning in America.* New York: Hill and Wong, 1957. (Originally published 1918)

Waitzkin, H. B. "Doctor-Patient Communication: Clinical Implications of Social Scientific Research." *Journal of the American Medical Association,* 1984, *252*(17), 2441–2446.

Waitzkin, H. B. "Research on Doctor-Patient Communication: Implications for Practice." *Internist,* 1986, *27*(7), pp. 7–10.

Wall, A. and Evans, N. J. (eds.). *Toward Acceptance: Sexual Orientation Issues on Campuses.* Lanham, Md.: University Press of America, 2000.

Waltzer, H. *The Job of the Academic Department Chair.* Washington, D.C.: American Council on Education, 1975.

Ware, J. E., Jr., and Davies, A. R. "Behavioral Consequences of Consumer Dissatisfaction with Medical Care." *Evaluation and Program Planning,* 1983, *6,* 291–297.

Watzlawick, P., Beavin, J. H., and Jackson, D. *Pragmatics of Human Communication.* New York: Norton, 1967.

Wegner, J. W. "Rational, Accessible Ways to Rank Law Schools." *National Law Journal,* July 14, 1997, *19*(46), 822–823.

Weinstein, L. A. *Moving a Battleship with Your Bare Hands.* Madison, Wis.: Magna, 1993.

Weisinger, H. *Emotional Intelligence at Work.* San Francisco: Jossey-Bass, 1998.

Wheeler, D. W. "New Unit Administrators: How Long Do They Pursue the Challenge?" *Department Chair,* Fall 2001, *12*(2), 14.

Whitt, E. J. "Assessing Student Cultures." In J. H. Schuh and M. L. Upcraft (eds.), *Assessment in Student Affairs.* San Francisco: Jossey-Bass, 1996.

Williams, W. M., and Ceci, J. J. "How'm I Doing? Problems with Student Ratings of Instructors and Courses." *Change,* Sept.-Oct. 1997, *29*(5), 12–23.

Wilson, R. "It's 10 A.M. Do You Know Where Your Professors Are?" *Chronicle of Higher Education,* Feb. 2, 2001a. (http://chronicle.com/free/v47/i21/21a01001.htm)

Wilson, R. "Beggar, Psychologist, Mediator, Maid: The Thankless Job of a Chairman." *Chronicle of Higher Education,* Mar. 2, 2001b, *47*(25), A10-A12.

Wingspread Group on Higher Education. *An American Imperative: Higher Expectations for Higher Education.* Racine, Wis.: Johnson Foundation, 1993.

Winston, G. C. "Is Princeton Acting Like a Church or a Car Dealer?" *Chronicle of Higher Education Review,* Feb. 23, 2001. (http://chronicle.merit.edu/cgi2-bin/printable.cgi)

Witherspoon, P. D. *Communicating Leadership.* Boston: Allyn and Bacon, 1997.

Wolff, R. P. *The Ideal of the University.* New Brunswick, N.J.: Transaction, 1992.

Wolverton, M., and Gmelch, W. H. *College Deans: Leading from Within.* Westport, Conn.: American Council on Education, Oryx Press, 2002.

"Women Faculty Members Continue to Earn Less." *Business Officer,* May 2002, *35*(11), 16.

Zeithaml, V. A., Parasuraman, A., and Berry, L. L. *Delivering Quality Service.* New York: Free Press, 1990.

Zimmerman, J. "Relationship Investing and Shareholder Communication." *Journal of Applied Corporate Finance,* 1993, *6*(2).

Zlotkowski, E. "Mapping New Terrain: Service-Learning Across the Disciplines." *Change,* Jan.–Feb. 2001, *33*(1) 25–33.

Index

Faculty (continued)
leadership development of, 292–293, 321; recognizing as teachers, 20–21, 259, 260, 385; social competencies of, 223–224; structural distinctions between, 263; teaching assistants and, 264–271; workplace satisfaction of, 111; *See also* Staff; Teachers
Families, key requirements of, 131
Feedback: academic leadership and, 305–306; Web-based mechanism for, 276–277
Financial services: *EHE* model applied to, 200–201; performance indicators for, 210
Fiske Guide to Colleges, 190
Franklin, Ben, 233
Free Speech Movement, 137
Freeland, Richard, 298
Frontline work units, 140

G

Garland, James C., 190–191
Garvin, David, 12
Gempesaw, Conrado M. (Bobby), II, 308, 309–314
Goals: appropriate setting of, 120–121; benchmarking, 191; critical, 140, 145, 147; leadership development, 303–304; learning organizations and, 12–14, 115, 383; workplace competencies and, 70–71
Goleman, Daniel, 300
Governance structures, 290–291
Grade point averages, 100
Graduate students: collaboration between, 223–224; developing teaching skills of, 264–271; enhancing quality of instruction for, 264–271; most memorable experiences of, 257–258; *See also* Students; Undergraduate students
Graduates: opinion survey of, 75–76; percentage of, by major, 66; preparing for the workplace, 67–69

Greene, Howard, 190
Greene, Matthew, 190

H

Haislar, Adolph, 177, 190–201
Haley, W. James, 177, 190–201
Harvard Business School Council on Competitiveness, 96
Harvey, James, 361
Hawthorne Effect, 344
Health care: asymmetrical interactions in, 351; Baldrige program in, 158; communication competence in, 349–350; organizational structure in, 225; patient perspective of, 347–348; technical competence in, 349
Helping Hands program, 277
Herman, Richard H., 245
Herrling, John, 345–346
Hewertson, Roxi Bahar, 323
Higher education: academic excellence in, 23–24, 338–340; assessment process in, 16–18, 383–384; asymmetrical encounters in, 352; Baldrige program in, 158–160; broadening public appreciation for, 8–9, 31–48, 381–382; business and administrative affairs in, 332–337; business features compared with, 185–186; collaboration and community in, 18–20; communication process and, 249–251; contemporary challenges for, 6–27; dashboard indicators for, 102–112; excellence indicators in, 99–102; historical perspective of, 332–333; improvement activities in, 16–18, 383–384; leadership in, 22–23, 288–308; learning environments of, 11–16; marketplace expectations and, 5–6; missions and stakeholders of, 32–39; operational excellence in, 26–27, 353–355; organizational structure and, 224–229; planning process in, 16–18, 383–384; relationship